OTHER BOOKS BY ROSEMARY RADFORD RUETHER

The Church Against Itself

Communion Is Life Together

Gregory Nazianzus: Rhetor and Philosopher

*The Radical Kingdom: The Western Experience
of Messianic Hope*

*Liberation Theology: Human Hope Confronts
Christian History and American Power*

RELIGION
and SEXISM

IMAGES OF WOMAN
IN THE JEWISH AND
CHRISTIAN TRADITIONS

Edited by

Rosemary Radford Ruether

SIMON AND SCHUSTER | NEW YORK

We wish to thank the original publishers for permission to quote from the following:

Daedalus, Journal of the American Academy of Arts and Sciences: Erik H. Erikson, "Autobiographic Notes on the Identity Crisis," in *The Making of Modern Science: Biographical Studies*, Boston, Mass., Fall 1970.

Harper & Row, Publishers, Inc.: Richard I. Evans, *Dialogue with Erik Erikson*, and Robert Bellah, *Beyond Belief*.

W. W. Norton & Company, Inc.: Erik H. Erikson, *Childhood and Society*, *Gandhi's Truth*, *Identity: Youth and Crisis*, and *Young Man Luther*, and Joan M. Erikson, *Saint Francis et His Four Ladies*.

Tavistock Publications Ltd.: Clifford Geertz, "Religion as a Cultural System," in Michael Banton, ed., *Anthropological Approaches to the Study of Religion*.

A Touchstone Book

Published by Simon & Schuster, Inc.
Simon & Schuster Building
Rockefeller Center
1230 Avenue of the Americas
New York, New York 10020

TOUCHSTONE and colophon are registered trademarks
of Simon & Schuster, Inc.

ISBN 0–671–21692–9
ISBN 0–671–21693–7 Pbk.
Library of Congress Catalog Card Number 74–2791
Designed by Irving Perkins
Manufactured in the United States of America
By The Book Press, Brattleboro, Vt.

4   5   6   7   8   9   10   11   12   13
            11   12   13   14   15   16   Pbk.

*THIS BOOK IS DEDICATED
TO MY MOTHER,
REBECCA CRESAP ORD RADFORD,
A WISE WOMAN.*

Contents

7

Preface

The essays in this volume have been written to fill a growing need for a more exact idea of the role of religion, specifically the Judaeo-Christian tradition, in shaping the traditional cultural images that have degraded and suppressed women. To what extent did Judaism and Christianity contribute directly to and promote this heritage of misogynism? To what extent, as is often argued, were they responsible for combating an earlier denigration of women and contributing to woman's gradual rise to a more respected position in modern times? Much of the current literature in the woman's movement has been written by women who are alienated from religion and who, although perhaps occasionally indicating a recognition of the role of the Church in this history of repression, have little historical or doctrinal information about this process. This leaves a serious gap in the understanding of the dilemma of woman's liberation, for religion has been not only a contributing factor, it is undoubtedly the single most important shaper and enforcer of the image and role of women in culture and society. If one takes either a more Marxist or a more psychological view and assumes that the real "cause" of misogynism lies on the level of the economic power struggle or on the level of an immature adolescent psyche in the male struggling for freedom from the mother, it still remains that it has been religion that has been the ideological reflection of this sexual domination and subjugation.

And it has been religion, as a social institution, that has been its cultural sanctioner.

Despite the assumption of most people that religion and sex do not mix any more than religion and politics, religion traditionally has been both highly political in its reality and highly sexual in its imagery. Sublimated sexual imagery is central to religious language, even if one prescinds from the more radical statement that religion "is" sublimated sexuality. From the earliest stages, the sexual dialectic has contributed to religion its chief imagery and psychic energy, and this in turn has had a profound effect on the way in which actual men and women have been able to experience their respective existences. Judaism and Christianity are no different from other religions in this pervasive sexual imagery, although they have been distinguished from most religions in their elevation of an exclusively male, patriarchal God, without female consort, as the sole ruler of the heavens, and a corresponding repression of feminine imagery of the divine and of feminine roles in worship. The essays in this volume are an attempt to give, in the compass of a single work, a glimpse of the history of this relationship of patriarchal religion to both feminine imagery and to the actual psychic and social self-images of women. There is also an attempt to suggest, particularly in the final chapter and the concluding parable, the ways in which patriarchal religion must be reshaped to overcome its unjust and debilitating effects on women. Needless to say, this group of essays is only the beginning of what is hoped will be a growing body of research into this topic which will begin to shape the teachings of Western culture in universities, as well as the actual practices of churches and other social institutions.

The authors of these essays are scholars in the particular areas of historical theology in which they write. They represent a small but growing body of women who are professors of religion in seminaries and departments of religion or in related fields, as well as men who have also felt the need to come to a more just understanding of this function of religion.

Patricia Martin Doyle taught in the field of religion and psychology at the Divinity School at Harvard University and is currently teaching in that field at the School of Theology at Claremont, California.

Phyllis Bird holds her theological doctorate from the Divinity School at Harvard University and is currently a professor of Old Testament at Perkins School of Theology in Dallas, Texas.

Bernard P. Prusak received his doctorate from Lateran University in Rome and is a professor in the Department of Religious Studies at Villanova University, in Pennsylvania. His essay on the image of women in the pseudepigraphical literature of the inter-testamental period was requested for this volume after he delivered it in the "Working Group on Women and Religion" at the annual conference of the American Academy of Religion in Los Angeles (September 1972).

Constance F. Parvey is a graduate in New Testament Studies from the Divinity School at Harvard University and is a consultant for the Lutheran Church of America. She is a frequent lecturer and contributor to religious journals in the areas of religion and contemporary affairs and has recently been called to the pastorate of the University Lutheran Church in Cambridge, Massachusetts.

Rosemary Radford Ruether holds a doctorate in Classics and History of Christian Thought from the Claremont Graduate School in Claremont, California. She is a professor of Historical Theology at Howard University School of Religion in Washington, D.C., and has taught Theology and Women's Studies at the Harvard Divinity School and the Yale Divinity School.

Judith Hauptman is Instructor of the Talmud in the Teachers' Institute of the Jewish Theological Seminary in New York City and one of the first women in Conservative Judaism to teach in this field.

Eleanor Commo McLaughlin holds her doctorate in Medieval History from Harvard University. She has taught at Wellesley College and holds a research fellowship in Church History and Women's Studies at the Harvard Divinity School.

Clara Maria Henning is one of the few Roman Catholic women with a graduate degree in Roman Catholic Canon Law and has worked as a canon lawyer for the Diocese of Detroit.

Jane Dempsey Douglass holds a doctorate in Church History from Harvard University and is Professor of Church History, specializing in Reformation thought, at the School of Theology at Claremont, California.

Joan Arnold Romero is a professor of Theology at the United

Theological Seminary in Dayton, Ohio. She is a candidate for a doctorate in Latin American Liberation Theology at the Divinity School of Harvard University.

Judith Plaskow Goldenberg is a doctoral candidate at Yale University and has been an instructor in Theology at Sir George Williams University in Montreal, Canada. She is a research associate in Theology and Women's Studies at the Harvard Divinity School. She developed her parable "The Coming of Lilith" while attending the conference on women and religion sponsored by Church Women United at Grailville, Ohio, in the summer of 1972. This parable turns male misogynist mythology upside down, revealing it for what it is, a projection of male insecurity and demands for dominance. But Judith Goldenberg also shows that the fearsomeness of Lilith in the male imagination preserves a recognition of suppressed power and creativity in women. This power and creativity must be released from its alienated limbo and "brought back into the garden" to become a constructive force in building a new humanity on a new earth. If Eve's fall represents the dehumanization of women under patriarchy and patriarchal religion since the beginning of civilization, the coming of Lilith must stand for women's reclamation of their creativity autonomy and intellectual energy as a reciprocal selfhood, which, when repressed and banished by male dominance, could only appear as a vengeful hostile being in the guilty imaginations of men, and could only express itself in subversive ways in an enslaved womankind.

This book, then, is not primarily about what women really are. Rather it is about what women have appeared to be in the androcentric perspective of a male-dominated universe, and what they have been made to be in this context. This is the history of the shattered image, because woman, in being made to represent the projections of what men are not, his fears and aspirations, became a mirror-being without real selfhood of her own, the amalgam of the contradictions of men. Simultaneously the "Devil's Gateway" and the Virgin Mother, the hated and the adored, woman becomes, in Western mythology, a chimera without substance. But by looking back at these images, by establishing an autonomous subjectivity and standpoint from which to study, evaluate and judge these images, women today also shatter this mirror and, with it, shatter their own false mirror role. They establish the basis for a new humanity beyond patriarchy which must be based on dialogue and reciprocal consciousness.

ROSEMARY RADFORD RUETHER
September, 1973

Women and Religion: Psychological aud Cultural Implications

PATRICIA MARTIN DOYLE

The question raised by the essays in this volume on images of women in the Judaic-Christian tradition is the single most radical question that can be asked in our own time and for the foreseeable future. In these essays it assumes many forms, but all have one basic issue in mind. In its simplest terms, the authors ask, "How shall we evaluate and reform religious life in terms of the full dignity, equality and liberation of women and men?" Correlatively, the question applies to all cultural and individual values, ethics, styles of life, interpretations of meaning, organized modes of being, or in short, every aspect of life and reality as it is both consciously and unconsciously lived and perceived. These are not disparate issues but various aspects of the one basic question that can and must be asked.

The debate on women and religion is the single most important and radical question for our time and the foreseeable future precisely because it concerns religion and because it affects all possible people and peoples. As many theologians and social scientists would argue, religion concerns the deepest and most ultimate aspects of human life, individually and collectively. It provides "a set of symbolic forms and acts that relate man to the ultimate conditions of his existence,"[1] which are of the most profound importance to man. As Clifford Geertz states:

> A religion is a system of symbols which acts to establish powerful, pervasive and long-lasting moods and motivation in men by formulating conception of a general order of existence and clothing these conceptions with such an aura of factuality that the moods and motivations seem uniquely realistic.[2]

To raise the issue of women in relation to religious systems therefore challenges the most important and profound aspect of life. As William James, quoting Tolstoy, says, religion is "that by which men live."[3] Feminist analysis of culture and society stops prematurely if it does not dare to tackle religion. When feminists take on religion they oppose the most deeply held motivations, beliefs and life orientations. It is this dimension of religion that makes the debate the most radical of all feminist encounters with cultural and individual thought and feeling. We should not be surprised if the dispute thus results in radical resistance within the churches and individual men and women, as well as in the possibility of radical cultural, psychological and religious transformations for others. Nonetheless religious consciousness cannot help but be changed by the impact of the question, and even those who resist change will have to struggle with the issue if and when they decide to repudiate women and the feminist challenges to religion, culture and individual orientations.

The problem of women vis-à-vis religion is also the most important question that can be raised, simply because it affects more people than any other issue. Every woman and man in Western culture who is influenced by the Judaic-Christian tradition is at least indirectly affected by the issues raised in this and similar books. By extension to other religious systems, it could affect all cultures and all present and future persons. It may be trite to say that half of the world's population is composed of women, but this fact alone transforms the women issue into an overriding concern for humanity. Yet it is not limited to women. Nobody is immune, for men as well as women are involved in the possible transformation of all aspects of their thinking, feeling and acting, individually and collectively. A new, radical and fundamental question faces the people of the world.

In the essay that follows I hope to explore some of the psychological and cultural justifications and implications of the debate on women and religion and examine the balance of female/male imagery in the Judaic-Christian tradition. I will focus primarily upon the relevant psychological work and ideas of Erik and Joan Erikson in regard to the issues of women and religion, although occasional reference will be made to the works of Paul Tillich insofar as Erikson's perceptions need to be set within theological contexts.[4] Such an analysis is entirely appropriate to theology, for as the late Paul Tillich argued, "Christianity cannot be considered in isolation from the general religious and cultural, psychological and sociological development of humanity."[5] Today cultural and psychological feminist concerns are central to the religious situation and development of our time.

IDENTITY AND IDEOLOGY

Erikson attends primarily to the psychological and cultural implications and sources of the relative male-female balance within religious consciousness. He shares with Christian theology certain basic models of masculinity and femininity, but his psychology of religion goes considerably beyond most theologians on the question at various points, particularly in terms of the relation between identity and ideology.

Erikson formulated the idea that adolescents go through an identity crisis that is related to possible and actual ideological commitments (including those of religion) within each individual's peculiar cultural setting. The notion has had a far-reaching impact on the psychosocial situation of our time. Psychologically, it diagnosed a previously unrecognized psychosocial phenomenon inherent in normal maturation which has both healthy and pathological dynamics of its own. Socially, self-conscious questioning of identity and ideological commitments has spread with word of its diagnosis, almost by contagion. Culturally, it gave impetus to studies of the relation between identity and ideology by social scientists and others engaged in the study of religion and ideology. Not least among its results, the concept has provided a theoretical rationale for both blacks and women to look at prevalent ideologies in terms of how they impinge upon identity formation for non-white and nonmale groups in our society.

Erikson defines identity as that partly conscious and partly unconscious inner sense of personal continuity, sameness and uniqueness that is confirmed daily in one's actions and in the mutual affirmations of others. It is the affirmative sense of "This is who I am," or "This is the real me," which a person possesses when feeling most real, energetic and confident. It reaches into one's past and into the future as a perception that one's self is both given and chosen. *Given,* for there is the sense of an unshakable basis to the self that is mutually recognized by oneself and others as inherently one's own. *Chosen,* for there is the sense that the person actively wills to be the person that is given. Passive inheritance, conditioning and conditions are turned into an active stance. One can "make one's identity happen" within one's own cultural and historical period.

Identity has its own dynamics and conflict and its own developmental period—that of adolescence and youth—when it comes to a crisis and resolution. The nature and degree of the crisis is more noticeable and acute in some times, places and groups than in others, and usually depends on ideological factors as well as on social changes within the defined "realities" of a given cultural situation. As Erikson says:

> The nature of identity conflict often depends on the latent panic pervading a historical period. Some periods in history become identity vacua caused by three basic forms of human apprehension: *fears* aroused by new facts, such as discoveries and inventions (including weapons) which radically expand and change the whole world-image; *anxieties* aroused by symbolic dangers vaguely perceived as a consequence of the decay of existing ideologies; and the *dread* of an existential abyss devoid of spiritual meaning.[6]

Such factors are all obviously related to ideological or (what was earlier defined as) religious symbol systems undergirding and guiding particular cultures.

For his part, Erikson defines ideology in slightly varying ways, depending upon whether he is calling attention to the individual or cultural implications of ideology. His general definition is that

... an ideological system is a coherent body of shared images, ideas, and ideals which, whether based on a formulated dogma, an implicit Weltanschauung, a highly structured world image, a political creed, or, indeed, a scientific creed (especially if applied to man), or a "way of life," provides for the participants a coherent, if systematically simplified, over-all orientation in space and time, in means and ends.[7]

In his case history of the relation of identity and ideology presented in *Young Man Luther* Erikson says:

In this book, *ideology* will mean an unconscious tendency underlying religious and scientific as well as political thought: the tendency at a given time to make facts amenable to ideas, and ideas to facts, in order to create a world image convincing enough to support the collective and individual sense of identity. Far from being arbitrary or consciously manageable (although it is as exploitable as all of man's unconscious strivings), the total perspective created by ideological simplification reveals its strength by the dominance it exerts on the seeming logic of historical events, and by its influence on the identity formation of individuals (and thus on their "ego-strength"). In this sense, this is a book on identity and ideology.[8]

In both of the definitions above, ideology is related to the sense of individual and communal identity. In perhaps his most systematic statement of the relations between ideology and identity, especially as they are seen in terms of the peculiar developmental period of youth, Erikson draws eight consequences of ideology for identity:

... we can ascribe to ideology the function of offering youth (1) a simplified perspective of the future which encompasses all foreseeable time and thus counteracts individual "time confusion"; (2) some strongly felt correspondence between the inner world of ideals and evils and the social world with its goals and dangers; (3) an opportunity for exhibiting some uniformity of appearance and behavior counteracting individual identity-consciousness; (4) inducement to a collective experimentation with roles and techniques which help overcome a sense of inhibition and personal guilt; (5) introduction into the ethos of the prevailing technology and thus into sanctioned and regulated competition; (6) a geographic-historical world image as a framework for the young individual's budding identity; (7) a rationale for a sexual way of life compatible with a convincing system of principles; and (8) submission to leaders who as super-human figures or "big-brothers" are above the ambivalence of the parent-child relation. Without some such *ideological commitment,* however implicit in a "way of life," youth suffers a *confusion of values* . . . which can be specifically dangerous to some but which on a large scale is surely dangerous to the fabric of society.[9]

The above description can stand on its own, but for our purposes further attention should be drawn particularly to two of the consequences of ideology upon identity—those listed above as (2) and (7).

An ideology formulates consciously and unconsciously the dangers and evils of a particular individual and social world as much as it does the ideals. Erikson believes that any given system combines with its ideals an "irrational self-hate of one's negative identity and the irrational repudiation of inimical otherness."[10] People, in other words, define themselves (consciously as much as unconsciously) in terms of what they will try *not* to be or become, although they know that in fact they have such alternative possibilities within themselves. People define themselves and their culture negatively as well as positively. There is an inner and outer enemy, as well as an inner and outer ideal, which remains part of one's self-definition and is an impediment to individual and cultural wholeness. Erikson states:

> Identity formation normatively has its negative side which throughout life can remain an unruly part of the total identity. The *negative identity* is the sum of all those identifications and identity fragments which the individual had to submerge in himself as undesirable or irreconcilable or by which atypical individuals and marked minorities are made to feel "different." In the event of aggravated crises, an individual (or, indeed, a group) may despair of the ability to contain these negative elements in a positive identity. A specific rage can be aroused wherever identity development loses the promise of a traditionally assured wholeness: thus an as yet uncommitted delinquent may become a criminal. Such potential rage is also easily exploited by psychopathic leaders, who become the models of a sudden surrender to total

doctrines and dogmas in which the negative identity becomes the dominant one.[11]

As Erikson acknowledges, the negative identities of white males in our own culture are projected and enforced upon minorities and women even as they are denied, repressed and resisted into unconscious, hateful identifications by white males. In his brief essays on race and women[12] Erikson makes it clear that he believes that the assignment of negative identities and qualities identified with minorities and women does almost as much irreparable damage to white males and our contemporary culture as it does to women and minorities.

Erikson argues, in the case of minority and race specification, that a "pseudospecies" of mankind has resulted for various groups in terms of positive and negative group identities and identifications. Those who are not identical with white males are defined as not really or fully human, and are therefore subject to exclusion from humanity and to elimination. Nazi practices illustrate the extreme to which pseudospecification can go. The developments of the nuclear age, however, entail the possible annihilation of all people and make it mandatory to define all peoples as richly varying but fully human co-members of one species in a new and wider identity.

Within Western culture, minorities and women have been subject to pseudospecification and negative identification. Response to pseudospecification by whites has caused minorities to perceive themselves as "invisible," "nameless" and "faceless," lacking even in solid substantiality. Against such "nobodyness" blacks and others strive to reconquer a "surrendered identity."[13] Response to the asserted superiority of white males has mostly resulted in a sense of negative identity and the rage at foreclosure of positive possibilities that such a negative identity entails. Against both options, "Black is beautiful" tries to reclaim positive identity. Erikson notes that

> the oppressor has a vested interest in the negative identity of the oppressed because that negative identity is a projection of his own unconscious negative identity—a projection which, up to a point, makes him feel superior but also, in a brittle way, whole.[14]

It is important to note that, while Erikson challenges the cultural bias of the perception, the negative identity of blacks includes many elements identified as "feminine" by white male culture, including submissiveness, deprecation of personal worth, emotional intensity and "feminine" vocational goals of performance within the arts.[15] It may be legitimate to push the question from the usual explanatory analysis of the relative predominance of mothers within black culture to the question of whether minorities and women share a common psychological and cultural fate as that negative identity of white males which is primarily and primordially based upon defining oneself as not-female. It is sex rather than race that first defines what is unacceptable for most children to be, and it may be sex-linked identifications that define and contaminate those of race.

As to the provision of "a rationale for a sexual way of life compatible with a convincing system of principles," Erikson, for one, is quite certain that women have been mercilessly exploited even when they have enjoyed "secondary gains of devious dominance" through capitulation. He says:

> Woman, throughout the ages (at any rate, the patriarchal ones), has lent herself to a variety of roles conducive to an exploitation of masochistic potentials; she has let herself be confined and immobilized, enslaved and infantilized, prostituted and exploited, deriving from it at best what in psychopathology we call "secondary gains" of devious dominance. This fact, however, could be satisfactorily explained only within a new kind of biocultural history which (and this is one of my main points) would first have to overcome the prejudiced opinion that woman must be, or will be, what she is or has been under particular cultural conditions.[16]

Few statements of the negative identity and role of women carry such sweeping charges for both males and females as Erikson's on the exploitation of women.

Erikson states that in general, "in some periods of history and in some phases of his life cycle, man needs . . . a new ideological orientation as surely and as sorely as he must have air and food."[17] There is no doubt for Erikson that we are now in such a period, and that the new ideological and identity system must take positive account of suppressed negative identities for white males and the positive identity and role of women. As he states in the opening paragraph of his essay on women:

>   There are a great number of economic and practical reasons for an intensified awareness of woman's position in the modern world. But there are also more elusive and darker reasons. The ubiquity of nuclear threat, the breakthrough into outer space, and increasing global communication are all bringing about a total change in the sense of geographic space and historical time, and thus they *necessitate nothing less than a redefinition of the identity of the sexes within a new image of man* [italics mine]. . . . But it is clear that the danger of man-made poison dropping invisibly from outer space into the marrow of the unborn in the wombs of women has suddenly brought one major male pre-occupation, namely, the "solution" of conflict by periodical and bigger and better wars, to its own limits. The question arises whether such a potential for annihilation as now exists in the world should continue to exist without the representation of the mothers of the species in the councils of image-making and decision.[18]

Three characteristic themes find expression in this paragraph. They are, first, that male ideologies and identities have reached their logical and tolerable existential limit and have become exceedingly dangerous as they are acted out in complete disregard for the concerns of women. Second, that despite relative emancipation, "woman, in many ways, has kept her place within the typologies and cosmologies which men have had the exclusive opportunity to cultivate and idolize."[19] Women need to cultivate and help formulate new identities and new ideologies in light of the new valuations and understandings of women and the world not only for themselves but for the sake of a new and more holistic image of both women and men and a new understanding of the meaning of life. Third, new social and cultural forms must emerge in which women can claim full equality, dignity, specific creativity, and actualization of their specific interests and concerns. Erikson hopes that the combined thrust of these developments will enable nothing less than a newly livable and creative present and future for subsequent generations. To pin hope for the future of the world on women may sound extreme or unduly optimistic about women to some, but Erikson believes little else can be done. The continued exclusion and negation of women and the concerns of women in a totally masculine culture may almost inevitably lead to the end of the human (and other) species in a nuclear holocaust or some other form of destruction.

At this point it may be essential to state Erikson's own hypotheses concerning male and female identity so that the religious, cultural and psychological implications of his analysis may become clearer. In so doing, however, one must be aware that, as Erikson notes, the process of identity formation and ideological commitment has been studied almost exclusively in relation to males. Theories about women and/or the contrast between males and females are hypotheses for study and reflection rather than scientific or dogmatic truths that have been empirically verified.

MALE AND FEMALE DIFFERENCE

Erikson, like Freud before him, attempts to define the "intrinsically feminine" and the "intrinsically masculine" essence of women and men in terms of the anatomical dissimilarity of their genital organs. He argues that males and females organize space according to the morphology of their bodies, and that this affects one's psychosocial development and orientation to "inner" and "outer" space. The original basis of this thesis was his perception of play differences among 150 ten- to twelve-year-old children of each sex in a developmental study at Berkeley.[20] Each sex constructed 450 "exciting movie scenes" in which those of two thirds of the boys and girls could be commonly and easily differentiated. Boys tended to build ruins or tall structures that were liable to collapse, or depict action scenes in exterior situations that had strong motion (by Indians, animals, motorcars), with its channelization or arrest (by policemen). The need for caution outdoors was apparent. Girls tended to build peaceful interiors that were open, simply enclosed or excitingly intruded upon (by men or animals), with females engaged in enjoyable or productive pursuits inside (e.g., playing the piano). Feminine "goodness" indoors was apparent. Boys adorned high structures; girls, gates. Erikson goes on to state:

It is clear by now that the spatial tendencies governing these constructions . . . in fact, closely parallel the morphology of the sex organs: in the male, *external* organs, *erectable* and *intrusive* in character, *conducting* highly *mobile* sperm cells; *internal* organs in the female, with a vestibular *access* leading to *statically expectant* ova. Does this reflect an acute and temporary emphasis on the modalities of the sexual organs owing to the experience of oncoming sexual maturation? My clinical judgment (and the brief study of the "dramatic productions" of college students) incline me to think that the dominance of genital modes over the modalities of spatial organization reflects a profound difference in the sense of space in the two sexes, even as sexual differentiation obviously provides the most decisive difference in the ground plan of the human body which, in turn, codetermines biological experience and social roles.[21]

Erikson believes that adult men and women, as well as boys and girls, tend to follow the spatial morphology of their bodies in their psychic, social, cultural and religious life. Anatomy is not wholly destiny, as Freud argued, nor history alone one's destiny, as Napoleon stated, but "anatomy, history and personality are our *combined destiny.*" One is never not a male or a female but always one or the other, and adult commitments reflect this for better and for worse. Regardless of the propensities and achievements of particular individuals, the majority of men and women (versus exceptional individuals) live out sex-specific orientations. Erikson states: "The emphasis here is on predisposition and predilection, rather than on exclusive ability, for both sexes (if otherwise matched in maturation and intelligence) learn readily to imitate the spatial mode of the other sex." Such imitation forms a strong basis for communication and agreement between the sexes. A number of exceptional individuals of especial talent and/or weakness are primarily oriented to the concerns, values and spatial perceptions of the opposite sex. They bear witness to the legitimate heritage of all men and women to actualize their lives in the fullest possible way. Erikson states: "Each sex can transcend itself to feel and to represent the concerns of the other. For even as real women harbor a legitimate as well as compensatory masculinity, so real men can partake of motherliness—if permitted to do so by powerful mores."[22]

Freud based much of his psychology on the male's possession of a penis as the foundation of his psychic life. Erikson goes considerably beyond Freud in looking at psychosocial as well as psychosexual foundations and stages in the development of male identity, psychic and social life. Adult manhood cannot be reduced to simple sexual functioning or the Oedipal stage of development. Nonetheless Erikson believes that there are some rather stark and embarrassingly simple correlations to be drawn between male sexuality and our present cultural belief systems and behavior. Moreover, he believes that these male cultural patterns have about reached their limit of value, utility and rationality, unless society becomes considerably modified by feminine input. As he states:

> Here I say little about men; their accomplishments in the conquest of geographic space and of scientific fields and in the dissemination of ideas speak loudly for themselves and confirm traditional values of masculinity. Yet the play-constructing boys in Berkeley may give us pause: on the world scene, do we not see a supremely gifted yet somewhat boyish mankind playing excitedly with history and technology, following a male pattern as embarrassingly simple (if technologically complex) as the play constructions of the preadolescent? Do we not see the themes of the toy microcosm dominating an expanding human space: height, penetration, and speed; collision, explosion—and cosmic super-police?

> The special dangers of the nuclear age clearly have brought male leadership close to the limit of its adaptive imagination. The dominant male identity is based on a fondness for "what works" and for what man can make, whether it helps to build or destroy . . . In view of the gigantic one-sidedness which is threatening to make men the slave of his triumphant technology, the now fashionable discussion, by women and by men, as to whether woman could and how she might become "fully human" is really a cosmic parody.[23]

Erikson's critique of the dominant male identity and ideological commitments in our time tends to be based on the practical results of the one-sided development of psychosocial possibilities. He speaks of self-made men ruthlessly striving for mastery, competence and power who willfully suppress and conquer all that gets in their way. He speaks of the boyishness of perpetually adolescent males who have such a fondness for technology and "what works" that they play with instruments of wider and wider destructiveness. This framework even—or perhaps, especially—infects the perception of God, so that the Ultimate is invoked to substantiate a destructively masculine world. As Erikson says: "Man's Ultimate has too often been visualized as an infinity which begins where the male conquest of outer space ends, and a domain where an 'even more' omnipotent and omniscient Being must be submissively acknowledged."[24] Such a gigantic one-sidedness, Erikson notes, has brought us to our current appalling situation in which the traditional feminine values of realism in householding, responsibility in upbringing, resourcefulness in keeping and making the peace, devotion to healing, creativity in fostering life, hitherto ignored, must find a new emphasis and input into our cultural life.[25]

On the feminine side, Erikson emphasizes the dissimilarity of his views to those of Freud and his followers. Freud spoke of women in terms of their negative sexual identity. He saw women as defective men, as the sex that did not have what men possessed —namely, a penis—and that felt and were irrevocably damaged and made envious by the perception of their lack. Erikson allows himself to wonder at the analysts' "phobic avoidances" of the positive somatic identity of women,[26] and at their lack of perception that "behind man's insistence on male superiority there is an age-old envy of women who are sure of their motherhood while man can be sure of his fatherhood only by restricting the female."[27] Erikson calls Freud Victorian, patriarchal, and unduly influenced by women patients who were partly sick because they were in fact completely dominated and subjugated. "Freud's general judgment of the identity of women was," he states, "probably the weakest part of his theory." Erikson argues that many women are envious of men, but that this is entirely natural for any girl, who can

> . . . see that a boy, just because of his anatomical appendage, was considered more important. . . . women could not help harboring that inner rage which comes from having to identify with your negative image of you. And, as usual, the exploiter offered

more complex compensation in his own terms, offering (to high and low) the ideal of the lady, or the keeper of the house, or the courtesan.[28]

He goes on to say:

. . . such envy exists in all women and is aggravated in some cultures; but the explanation of it in male terms or the suggestion that it be borne with fatalism and compensated for by a redoubled enjoyment of the feminine equipment (duly certified and accepted as second rate) has not helped women to find their places in the modern world, for it has made of womanhood an ubiquitous compensation neurosis marked by a bitter insistence on being "restored."[29]

Such remarks should be placed within the context of Erikson's diagnosis of negative identity and pseudospecification, for it is clear that it is women who have borne the major brunt of both down through history.

Erikson, for his part, argues that women have a *positive* somatic identity based on the possession and attunement of women to "an inner productive space," or the womb. According to Erikson, women's orientation to inner space is the basis of maternity, and means among other things that

. . . the very importance of the promises and the limitations of the inner productive space exposes women to a sense of specific loneliness, to a fear of being left empty or deprived of treasures, of remaining unfulfilled and of drying up. . . . clinical observation suggests that in female experience an "inner space" is at the center of despair even as it is the very center of potential fulfillment. Emptiness is the female form of perdition—known at times to men of the inner life . . . but standard experience for all women. To be left, for her, means to be left empty, to be drained of the blood of the body, the warmth of the heart, the sap of life. . . . Clinically, this "void" is so obvious that generations of clinicians must have had a special reason for not focusing on it.[30]

This particular form of the sense of possible creativity of the "inner productive space" or emptiness is not totally peculiar to women. Both sexes, according to Erikson, legitimately participate in the sexuality of the other, and men of special giftedness or weakness also specialize in "that inwardness and sensitive indwelling . . . usually ascribed to women," although it "also exists in some form in all men." But, Erikson argues, "the point is that in women the basic schema exists within an over-all optimum configuration such as cultures have every reason to nurture in the *majority of women,* for the sake of collective survival as well as individual fulfillment."[31]

RELIGION AND THE FEMININE

The feminine "inner productive space" has religious as well as psychological and cultural value and implications for the Eriksons. In the following subsection of the essay I will explore a few of Erikson's explicit references to religion and femininity in terms of the four themes of maternity, mysticism, religious "actualism" and sanctity. In each area sex or sex-linked propensities are religiously significant, according to Erikson.

In Erikson's view, every mother (and maternity in general) mediates and embodies the primary religious response to life for all infants in their care. This is partly because it is the mother with whom every individual first starts life and with whom the child has that first relation that becomes the basis for subsequent development and establishment of patterns of relationship. The child learns basic trust and mistrust during this stage which "forms the basis in the child for a sense of identity which will later combine a sense of being 'all right,' of being oneself, and of becoming what other people trust one will become." The child starts life in a symbiotic union with the mother in which the child has no separate identity but only an identity of "being part of the mother." Gradually the child establishes a rudimentary sense of separate identity, partly through the process of weaning and teething. The child is introduced into a sense of inner division within himself. The result for all children is a "universal nostalgia for a paradise forfeited. It is against this powerful combination of a sense of having been deprived, of having been divided, and of having been abandoned—that basic trust must maintain itself through life."[32] Such a basic trust is given, maintained and restored, in Erikson's view, by the mother's own sense of trust and oneness with the world. Whether conscious or not, the mother mediates her own religious commitments to the child. Erikson states:

> The parental faith which supports the trust emerging in the newborn has throughout history sought its institutional safeguard (and, on occasion, found its greatest enemy) in organized religion. Trust born of care is, in fact, the touchstone of the *actuality* of a given religion. All religions have in common the periodical child-like surrender to a Provider or providers who dispense earthly fortune as well as spiritual health; some demonstration of man's smallness by way of reduced posture and humble gesture; the admission in prayer and song of misdeeds, of misthoughts, and of evil intentions; fervent appeal for inner unification by divine guidance; and finally, the insight that individual trust must become part of the ritual practice of many, and must become a sign of trustworthiness in the community. . . . Primitive religions, the most primitive layer in all religions, and the religious layer in each individual, abound with efforts at atonement which try to make up for vague deeds against a maternal matrix and try to restore faith in the goodness of one's strivings and in the kindness of the powers of the universe.[33]

Given Erikson's view of the primacy of the mother-child relation for the individual's relation to religion and life, it is not surprising that both Erik and Joan Erikson focus upon the role of Mary the Madonna as representing in theological, ideological and devotional terms the embodiment of the primary "religious fact." Hence, Joan Erikson in *St. Francis et His Four Ladies* celebrates the elevation of Mary in medieval piety, and especially the devotion of Francis, to a position of pervasive influence and power. She says: "Around such a Heavenly Personage all the mystery and symbolism of ancient pre-Christian female deities could converge and restore a unity of rational and emotional spirituality denied by the Judaic roots of Christianity."[34] That the renaissance of mother religion was relatively brief is cause for Erik Erikson to lament that "wherever Luther's influence was felt, the Mother of God (that focus of women's natural religion-by-being-and-letting-be) was dethroned."[35]

In *Young Man Luther* Erik Erikson points out that the overwhelming thrust of Luther's theological formulations was almost exclusively masculine in centering upon the father-son relation in religion and life. Both father and son roles were transformed and revitalized in imaginative new ways within a whole new socio-economic and cultural setting to which Luther's new self-consciousness contributed. Feminine roles, identity and theological presence, on the other hand, were both ignored and impoverished. The demotion of Mary was only one—if the primary—symptom of the exclusion of the feminine. Erikson states:

> Kierkegaard's comment that Luther invented a religion for the adult man states the limitation as well as the true extent of Luther's theological creation. Luther provided new elements for the Western male's identity, and created for him new roles; but he contributed only one new feminine identity, the parson's wife —and this solely perhaps because his wife, Katherine of Bora, created it with the same determined unself-consciousness with which she made the great Doktor marry her. Otherwise, the Lutheran revolution only created ideals for women who wanted to be like parsons if they couldn't be like parsons' wives.[36]

A woman could aspire to the masculine identity of a professional religious male if she couldn't be the wife of one! In neither case were women offered positive identities in their own right or positively valued.

Erikson's criticism above represents one of the many agreements between Erikson and Tillich as to the harmful effects of the self-conscious purge and elimination of "the female element in the symbolic expression of ultimate concern," especially as the female element is represented in the role of the Virgin Mary. Tillich believed the purge drove many Protestants to other forms of religion that at least minimally express feminine elements, especially mystical sensitivity,[37] but that elimination of Mary was so nearly complete in Protestant religious consciousness that Mary could not be revived as a religious symbol for Protestants. His own work is pervaded by a "hidden Mariology" insofar as he, in effect, substitutes the "motherhood of God" for "the demanding father image" with his emphasis on the ground and power of being itself. As he notes, "In so far as it (the concept ground of being) is symbolical, it points to the mother quality of giving birth, carrying and embracing, and, at the same time, of calling back, resisting independence of the created, and swallowing it."[38]

Historically, mythically and psychologically, Erikson and Tillich may be right that the motherhood of God is the first statement that can be made about divinity. In an ecologically sensitive age, Mariology as well as Mother Earth religion may be appealing and worthy of resuscitation. I expect, however, that many (and not just feminists) would find exclusive association of divinity with motherhood as confining and tyrannical as the father image many now try to escape, so that the task is to find imagery that transcends sex-specific capacities and awareness.

Mystics, saints and religious actualists, for the Eriksons, share specific sensitivity to feminine modes of perception of the divine. Actualization of maternal capacities plays a part in varying ways for each of these kinds of religious consciousness. The key claim, however, is broader and centers upon the ambiguous role that the "inner productive space" plays in religious perception. As noted earlier, Erikson believes that "emptiness is the female form of perdition—known at times to men of the inner life . . ., but standard experience for all women." So, too, blessedness, grace or the Ultimate may be characterized as a receptivity to the Divine in the Immediate that Erikson believes is "natural" to women's experience, although men also may share this perception. He says, "The Ultimate . . . may well be found also to reside in the Immediate, which has so largely been the domain of woman and the inward mind."[39] It is noteworthy that Erikson not only shares this presumption with Tillich but sets forth this belief in writing to "answer" Tillich's spoken worry that psychoanalysis may be undermining sensitivity to the Ultimate. Perhaps Erikson is saying that "proper" psychological understanding can lead to increased religious sensitivity.

Tillich, for his part, claims that one-sided masculine consciousness in Protestant religion, culture and moralistic personalism has been antithetical to perceiving and valuing the sacred in the Immediate. It is hostile to mystical experience and tendencies and "distrustful of the ecstatic element of the Spiritual Presence."[40] Such a mind-set impedes certain kinds of experience of grace and drives others to apersonal mysticism. The repudiation of the feminine thus has profound religious implications for Tillich and Erikson, as does cultivation of feminine perception.

In the case of mysticism, Erikson's insight into the centrality of the "inner productive space" and the perdition of emptiness points to new possibilities for understanding mystics and mystical experience both psychologically and theologically. The "dark night of the soul" and the "emptiness that attracts grace" can be illumined by this motif as it is found in such mystics as John of the Cross, Eckhart, and Simone Weil. Similarly, experiences of grace, including the "mystical marriage" of the feminine soul to God and the "birth of God" in the soul may be psychologically understood in a new way in the writings of such mystics as Bernard, Eckhart, Teresa, John of the Cross, and others. The psychology of religion and psychohistorical studies of religious figures could be considerably advanced by this particular insight.

"Religious actualists," as well as mystics, manifest the "feminine" concentration upon the Immediacy of the Divine, according to Erikson. Such people make "real," through effective action and inventive symbolism, the renewing consciousness and maximization of the Ultimate in daily life and the higher and greater unity among men. For the Eriksons, both Gandhi and Francis[41] had the genius to create new and dramatic rituals to symbolize the presence of the Ultimate in the smallest details of daily life. This takes an artistic and creative genius that is by no means "common to all women" and yet which, for the Eriksons, calls upon the same imaginative energies that all mothers exercise in relation to newborn children in creating rituals of interaction.[42] Such rituals make actual and mediate to child and follower alike the goodness, unity and meaning of the infinite within the finite moments, relations and "facts" of the everyday world.

Although by no means restricted to it, the cultivation of sanctity also has a feminine component, according to the Eriksons. In *Gandhi's Truth*, Erikson asserts that the religious presence of saints

> . . . has an affinity to the experience of women, who in their hereness and practical religiosity weave together in the chores of daily life what really "maintains the world," and who—while

heroes court death—can experience death as an intrinsic part of a boundless and boundlessly recreative life.[43]

Gandhi, for one, self-consciously assumed a maternal presence for his followers, personally and culturally appropriating the role of the mother as "the deepest, the most pervasive, and most unifying stratum of Indian religiosity."[44] In so doing, Gandhi (like other saints before him) transferred private maternity and "householder-ship" to the larger public world. Every person became a kinsman, a son or daughter, a brother or sister, to be sanctioned within the maternal presence. Erikson believes such a stance is common to saints, although perhaps especially exhibited in somebody like Gandhi. He says:

> . . . I wonder whether there has ever been another political leader who almost prided himself on being half man and half woman, and who so blatantly aspired to be more motherly than women born to the job, as Gandhi did. . . . He undoubtedly saw a kind of sublimated maternalism as part of the positive identity of a whole man, and certainly of a *homo religiosus*. But by then all overt phallicism had become an expendable, if not a detestable matter to him. Most men, of course, consider it not only un-necessary, but in a way, indecent, and even irreverent, to disavow a god-given organ of such singular potentials; and they remain deeply suspicious of a sick element in such sexual disarmament. And needless to say, the suspicion of psychological self-castration becomes easily linked with the age-old male propensity for con-sidering the renunciation of armament an abandonment of male-hood. Here, too, Gandhi may have been prophetic; for in a mechanized future the relative devaluation of the martial model of masculinity may well lead to a freer mutual identification of the two sexes.[45]

Several elements in this remarkable statement call for further attention. Among them are Erikson's statement that "Gandhi un-doubtedly saw a kind of sublimated maternalism as part of the positive identity of a whole man, and certainly of a *homo religi-osus*," and Erikson's claim that "Here, too, Gandhi may have been prophetic" of a movement toward a "freer mutual identification of the two sexes." Both are terribly important.

But first it is important to ask, in the light of such a statement, whether it might be the case that Erikson's appeals to women to assume in public realms the maternal values and presence of the private realm of women is not basically an appeal for sanctity. Erikson wants both women and men to be able to be maternally present to the household of all peoples. He ventures to express a hope:

> Maybe if women would only gain the determination to represent publicly what they have always stood for privately in evolution and in history (realism in householding, responsibility of upbringing, resourcefulness in peacekeeping, and devotion to healing), they might well add an ethically restraining, because truly supra-national, power to politics in the widest sense.[46]

One may greet such a statement with cynicism or hope. In either case, the full actualization of feminine values and concerns in the world may represent a new kind of practical religious vocation for Erikson which partakes in sanctity. One might add, however, that the ability and willingness of women (and men) to assume public affirmative responsibility for "feminine values" presumes a certain cultivation of "masculine" abilities and orientations, such as willingness to participate in the "external world" outside the home and techniques of conflict as well as cooperation. Feminine sanctity as well as masculine sanctity calls for a new, "androgynous" or "bisexual" unity in religious, secular and psychological capacities, skills and consciousness.

ANDROGYNOUS OR BISEXUAL RELIGION AND CONSCIOUSNESS

Erikson's remarks above lend psychological and cultural support to a new valuation of the feminine and to a theology of the "motherhood of God." Perhaps the major question to ask of Erikson, however, is whether his theory supports bisexual or androgynous being, religiously and individually. Little work has yet been done psychologically or theologically to determine exactly what bisexual or androgynous being looks like. At this point one simply assumes that the term implies either (1) that "masculine" and "feminine" traits are combined in a new "mix" that allows and encourages women to become "masculinely feminine" and men to become "femininely masculine" or (2) that sexual difference will disappear in a new and wider "unisex" identity that "transcends" sex-specific reference. Each of us probably has his or her own preference and fears about either alternative. At this point, however, it may behoove us not to decide upon the precise future shape of human perception and activity but to ask about the general needs and trends of contemporary society and the future. It seems to me that both Erikson and Tillich support a general move toward androgyny or bisexuality in psychological, cultural and religious being, at least in qualified ways.

Erikson is clear that all people, despite somatic differences between males and females, are basically androgynous in nature, and that most people will choose to actualize both masculine and feminine aspects of themselves if they are encouraged or allowed to do so by their culture. For Erikson, women do not cease being women, nor do men cease being men, but "each sex can transcend itself to feel and to represent the concerns of the other. For even as real women harbor a legitimate as well as compensatory masculinity, so real men can partake of motherliness—if permitted to do so by powerful mores."[47]

As noted above, Joan and Erik Erikson see the sanctity of both Francis and Gandhi as partly constituted by their reconciliation and actualization of the feminine capacities, as well as the masculine, within themselves. In describing Francis, Joan Erikson remarks on the combined reconciliation and actualization of both masculine and feminine qualities in great artists and saints. She says:

> . . . But there is another . . . related side to this saint which has for some people blurred his image. I mean a rather mysterious feminine quality which in the eyes of many has characterized him as a mild and passive figure. And yet was this very femininity not one of the sources of his peculiar strength? . . . For to bring talent to creative fruition requires a merging, a consolidation of the inherent polarities within the artist and every man—the masculine and feminine elements of his nature.

And artist and saint have something else in common. They must and do reconcile, at whatever cost of distress and frustration, the masculine and feminine in themselves. True, the male artist can always regain his masculine stature by embodying his tenderest insights in forceful and sometimes grandiose form, which he often does with a marked recovery of his vanity and rebelliousness. For the woman the feminine propensity to bend with the gale will be allied with great firmness in truly creative mothering and all other creative activities. However, the saint who is an artist too must not only wed the two sides of our basic bisexuality which struggle for reconciliation in all of us, but he must also manage a harmonious alliance of self-denying asceticism and receptive sensuality.[48]

The particulars of Francis' mode of sanctity may not be repeated in our time, but the Eriksons point to a quality of previously recognized saints which I believe will increasingly become real for ordinary as well as unique individuals: the wedding of the "two sides of our basic bisexuality which struggle for reconciliation in all of us." Such a movement will not be limited to men actualizing maternal or feminine as well as masculine qualities. Men do need to attune themselves to feminine values and qualities so that they might become more whole. But women, too, need to live out masculine values and qualities in reconciliation with feminine aspects of their lives.

That the Eriksons see androgynous or bisexual life as characteristic of saints seems to me to point to the sacred or ultimate dimensions of a "new" structure of personality and religious consciousness which previous saints may have "anticipated" as characteristic of religious life, or perhaps better, of spiritually free and freeing life within the Kingdom of God. Erikson suggests something similar when he says that Gandhi's life in its bisexuality may be prophetic for the future of a "freer mutual identification of the two sexes" that is part of the destiny of *homo religiosus*. Perhaps the saints point to our own religious, cultural and psychological future as androgynous or bisexual beings.

Erikson's theological colleague, Tillich, suggests a similar development in future theology in terms of androgynous or bisexual being. He says, "The question can only be whether there are elements in genuine Protestant symbolism which transcend the alternative male-female and which are capable of being developed over against a one-sided male-determined symbolism."[49]

In line with such a question, Tillich states that his reformulation of the doctrine of the Holy Spirit self-consciously attempts to transcend sex-specific orientations and be androgynous or bisexual in character. The Spiritual Presence and the Spiritual Community contain many elements that Tillich himself usually thinks of as feminine—mystical sensitivity, ecstasy, immediacy, union and communion, the sanctification of all life here and now, the rule of love over moral law, and so forth. "Masculine elements" are also included in prophetic sensibility, ethical action and discernment, attunement to the realities of history, and so on. But both "masculine" and "feminine" elements are transcended as they are combined in a new "mix." One can imagine men and women living in the Spiritual Presence and the Spiritual Community who are able to unite within themselves and their culture the previously warring alternatives of separate male or female consciousness alone. I believe such a consciousness is prophetic of our future, that a new era awaits realization, in which the promise of Galatians 3:28 may be fulfilled, that "There is neither Jew nor Greek, there is neither slave nor free, there is neither male nor female, for you are all one in Christ Jesus."

SUMMARY

There are profound religious, cultural and psychological implications to the question raised by the essays in this book. We have seen that Erikson believes that the exclusive masculinization of Protestant religion and culture since the Reformation has been one-sided and dangerous for humanity. Cultivation of the feminine in religious symbolizations and consciousness, in future ideologies and identities, is urgently needed if humanity is to be saved from possible catastrophe and become more whole. Practically speaking as well as idealistically speaking, two developments are necessary. First, the women's movement needs to succeed in claiming full equality and dignity for women and their concerns in every aspect of life—in religion, ideology and identity, as well as in the more "practical" social and cultural spheres of private and public life.

Second, given full recognition of feminine values and concerns, both men and women must be free to live androgynously in everyday life and in response to the ultimate dimensions of life in ways that combine and transcend specific masculinity and femininity.

NOTES

1. Robert N. Bellah, *Beyond Belief: Essays on Religion in a Post-Traditional World* (New York: Harper & Row, 1970), p. 21.
2. Clifford Geertz, "Religion as a Cultural System," in Michael Banton, ed. *Anthropological Approaches to the Study of Religion*, A. S. A. Monographs, III (London: Tavistock Press, 1966), 4.
3. William James, *The Varieties of Religious Experience: A Study in Human Nature*, Gifford Lectures for 1901–1902 (Modern Library ed., 1936), p. 184.
4. Paul Tillich: *Systematic Theology*, III (Chicago: University of Chicago Press, 1963), 293–294. For a longer explication of Paul Tillich's views, see the essay by Joan Arnold Romero in this book. It is appropriate to refer occasionally to Tillich's views within an essay devoted primarily to Erikson not only because of certain stated similarities between the views of Erikson and Tillich but also because the personal dialogue they engaged in while at Harvard was significant enough to cause parts of it to appear in print.
5. Paul Tillich, The Protestant Era (Chicago: University of Chicago Press, 1948), p. xxiii.
6. Erikson, "Autobiographic Notes on the Identity Crisis," *Daedalus* (Fall 1970), p. 733.
7. *Identity: Youth and Crisis* (New York: Norton, 1963), pp. 189–190.
8. Erik Erikson, *Young Man Luther* (New York: Norton, 1958), p. 22.
9. *Identity: Youth and Crisis*, pp. 187–188.
10. Ibid., p. 189.
11. "Autobiographic Notes," p. 733.
12. "Womanhood and the Inner Space" and "Race and the Wider Identity," in *Identity: Youth and Crisis*, pp. 261–320.
13. Ibid., pp. 295–299.
14. Ibid., p. 304.
15. Ibid., pp. 305–308.
16. Ibid., p. 284.
17. *Young Man Luther*, p. 22.
18. *Identity: Youth and Crisis*, p. 261.
19. Ibid., p. 262.

20. *Childhood and Society* (New York: Norton, rev. ed. 1963), pp. 97–108.
21. Ibid., p. 106.
22. *Identity: Youth and Crisis*, pp. 285, 273, 286.
23. Ibid., pp. 274, 262–263.
24. Ibid., pp. 293–294.
25. Ibid., pp. 261–264, 289–293.
26. Ibid., p. 278.
27. Richard I. Evans, *Dialogue with Erik Erikson* (New York: Dutton, 1969), p. 44.
28. Ibid., pp. 43–45.
29. *Identity: Youth and Crisis*, pp. 278–279.
30. Ibid., p. 278.
31. Ibid., p. 282.
32. *Childhood and Society*, pp. 249–250.
33. Ibid., pp. 250–251.
34. Joan Erikson, *St. Francis et His Four Ladies* (New York: Norton), p. 108.
35. *Young Man Luther*, p. 71.
36. Ibid.
37. *Systematic Theology*, III, 293–294.
38. Ibid.
39. *Identity: Youth and Crisis*, p. 294.
40. *Systematic Theology*, III, 294.
41. Erik Erikson, *Gandhi's Truth* (New York: Norton, 1969), pp. 425–436, and Joan Erikson, *St. Francis et His Four Ladies*, pp. 117 ff.
42. "The Development of Ritualization," in *The Religious Situation 1968*, ed. Donald Cutler (Boston: Beacon Press, 1968), pp. 771–773.
43. *Gandhi's Truth*, p. 400.
44. Ibid., p. 402.
45. Ibid., pp. 402–403.
46. *Identity: Youth and Crisis*, p. 262.
47. Ibid., pp. 285–286.
48. *St. Francis et His Four Ladies*, pp. 48, 128–129.
49. *Systematic Theology*, III, 293.

Images of Women in the Old Testament

PHYLLIS BIRD

For most of us the image of woman in the Old Testament is the image of Eve, augmented perhaps by a handful of Bible-storybook "heroines," or villainesses, as the case may be (Sarah, Deborah, Ruth, Esther, Jezebel, Delilah). Some may also perceive in the background the indistinct shapes of a host of unnamed mothers, who, silent and unacknowledged, bear all the endless genealogies of males. But it is the named women, by and large, the exceptional women, who supply the primary images for the usual portrait of the Old Testament woman. These few great women together with the first woman (curiously incompatible figures in most interpretations) fill the void that looms when we consider the image of woman in the Old Testament. For the Old Testament is a man's "book," where women appear for the most part simply as adjuncts of men, significant only in the context of men's activities.

This perception is fundamental, for it describes the terms of all Old Testament speech about women. The Old Testament is a collection of writings by males from a society dominated by males.[1] These writings portray a man's world. They speak of events and activities engaged in primarily or exclusively by males (war, cult

41

and government) and of a jealously singular God, who is described and addressed in terms normally used for males.[2]

But women appear in these pages more frequently than memory commonly allows—and in more diverse roles and estimations.[3] In some texts the woman of ancient Israel is portrayed simply as a class of property. In others she is depicted as possessing a measure of freedom, initiative, power and respect that contemporary American women might well envy. This essay attempts to examine that full range of Old Testament images of women, with attention to the contexts in which they were formed and formulated and the meaning given to them by the various "authors."

Only a reading of the Old Testament can give an adequate impression of the variety of viewpoints and expression represented in its words about women and also expose the common threads that run through them. Here we can do no more than sample that literature. The short selections offered below aim only to suggest the compass of the evidence upon which the following analysis is based.

> Most blessed of women be Jael
>   the wife of Heber, the Kenite,
>   of tent-dwelling women most blessed.
>   . . . . .
> She put her hand to the tent peg
>   and her right hand to the workman's mallet;
> she struck Sisera a blow,
>   she crushed his head,
>   she shattered and pierced his temple. (Judg. 5:24, 26)[4]

> I brought you up from the land of Egypt,
>   and redeemed you from the house of bondage;
>   and I sent before you Moses, Aaron, and Miriam. (Mic. 6:4)

> Now when the Queen of Sheba heard of the fame of
> Solomon concerning the name of the Lord, she came
> to test him with hard questions. She came to
> Jerusalem with a very great retinue, with camels
> bearing spices, and very much gold, and precious
> stones . . . (I Kings 10:1-2)

So Bathsheba went to King Solomon, to speak
to him on behalf of Adonijah. And the king
rose to meet her, and bowed down to her;
then he . . . had a seat brought . . . and she
sat on his right. (I Kings 2:19)

Everyone who curses his father or his mother
shall be put to death. (Lev. 20:9)

The peasantry grew plump in Israel
   they grew plump on booty
When you arose, O Deborah,
   arose, a mother in Israel. (Judg. 5:7)[5]

Out of the window she peered,
   the mother of Sisera gazed through the lattice:
"Why is his chariot so long in coming?
   Why tarry the hoofbeats of his chariots?"
Her wisest ladies make answer,
   nay, she gives answer to herself,
"Are they not finding and dividing the spoil?—
   A maiden [lit., womb] or two for every man . . ."
                                          (Judg. 5:28–30)

Now King David was old and advanced in years;
and although they covered him with clothes, he
could not get warm. Therefore his servants said
to him, "Let a young maiden be sought for my lord
the king . . . let her lie in your bosom, that my lord
the king may be warm." So they sought for a beautiful
maiden throughout all the territory of Israel, and
found Abishag the Shunammite, and brought her to the
king. (I Kings 1:1–4)

. . . the men of the city, base fellows, beset the house
round about, beating on the door; and they said
to the old man, the master of the house, "Bring
out the man who came into your house, that we
may know him." And the man, the master of the
house, went out to them and said to them, "No,
my brethren, do not act so wickedly . . .

here are my virgin daughter and his concubine;
let me bring them out now. Ravish them and do
with them what seems good to you; but against this
man do not do so vile a thing." (Judg. 19:22–24)

When you go forth to war against your enemies . . .
and you take them captive, and see among
the captives a beautiful woman, and you have
desire for her and would take her for yourself
as wife, then you shall . . . [permit her to]
bewail her father and mother a full month; after
that you may go in to her and be her husband,
and she shall be your wife. Then, if you have no
delight in her, you shall let her go where she
will; but you shall not sell her for money, you
shall not treat her as a slave, since you have
humiliated her. (Deut. 21:10–14)

When Rachel saw that she bore Jacob no children,
she envied her sister; and she said to Jacob.
"Give me children, or I shall die!"

Then God remembered Rachel and God hearkened to her
and opened her womb. She conceived and bore a
son, and said, "God has taken away my reproach." (Gen. 30:1–2,
22–23)

. . . If a woman conceives and bears a male child, then she
shall be unclean seven days . . . But if she bears a
female child, then she shall be unclean two weeks. (Lev. 12:2, 5)

A certain woman threw an upper millstone upon
Abimelech's head and crushed his skull. Then he
called hastily to the young man his armor-bearer,
and said to him, "Draw your sword and kill me,
lest they say of me, 'A woman killed him.' " (Judg. 9:53–54)

My people—children are their oppressors,
    and women rule over them.
O my people, your leaders mislead you,
    and confuse the course of your paths. (Isa. 3:12)

Now when Athaliah the mother of Ahaziah saw that
her son was dead, she arose and destroyed all the
royal family. . . . [and she] reigned over the land
for seven years. (II Kings 11:1, 3)

The Lord has created a new thing on earth:
    a woman protects [lit., encompasses] a man. (Jer. 31:22)

A good wife . . .

. . . . .

She considers a field and buys it;
    with the fruit of her hands she plants a vineyard.
She girds her loins with strength
    and makes her arms strong.
She perceives that her merchandise is profitable. (Prov. 31:10,
16–18)

Rejoice in the wife of your youth,
    a lovely hind, a graceful doe.
Let her affection fill you at all times
    with delight,
    be infatuated always with her love. (Prov. 5:10–19)

A continual dripping on a rainy day and a
    contentious woman are alike. (Prov. 27:15)

The daughters of Zion are haughty
    and walk with outstretched necks,
    glancing wantonly with their eyes,
Mincing along as they go,
    tinkling with their feet. (Isa. 3:16)

The lips of a loose woman drip honey,
    and her speech is smoother than oil;
but in the end she is bitter as wormwood,
    sharp as a two-edged sword. (Prov. 5:3–4)

How fair and pleasant you are,
    O loved one, delectable maiden!
You are stately as a palm tree,
    and your breasts are like its clusters.
I say I will climb the palm tree

and lay hold of its branches
Oh, may your breasts be like clusters
      of the vine
    and the scent of your breath like
      apples,
and your kisses like the best wine . . . (S. of S. 7:6–9)

. . . I found him whom my soul loves.
I held him, and would not let him go
    until I had brought him into my
      mother's house,
    and into the chamber of her that
      conceived me. (S. of S. 3:4)

The daughter of any priest, if she profanes
herself by playing the harlot, profanes her
father; she shall be burned with fire. (Lev. 21:9)

I will not punish your daughters
    when they play the harlot,
nor your brides when they commit adultery;
for the men themselves go aside with harlots,
    and sacrifice with cult prostitutes. (Hos. 4:14)

So God created man in his own image, in the image
of God he created him; male and female he created
them. (Gen. 1:27)

The variety of images apparent even in this limited selection of texts suggests that no single statement can be formulated concerning *the* image of woman in the Old Testament. At the same time an attempt must be made to discover what unity and coherence may exist within this plurality of conceptions. This process cannot be short-circuited by simply focusing upon the image of woman presented in the creation narratives. While those accounts have been rightly recognized to contain statements of primary importance concerning the nature of man and woman, their place within the total Old Testament literature has been virtually ignored. The task of this essay—to present the *Old Testament's view*—requires that an effort be made to locate the creation accounts within the larger testimony of the Old Testament.

One consequence of such an effort must be the recognition that Eve—or the first woman—is nowhere referred to in the Hebrew Old Testament outside the accounts of origins found in Gen. 1–4.[6] Because of this limited context of reflection upon the original woman, these too familiar passages are treated last in this essay, after a picture of woman has been formed from references contained in the legal, didactic, historical and prophetic writings.

The diversity in the Old Testament conceptions of women may be attributed in part to differences in the time of composition of the writings and in part to differences in socioreligious context. The texts span close to a millennium in their dates of composition (twelfth to third century B.C.), while particular themes, motifs, images and languages may derive from even earlier periods and cultures. However, since the "prehistory," of these texts can be assessed only by speculation that moves beyond adequate controls and scholarly consensus, they must be judged in their present form as products of that society known to us as Israel and as reflecting primarily the beliefs and practices of the period of their composition.[7]

That millennium saw enormous changes in the social, economic, political and religious life of Israel. The texts on which this study is based reflect social patterns and images of seminomadic tribal society and of settled peasant agriculturalists. They mirror the modest and homogeneous life of the village, but also the cosmopolitan and stratified society of the capital and major cities. They embody the religious and cultural heritage of Mesopotamia and of Canaan and presuppose the differing political organization of autonomous clans, tribal league, independent monarchies, and the exile communities and subject provinces of a series of foreign imperial states. With these political changes went changes in the economic and religious life. New forms of social and religious organization emerged, new offices, new roles, new classes, new ideas and definitions—of man, and woman, of God and of his people. Some of the differences in the Old Testament conceptions of women must be attributed to these changes.

They may also be related to the individual authors, to the nature of the literature in which they are found, and to the particular situations they address. Thus prescriptive statements must be distinguished from descriptive, and attention must be given to the fact that different literary genres (e.g., myths, proverbs, admonitions and instruction, hymns, law, history, tales, sermons and prophetic discourse) follow rules of their own and reflect in different ways and different paces the changing images of the society. Hence the references considered below have been roughly grouped by literary types.[8]

THE IMAGE OF WOMAN IN THE OLD TESTAMENT LAWS

Though the laws of the Old Testament give only a partial view of the norms of ancient Israel, they are nevertheless a primary source for reconstructing the ideals and practices of that society. They are preserved, for the most part, in several large "codes," or collections, ranging in date from premonarchic (before 1,000 B.C.) to postexilic (500–400 B.C.) times.[9] Each collection, however, in its own prehistory has taken up material of different ages, and each combines laws of different types, including both "secular" law (the "law of the [city] gate"—where deliberation of cases took place) and religious law (the law of the sanctuary or religious assembly). Despite this variety, however, none of the "codes" can be considered comprehensive. All are samplers of one kind or another. All presuppose the current existence of a system that they seek not to formulate but to preserve from dissolution and destruction. Thus the laws frequently deal with areas in which changes have occurred or threaten, while the common assumptions of the society are left unspoken and must often be inferred from the special cases treated in the collections.

In many respects Israelite law differs little from that of ancient Mesopotamia and Syria. It is testimony to Israel's participation in a common ancient Near Eastern social and cultural milieu. Salient features of this shared culture revealed in Israel's laws are patriarchy (together with patrilineal descent and patrilocal residence as the usual norm), a more or less extended family, polygyny, concubinage,[10] slavery (under certain conditions), and the thoroughgoing institutionalization of the double standard. Israel's laws differ most notably from other known law codes in their unusual severity in the field of sexual transgression and in the severity of the religious laws that prescribe and seek to preserve the exclusive and undefiled worship of Yahweh, the national deity. These two unique features are interrelated, and both had significant consequences for women in ancient Israel.[11]

The majority of the laws, especially those formulated in the direct-address style of the so-called apodictic law (the style used primarily for the statement of religious obligations), address the community *through its male members*.[12] Thus the key verbal form in the apodictic sentence is the second person *masculine* singular or plural. That this usage was not meant simply as an inclusive form of address for bisexual reference is indicated by such formulations as the following:

Thou shalt not covet thy neighbor's wife. (Exod. 20:19)

You shall not afflict any widow or orphan.
If you do . . . then your wives shall become
widows and your children fatherless. (Exod. 22:22–24 [Heb. 21–23])

You shall be men consecrated to me. (Exod. 22:31)

Similarly, the typical casuistic law (case law) begins with the formula "If a *man* does X . . ." The term used for "man" in this formulation is not the generic term, *'ādām*, but the specifically and exclusively masculine term, *'iš*. Even if one argues that these laws were understood to apply by extension to the whole community, it must be noted that the masculine formulation was apparently found inadequate in some circumstances. Thus *'ādām* is substituted for *'iš*, or the terms "man" and "woman" (*'iš, 'iššāh*) are used side by side where it is important to indicate that the legislation is intended to be inclusive in its reference.[13]

The basic presupposition of all the laws, though modified to some extent in the later period, is a society in which full membership is limited to males, in which only a male is judged a responsible person. He is responsible not only for his own acts but for those of his dependents as well. These include wife, children and even livestock, in the extended and fluid understanding of household/property that pertained in ancient Israel (Exod. 20:17, 21:

28–29). The law addresses heads of families (the family is called appropriately a "father's house" in the Hebrew idiom), for it is the family, not the individual, that is the basic unit of society in old Israel.[14]

But this definition of society as an aggregate of male-dominated households was modified in Israel by a concept of the society as a religious community, a religious community composed in the first instance exclusively of males, or perhaps originally all adult males.[15] This is the understanding of the covenant congregation, or the "people" (*ͨam*), Israel, addressed by Moses on Sinai:

> So Moses went down from the mountain to the
> people (ͨam). . . . And he said to the people
> (ͨam), "Be ready by the third day; do not go
> near a woman." (Exod. 19:14–15)[16]

It also coincides with the understanding of the "people" (*ͨam*) as the warriors of the community, a usage illustrated in certain texts pertaining to the premonarchic period.[17]

> The Lord said to Gideon, "The people (ͨam) are
> too many for me to give the Midianites into
> their hand." (Judg. 7:2)

> Sisera called out all his chariots . . . and all
> the men (ͨam) who were with him . . . (Judg. 4:13)

In both cult and war the "true" nature of Israel manifested itself.[18]

The coincidence in Israel of these two male-oriented and male-dominated systems (the sociopolitical and the religious) created a double liability for women, enforcing upon them the status of dependents in the religious as well as the political and economic spheres. Discrimination against women was inherent in the socio-religious organization of Israel. It was a function of the system. And though this systemic discrimination need not be represented as a plot to subjugate women—and thereby liberate the male ego—the system did enforce and perpetuate the dependence of women and an image of the female as inferior to the male.

This is illustrated in the legal material by laws dealing with inheritance, divorce, sexual transgressions, religious vows, cultic observances and ritual purity. One of the chief aims of Israelite law is to assure the integrity, stability and economic viability of the family as the basic unit of society. In this legislation, however, the interests of the family are commonly identified with those of its male head. His rights and duties are described with respect to other men and their property. The laws focus mainly upon external threats to the man's authority, honor and property, though they may occasionally serve to define and protect his rights in relation to members of his own household (slaves: Exod. 21:20–21; children: Deut. 21:18–22; wife: Num. 5:11–31). Only in rare cases, however, are the laws concerned with the rights of dependents (Exod. 21:26–27; Deut. 21:10–14, 15–17 and 22:13–21).[19]

The wife's primary contribution to the family was her sexuality, which was regarded as the exclusive property of her husband, both in respect to its pleasure and its fruit. Her duty was to "build up" his "house"—and his alone. This service was essential to the man in order for him to fulfill his primary role as paterfamilias. It was as a consequence jealously guarded. Adultery involving a married woman was a crime of first magnitude in Israelite law (Lev. 20:10; Exod. 20:14), ranking with murder and major religious offenses as a transgression demanding the death penalty—for both offenders.[20] The issue was not simply one of extramarital sex (which was openly tolerated in certain circumstances). The issue was one of property and authority. Adultery was a violation of the fundamental and exclusive right of a man to the sexuality of his wife. It was an attack upon his authority in the family and consequently upon the solidarity and integrity of the family itself.[21] The adulterer robbed the husband of his essential honor, while the unfaithful wife defied his authority, offering to another man that which belonged only to him—and that which constituted her primary responsibility toward him.

The corollary of the unwritten law that a wife's sexuality belongs exclusively to her husband is the law that demands virginity of the bride.[22] The wife found guilty of fornication is, like the adulteress, sentenced to death. In this case, however, the crime is not simply against her husband but against her father as well.

Extramarital sex is treated quite differently when a husband's rights are not involved. The man who violates an unmarried girl must simply marry her, making the proper marriage gift (*mōhar*) to her father. The only penalty he suffers is that he may not divorce her (Deut. 22:28–29).[23] Prostitution seems to have been tolerated at all periods as a licit outlet for male sexual energies, though the prostitute was a social outcast, occupying at best a marginal place in the society. Hebrew fathers were enjoined not to "profane" their daughters by giving them up to prostitution, and the prophets used the figure of harlotry to condemn Israel's "affairs" with other gods.[24]

Taken together, the various laws that treat of extramarital sex evidence a strong feeling in Israel that sexual intercourse should properly be confined to marriage,[25] of which it was the essence (Gen. 2:24) and the principal sign.[26] Thus the victim of rape, the slave girl or the female captive taken for sexual pleasure, must become or must be treated as a wife (Exod. 21:7–11; Deut. 21: 10–14). Polygyny was a concession to the man's desire for more than one sexual partner, with concubinage a modification or extension of this.[27] Perhaps prostitution was tolerated as a poor man's substitute. It must certainly have been strengthened by the increasing institution of monogamous marriage as the general norm.

The laws dealing with sexual transgressions represent a strong statement of support for the family. But they are all formulated from the male's point of view, the point of view of a man who jealously guards what is essential to the fulfillment of his role in the family. Thus a jealous husband who suspects his wife of infidelity, but has no proof of it, may require her to submit to an ordeal. If she is "proved" innocent by this procedure, the husband incurs no penalty for his false accusation (Num. 5:12–31).[28] Infidelity by the husband is not considered a crime.

Divorce was recognized in ancient Israel and regulated by law, at least in the later period of the monarchy. The extent of the practice and the circumstances in which it was sanctioned remain unclear; there is no doubt, however, that it was an exclusively male prerogative. Some scholars have interpreted the "indecency" (*ʿerwāh*) given as the ground for divorce in the law of Deut. 24:1–4 as a reference to sexual infidelity.[29] If so, it would represent a modification of the more severe law of adultery found in Lev. 20. Others have suggested barrenness.[30] The Israelite man must commonly have understood his conjugal rights to include the right to progeny, especially male progeny. A wife who did not produce children for her husband was not fulfilling her duty as a wife. In early Israel it was apparently customary for her to offer him a female slave to bear for her (Gen. 16:1-3 and 30:1-3); or the husband might simply take another wife (where economically feasible [I Sam. 1:2])—or secure the services of a harlot (?) (Judg. 11:1-3). In the monogamous family of the later monarchy divorce must have been a more frequent alternative. All the Old Testament references to divorce are found in sources stemming from this period or later (Deut. 24:1-4; Jer. 3:8; Isa. 50:1; possibly Hos. 2:2).

The integrity of the family was also secured by inheritance laws that insured against the alienation of family property, that essential property which assured to each father's house its "place" in Israel. The basic inheritance laws are not contained in the Old Testament legal codes, but can be inferred from extralegal references and from a number of laws dealing with special cases in the transfer of family property (Num. 27:1-11 and 36:1-9; Jer. 32:6-8; Ruth 4:1-6). Two of these concern the inheritance of daughters. Since a daughter left her father's house at marriage to become a member of her husband's family, she normally received no inheritance. (Neither did the wife, since property was transmitted in the male line.) By special legislation, however, daughters were permitted to inherit where sons were lacking (Num. 27:1-11).[31] But they were only placeholders in the male line, which was thereby enabled to continue in their children.[32] The rare institution of the levirate (the marriage of a widow to the brother of her dead husband) may also have been designed to preserve the property of a man to his name—that is, for his male descendants.

In the patriarchal family system of Israel a woman had only a limited possibility of owning property, though responsibility for managing it may have been assumed with some frequency.[33] Normally, however, a woman was dependent for support upon her father before marriage and her husband after marriage. As a consequence, the plight of a widow without sons might be desperate. Her husband's property would pass to the nearest male relative, who was apparently under no obligation to maintain his kinsman's wife. She would be expected to return to her own family. The frequent impossibility of this solution, however, is suggested by the special plea for defense of the widow that occurs repeatedly in the ethical injunctions of the Old Testament (e.g., Isa. 1:17; Jer. 7:6 and 22:3; Zech. 7:10; Exod. 22:22).

The laws also illustrate, both explicitly and implicitly, disabilities of women in the religious sphere. As noted above, the oldest religious law was addressed only to men, while the sign of membership in the religious community was circumcision, the male initiation rite. Only males were required by the law of Deut. 16:16 to attend the three annual pilgrim feasts, the primary communal religious acts of later Israel.[34] Consonant with this bias was the assumption of the cultic law that only males might serve as priests (eventually restricted to the "sons of Aaron"). However, in keeping with the understanding of the family as the basic social unit, the priest's whole household shared in the holiness of his office and in the obligations imposed by it. Thus a priest's daughter who "defiled" herself by fornication incurred the sentence of death, since she had also defiled her father by her act (Lev. 21:9; see also 22:10–14).

Women also suffered religious disability that was only indirectly sex-determined. Israelite religion, following widespread ancient practice, excluded from cultic participation all persons in a state of impurity or uncleanness—that is, in a profane or unholy state. Various circumstances were understood to signal such a state, during which time (usually limited) it was considered unsafe to engage in cultic activity or have contact with the cult. Israel's laws recognized leprosy and certain other skin diseases, contact with a corpse, bodily emissions of all types (both regular and irregular, in members of both sexes), sexual intercourse and childbirth as among those factors that caused uncleanness (Lev. 12–15). The frequent and regular recurrence of this cultically proscribed state in women of childbearing age must have seriously affected their ability to function in the cult.

An explicitly discriminatory expression—or "extension"—of the idea of ritual uncleanness is found in the law determining the period of impurity occasioned by childbirth (Lev. 12:1–5). Seven days are prescribed for a mother who has borne a son, but fourteen for the mother of a female child. Another cultic law that gives explicit statement to the differential values placed upon males and females is the law of Lev. 27:2–8, which determines monetary equivalents for vows of persons to cultic service. According to this reckoning the vow of a male aged twenty to sixty years was valued at 50 shekels, while that of a woman in the same age bracket was worth only 30 shekels.[35] Thus it appears that a male of any age was more highly valued than a female.[36]

The reason for this differential valuation must have been in large part economic, though a psychological factor is also evident. As in most premodern, labor-intensive societies, a large family was prized, since it offered a superior labor supply and flexibility and sustaining power when faced with serious threats to its existence. The large family carried more weight in the community and assured honor to its head—and to his spouse.[37] Many descendants also assured the continuity of the father's house and name. But only males could perform this task, and only males remained as primary economic contributors. On both economic (labor value) and psychological grounds the significant size of the family was reckoned in terms of males.[38] Females were necessary as child-bearers and child rearers, but they always had to be obtained from outside the family—and at a price. A man's own daughters left his house to build up another man's family. Thus an excess of female dependents was a luxury and/or a liability.

The picture sketched above is not a complete portrait of woman in ancient Israel; nevertheless it does present the essential features. Additions and qualifications are necessary at many points. Most stem from sources outside the legal material and are treated later, but a few, explicit or implicit in the laws themselves, must be noted here.

The ancient command to honor one's parents (Exod. 20:12; Deut. 5:16) recognizes the female as the equal of the male in her role as mother. It places the highest possible value upon this role, in which her essential function in the society was represented—the reproductive function.[39] The welfare of family and society and the status of the husband depended upon her performance of that task. Consequently she was rewarded for it by honor and protected in it by law and custom which "exempted" her (indirectly) from military service and "excused" her from certain religious and civic obligations.

Laws of this type, though positive (or compensatory) in their discrimination, may be classed together with those that discriminate negatively as laws in which the sociobiological role of the individual or his/her social value (= productivity) is a significant factor in the legal formulation. In a society in which roles and occupations are primarily sexually determined, sexual discrimination is bound to be incorporated in the laws. At the same time, however, laws that do not regard the person, but only acts or states, may be "egalitarian" in their conception.[40] This is illustrated in the old laws of Exod. 21:26 and 21:28, which assess penalties on the basis of injury suffered, without regard to the sex of the injured person. Egalitarianism, or nondiscrimination, is characteristic of most of the laws concerning ritual impurity and is a consistent feature of the laws dealing with major ethical, moral and cultic infractions. Thus illegitimate association with the supernatural incurred the same penalty whether the practitioner was male or female (Lev. 20:27; Deut. 17:2–7), and cult prostitutes of both sexes were equally proscribed (Deut. 23:17). Illicit types of sexual intercourse, with their equal and severe penalty (death) for both offenders, may also have been viewed as belonging to this category of offenses—that is, as practices of the surrounding peoples, abhorrent to Yahweh (Lev. 18:6–18, 20:10–21; Deut. 22:30).[41]

The only statements of equal "rights" in Old Testament law are indirect and qualified. They, too, pertain to the cultic sphere. The laws of Num. 6:2 ff. and 30:3–15 (both belonging to the latest of the law codes) indicate that women, as well as men, might undertake on their own initiative binding obligations of a religious nature. Num. 30:3–15 qualifies this, however, by upholding—but limiting—the right of a husband or father to annul a vow made by his wife or daughter (thereby allowing the interests of family to take precedence over the interests of the cult).[42]

The picture of woman obtained from the Old Testament laws can be summarized in the first instance as that of a legal nonperson; where she does become visible it is as a dependent, and usually an inferior, in a male-centered and male-dominated society. The laws, by and large, do not address her; most do not even acknowledge her existence. She comes to view only in situations (a) where males are lacking in essential socioeconomic roles (the female heir); (b) where she requires special protection (the widow); (c) where sexual offenses involving women are treated; and (d) where sexually defined or sexually differentiated states, roles and/or occupations are dealt with (the female slave or captive as wife, the woman as mother, and the sorceress). Where ranking occurs she is always inferior to the male. Only in her role as mother is she accorded status and honor equivalent to a man's. Nevertheless she is always subject to the authority of some male (father, husband or brother), except when widowed or divorced— an existentially precarious type of independence in Israel.[43]

THE IMAGE OF WOMEN IN PROVERBS

References to women in the Book of Proverbs are limited and stereotyped. Three major types dominate: (1) the mother, (2) the wife, and (3) the "other/foreign" woman.

The woman is portrayed in Proverbs as a teacher, whose instruction a son is commended to heed. In this role she is typically ranked alongside the father (in the normal parallelism, father . . . mother [1:8, 6:20]), though in the instruction of 31:1–9 it is the mother alone who is mentioned as author of the advice. Elsewhere mother and father together represent the parents, who take delight in a wise son (10:1, 15:20, 23:24–25) and to whom honor is due (20:20; see also Exod. 20:12). In Proverbs, as in the laws, the mother is described in positive terms only. But here it is clear that the term "mother" does not refer primarily to her reproductive function but to her role in the nurture and education of the child. She is not merely the womb that bears a man but a source of wisdom essential to life.

The wife is depicted in a more varied and ambivalent light. The "good" wife, or "woman of quality," is described as the crown of her husband (literally, "master") and is contrasted with the wife "who brings shame," that is, who degrades rather than enhances her *husband's* reputation (12:4). She is also described as prudent (19:14) and gracious (11:16), with honor as her gain (11:16). Obtaining such a wife is deemed a gift from God (18:22, 19:14).

A detailed list of the activities and skills of the "wife of quality" is found in the acrostic poem of Prov. 31:10–31. Here we see a woman of the upper class, presumably from the time of the monarchy. She is manager of the household, directing the work of servants and seeing to it by industriousness and foresight that her family is well provided for in food and clothing. She engages in business transactions, apparently on her own initiative, buying land, setting out a vineyard with the profits reaped from her undertakings, and manufacturing clothing. She is generous and ready to help the poor and needy, possesses strength and dignity, is a wise and kind teacher. In consequence of her good character and her provision for her household, her husband is "known in the gates." He trusts her and profits by her. Recognizing his good fortune ("a good wife is far more precious than jewels" [vs. 10]), he praises her in company with his children. In this portrait the sexual attributes of the wife are not mentioned. She is characterized in wholly nonsexual terms as provisioner of home and husband, toward whom all her talents and energies appear to be directed. In this role "she does him good" (vs. 12).

A "bad" wife is also described in Proverbs, but not as a general type. She is identified primarily in terms of a single trait—contentiousness. The contentious woman is likened to a "continual dripping on a rainy day" (19:13, 27:15). It is better to live in a desert land or in the "attic" than to share a house with her (21: 9, 19, 25:24). The bad wife is characterized as "one who causes shame" (12:4); she disgraces not only herself but her husband— which is the main point of the admonition.

In only one passage in Proverbs is the wife described as a sexual partner. The counsel to fidelity in 5:15–19 contrasts the "wife of your youth" with the "loose woman," advising the husband to "drink water from [his] own cistern" and not to let his streams flow for others (vss. 15–16; cf. Sir. 26:19–21). He should let her breasts delight him and be intoxicated always (and only) by her love. The ideal portrayed here is that of sexual pleasure identified with marriage; and it is monogamous marriage that is presumed.

This counsel to fidelity is paralleled by the admonition to beware the seductions of the "other/foreign" woman—the most common word concerning women found in the instruction literature (2:16, 5:3–6, 5:20, 6:24, 7:5, 22:14, 23:27–28; cf. 31:3; Eccles. 7:26; "harlot": 7:10–23, 29:3). Characterized by the RSV translation as a "loose woman" or "adventuress,"[44] she is depicted as luring men to destruction (her house/path leads to death: 2:16,

5:3; cf. 7:22, 9:18, 22:14, 23:28) by her "smooth talk" (2:16, 5:3, 6:24, 7:5; cf. 7:21). She accosts her victim in the squares and marketplace and lies in wait at the street corners to entice him into her house (7:12, 9:14–15).

The loose woman in Proverbs personifies "folly" and is contrasted with the "wise woman," or "wisdom" personified (9:1–6; 13–18), while association with harlots and love of wisdom describe antithetical behavior (29:3). But wisdom is not simply the antithesis of the folly characterized by the loose woman; it is the antidote. Throughout these admonitions runs the idea that wisdom will protect a man from the disaster she portends.

As the counsel to fidelity shows, the condemnation of the "strange" woman and her ways is not a condemnation of erotic love but of its abuse—its employment as the tool of an unscrupulous woman, out of the man's control.[45] In Proverbs sex is subordinated to wisdom. It is not extolled, like wisdom, as a good in itself, but is praised and appreciated only when channeled and controlled within the confines of marriage. The control essential to its enjoyment (in this view) must be exercised by the man, to whom the words of advice are directed.[46]

Two references are made to an adulteress. In 6:26 she is compared with the harlot; while the latter takes a man's money ("may be hired for a loaf of bread"), the former may cost him his life. The thought, which is amplified in the following verses, is that adultery constitutes theft, and the wronged husband will avenge himself upon the adulterer. In 30:20 the adulteress is portrayed as an amoral woman who refuses to acknowledge her guilt: "She eats, wipes her mouth, and says, 'I have done no wrong.' "

The wisdom sayings and instruction literature of Proverbs give a somewhat different picture from that of the laws. A more homogeneous social milieu is assumed here: urban, monogamous and relatively comfortable. It is a literature of the upper class predominantly; and it addresses men exclusively. A man's success depends upon heeding his parents' instruction and obtaining a good wife. His fortune is seen as determined in large measure by his relationships with women, relationships determined both by accident (providence) and choice. Practical and moral suasion are employed here to guide that choice. The evils he is warned to recognize and avoid apparently carry no legal penalties. Adultery is redressed only by a husband's jealousy, and prostitution, conceived as the primary threat to a man, appears to flourish unsanctioned. Women are not chattel in Proverbs, nor are they simply sexual objects; they are persons of intelligence and will, who, from the male's point of view expressed here, either make or break a man. The man must learn to recognize the two types and abstain from harmful relationships. He does so by means of wisdom, wisdom gained first and foremost from his parents—of both sexes.

THE IMAGE OF WOMAN IN THE HISTORICAL WRITINGS

The historical writings amplify greatly the picture of woman obtained from the laws and proverbs. The descriptions they offer of the women of their day and of the legendary figures of times past add richness of color and detail to the outline already sketched, confirming in many instances the initial broad strokes, but demanding reassessment and redrawing of some features. The composite portrait contained in these writings displays variety and ambiguity in the image and status of women not apparent in the laws.

Despite the quantity and diversity of the references and despite occasionally vivid and individualistic portrayals, the great majority of women referred to in the historical writings appear in reality more as types than as "real," historical individuals. Even where a woman—or a woman's name—has attained legendary stature, where force of character or peculiarity of vocation or position has procured a unique place for her, or where an author, following his own sympathies or artistic aims, has lingered over a particular female figure, the roles played by women in these writings are almost exclusively subordinate and/or supporting roles. Women are adjuncts to the men: they are the minor (occasionally major) characters necessary to a plot that revolves about males. They are the mothers and nurses and saviors of men;[47] temptresses, seducers and destroyers of men;[48] objects or recipients of miracles performed by and/for men;[49] confessors of the power, wisdom and divine designation of men.⁵⁰ They are necessary to the drama, and may even steal the spotlight occasionally; but the story is rarely about them.⁵¹

Only Deborah and Jezebel stand on their own feet—possibly also Miriam and Huldah. But far too little evidence survives about them to assess their actual position in Israelite society or their representativeness. The Queen of Sheba also appears as an independent figure, but this legendary foreigner cannot be placed within the context of Israelite society; she is introduced only as an exotic rival of Solomon in wisdom and wealth, a figure who must have the status of an equal or near equal in order to test him and acknowledge his superiority (I Kings 10:6–9).

The two most common images of woman in the historical writings are those of wife and mother, frequently combined when the woman is portrayed as a historical individual. Other types, such as the barren woman, the foreign woman, and the widow, represent subtypes or modifications of these two. Identification of women by occupation or profession other than wife-mother is found in a small though significant group of references.

The primary characteristics of the mother in the historical writings are compassion, solicitousness and jealousy for her children; she also appears (indirectly) as a teacher or determiner of character and as a figure of authority and respect—usually in conjunction with the father (i.e., as co-parent). (See I Kings 19:20; I Sam. 22:3–4; Judg. 14:2–3, 16.) The special feeling of the mother for her child—and for a son in particular—is given frequent and varied expression: the mother of Sisera suppressing her premonition of disaster with self-assuring visions of the scenes of victory (Judg. 5:28–30); Rachel weeping inconsolably for her children (Jer. 31:15); Rizpah in mourning vigil over the bodies of her dead sons, moving both heavens and king to acts of sympathy (II Sam. 21:8–14); the "true" mother in Solomon's famous test revealing herself by her willingness to give up her own child to another woman in order to save his life (I Kings 3:16–27); the wealthy woman of Shunem cradling her dying child in her lap (II Kings 4:18–20).⁵² These adumbrations of the pietà show no distinctions of social status. Queen mother (Judg. 5), concubine (II Sam. 21) and harlot (I Kings 3) all exhibit in these representations a common maternal feeling, a special and enduring bond with the fruit of their womb that makes the loss of children a woman's greatest loss. In this bereavement all women are alike, and all are equal.

Suffering also marks the other primary image of the mother, the image that predominates in the prophetic writings. It is the woman (Isa. 13:8, 21:3, 26:17; Jer. 4:31, 30:6, 48:41; Mic. 4:9–10; etc.) in childbirth who has fixed the poet's attention. Her pangs represent for him the greatest anguish known to man, and their vivid portrayal expresses the deep pain and turmoil of all persons in extremity. The male writer sees in them not only pain but helplessness and fear, so that he contrasts the woman in childbirth with the warrior, strong and courageous, and mocks the fearful army by calling them women (Nahum 3:13; see also Jer. 30:6).

Socioeconomic factors certainly played a role in Israelite attitudes toward children and toward motherhood. The loss, or threatened loss, of an only child, especially when the woman was a widow, might be an occasion for panic as well as pathos, for the mother's life and/or welfare might depend upon the life of the child (II Sam. 14:2–17; II Kings 4:18–25). The barren woman shared with the woman made childless by bereavement the same precarious future. In addition, however, she suffered immediate social and psychological deprivation for her failure to achieve motherhood.

Barrenness was a shame and a reproach in Israel (Gen. 30:1–2, 22–23; I Sam. 1:3–7, 11); it was interpreted as divine punishment or at least a sign of divine displeasure (Gen. 16:2, 20:18, 30:26; I Sam. 1:5; II Sam. 6:20–23). It brought gloating derision from other women, especially from co-wives who had proved their fertility (I Sam. 1:6; cf. Gen. 30:1, 8 and 16:4), and it threatened the woman's status as a wife (Gen. 30:1–2; 15–20). The barren woman was deprived of the honor attached to motherhood—the only position of honor generally available to women, representing the highest status a woman might normally achieve. Consequently the expression "a mother in Israel" could be used metaphorically to describe a woman or a city (grammatically feminine) of special veneration[53] (Judg. 5:7; II Sam. 20:19), and the reversal of a woman's fortunes might be depicted in the image of a barren woman giving birth to seven sons (I Sam. 2:5). But motherhood brought more than honor, more than security and approval of husband and society. It brought authority. It offered the woman her only opportunity to exercise legitimate power over another person.[54] In the hierarchically organized patriarchal family, in which women of every age and status were subject to the authority of a male superior, this must have been a significant factor in a woman's desire for children. The only relationship in which dominance by the woman was sanctioned was the mother-child relationship.

The authority of the mother over her children is illustrated by relatively few examples, most of which pair the woman in this role with the father (there is no common term for "parents"). Her influence on the character of the child is indicated only indirectly in the historical writings.[55] Direct power and influence over the life of the child may be seen in a mother's dedication of a child to cultic service (I Sam. 1:11), in her efforts to affect the choice of a son's wife (Gen. 27:46–28:2; cf. Judg. 14:3), and in attempts to have her own son (in a polygynous family) or a favorite son declared principal heir (Gen. 21:10; I Kings 1:15–20).

The interests of a mother in the fortunes of her son are especially apparent when he is a potential heir to the throne, since his ascension elevates her to the honored position of queen mother. This position appears to have been a recognized institution, at least in the Judaean monarchy, in which the queen mother was referred to by the title "[great] lady" (*gᵉbīrāh*), and her name was included in the regnal formulas of each king.[56] The deference accorded the queen mother is illustrated in the account of Bathsheba's reception by her own son, King Solomon (I Kings 2:19). The potential power inherent in the position is evidenced in Athaliah's successful seizure of the throne (and six-year reign) on the death of her son, King Ahaziah (II Kings 11:1–3).

The primary category to which all these women belong is that of wife. It is the comprehensive category that describes the destiny of every female in Israel.[57] Yet the image of the wife is an elusive one. As wife alone she is all but invisible. Neither eulogized nor deprecated, she rarely appears unless thrust forward by some peculiarity of family, character, position or deed or unless required to link two male figures (I Kings 3:1, 4:11; II Kings 8:18; I Sam. 18:20–27; II Sam. 3:13 ff.) or two generations of males.[58] Wives figure most prominently in the patriarchial narratives, primarily because they are by their nature *family stories,* created and/or employed for the purpose of creating a history based upon a genealogical scheme. In these tales the wives are seen primarily, though not exclusively, as mothers, while daughters appear only as wives—accounting for external relations.[59] Wives also figure in the tales incorporated into the books of Judges, Samuel and Kings and play significant parts in the court narrative of David, which also partakes of the story genre. But they are almost totally lacking in the "political" history of Joshua-Kings, except for an occasional word of warning about the danger of foreign wives—or of marriage with foreigners in general.

Hebrew has no special term for "wife," but uses the common word for "woman" (*'iššāh*) in genitive "construct" with the name of the husband ("woman of NN")—a formula that can be applied to a concubine (*pilegeš*) as well as a full wife. There is also no specific term for "husband," though the relational term *ba'al* ("master") was frequently used in the corresponding genitival construction instead of the general word for man, (*'iš*) ("man/master of NN"). This usage is indicative of the nature of the husband-wife relationship in Israel. It suggests why the marriage relationship was appropriated as a metaphor for the covenant relationship of Yahweh to Israel, a relationship characterized by intimacy—and subordination.

The Hebrew wife has often been characterized as essentially a chattel. And in some respects this view is justified. Wives, children, slaves and livestock described a man's major possessions (Exod. 20:17). Wives, or simply "women," are found in lists of booty commonly taken in war (Deut. 20:14; cf. Deut. 21:10–14; I Sam. 30:2, 5, 22: I Kings 20:3, 5, 7; II Kings 24:15), and wives are counted—along with concubines, silver and gold—as an index of a man's wealth (I Kings 10:14–11:8).[60] In these and other references in which mention of a wife serves simply to complete a reference to family, household or possessions, she is usually anonymous and is not formally distinguished from other property.

Despite legal, economic and social subordination, however, wives were not simply property. They could not be bought and sold, and it is doubtful that they could be divorced without substantial cause. Later law required a formal writ of divorce (Jer. 3:8; Isa. 50:1; see also Deut. 24:1–4).[61] But the rights of concubine and wife were not fixed by contract (as in later Jewish practice) or by any surviving law. They were presumably customary and negotiated by agreements between the husband and the wife's family. A wife's rights and freedom within the marriage would depend in large measure upon the ability of her family to support and defend her demands. Thus the daughter of a rich and powerful man could expect better treatment as a wife. Her status as a wife would reflect the status of her family.

The wives depicted in the historical writings exhibit a wide variety of characteristics, yet a coherent picture is not difficult to obtain. The good (ideal) wife is well illustrated by Abigail, wife of Nabal (and later of David) (I Sam. 25:2–42), with supplementary traits drawn from other examples. She is intelligent, beautiful, discreet, and loyal to her husband (despite his stupidity and boorish character in the case of Nabal; see Jer. 2:2). Prudent, quick-witted and resourceful, she is capable of independent action, but always acts in her husband's behalf. The good wife does not attempt to rule her husband, nor does she openly oppose him. She defers to him in speech and action, obeys his wish as his command, and puts his welfare first. She employs her sexual gifts for his pleasure alone and raises up children to his name.[62]

The Old Testament historical texts portray the woman as intelligent, strong-willed and capable, and especially endowed with the gift of persuasion (see II Sam. 14:1–20, 20:16–22; I Kings 1:11–31). As a consequence, she was also potentially dangerous to the man, since, if she wished, she could use her sexual and intellectual gifts to undo him or to gain her own ends at his expense. Against this female power not even the strongest man could stand (Judg. 16:4–21). The danger presented by the woman to the man was greatest where the relationship was most intimate, namely, in marriage. And there the threat had a second root. For the wife was always to some degree a stranger in her husband's household, an outsider who maintained bonds of loyalty to her father's house and who might consequently be used by her kinsmen. This danger from the wife's external connections was magnified if she was a foreigner, a fact that is reflected in a demonstrated preference for ingroup marriage (Gen. 24:1–4, 26:34–35 and 27:46–28.5; Judg. 14:1–3)[63] and in numerous laws, preachments, and "case histories" that warn against the disastrous consequences of marriage with foreigners (Judg. 3:5–6; Ezra 9–10, esp. 9:1–2; Num. 31:15–16; see also I Kings 11:1–8).

The historical writings rarely portray the wife as a sexual partner or lover, though they assume (as ideal) a high correspondence between love and marriage.[64] In general they give too little information about the marriage relationship to permit substantial conclusions. Israelite marriage was essentially an arrangement between two families, usually initiated by the man or his parents (Judg. 14:12; Gen. 34:1–4, 8; Gen. 24). This male locus of the initiative is illustrated by the verbs and the actions that commonly describe the incorporation of the woman into the new household: she is "given," "taken," "sent for," "captured"—and even purchased, in the case of a slave wife. Some texts suggest, however, that the woman's role was not wholly passive or lacking in initiative (II Sam. 11:2–5; I Sam. 18:20),[65] that she could refuse an "offer" (Gen. 24:5, 57–58) and make demands of her own (Judg. 1:15). Though a woman could not divorce her husband, the mistreated wife might simply return to her father's house (Judg. 19:2).[66]

Polygyny is a recurrent feature in the narratives of the premonarchic period, and efforts to assure equal rights to multiple wives (and/or their children) are evidenced both in the laws and the narratives (Gen. 30:15; Deut. 21:15; cf. Gen. 29:30–31).[67] By the eighth century B.C., however, and probably a good deal earlier, monogamous marriage was clearly the norm and the ideal.[68] It is presupposed by Hosea's use of the marriage analogy to speak of Yahweh's exclusive and demanding relationship to Israel. This metaphor of Israel as the bride or wife of Yahweh, which is also employed by Jeremiah (2:2, 3:1, 4, 6–10) and Ezekiel (ch. 16), is always found in the context of an indictment of Israel's unfaithfulness. She is described in alternating images as harlot and adulteress, though the language of harlotry predominates.[69] The choice of the latter metaphor may be related to the conspicuous feature of cult prostitution in Canaanite religion,[70] but the fact that it becomes prominent only in the eighth century while dominating later theological language suggests that it should be correlated with the use of the bride/wife motif.

The harlot was the primary symbol of the double standard in Israel. She was in every period a figure of disrepute and shame

(Gen. 34:31; Judg. 11:1; I Kings 22:38; Isa. 1:21; Jer. 3:3; Ezek. 16:30), at best merely ostracized, at worst (in circumstances involving infidelity and defilement) subjected to punishment of death (Gen. 38:24; see also Lev. 21:9). But the harlot was also tolerated in every period by men who incurred no legal penalties—or even censure—for the enjoyment of her services (Gen. 38:15 ff.).[71] Her status and image gained nothing, however, from this tolerance. The two best-known stories of harlots (Rahab, who saved the spies of Joshua [Josh. 2:1–21], and the two harlots who presented their case to Solomon for judgment [I Kings 3:16–27]), often cited as evidence of their acceptance in Israelite society, also presuppose their low repute. In both accounts the harlot heroines are made to demonstrate in their words and actions faith, courage and love that would scarcely be expected of the average upright citizen and thus is all the more astonishing and compelling as the response of a harlot—that member of society from whom one would least expect religious and moral sensitivity. They serve the storyteller's purpose in much the same way as does the poor widow —that member of society whose existence is most precarious and who is consequently a favorite for depicting great faith and generosity.

In addition to the primary roles of wife and mother, women appear in the historical writings in a number of other, more specialized roles, occupations and professions. Except in the case of the harlot, these are normally not alternatives to the wife-mother role, but represent complementary or supplementary activities. Foremost among these is the prophetess, of whom the Old Testament canon knows three by name:[72] Deborah (Judg. 4:4–16), in the premonarchic period; Huldah (II Kings 22:14–20), in the late monarchic period (seventh century B.C.); and Noadiah (Neh. 6:14), in the postexilic period (fifth century B.C.). Too little is known about any of them to speak confidently or in detail about women in this role. But some general statements are possible. None of the authors who introduce these figures into their writings gives special attention to the fact that these prophets are women—in contrast to Old Testament commentators, who repeatedly marvel at the fact.[73] Despite some compounding in the traditions relating to Deborah and consequent difficulty in interpreting her role(s), the descriptions of the words and activities of the three

named prophetesses coincide closely with those of their male contemporaries in the same profession. There is no evidence to suggest
that they were considered unusual in this role.

But if female prophets were accepted in Israel, they were also
rare. No collections of their words have survived among the prophetic books of the Old Testament—at least none identified by a
woman's name. Discrimination might be argued, discrimination
that was broken through only in the periods of national crisis,
when the three known prophetesses emerged. But Israel knew
other crises when no women arose to prophesy. Most likely, female
prophets were always few in number, and presumably not associated with guilds and disciples who might have collected and preserved their oracles. Their exercise of their calling must have been
at best part-time, at least during child-rearing years, and may not
even have begun until later in life.[74] For the Israelite woman such
a profession could only have been a second vocation. Early marriage, with its demand upon women of a primary vocation as wife
and mother, would have excluded the early cultivation of the gift
of prophecy.[75] But its authenticity was not subject to doubt on the
basis of sex. Prophecy was a charismatic gift, and as such, no
respecter of persons. The person who had a message from God
would be sought out, heeded and accorded recognition if his/her
message was understood to have validity. The message authenti-
cated the messenger. The Old Testament accounts of female
prophets are testimony to Israel's recognition that God could and
did communicate with females as with males, entrusting to them
messages of vital concern to the whole community.

Prophecy may be contrasted with cultic service as the only
religious profession generally open to women throughout Israel's
history. There are some suggestions that women did function in
the cult of the earlier period: the portrayal of Miriam alongside the
priestly figure of Aaron in Num. 12:1-2,[76] and reference to "serving
women" in the tent of meeting (Exod. 38:8; cf. I Sam. 2:22). But
any early openness to women in the cult seems to have been fore-
closed by a strong reaction during the period of the monarchy to
the religious practices of Canaan, especially to fertility rites that
involved female cult personnel. Thus the women referred to in
association with the cult of the monarchic period are all described
as illicit practitioners of non-Israelite rites.[77] Reference to female

(temple) singers is found in works of the postexilic period (Ezra 2:65; Neh. 7:67, I Chr. 25:5), though they are associated there with the pre-exilic (and exilic) cult. This service, performed both by males and females, was in any case clearly auxiliary to the main cultic office.

Women were also recognized as practitioners of occult arts ("mediums" and "sorceresses"), though they were banned in Israel together with their male counterparts (I Sam. 28:7; Exod. 22:18; cf. Deut. 18:10; II Chr. 33:6).[78] The functioning of women in this capacity is analogous to that of the prophetess; the profession was in both cases based upon the exercise of a special "gift."[79] A related specialization of women, though less distinctly "professional," is illustrated by the "wise woman" (II Sam. 14:2, 20:16). The women so designated seem to have been noted especially for astute counsel, persuasiveness and tact.[80] Their reputations, built upon demonstrated skill or the efficacy of their words, might extend well beyond the boundaries of their own towns (II Sam. 14:2). Thus wisdom was recognized as a gift that, like prophecy, was in no way restricted to men. It was honored and sought out whenever it manifested itself.

Other professional specializations of women (all part-time) were more closely related to the primary roles played by women in the society. These include professional mourners, or "keening women" (Jer. 9:17), midwives (Gen. 35:17, 38:28; Exod. 1:15–21) and nurses (Ruth 4:16; II Sam. 4:4; Gen. 24:59, 35:8; Exod. 2:7; II Kings 11:2; II Chr. 22:11). Female slaves or servants, particularly those of the king's household, were apparently trained in a variety of specialties, as "perfumers," bakers and cooks (I Sam. 8:13). In addition to these, female singers are mentioned as entertainers in II Sam. 19:35 and Eccles. 2:8.

The hundreds of references to women in the historical and prophetic books present many and varied images. Central to most, however, and underlying all are the images of wife and mother (or wife-mother), with the harlot as a kind of wife surrogate or anti-wife image. These two primary roles defined most women's lives, though in varying degrees and with varying meaning, depending on the size, structure, function and status of the particular family. That is, for most women the sexually determined roles of wife and mother also described their *work*, since the division of labor was based almost exclusively on sex. In the limited roles open to her, however, the ancient Israelite woman contributed more substantially and more significantly to the welfare of family and society than the modern Western woman in the same role. She was not simply a consumer but a primary producer or manufacturer of much of the essential goods required by the household; in addition, she had charge of the basic education of the children. She apparently had considerable power, authority and freedom of decision in this important realm that she managed,[81] and she could make significant decisions about her own life and that of her children (by religious vows, specifically)—though her husband (or father) was granted veto power in some cases.

While in certain limited circumstances a woman might be thought of only as a sexual object (Judg. 5:30; I Kings 1:2-4; see also Gen. 19:8; Judg. 19:24), nonsexual attributes predominate in most Old Testament references to women; in particular, intelligence, prudence, wisdom, tact, practical sense and religious discernment recur in numerous characterizations of women, often replacing or preceding descriptions of physical appeal. The women of these texts are not depicted as silly or frivolous, except perhaps in the prophetic caricatures of the harlot or of the pampered ladies of the upper class (Isa. 3:16-4:1; Amos 4:1). Women may be portrayed as unscrupulous, but they are rarely, if ever, characterized as foolish.

Despite the family locus of most of the woman's activity, the knowledge and abilities of women were not confined to the family circle or limited to expression in strictly female activities. The possession of special gifts and powers beneficial to the larger community was recognized and acknowledged in women as well as men, with the result that some professional specialization was possible for a few women along with their primary occupation of wife and mother. Most of these involved the exercise or employment of special kinds of knowledge: practical wisdom (the "wise women" of Tekoa and Abel); ability in deciding legal disputes (Deborah as judge); power to receive divine communications (Deborah as prophetess, Miriam, Huldah, and possibly Noadiah); and ability to call up spirits from the dead (the medium of Endor).

Judged by economic criteria or in terms of interest in continuity of house and name, the woman of the Old Testament was deemed inferior to the man. In the realm of the cult her activity was restricted. And from the viewpoint of the law she was a minor and a dependent, whose rights were rarely acknowledged or protected. These several systems in which woman's roles and status have been described represent in large measure cultural givens, which cannot be ignored. They mark the base line for any discussion of the image of Old Testament woman; but they do not describe all situations or all points of view.[82] In many situations the woman was in fact and/or in theory an equal, despite manifold and combined pressures to treat her as an inferior.[83] She was recognized as equal (or superior) in the possession and employment of certain kinds of knowledge and in religious sensibility and sensitivity. In love she might also be an equal,[84] and could exploit (Judg. 16:4–22) as well as suffer exploitation. She was in general charged with the same religious and moral obligations as men, and she was held responsible for her acts.[85] Man in the Old Testament recognizes woman as one essentially like him, as a partner in pleasure and labor, one whom he needs, and one who can spell him weal or woe. From his point of view—the only point of view of the Old Testament texts—the woman is a helper, whose work as wife and mother is essential and complementary to his own. In a sense she completes him—but as one with a life and character of her own. She is his opposite and equal.

THE IMAGE OF WOMAN IN THE ACCOUNTS OF CREATION

Against the multitude of Old Testament references to women, actual and ideal, contemporary and past, the Bible has set two accounts of the first woman. Each belongs to a larger creation "story," and each shares many common features with similar accounts from the ancient Near East. In the mythopoeic world that was Israel's cradle, accounts of origins did not simply explain what happened in the beginning; they were statements about the nature of things as they "are" (or as they should be). In the recitation or re-enactment of the myth the original drama of creation was repeated and the present order maintained through re-creation. Thus the Babylonian account of the creation of the world was a central feature in the liturgy of the New Year celebration, serving to insure that the forces of order (the created, present order) would prevail for another year over the forces of chaos (associated especially with the spring floods), and the account of the creation of mankind was the text of an incantation, recited by a midwife to assure a good birth.[86] The primary concern of a myth is not with the past but with the present.

Israel's accounts of creation draw heavily upon the myths current at their times of composition. The same basic themes occur, the same developments—even the same language is used in some cases. But the meaning of the biblical accounts differs radically from that of their prototypes, because the context of their employment is different. The Genesis accounts are no longer myth, but history—or a prologue to history. Creation has become the first of a series of events that extend on down to the writer's own day. That intervening period is never wholly collapsed in the biblical view. Creation stands always and only at the beginning—remote, complete, unrepeatable, the first of God's works. The God who performed that work continues to labor and to act, but in new ways. History is the drama of the interaction of God and the world that he created, the world to which he gave a life and a will of its own. The creation stories tell of man's place in that created world of nature and of his-her essential character. This is spelled out in Gen. 3 by an account of the first acts taken by that autonomous creation.

While the two creation accounts of Genesis differ markedly in language, style, date and traditions employed, their basic statements about woman are essentially the same: woman is, along with man, the direct and intentional creation of God and the crown of his creation. Man and woman were made for each other. Together they constitute humankind, which is in its full and essential nature bisexual.

The well-known word of the Priestly writer (P) in Gen. 1:27 is eloquent and enigmatic in its terseness: "God created mankind (*'ādām*) in his own image . . . male (*zākār*) and female (*neqēbāh*) he created them." Two essential statements, and that is all. No exposition is given, no consequences stated, only the prefatory statement in verse 26 proclaiming the intentionality of this creation. The first statement has as its primary point the assertion that the human animal is distinguished from all others in being modeled or patterned after God himself ("in his image" is an adverbial clause describing the process of fashioning). In contrast to the other creatures, man's primary bond is with God and not with the earth; man's purpose in creation is to rule the earth. The second major statement is an expansion and a specification of the first. It does not relate a subsequent act of creation but only a subsequent thought of the narrator; and it does not explicate the meaning of the image. It simply makes the essential point that the genus, *'ādām*, is bisexual in its created nature.[87] There is no androgynous original creation in P.

The older, Yahwistic (J) account of creation in Gen. 2–3 is of a wholly different genre—a narrative. Here the art of the story-teller is seen in a work of great beauty and pathos, a narrative of beguiling simplicity, filled with yearning, compassion and dramatic tension—the "soul" version of creation, in contrast to the cool, cerebral account of the priestly writer. In J's account the creation of man (*'ādām*, deliberately ambiguous here)[88] is the beginning and the end of the story, with all of God's other creative acts bracketed in between. Here God's primary creation remains incomplete until, by a process of trial and error which populates the earth with creatures, that one is finally found for whom the man has waited and longed, namely, woman. With the creation of woman, man is finally his true self, a sexual and social being (*'îš*). J's account is a drama of the realization of the divine intention in creation.

The man in this creation drama recognizes the woman as his equal, as a "helper fit for him" (2:18). She is emphatically not his servant. "Helper" (*cēzer*) carries no status connotations, while the Hebrew expression translated "fit for" means basically "opposite" or "corresponding to." The statement simply expresses the man's recognition (the story is told from his point of view exclusively) that he needs her and that she is essentially like him. She is the "thou" that confronts him and the other that completes him. The story represents her as derived but not inferior. The fact that she is formed directly from the man is meant to emphasize the essential identity of man and woman. Woman is not a separate order of creation like the animals, each of which was created, like *'ādām*, from the earth. The scientific and symmetrical language of P, with his concept of one genus ('ādām) in two sexes ("male" and "fe-male"), is not used here, but the same idea is expressed in dynamic and dramatic language. The essential oneness of the two distinct persons (identified by the sociosexual terms "man" and "woman") is proclaimed in the man's recognition of and emotional response to the fact: "This one at last is bone of my bones and flesh of my flesh"![89]

In J's work the drama of creation forms part of a larger story of origins. The Yahwist's word about man and woman in their essential nature is not finished with the simple statement of their existence or of the "original" state of their existence; it is spelled out, as the account of creation itself, in the language of events. The true nature or character of man and woman is revealed only as they begin to interact with each other and with their environ-ment as feeling, rational and responsible beings. In this action/ interaction their latent capacity for judgment, for disobedience and for self-interest is actualized, and the pain and frustration that the author knows as a mark of human existence becomes a part of the history of the first couple and of mankind.

The author of this well-known and often misinterpreted ac-count shared the age-old notion that misery is a sign of sin or guilt. Mankind's suffering was therefore conceived as punishment. The crime that the Yahwist depicts is the crime of disobedience, a crime committed by both man and woman.[90] The order of their transgressing is unimportant for the question of their guilt; the consequences of their acts (knowledge, shame—and pain) are de-scribed only when *both* have eaten the forbidden fruit.[91] The manner and the explanation of the responses of the pair is also inconsequential for the question of their guilt and punishment. Each individually and knowingly disobeys the divine command. But the way in which the response of each is portrayed may be understood to indicate something of the author's—or the tradi-tion's—view of the character of man and woman. The woman in this portrait responds to the object of temptation intellectually and reflectively, employing both practical and esthetic judgment. The man, on the other hand, passively and unquestioningly accepts what the woman offers him.[92]

In their common act of disobedience the man and woman become fully human, identifiable with men and women of the author's own day. Losing their original innocence, they become knowledgeable, responsible, and subject to pain and the contradictions of life. The "punishment" described in the poem of 3:14–19 simply represents the characteristic burdens and pain of man and woman as traditionally perceived in Israelite society. Ample testimony is offered by other Old Testament texts that the pangs of childbirth were viewed as the most common and acute pain suffered by women. They were at the same time indicative of the woman's primary and essential work in the society—procreation. By no means an inclusive definition of her work, it was nevertheless that to which all other work and all other roles were subordinated. The man's pain is described analogously as related to his work—gaining a living from the soil. The work of the pair is here simply described as the work of survival, biological (the work of the female) and material (the work of the male). But it is not simply the pain of toil that the author describes, it is the pain of alienation in that toil. The ground, the source of the man's life and work, has become his antagonist rather than his helper, and the man, the source of the woman's life and work, has become her ruler rather than her friend.[93]

The words of Gen. 3 are descriptive, not prescriptive. J's story of the first couple is heavily etiological; it offers an explanation for the primary characteristics of the human situation as Israel knew it. And this minimal statement shows substantial agreement with the fuller account gleaned from other Old Testament writings. But it is not normative. Israel did not use this legend to justify the existing order or to argue for woman's subordination. She did not need to. She understood the states described—for both man and woman —as givens. J's view was larger than the common one, however, and marked by a profound sense of the wrongness of this order: given, but not willed, the tragic consequence of man's exercise of his-her God-given reason and will. This was also not J's final word about the human situation. In its present setting the story has lost much of its etiological significance, for it is no longer simply a description of things as they are but is the first act in a world-historical drama that the historian has created as the context for Israel's history. For J, the central figure in that drama is Yahweh, God, who continues to will, to act and to create. Adam and Eve are the beginning of his works, not the end. Yahweh goes on in a play of many acts to create a new people and to enter into a new relationship with them.

It is with that same understanding of the dynamic character of history that the prophets speak of God's continued action in their own day, an action portrayed typically as judgment upon a people who had replaced theological norms with sociological ones (security, status, wealth, etc.). Neither the prophets nor the theologians, such as J and P, succeeded in wholly escaping the culturally determined understanding of male and female roles that they had inherited. And their greater egalitarianism should not be too sharply contrasted with the overtly discriminatory laws and practices recorded in other Old Testament literature, since there, too, male-dominated language and structures disguised to a considerable degree the actual power, freedom and respect of women in the society—respect based largely, though not solely, upon complementarity of roles. But distinctions of all types lend themselves to exploitation and to the creation of differential ethical standards. The historians of the Old Testament look behind the present state of division and alienation to an original and intended equality and harmony in creation, while the prophets focus upon the existing state of inequality and exploitation, addressing it with a concept of justice manifested in judgment—justice understood as a new act that God will perform to purge his creation, an act of retribution and rectification. The proud will be abased (Isa. 4:17), and the "men of distinction" will head the exile train (Amos 6:4–7); but she who is now an outcast in men's eyes will not be punished for her sin (Hos. 4:14).

Some among the prophets saw beyond the present day, beyond the present order and the impending judgment. They looked to a new act of God in creation, to a new order with new possibilities for human existence, radical possibilities that would abolish the present alienation and exploitation based on distinctions of species, age, sex and social status. These prophetic visions speak of the knowledge of God in every heart, requiring no class of teachers to expound it (Jer. 31:31–34); of God's spirit free to all, so that old and young, male and female, bound and free shall prophesy (Joel 2:28–29); of lion and lamb, wild beast and helpless child living together in harmony and without fear (Isa. 11:6–9); and the reversal of the prevailing sexual roles: "a woman protects a man" (Jer. 31:22).[94]

The statements concerning the first man and woman must be read together with the statements of God's interaction with the world of his creation, his promises and his demands, his sending of saviors and spokesmen (both male and female), his judgments, his forgiveness and his new creation. Israel's best statements about woman recognize her as an equal with man, and with him jointly responsible to God and to cohumanity. That Israel rarely lived up to this vision is all too apparent, but the vision should not be denied.

NOTES

1. The term "patriarchy" is appropriate to designate such a society, but it is avoided here because of the fact that widespread indiscriminate use of the term has led to the blurring of significant social and cultural distinctions among various "patriarchal" societies. Whatever the terms employed, however, the characterization of ancient Israel as a male-centered and male-dominated society is meant as a descriptive statement. The aim of this essay is not to decry or to advocate but simply to record the perceptions of women found in the Old Testament writings and to analyze them in terms of their sources and consequences in ancient Israelite society and religion. Speculation concerning origins is renounced, and *Nachgeschichte* (the subsequent history of the ideas) is left to students of more recent periods in the tradition.
2. Exceptions to this latter rule are invariably deemed noteworthy by commentators. The extent and the meaning of gynomorphic language applied to the Deity has still to be assessed. See Phyllis Trible, "Depatriarchalizing in Biblical Interpretation," *Journal of the American Academy of Religion* XLI (1973), pp. 31–34. Whether the Old Testament use of feminine metaphors for God (always "mother" images, never "wife") is the product of Israelite monotheism or is a more general characteristic of language about certain types of deities (e.g., creator gods or tutelary deities) also needs to be explored.
3. See E. Deen, *All the Women of the Bible* (New York: Harper, 1955).
4. All citations are from the Revised Standard Version of the Bible (RSV) unless otherwise noted.

5. The translation is that of Marvin Chaney in *Israel's Earliest Poetry* (unpublished Ph.D. dissertation, Harvard, June 1974), based on a new understanding of the Hebrew; used by permission of the author.

6. Two references occur in later writings contained in the Greek canon: Tob. 8:6 and Sir. 25:24; cf. II Cor. 11:3, I Tim. 2:13, and numerous references in the Pseudepigrapha (see index to R. H. Charles, ed. *The Apocrypha and Pseudepigrapha of the Old Testament in English*, Vol. II [Oxford, 1913]). References to Adam are more frequent, but only Job 31:33, in the Hebrew Old Testament, refers to him apart from genealogies and the original creation stories.

7. Thus all speculation concerning an "original" matriarchy is rejected in this essay as inconsequential for the period and the society under consideration.

8. A chronological arrangement, while desirable, has not proved feasible, because of the frequent impossibility of determining dates for individual texts. Of the four groupings created for this study (laws, proverbs, "historical" texts, and accounts of origins) the third is, unfortunately, too omnibus. Based primarily upon references in the historical books, it incorporates some material from the prophetic writings, which have received no separate treatment because of limitations of time and space. The third section of the canon, apart from the book of Proverbs, has also suffered neglect for the same reasons, though occasional references from that corpus have found their way into the discussion at places. These omissions are acknowledged with regret.

9. M. Noth, *The Laws in the Pentateuch and Other Studies* (Philadelphia: Fortress Press, 1966), p. 8.

10. Polygyny and concubinage appear to have been more common in early Israel and are not mentioned in later texts, except in connection with the royal household.

11. Israel's view of the proper place of sex and the harsh penalties laid upon sexual offenders presumably reflect a deliberate antithesis to the practices of the surrounding peoples (specifically Canaanites), but they may also be rooted in Israel's peculiar understanding of herself as a "holy people." Sexual offenses are religious offenses in Israel. They are not private matters but matters of vital concern to the whole community. See Noth, *Laws*, p. 55.

12. The whole community was bound by the law, however, sometimes explicitly and sometimes implicitly. E.g., the absence of any mention of the wife in the Sabbath law (Exod. 20:10; Deut. 5:14), though sons and daughters and male and female slaves are listed, suggests that the wife was treated as one person with the man ("you," second person masculine singular), who is addressed by the law. (Whatever the interpretation, she is clearly not an independ-

ent person in this formulation.) In the postexilic community the inclusive reference is made explicit; the assembly ($q\bar{a}h\bar{a}l$) convened to hear the reading of the law is described as consisting of "both men and women and all who could hear with understanding" (Neh. 8:2–3). In this late period the concept of the religious assembly itself has apparently been broadened to include women.

13. Compare Lev. 13:9 (*'ādām*) and Lev. 13:38 (*'iš*, *'iššāh*) with Lev. 13:40 (*'iš*). See also Num. 6:2 (*'iš*, *'iššāh*).

14. Compare the idea, familiar even in contemporary Western society, of the citizen as property owner and/or family head. On the family and the place of the family in ancient Israel see J. Pedersen, *Israel*, I–II (Copenhagen, 1926; Oxford, photo reprint, 1964), 46–96. See also R. de Vaux, *Ancient Israel. Its Life and Institutions* (New York: McGraw-Hill, 1961), pp. 19–40, 53 ff. Israelite family life and institutions are illuminated by references to recent and contemporary Middle East families in R. Patai, *Sex and Family in the Bible and in the Middle East* (Garden City, N.Y.: Doubleday & Co., 1959).

15. Circumcision as the sign of the covenant (Gen. 17; Lev. 12:3; cf. Exod. 12:48) makes this explicit. This practice is in other societies a "rite of passage," performed at puberty and signaling the initiate's entry into the tribe as a full, adult member with all attendant privileges and duties, including marriage. See Exod. 4:26 and Josh. 5:2–7.

16. I.e., the men are to keep themselves "holy." Sexual intercourse was considered defiling in Israel. See Lev. 15:18; I Sam. 21:4–5; II Sam. 11:11.

17. The *ʿam* is first and foremost a kinship group—in a patriarchal society, "the sons of NN." It may be used in an inclusive sense as a designation for the whole community, including women (Judg. 16:30), or it may be restricted to the men, the community at worship and at war (Pedersen, *Israel*, I–II, 54–56).

18. See the evolutionary interpretation given to this phenomenon by Herbert Richardson, *Nun, Witch, Playmate* (New York: Harper & Row, 1971), p. 14: "What happened in ancient Israel was that the male group displaced the tribe as the primary social institution. It displaced the tribal family into a secondary position so that the family existed within the male group rather than vice versa."

19. The laws of Num. 27:1–11 and 36:1–9 are not concerned with the daughter's rights but with the father's, while the prohibition of Lev. 19:29 is a cultic proscription, not a defense of a minor's rights.

20. See Lev. 18:20. M. Noth, *Leviticus* (Philadelphia: Westminster Press, 1965), p. 150, sees the reference to the woman in 20:10 as an addition to the older law, representing a later interpretation, namely, that the woman is to be viewed not only as the object but as a fellow subject in the proceedings for breach of marriage. The

actual practice and presuppositions reflected in historical, prophetic, and proverb texts point to a milder punishment, at least in the periods represented by those texts. See Jer. 3:8 and Hos. 2:2–7.

21. Incestuous sexual relationships, which were judged with equal severity (Lev. 18:6–18 and 22:10–21), may have been understood in a similar way as threatening the complex relationships of rights and authority within the extended family, and thus the order and stability of the family. See Pedersen (*Israel*, I–II, 65), who stresses the psychological aspect of these offenses. For another explanation, see below, p. 52.

22. Likewise unwritten, but implied in Deut. 22:13–21.

23. See Exod. 22:16–17 and II Sam. 13:11–16. Genesis 34:1–7; 25–27 expresses a more severe attitude toward rape. In no case, however, are the girl's interests regarded by the law.

24. See below, p. 55, pp. 64–65, and note 69. There is considerable fluidity in the metaphorical use of the terms for adultery and prostitution to describe idolatrous worship and "idolatrous" political relationships (see Hos. 2:2; Jer. 3:8–9, Ezek. 16:30–35). Israel's relationships with other gods and nations are usually described as harlotry, thus emphasizing the brazen and habitual character of the act. This figure presumes that the "marriage" bond with Yahweh has long been broken or disregarded. The figure of the adulteress lays more stress upon the "marital" relationship and the exclusive nature of its claim.

25. The common ancient Near Eastern understanding of the sexual act as holy (or at least potentially so) was emphatically rejected by Israel, though the Canaanite terms *qᵉdēšîm* (m.) and *qᵉdēšôt* (f.) ("holy/consecrated ones") were used to refer to illicit cult prostitutes. Sex in Israel belonged to the order of the profane, not the holy. Its proper uses included both enjoyment and procreation. Emphasis upon the former accounts for such literature as the Song of Solomon and also explains Israel's concession (in the male interest) to prostitution. For the most part, however, extramarital sex was discouraged for practical, moral and religious reasons.

26. Sexual union as the sign of marriage is suggested by the designation of the wife as her husband's "nakedness" (Lev. 18:7, 14, 16). See Pedersen, *Israel*, I–II, 65.

27. In some circumstances concubines were treated much as wives (Judg. 19:2–9), though they did not have the full rights of free persons. There is some indication that the king's concubines were inherited by his successor, at least in the early days of the monarchy (II Sam. 16:21–22; See also II Sam. 3:7–8 and I Kings 2:13–22), but this practice (which may have extended to all the king's wives on occasion [II Sam. 12:8]) was probably a special feature of the royal household. See Patai, *Sex and Family*, pp. 41–43.

28. See the later law of Deut. 22:13–21, however, where the husband

who slanders his wife with a false accusation of unchastity incurs a double penalty—corporal punishment and a fine.

29. See Patai, *Sex and Family*, p. 120 (citing Hos. 2:4 ff.; Isa. 50:1; and Jer. 3:8—all prophetic similes) and Gehard von Rad, *Deuteronomy* (Philadelphia: Westminster Press, 1966), p. 150.

30. Pedersen thought this to be the most common reason for divorce, but could refer only to Gen. 29:34 as evidence (*Israel*, I–II, 71). Patai (*Sex and Family*, p. 120) notes that divorce for barrenness is never mentioned, but argues that the emphasis on procreation and the insecurity of the childless woman indicated in the patriarchal stories make barrenness a most probable cause for dismissal. In this connection it should be noted that the several conspicuously barren wives of the Old Testament all bear eventually (e.g., Sarah, Samson's mother, Hannah, and the "great" woman of Shunem). Their barrenness is a literary device that retards the action of the story, heightens anticipation and suspense, and gives a miraculous character to the birth. In most cases the real interest of the story is in the child that is finally born. Attention is focused upon him through this device. His existence is made to depend upon a special act of God in opening his mother's womb.

31. This special provision for female inheritance was further modified in the interests of tribal solidarity and the preservation of tribal land by a specification that the inheriting daughter marry within her father's tribe (Num. 31:1–9). From this it is clear that the daughter's husband was regarded as the real heir.

32. The property would otherwise pass to the father's nearest male relative and thus be lost to his name.

33. Von Rad (*Deuteronomy*, p. 107) notes that the "updating" in Deut. 15:12–17 of the old law of the Hebrew slave (Exod. 21:1–11) presupposes that the woman has in the meantime become capable of owning landed property and is thus able to sell herself into slavery for debt just as a male. Cf. II Kings 8:3–6 (though in this case the property claimed by the widow might possibly belong to her minor son).

34. Women may have been excused from this obligation in view of their more highly deemed—and confining—services to home and children. But the fact that they were dispensable in the practice of the cult would support any notion of their inferiority in that realm. Note, however, that against the law of Deut. 16:16, the custom of a single annual visit to a local sanctuary is described in I Sam. 1:3–8 (from the period of the judges), in which the man was regularly accompanied by his wife or wives. Only the man sacrificed, however (vs. 4).

35. Further gradations by age and sex make it clear that it was labor value that was reckoned by this table of equivalents.

36. See Neh. 5:1–5, in which the impoverished Jews complain that in

order to pay their debts they are being forced to sell their sons and daughters into slavery—and that some of their *daughters* have *already* been enslaved. The relatively greater expendability of females may also have found expression in female infanticide by abandonment, a practice attested among contemporary peoples of the Middle East and suggested for the Old Testament period by the image of the female foundling in Ezek. 16 (Patai, *Sex and Family*, p. 136).

37. See the blessing of Gen. 24:60: "[May you] be the mother of thousands of ten thousands."

38. See, for example, Gen. 46:8–27, in which wives are explicitly omitted from the tally given in vs. 26, and only one daughter is included among the 70 persons counted! See also Neh. 7:6–37, in which the number of persons returning from the exile is counted by families of men only.

39. Cf. Gen. 3:20, in which Eve's name is interpreted to mean "mother of all living."

40. It must be noted, however, that inequality of opportunity may make equal responsibility discriminatory in effect.

41. For a different interpretation, see note 21, above.

42. The widow and the divorcée are alone free to make binding vows, since they alone bear no immediate responsibility to a male whose interests might be hurt by the action (vs. 9).

43. The prostitute, as a pariah, existed for the most part outside the primary authority structures of the society.

44. The Hebrew word used in most of these passages means simply a "stranger" or "foreigner"; only in 7:10–22 and 29:3 is the professional term "harlot" (*zōnāh*) employed. Scholars dispute whether the woman in question was actually a foreigner or simply a woman whose mores made her a social outcast and therefore an "outsider" (see W. McKane, *Proverbs* [Philadelphia: Westminster, 1970], pp. 285, 287). Some see in the descriptions of her a reference to a devotee of a foreign cult and thus a cult prostitute (ibid., pp. 284, 287). For the discussion here it is sufficient simply to designate her as the "other" woman, contrasting her with the wife. The admonitions against association with her are not religious or ethical but "practical." "She'll be the death of you," they predict.

45. See B. Childs, *Biblical Theology in Crisis* (Philadelphia: Westminster, 1970), pp. 186–190.

46. Ibid. In striking contrast to Proverbs, the Song of Solomon extols erotic love for itself as the most prized of human possessions. Its power and beauty are expressed in a relationship of complete mutuality, controlled neither by the man nor by the woman, and therefore (necessarily) apart from the marriage relationship with its structure of male domination and female subordination. In the Song the lovers alternate in initiating acts of lovemaking. There

the woman is portrayed as seeking out her beloved in the very same language used by Proverbs to describe the aggressive enticement of the harlot—but with no hint of condemnation. For further comparison of the parallel passages in Proverbs and Song of Solomon, see Childs, ibid., pp. 190–196. See also Trible, "Depatriarchalizing in Biblical Interpretation," pp. 42–47.

47. E.g., Jehosheba (II Kings 11:2), Rahab (Josh. 2:1–21), Moses' mother and sister and Pharaoh's daughter (Exod. 2:2–10).

48. E.g., Delilah, Jael, the woman of Thebez (Judg. 9:53), Jezebel.

49. E.g., the widow of Zarephath (I Kings 17:8–24; See also II Kings 4:1–7), the "great" woman of Shunem (II Kings 4:8–37), Sarah, Samson's mother (Judg. 13:2–3).

50. E.g., Rahab (Josh. 2:8–13), Abigail (I Sam. 25:28–29), the Queen of Sheba.

51. The exceptions, Ruth and Esther, are both encountered in works of a distinct literary genre, the novella, in which they are the central figures.

52. See also Hannah in her yearly visits to the child she had vowed to the service of Yahweh (I Sam. 2:19) and Moses' mother boldly trusting in the compassion of another woman to save the life of her own son (Exod. 2:1–10).

53. Or, perhaps, one who protects, saves or succors. Cf. Isa. 22:21 and Job 29:16.

54. Indirect or "underhanded" means of exercising power are the devices commonly employed by women in patriarchal societies. See Pedersen, *Israel*, I–II, 69.

55. In a rare acknowledgment of a woman's effect upon the political and moral life of the nation, the Deuteronomic historian judges the sibling kings, Ahaziah and Joram, in terms of the (evil) example of *both* parents, Ahab and Jezebel (I Kings 22:52; II Kings 3:2,13; see also II Kings 9:22 ff.). The widespread practice of cursing a man by cursing his mother may also be an acknowledgment of the mother's influence on the child. Compare Saul's reproach of Jonathan in II Sam. 20:30, "you son of a perverse, rebellious [= possibly "runaway"] woman," with the English deprecations "s.o.b." and "bastard."

56. The name of the queen mother is omitted from the formulas of two southern kings, Ahaz (II Kings 16:2) and Jehoram (II Kings 8:16–18). Jehoram's *wife's* name is given, however, which is unique in these records (she was the daughter of the notorious northern king Ahab). Normally the king's wives were of no interest to the official chroniclers or to the Deuteronomic historian. Only David's wives are known, because of the roles they play in the extended biographical history of David's rise and reign.

57. Exceptions only confirm the rule. See Judg. 11:37–40.

58. Rachel and Leah, together with their servants Bilhah and Zilpah,

are in the first instance simply mothers of the twelve "sons of Israel," and are only secondarily fleshed out with individual characteristics as wives of Jacob. See M. Noth, *Das System der zwoelf Staemme Israel* (Stuttgart: Kohlhammer, 1930), p. 7.

59. See Gen. 34 (Dinah and Shechem—though the relationship failed to result in marriage, according to this account).

60. Despite the moralistic interpretation given by the editor, the enumeration of Solomon's wives and concubines was certainly intended to suggest his great means as well as his great appetite.

61. Even concubines and female prisoners of war taken as wives had limited rights, by virtue of their sexual union with the master, that distinguished them from ordinary slaves—or other property.

62. A case of extreme loyalty in this respect is exemplified by Tamar, who in desperation to fulfill her duty to her dead husband lures her father-in-law to impregnate her (Gen. 38). See Pedersen, *Israel*, I–II, 79.

63. Even half-sibling marriage seems to have been tolerated in David's time (II Sam. 13:13), though later law prohibits it (Lev. 18:9, 20:17). See Pedersen, *Israel*, I–II, 64–65.

64. Compare Judg. 16:1 ff. and 16:4 ff. A man "goes in to" or "lies with" a harlot, but he is expected to take the woman he "loves" as a wife. Where he does not, the relationship is clearly an abnormal one (II Sam. 13:1 ff. and 15–16). The major exception to this rule is found in the Song of Solomon, where love is extolled without thought of marriage.

65. In this case Michal's obvious love for David is exploited by her father, Saul, who makes an exorbitant demand as the bride price.

66. But a father might also step into the marriage and give a neglected daughter to another man (Judg. 15:1–2; I Sam. 25:44).

67. See Patai, *Sex and Family*, p. 44.

68. The major exception is the royal family (II Kings 24:15).

69. See p. 55, above. The harlot as a metaphor for Israel is found in Isaiah, Hosea, Micah, Jeremiah, Ezekiel and Nahum. The verb *zānāh* ("to play the harlot") is used to speak of apostasy in Judg. 2:17, 8:27, 33; Exod. 34:15–16; Deut. 31:16; Lev. *passim*; Num. 15:39, 25:1; Hos. 1:2, 4:12 and 15, 9:1; Jer. 2 and 3 (4 times); Ezek. (15 times); Ps. 106:39; I Chr. 5:25.

70. Note, however, that our chief source of information is the highly biased accounts of Hebrew prophets and theologians, who frequently describe all non-Yahwistic worship as simply prostitution.

71. See Patai, *Sex and Family*, p. 147. Patai argues that attitudes toward harlotry became more lenient in the later period of the monarchy, by which time harlots were an accepted part of urban society (I Kings 22:38; Isa. 23:16; Exod. 16:24–25; Jer. 3:2, 5:7; Prov. 2:16, 5:3, 8, 6:24–25; 7:5, 10, 11, 12, 9:14, 15; Sir. 9:3–9, 19:2 26:9). His argument that later Hebrew attitudes toward

prostitution involved no essentially moral judgment is supported only by citations from Prov. and Sir., both of which represent a genre of literature characterized by practical rather than moral judgments.

72. The enigmatic unnamed prophetess (*hann^ebîāh*) of Isa. 8:3 is excluded from this analysis since nothing is known about her *prophetic* activity and her identity and role are disputed.

73. "Why did a chief priest inquire of a woman? And who was she? The question has been asked since at least Kimchi's day" (J. A. Montgomery, *A Critical and Exegetical Commentary on the Book of Kings* [Edinburgh: T. & T. Clark, 1960], p. 525).

74. Deborah and Huldah are both referred to as married women; it is generally assumed that all women of marriageable age and condition were married.

75. This pattern may be contrasted with that of the prophet Jeremiah, who knew himself to have been called as a "youth" (Jer. 1:7) and whose vocation obliged him to renounce normal family life (16:2). Other male prophets are known to have been married. But marriage was never considered a vocation for males, as it was for females, and would generally have interfered far less with their "choice" and exercise of a profession.

76. Her "punishment" (vss. 9–14), in which she is made cultically unclean and excluded from the holy camp, also suggests a cultic interpretation of her role. In Exod. 15:20 she is described as a prophetess, but the meaning of the term for this early period is disputed. See Mic. 6:4.

77. These included the *q^edēšāh* ("holy/consecrated" woman) (Deut. 23:18 [Heb.; Eng.:vs. 17]; Hos. 4:14; cf. Gen. 38:21, 22) and devotees of the Canaanite mother goddess, Asherah (II Kings 23:7). In addition to cult personnel, women are also singled out as worshippers of foreign gods in Ezek. 8:14 (women weeping for Tammuz, a Sumerian god, whose death was annually lamented by women) and Jer. 7:18, 44:17–19 (women making offerings to the Queen of Heaven, a female deity of Assyro-Babylonian or Canaanite provenance). It is significant that the syncretistic rites with which Israelite women are explicitly connected are associated solely with female deities or with deities whose cult was predominantly female. See T. Jacobsen, *Toward the Image of Tammuz and Other Essays on Mesopotamian History and Culture* (Cambridge, Mass.: Harvard University Press, 1970), pp. 29, 73–101. Compare also the practice of Elephantine Jews, whose cult included a female deity. See R. Patai, *The Hebrew Goddess* (New York: Ktav, 1967), and W. F. Albright, *Archaeology and the Religion of Israel* (2d ed., Baltimore: Johns Hopkins, 1946).

78. The old law of Exod. 22:18 refers to "sorcery" alone of the magic arts, citing it along with bestiality and sacrifice to other gods (vss.

19–20) as practices demanding death. The clause concerning sorcery stands out from the rest by its feminine formulation ("you shall not permit a sorceress to live"). The practice was presumably considered a female specialty at that time. The later list of seven proscribed types of magic or divination in Deut. 18:10 is entirely masculine in its formulation (and probably inclusive in its intended reference). By this time, at least, sorcery and necromancy were clearly not regarded as exclusively female arts. See *Interpreter's Dictionary of the Bible (IDB)*, ed. G. A. Buttrick (New York and Nashville: Abingdon, 1962) I. Mendelsohn, "Magic, Magician," III, 223–225; "Familiar Spirit," II, 237–238; and "Divination," I, 856–858.

79. See Mendelsohn, "Magic," *IDB*, III, 224. The "gift" employed by the magicians consisted largely of special techniques, knowledge, or talismans that could be learned or acquired and passed on. As a consequence, sociological factors, including sexual distinctions, might be expected to play a larger role in the identification and classification of these manipulative artists than of the charismatics (prophets).

80. The adjective "wise" as applied to both men and women covers a wide variety of meaning and usages. While it frequently designates a class of counselors found in the court (see Judg. 5:29, where it describes the ladies who counsel the queen mother of Sisera), it may also be used of persons skilled in various arts and crafts (such as the keening women of Jer. 9:17 or the spinners of Exod. 35:25), and may be used in an even broader sense of one who is prudent, discerning, capable in solving problems and in counseling profitable action. See S. H. Blank, "Wisdom," *IDB*, IV, 852–861.

81. As a consequence, it is women who are the saviors of men when the threat is felt within the house or living quarters, the woman's province. See Exod. 1:15–2:10; Josh. 2:1–7, 15–16; I Sam. 19:11–17; II Sam. 17:17–20; II Kings 11:1–3. But the home can also be a battlefield if the woman chooses (Judg. 4:18–21, 5:24–27; see also Judg. 16:4–22).

82. Notably absent from all these references to women is any conscious reflection upon woman's place and being in society, including any theological interpretation of her purpose and portion.

83. The actual status of women is exceedingly difficult to judge in a patriarchal and patrilineal society, where systematic bias in favor of the male characterizes language, laws and most formal structures and relationships. The compensation that necessarily exists in such a system is rarely visible in formal documents and is hard to assess. Whether formalized or informal, it generally serves to re-enforce the system by making it bearable for those discriminated against. Thus the honoring of the mother is a necessary compensation, since the mother's role is an essential one to the maintenance of

the society. Informal compensation is represented in the "under-handed" tactics used by women to get their way. But significant attempts were also made in Israel, against prevailing cultural norms, to recognize women as equals in the covenant community. Glimpses of this can be seen in some of the laws and especially in prophetic judgments (Hos. 4:14) and prophetic eschatology (Joel 2:28–29 and Jer. 31:32).

84. See especially the Song of Solomon. Phyllis Trible ("Depatri-archalizing in Biblical Interpretation," p. 47), sees in these poems an expression of Paradise regained, of the possibility of nonex-ploitative male-female relationship.

85. See, for example, the nondiscriminating laws and Isa. 3:16–4:1, 32:9–12; Amos 4:1–3; Jer. 44:20–30.

86. The text as it has been transmitted is complete with rubrics ad-dressed to the midwife and the pregnant woman.

87. The P formulation implies an essential equality of the two sexes. But its implications were only partially perceived by the priestly writer, whose own culturally determined ideas concerning appro-priate roles and activities of men and women generally fail to reflect this insight. Thus male genealogies and an exclusively male priesthood dominate the rest of his work.

88. *ādām* in Gen. 2 is both the genus and the first individual, who appears as male and not androgynous, though the woman is formed from him. That he is conceived as a man in this naïve version is clear from the statement concerning his loneliness (2:18); but he is not yet sexually aware. His true nature as a sexual being is manifest only as he is confronted by the woman. Thus he is at once truly male and truly man when joined by woman.

89. Gen. 2:23; see also vs. 24. In J's view the sexual act that unites man and woman is the sign of an intended and original union. The man and the woman do not simply exist alongside one another as partners in work—though they are that; nor is their sexuality created primarily for procreation (as in P). They are created *for* each other, to complete each other. Their union in "one flesh" is a reunion. The fact that this is expressed by a man from his point of view should not obscure the basic intention and significance of the statement.

90. The crime is devoid of malicious intent, and is "softened" still further by the introduction of an instigator external to the man and woman. The serpent is the seducer, and he is made to bear the blame and punishment for the seduction. But the pair who succumbed to his tempting must pay the consequences of their common sin, the sin of disobeying the divine command.

91. The sequence of events in the narrative and the roles of the man and woman in it derive, presumably, from a much older story, whose basic characters and meaning have been radically trans-

formed in this Israelite appropriation of it. See J. S. Bailey, "Initiation and the Primal Woman in Gilgamesh and Genesis 2–3," *Journal of Biblical Literature* LXXXIX (1970), 137–150.

92. In Trible's characterization ("Depatriarchalizing in Biblical Interpretation," p. 13) the man's one act is "belly-oriented," while the response of the woman is that of a theologian. I doubt that the minimal description given here of the man's response can support substantial inferences concerning the character of the man. According to Trible, "the man is passive, brutish, and inept," in contrast to the woman, who is "intelligent, sensitive, and ingenious" (ibid.). The man acts here in his normal role at mealtime: he accepts the food offered to him by his wife. No qualification is necessary of the general rule of male dominance in a patriarchal society. More important, however, is the fuller description of the woman's reponse. It, too, presents a picture that is consonant with the portrait of woman found in other Old Testament sources, where she is indeed "intelligent, sensitive and ingenious."

93. The ambiguity in human existence and the interrelatedness of pleasure and pain are more clearly shown in the case of the woman, since her work is described in relational terms. That definition is given in the culture and the tradition with which the author had to work. The focus of this passage is upon the couple's work, not upon the male-female relationship. Consequently the asymmetry in the description of the man's and the woman's lot should not be overinterpreted. The man's desire for the woman is quite as prominent in this author's mind (2:23–24) as the woman's desire for the man (3:16).

94. Literally, "a woman encompasses a man." See W. L. Holladay, "Jer. 31:22b Reconsidered: 'The Woman Encompasses the Man,'" *Vetus Testamentum* XVI (1966). 236–239.

Woman: Seductive Siren
and Source of Sin?

Pseudepigraphal Myth and
Christian Origins

BERNARD P. PRUSAK

In the third chapter of the Book of Genesis we find the story of a serpent who engages a woman in conversation and induces her to eat the fruit of the only forbidden tree in the garden, the tree of the knowledge of good and evil.[1] F. R. Tennant notes that two features of this Hebrew Fall story are likewise common to Greek mythology, namely, the agency of woman in the cause of evil and the acquisition of knowledge as the means of temptation to it.[2] When the Sirens address Odysseus in the *Odyssey* they sing:

> Bring your ship in, so you may listen to our voice.
> No one has ever yet sped past this place in a black ship
> Before he listened to the honey-toned voice from our mouths,
> And then went off delighted and knowing more things.
> For we know all the many things that in broad Troy
> The Argives and the Trojans suffered at the will of the gods.
> We know all that comes to be on the much-nourishing earth.[3]

Unfortunately, acceptance of the invitations in either Genesis or the *Odyssey* courts disaster. Adam and Eve become ashamed of their nakedness and fail in their attempt to hide from God (Gen. 3:7, 10–11). God confronts the woman and asks her what she has done. She replies, "The serpent beguiled me, and I ate" (Gen. 3:13). After cursing the serpent, God turns to the woman: "I will greatly multiply your pain in childbearing; in pain you shall bring forth children, yet your desire shall be for your husband, and he shall rule over you" (Gen. 3:16).

Women also serve the cause of evil in the legend of the giants recounted in Gen. 6:1–4.

> When men began to multiply on the face of the ground, and daughters were born to them, the sons of God saw that the daughters of men were fair; and they took to wife such of them as they chose. Then the Lord said, "My spirit shall not abide in man for ever, for he is flesh, but his days shall be a hundred and twenty years." The Nephilim were on the earth in those days, and also afterward, when the sons of God came in to the daughters of men, and they bore children to them. These were the mighty men that were of old, the men of renown.

This fragment of mythology explained the growth of evil on the earth, which again culminated in physical woes, the Flood.

In the second century before the Christian era Jewish interest in the cause of evil was heightened. A playful exegesis, or Haggada, about Genesis developed both in rabbinic literature and in the apocalyptic works of the time. For most of us, who are very comfortable with the Augustinian notion of original sin rooted in Gen. 3 and Rom. 5, the approach of this Jewish literature may seem rather strange. The pseudonymous Book of Enoch (I Enoch or Ethiopic Enoch) contains only passing references to the Paradise story.[4] Chapter 6 of Genesis, rather than ch. 3, is used as the *terminus a quo* in explaining the origins of evil. In chs. 6–11 and 106:14–18, in which I Enoch incorporates the lost Book of Noah, and in ch. 15, which recapitulates the entire story by means of Enoch's dream vision, we find an embellishment of the Nephilim myth. The "sons of God" are angels, or immortal, spiritual watchers, who descended from heaven to satisfy their lust for the beautiful women of earth.[5] Having entered a mutual pact to carry out rape with their leader Semjaza, two hundred watchers descended upon Mount Hermon. They slept with the women of earth, defiled themselves, and revealed all kinds of charms and enchantments to the women (I Enoch 6:6–7:2, 16:2–3). The women gave birth to giants, three thousand ells tall, who turned against mankind and filled the earth with blood and lawlessness (7:2–6). One of the fallen watchers, Azazel, who in certain passages is called "leader," taught men "to make swords, and knives, and shields, and breastplates, and made known to them the metals [of the earth] and the art of working them, and bracelets, and ornaments, and the use of antimony, and the beautifying of the eyelids, and all kinds of costly stones, and all coloring tinctures" (8:1, 10:7).[6] As in Genesis and the *Odyssey*, evil, women, and knowledge are a package deal. War, jewelry, cosmetics, and sex are Azazel's lessons.

Michael, Uriel, Raphael, and Gabriel, who are looking down from heaven, are horrified and report the chaos on earth to God (ch. 9). Uriel is dispatched to help Noah escape the flood by which God plans to destroy and purify everything on earth (10:1–3). Raphael is ordered to banish Azazel to the wilderness until the Day of Judgment, when he will be cast into fire. Gabriel is assigned to destroy the children of the watchers by inciting the giants to war among themselves until they all perish. Michael binds Semjaza and his associates in preparation for an eternal prison of fire (10:4–16, 13, 15–16, 19:1, and 21). However, as we are later told in Enoch's dream visions, evil spirits go forth from the souls of the dying giants' flesh and continue to wreak havoc upon humanity, and so evil perdures (15:8–16:1). God shows no mercy to the watchers who descended from heaven—the only place assigned spiritual beings. For seeking wives they will be assigned to eternal fire (15:2–7, 16:2–4). The women of the angels who went astray are destined to become Sirens (19:2).[7]

The Book of Jubilees, a midrashic Targum on Genesis, basically retains this curious account of the origin of evil, but with some modifications.[8] In Jubilees God himself sent the angels, or watchers, upon the earth "to instruct the children of men, and that they should do judgment and uprightness" (Jub. 4:15 and 5:6). Only later did they choose wives from the daughters of men, who bore them sons that were giants (4:22 and 5:1). "And lawlessness increased on the earth and all flesh corrupted its way, alike men and cattle and beasts and birds . . . and every imagina-

tion of the thoughts of all men [was] thus evil continually" (5:2).[9]
To remedy the situation the fallen angels were bound in the
depths of the earth (5:6). All humans except Noah and those in
the Ark were destroyed by a flood, while the giants slew each other
by the sword of war that God sent into their midst (5:6–9). As in
I Enoch, the spirits of these sons of the disobedient watchers live
on and begin to lead the children of Noah's sons into error (7:27
and 10:1–2).[10] After Noah's intercession on behalf of his sons,
God casts nine-tenths of the evil spirits, or demons, who are
"malignant and created to destroy," into the place of condemnation. He makes an agreement with their chief, Mastema, or Satan,
permitting 10 percent of them to remain on earth to assist him in
corrupting and leading astray the wicked until the time of his final
judgment (10:3–9). Only in the time of the messianic kingdom
will men finally live in peace and joy, "and there shall be no Satan
nor any evil destroyer" (23:29). In the meantime Noah is instructed by the angels of God regarding the medicines needed to
combat the diseases and seductions caused by the malignant spirits
(10:10–13).[11]

Jubilees, in what some regard as its more primitive core, also
contains the Fall story of Adam and Eve in basically the same form
as appears in Gen. 3 (see Jub. 3).[12] However, the name of the
forbidden tree is omitted, and Eve covers herself before she gives
Adam the fruit of the tree (Jub. 3:21). Along with all the physical
woes that befall Adam, Eve, and the serpent as a result of God's
curses, all the animals also lose the power of speech (Jub. 3:28).

In its final redaction Jubilees keeps the Paradise story of Gen.
3, which relates the first instance of evil in the world, separate from
the watcher myth of Gen. 6, which explains the subsequent
intensification of degeneracy leading to the Flood.[13] The serpent
and Satan remain distinct figures in two different stories in this
stage of development. But the process of embellishment on Gen. 6
will progress a bit further before the watcher myth fades, or rather,
coalesces into the story of Adam and Eve's Fall. The basically
Jewish works that we will now consider were assembled over
periods of time extending into the Christian era and therefore
contain some Christian interpolations in their final redactions.

Chapter 5 of the Testament of Reuben, from the Testaments

of the Twelve Patriarchs, makes women the prime culprits in its version of the watcher legend:[14]

> For evil are women, my children; and since they have no power or strength over man, they use wiles by outward attractions, that they may draw him to themselves. And whom they cannot bewitch by outward attractions, him they overcome by craft. For moreover, concerning them, the angel of the Lord told me, and taught me, that women are overcome by the spirit of fornication more than men, and in their heart they plot against men; and by means of their adornment they deceive first their minds, and by the glance of the eye instil the poison, and then through the accomplished act they take them captive. For a woman cannot force a man openly, but by a harlot's bearing she beguiles him. Flee therefore, fornication, my children, and command your wives and your daughters, that they adorn not their heads and their faces to deceive the mind: because every woman who useth these wiles hath been reserved for eternal punishment. For thus they allured the Watchers who were before the flood; for as these continually beheld them, they lusted after them, and they conceived the act in their mind; for they changed themselves into the shape of men, and appeared to them when they were with their husbands. And the women lusting in their minds after their forms, gave birth to giants, for the Watchers appeared to them as reaching even unto heaven.

Women are now the instigators of the watchers' fall, and are directly responsible for the subsequent spread of evil because of their seductive wiles. Whereas in I Enoch, Azazel, the fallen angel, taught the use of cosmetics and beauty aids after the molestation, women here use these means to seduce the angels.

But such explanations of the cause of evil, which enhanced the myth of the giants in Gen. 6, gradually fell into disfavor. Jewish apocalyptic literature, and also rabbinic literature, used a variety of models for explaining evil in the world. In the works we will now consider, the Fall story of Adam and Eve, from Gen. 3, predominates, but aspects of the watcher myth are retained and integrated, especially the element of female seduction. The writers were anxious to keep woman as the primary cause of evil.

In Eve's account of the Fall in the Apocalypse of Moses, sin seems to result from a sexual relationship between Eve and the tempter.[15] The serpent, who acted alone in the Paradise story of Genesis, is here used as a vessel by the devil. Satan speaks words through his mouth to deceive Adam (Apoc. Moses 16–17).[16] However, his only way of getting to Adam, whom he envies, is through Eve, when she is alone in her part of Paradise. He first convinces her that if she eats the fruit of the one forbidden tree she will be like God and know good and evil. Once Eve is anxious to eat the fruit, he changes his mind. Only if she swears an oath that she will give the fruit to Adam will he let her have it (Apoc. Moses 15 and 17:1–19:2).[17] Eve agrees and says, ". . . when he had received the oath from me, he went and poured upon the fruit the poison of his wickedness, which is lust, the root and beginning of every sin, and he bent the branch on the earth and I took of the fruit and I ate" (19:3). Eve immediately experiences shame at her nakedness and covers herself (ch. 20). But still she shares her secret with Adam and persuades him also to eat the fruit, which is "lust" (ch. 21). Adam eats, and straightaway his eyes are opened and he, too, knows his nakedness. "And to me [Eve] he saith, 'O wicked woman! what have I done to thee that thou hast deprived me of the glory of God?' " (21:6) The next part of the account paraphrases Genesis. However, the plea for mercy that God prescribes for Eve when he confronts her is extremely significant: "Lord, Lord, save me, and I will turn no more to the sin of the flesh." God then responds: "And on this account, from thine own words I will judge thee, by reason of the enmity which the enemy has planted in thee" (25:3–4). The serpent then loses his hands and feet because he was a vessel for the seduction of Eve (ch. 26).

In this account the fruit from the tree of knowledge is poisoned by lust, which implies that Satan sexually seduced Eve. Her prescribed confession corroborates such an interpretation. So does a remark made by Adam in the related Latin *Life of Adam and Eve:* "The complaint of Eve hath come to me. Perchance, once more hath the serpent fought with her."[18] The seduction element of the watcher legend has now been blended into the Adam and Eve story. The serpent is now identified as Satan. In the Latin *Life of Adam and Eve* he explains why he deceived Eve and, with her assistance, caused Adam to be expelled from his joy and luxury. Satan envies man, since he lost his glory for refusing to worship Adam as the image of God. Even Michael's urgings had not been able to convince him to worship what he considered inferior and younger in creation. Satan is now determined to rise above God by corrupting man, God's created image.[19]

Both the Apocalypse of Moses and the Latin *Life of Adam and Eve* exhibit the tendency to idealize Adam. Eve is constantly lamenting that she has brought misfortune, sickness, and death to Adam by her misdeed.[20] Adam doesn't let her forget it, since he even orders her to tell their children how she caused the Fall (Apoc. Moses 7:1, 14:2–3). In the Latin *Life of Adam and Eve*, Eve asks Adam if he would like to kill her for what she did. In the later Slavonic version Adam gets the idea by himself but decides that God doesn't wish it.[21]

The Book of the Secrets of Enoch (II Enoch or Slavonic Enoch) consists of a series of visions in which the apostate angels, and their leader, Satan, play a prominent role.[22] As in the Apocalypse of Moses, elements from the watcher legend are again interwoven with the Fall of Adam (II Enoch 7, 18, 29). We are told that Satan first tried to set his throne above God's, for which he and his heavenly cohorts were banished to the lower places. This took place before the angels sinned with the daughters of men, for which Satan is also held responsible.[23] That lamentable deed, which is now secondary and subsequent to the Fall of Adam and Eve, only climaxed his campaign to corrupt the earth. He had already brought evil to earth, motivated by his envy of Adam's lordship over that part of creation: "And he [the devil] understood his condemnation and the sin which he had sinned before; therefore he conceived thought against Adam. In such form he entered and seduced Eve, but did not touch Adam" (II Enoch 31:6, 41: 1–2). Adam's sin might be identified with his first taste of lust, having been introduced to it by Eve, who learned its sweetness from a sinful union with the devil. This is supported by the manner in which the author tries to lessen Adam's culpability: Satan never *touched* Adam. He was duped by Eve, who brought him death (II Enoch 30:18).[24]

Such an interpretation is explicit in the nuanced version of the Fall presented in the Apocalypse of Abraham. There the Fall of Adam and Eve is the starting point for the history of the human race. We again meet Azazel acting as the teacher of secrets, the role he was assigned in I Enoch. The Fall, which he instigates by revealing his secrets, seems identified with fleshly union between Adam and Eve.[25] This same motif is possibly reflected in the Syrian Apocalypse of Baruch (II Baruch), which maintains that the begetting of children and the passion of parents are results of the transgression of Adam (II Bar. 56:6).[26]

Except for the third and sixth chapters from Genesis none of the passages studied in tracing the role assigned woman as the cause of sin is drawn from what we, in contradistinction to the earliest Christians, consider canonical scripture. All the literature has been apocryphal or pseudepigraphal, since there is little development of our Genesis themes in the canonical books. (We might note that Jewish heroines, such as Esther and Judith, serve their people by exploiting their seductive charm.) Only the books of Ecclesiasticus and Wisdom of Solomon, accepted as canonical by some Christians, contain any pertinent references. Ecclesiasticus, or the Wisdom of Jesus Ben Sirach, says: "From a woman sin had its beginning, and because of her we all die." In the next breath the author speaks of male domination and female subservience: "Allow no outlet to water, and no boldness of speech in an evil wife. If she does not go as you direct, separate her from yourself."[27] While Ecclesiasticus emphasizes the role of woman in causing sin, the Wisdom of Solomon identifies the serpent as the envious devil who brings death to man, created for incorruption in *the image of God's own eternity* (or nature; *var.*).[28]

We must note that many of the themes we have considered are not the exclusive possession of the literature cited. They are a Haggada, or playful Midrash, that is common to both apocalyptic and rabbinic literature. The identification of the serpent with Satan, the devil's envy of Adam as the image of God, his seduction of Eve to cause Adam's downfall, and the broader angelic lust motif are likewise found in rabbinic literature.[29] For our purposes we have concentrated on what is one segment of a wider tradition. Furthermore, we recognize that rabbinic literature, and even other apocryphal books, had other explanations for the origin of evil, some of which did not depend upon either the Paradise story or the watcher myth (e.g., the *yetzer hara* [evil inclination] of IV Ezra 7:48 and 92).[30]

We have previously observed that the watcher legend gave

place to the Paradise story as the primary explanation of human corruption even in apocalyptic literature. But we must admit that the particular elements of the watcher myth that were retained by later writers and blended into the Fall of Adam story reflect a sort of theological prejudice that sought to justify female subjection to a degree surpassing the curse in Genesis. At the same time, seeing the imagination and zest that authors in a patriarchal society could summon for making women the scapegoats for all the wickedness in the world, one is given reason to suspect the seriousness and accuracy of the Genesis curse itself. Perhaps it is now time to relegate it to the same category as the notion of a six-day creation; it was the best an author could do in his culture.

Puzzled by the power of sexual drive and the mysteries of generation and birth, authors in a patriarchal society killed two birds with one stone. They explained the *de facto* existence of evil by indicting woman as its source, and thereby also had both a theological explanation and the justification for maintaining the cultural facts of male dominance and female subservience. Men of that time coped better with their dependence upon or need for woman as wife and mother if they had an excuse to intimidate her. This was accomplished by connecting sexual drive and generation with evil. If self-control was originally lost because of a powerful devil, then man's ego could breathe more easily when his present self-control seemed tenuous. Paradoxically, Eve's primeval duping of Adam guaranteed male hegemony, because Eve's supposed role in causing Adam's downfall was really a tool for intimidation. Every woman became an Eve, indicted as the cause of evil and the corrupter of men and angels. But now we must consider the influence of Jewish apocalyptic themes upon early Christianity's attitudes toward women.

That the Christian scriptures were influenced by the motifs we have studied is evident from the allusions to the watcher myth in the Epistle of Jude (vss. 6–7, 14) and II Peter (2:4) and from the references to the heavenly war in the Book of Revelation (ch. 12). Although the gospels reflect the demonology of the apocalyptic literature, Jesus is portrayed as being quite positive in his attitudes toward women. He freely converses with them, assigns them roles in his parables, and numbers them among his friends and close followers. With these observations, we refer you to a recent study

of that aspect.[31] We will turn our attention to the negative attitudes, which are more apparent in the literature of the Pauline
school.

It is to Paul's credit that he wrote the ringing declaration:
"There is neither Jew nor Greek, there is neither slave nor free,
there is neither male nor female; for you are all one in Christ Jesus"
(Gal. 3:28).[32] Yet when it suited his purpose, Paul would invoke
the *traditions* that insisted upon a subordinate role for women.
In I Cor. 11:4–10 he is concerned that women pray or prophesy
with their heads covered:

> Any man who prays or prophesies with his head covered dishonors
> his head, but any woman who prays or prophesies with her head
> unveiled dishonors her head—it is the same as if her head were
> shaven. For if a woman will not veil herself, then she should cut
> off her hair; but if it is disgraceful for a woman to be shorn or
> shaven, let her wear a veil. For a man ought not to cover his head,
> since he is the image and glory of God; but woman is the glory of
> man. (For man was not made from woman, but woman from man.
> Neither was man created for woman, but woman for man.) That
> is why a woman ought to have a veil on her head, because of the
> angels.

The meaning of the last verse has long been a problem to
exegetes. The text literally says that a woman ought to have
exousia (power) upon her head on account of the angels. Many
exegetes interpret *exousia* in the passive sense of a *symbol of
woman's subjection* or of *her husband's authority over her.*[33] Many
scholars follow Gerhard Kittel's interpretation of the word as
"veil."[34] Hans Lietzmann interprets the passage according to the
context of the Testament of Reuben 5, and says that the veil
affords women a magical power of protection against the fallen
angels, who were seduced by women in the first place.[35] Joseph
Fitzmyer, who provides an excellent review of all the opinions in
his study on Qumran angelology, objects to Lietzmann's interpretation, since, in his opinion, it would require the word "angels"
(*tous angelous*) to mean bad angels, or angels capable of sinning,
which he maintains is never the case in Paul.[36] He explains the
passage according to the Qumran Scrolls, and argues that a woman
with her head uncovered is like a person suffering from a bodily

defect. Such were never to appear before the angels who assist at gatherings of public worship.[37] Henry Cadbury develops a similar opinion from Scroll material. He maintains that women were considered inherently defective and unclean in Jewish and Essene thought and therefore were to hide themselves from the angels.[38]

Without pursuing the exegetical problem any further, we are still left with the question: Why is the uncovered head of a woman defective, especially when Paul himself maintains that her hair is her glory? (I Cor. 11:15) It appears that the influence of pseudepigraphal motifs should not be prematurely rejected. The veil was not worn lest angels fall again, but as a brand of shame or a scarlet letter for once having caused the Fall of Adam and of the angels. Paul seems concerned to maintain traditions and laws that are not prevalent among the gentile Corinthian Christians.[39] In I Cor. 14:34-35 we read:

> As in all the churches of the saints, the women should keep silence in the churches. For they are not permitted to speak, but should be subordinate, even as the law says. If there is anything they desire to know, let them ask their husbands at home. For it is shameful for a woman to speak in church.

In other texts the stress on male dominance and female subservience seems more clearly related to the pseudepigraphal stance, or at least to the wider Haggada that it reflects. In II Cor. 11:3 Paul notes that the serpent deceived Eve by his cunning.[40] But it is the first Epistle to Timothy, probably written by a disciple of Paul, which explicitly demands woman's submissiveness, arguing from her role in the Fall, and further tries to exonerate Adam at the expense of Eve (2:9-15):

> . . . women should adorn themselves modestly and sensibly in seemly apparel, not with braided hair or gold or pearls or costly attire but by good deeds, as befits women who profess religion. Let a woman learn in silence with all submissiveness. I permit no woman to teach or to have authority over men; she is to keep silent. For Adam was formed first, then Eve; and Adam was not deceived, but the woman was deceived and became a transgressor. Yet woman will be saved through bearing children, if she continues in faith and love and holiness, with modesty.[41]

The concern with beauty aids, which is also reflected in the advice given to the "weaker sex" in I Peter 3:1-7, strengthens our suggestion that the pseudepigraphical myths underlie the negativism toward women expressed here. It is significant that such arts were first revealed by the fallen angels in the pseudepigrapha.

If we can grasp only overtones of the pseudepigraphal myths in the New Testament, their influence is unmistakable in the later Church Fathers. In Justin Martyr the watcher theme of I Enoch and Jubilees is loud and clear:

> (God) committed the care of men and all things under heaven to angels whom he appointed over them. But the angels transgressed this appointment, and were captivated by love of women, and begat children who are those that are called demons; and besides, they afterwards subdued the human race to themselves . . . and among men they sowed murders, wars, adulteries, intemperate deeds, and all wickedness. (II *Apology* 5:3 ff.)[42]

Eve is allegorically presented as the virgin who, having been deceived by Satan, "conceived the word of the serpent and brought forth disobedience and death." Balance is provided by her parallel, Mary, who is the mother of him "by whom God destroys both the serpent and those angels and men who have become like the serpent."[43] Justin's dependence upon the watcher theme is shared by another apologist, Athenagoras, in his *Appeal on Behalf of Christians* (chs. 24, 25, 27).

Although he alludes to the watcher legend and explicitly mentions Enoch's mission to the angels, Irenaeus basically works with the story of Adam and Eve's Fall.[44] He includes the embellishments we saw in the Apocalypse of Moses and in the *Life of Adam and Eve*. Satan is a fallen angel whose sin was possibly the refusal to worship man as the image of God. He is now angry at God, whose order he disobeyed, and is envious of man's lordship over creation.[45] To spite God he wishes to corrupt God's image, man, but can only do it through Eve.[46] Eve is thoroughly deceived by Satan hidden within the serpent and plays right into Satan's hands by leading Adam into sin.[47] Eve was made the cause of death both to herself and to the entire human race.[48] Concupiscence and lust result from the first sin. Adam and Eve previously had had no imagination or conception of what is shameful.[49] Unfortunately, Adam, the naïve innocent, was caught in the middle of Satan's duel with God, and fell only because of Eve's treachery.[50]

Irenaeus systematically tries to exonerate Adam by pushing the blame onto the serpent and his accomplice, Eve.[51] He says that God interrogated Adam and Eve in order that "the blame might light upon the woman." "He interrogates her that she might convey the blame to the serpent."[52] ". . . but He took compassion upon man, who, through want of care no doubt, but still wickedly (on the part of another), became involved in disobedience; and He turned the enmity by which (the Devil) had designed to make (man) the enemy of God, against the author of it, by removing His own anger from man."[53] As in Justin's *Dialogue*, some balance is restored when Mary by her obedience brings forth Christ to undo what the virgin Eve brought about by her transgression.[54]

Clement of Alexandria likewise speaks of the angels who renounced the beauty of God for a beauty that fades. As a result, they fell from heaven to earth, where, having sunk into pleasures, they revealed to women the secrets they knew.[55] In a diatribe against jewelry Clement complains that certain ornaments used by women are nothing but a symbol of adultery. It is intriguing that he then refers to Eve:

> Yet, these women do not blush when they wear such conspicuous symbols of wickedness. Just as the serpent deceived Eve, so, too, the enticing golden ornament in the shape of a serpent enkindles a mad frenzy in the hearts of the rest of womankind, leading them to have images made of lampreys and snakes as decorations.[56]

Clement introduces an unusual variation upon a sexual explanation of the first sin when he hints that Adam was prematurely drawn by lust to have relations with Eve before God married them.[57] He speculates that the serpent tempted Adam to seek bodily pleasure, like the brute animals, and as a result Adam and Eve conceived before the time scheduled in God's timetable. N. P. Williams suggests that Clement may have borrowed this idea from the Apocalypse of Moses.[58]

While Clement insists, against the Gnostic Cassian, that the marriage act and generation were created by God and are therefore good, he admits that the circumstances of their first experience were unfortunate. Citing Jer. 20:14, he develops a theme that is rather familiar in later Fathers: "A curse on the day I was born, no blessing on the day my mother bore me." Psalm 51:5 and Job 14:4 are then seen to have reference to the first sin: "Behold I was brought forth in iniquity, and in sin did my mother conceive me. . . . Who can bring a clean thing out of an unclean?"[59] Every birth relates to the sinfulness of the first; every mother taints her offspring.

In comparison to others of his time, Clement is generally a mellow and balanced person with a positive attitude toward life. He seems to have admitted women into his lectures, and showed appreciation of their *equality in nature* and their capacity for wisdom (*Strom.* 4,8 and 19). At the same time, his attitude toward them is colored by a fear lest they become sirens and sources of sin. Their dresses should not be overly soft and clinging, and should be hemmed below the ankles rather than above the knees—as some maidens were wearing them even in his time! Women were to wear veils, but not circumvent their whole purpose by wearing purple ones, since colors attract attention and inflame the lusts.[60] In a passage discussing attire for church, Clement insists that women be entirely covered except when at home:

> For that style of dress is grave, and protects from being gazed at. And she will never fall, who puts before her eyes modesty and her shawl; nor will she invite another to fall into sin by uncovering her face. For this is the wish of the Word (I Cor. 11:5), since it is becoming for her to pray veiled. (*Paed.* 3,11)

In a section on wine-drinking and carousing Clement notes that woman by her very nature must be concerned with modesty to a much greater degree than is required even for a man endowed with reason. Why? "Because her shameless conduct shall not be hid." For a woman is quickly drawn into immorality even by only giving consent to pleasure (*Paed.* 2,2). That woman consistently comes out second best when compared to man is most evident from Clement's discourse on the manliness of beards:

His beard, then, is the badge of a man and shows him unmis-
takably to be a man. It is older than Eve and is the symbol of
the stronger nature. By God's decree, hairiness is one of man's
conspicuous qualities, and, at that, hairiness distributed over his
whole body. Whatever smoothness or softness there was in him
God took from him when he fashioned the delicate Eve from
his side to be the receptacle of his seed, his helpmate both in
procreation and in the management of the home. What was left
(remember, he had lost all traces of hairlessness) was manhood
and reveals that manhood. His characteristic is action; hers,
passivity. For what is hairy is by nature drier and warmer than
what is bare; therefore, the male is hairier and more warm-blooded
than the female; the uncastrated, than the castrated; the mature,
than the immature. Thus it is a sacrilege to trifle with the symbol
of manhood [the beard]. (*Paed.* 3,3)

The total effect of Clement upon this writer can be summed up in
a simple phrase: the motifs of the pseudepigrapha are alive and
still kicking—women.

In his later writings, of the Caesarean period, Origen seems to
have simply rediscovered what Clement had already accomplished.
Influenced by the practice of infant baptism in Palestine, Origen
sets aside the prenatal Fall theory of his earlier *De Principiis* and
and now speculates about the nature of the first sin in terms of the
need for purification from uncleanness. Following a line of thinking that is vaguely reminiscent of Clement, he believes there is
some hidden and secret cause for a woman who has conceived
of seed and brought forth to be called "unclean." Citing Psalm
51:5 and Job 14:4–5 as evidence, Origen concludes that her child
is also unclean and thus needs baptism.[61] From a passage in
his *Commentary on Canticles* 3, the source of such inherent birth
pollution might be identified with the theory that Eve was seduced
by the serpent, who by his persuasive suggestions poured the
poison of sin into her and infected all her posterity. This would
be in line with the motif of the Apocalypse of Moses.[62] Even when
Origen finally returned to a more literal interpretation of Gen. 3
in his *Commentary on Romans* (5,9), he points out that Adam
did not know his wife Eve or conceive Cain until after the sin.
Finally, in his *Contra Celsum* (6,43) Origen refers to the serpent,

who deceived the woman by a promise of divinity.[63] Her example is said to have been followed by the man. Noting that the scapegoat of Leviticus (16:18) was sent into the wilderness, to Azazel, he identifies Azazel as the tempter.

When one turns to Tertullian, the themes we have traced from the Pseudepigrapha appear with full force in both his Catholic and Montanist works. There is no nuanced subtlety about Tertullian's obsession with both virgins and married women wearing veils. In a cross section of his works we find him explaining Paul's directive that women at prayer be veiled "on account of the angels" by recalling the sinful union of angels and women from the watcher myth.[64] "It is right that that face which was a snare to them [angels] should wear some mark of a humble guise and obscured beauty" (*Adv. Marcionem* 5,8).

Tertullian is not anxious for married women and virgins to wear veils lest the angels fall again. He considers the veil a mark of shame for past conduct. This is evident from a passage in *De Virginibus Velandis* 7: "So perilous a face, then, ought to be shaded . . . that when standing in the presence of God, at whose bar it stands accused of the driving of the angels from their native confines, it may blush before the other angels as well." To justify his preoccupation with the dress and adornment of women he refers to Enoch, who taught that women learned about cosmetics and finery from the fallen angels.[65] If God wanted dresses made of purple and scarlet wool he would have created purple and scarlet sheep. Not only does Tertullian cite Enoch, but unlike Origen, he treats him as inspired.[66]

Tertullian also intertwines the watcher legend and its demonology with the Fall of Adam and Eve in Paradise, after the fashion of the later Jewish apocalyptic tradition (see *Adv. Marcionem* 5,18). He maintains that the power of the envious angel, the archcorruptor of the universe, has perverted man, the handiwork and image of God. Jealous of man's lordship over creation, the fallen angel wished to establish his own supremacy by corrupting man and, along with him, the entire material world.[67] Unable to launch a frontal attack directly on man, the devil gets at him through Eve. It is she who teaches Adam, who is not yet her husband, what she has learned from the Evil One (*De Patientia* 5). Cain is born as a child of wrath sprung from that impatience conceived of the devil's seed with the fecundity of evil. Tertullian similarly inserts sexual innuendos about Eve and the devil into an *allegorical* passage in which Eve is said to believe the serpent as Mary believed Gabriel:

The sin which the one occasioned by believing the other effaced by believing. Let no one say that Eve conceived nothing in her womb at the devil's word. The devil's word was the seed for her so that afterward she should give birth as an outcast and bring forth in sorrow. In fact she gave birth to a devil who murdered his brother; while Mary bore one who with time would bring salvation to Israel. (*De Carne Christ* 17)

Even though the destruction brought about by the female sex was restored to salvation by the same sex, that does not remove the ignominy and the need for expiation on the part of every woman alive:

. . . no one of you at all, best beloved sisters, from the time that she had first "known the Lord," and learned (the truth) concerning her own (that is, woman's) condition, would have desired too gladsome (not to say too ostentatious) a style of dress; so as not rather to go about in humble garb, and rather to affect meanness of appearance, walking about as Eve mourning and re-pentant, in order that by every garb of penitence she might the more fully expiate that which she derives from Eve,—the ignom-iny, I mean, of the first sin, and the odium (attaching to her as the cause) of human perdition. "In pains and anxieties dost thou bear (children), woman; and toward thine husband (is) thy inclination, and he lords it over thee." And do you not know that you are (each) an Eve? The sentence of God on this sex of yours lives in this age: the guilt must of necessity live too. You are the devil's gateway; you are the unsealer of that (forbidden) tree: you are the first deserter of the divine law: you are she who persuaded him whom the devil was not valiant enough to attack. You destroyed so easily God's image, man. On account of your desert—that is, death—even the Son of God had to die. (*De Cultu Fem.* 1, 1)

Tertullian is certainly not the last Father to show the influ-ence of our pseudepigraphal motifs. But we shall leave an analysis of those who followed for another time. Just a few comments about Augustine might be in order. His misogynism has usually been attributed primarily to the influence of Manichaeism upon his earlier life. Perhaps his prior life of debauchery simply guaranteed and intensified his amenability to a Christian tradition of negativism toward women already established in the time of Tertullian. Augustine rejects the watcher myth but still seems to be an heir to the motifs developed from it in later Jewish apocalyptic literature (De Civ. Dei 15,23). This might explain his theory that original sin is transmitted from parent to child through the concupiscence or lust that is a result of the first sin and invariably accompanies the act of generation.[68] In brief, further critical study is necessary to precisely determine the extent to which pseudepigraphal sources ultimately underlie Augustine's teaching that the sexual character of generation transmits sin.

We must also point out that there were other avenues used by the ancients to theologically justify woman's submissive role. Paul, in I Cor. 11:7–9, reflects an especially strong rabbinic theme developed from Genesis: man alone was made in the image of God; woman was derived from the rib of Adam and made for him. Therefore woman is subordinate because of her very mode of creation. This theme was amply developed by the Church Fathers, and as is the case in I Cor. 11, it perfectly complemented the seductive siren-source-of-sin model to clinch the case for woman's passive roles of silence and obedience.

The Genesis stories and all the myths that apocalyptic literature developed from them were written in a period of patriarchal culture. Women had been excluded from any public role that men might assume and thereby retain dominance over civil and religious society.[69] The religious writers of that time created myths that flowed from and buttressed their prejudices. Early Christianity's prejudice flowed from those same myths. Today the prejudices often exist apart from the myths. It is time to show that there is no foundation for the prejudice.

One might begin by observing that the Genesis stories, and all the apocalyptic motifs that developed from them, were attempts to articulate and somehow cope with the inner struggle that is part of life and its experiences. Especially within the debate on polygenism, Adam is more clearly seen as Everyman, Eve as Everywoman. As we learn to search for and value the *meaning* clothed in myth more than the vehicle that conveyed it, we may rightfully eliminate the prejudices regarding women. Evil and lust are still experienced as problems, but hopefully humanity has also matured somewhat in its manner of coping with sexuality. At least it is no longer necessary for men to create theological reasons for excluding women from any active role in civil or religious society in order to preserve their own dominance and cope with their sexual drives. Even the formerly patriarchal city-state has finally yielded to women's suffrage in our century. It would be unfortunate if theologians in some Christian communities justified a full *ministerial* role for women only with hindsight, when society absolutely required it, rather than assume the initiative in undoing the prejudice that their historical predecessors established so deeply in the cultural psyche.

NOTES

1. "But the serpent said to the woman, 'You will not die. For God knows that when you eat of it your eyes will be opened, and you will be like God, knowing good and evil.' So when the woman saw that the tree was good for food, and that it was a delight to the eyes, and that the tree was to be desired to make one wise, she took of its fruit and ate; and she also gave some to her husband, and he ate. Then the eyes of both were opened, and they knew that they were naked; and they sewed fig leaves together and made themselves aprons." (Gen. 3:4–7; see also Gen. 2:17). All scriptural citations in this article are taken from the Oxford Annotated Bible with the Apocrypha, Revised Standard Version, eds. Herbert G. May and Bruce M. Metzger (New York: Oxford University Press, 1965).
2. F. R. Tennant, *The Sources of the Doctrine of the Fall and Original Sin* (New York: Schocken Books, 1968; orig. ed. 1903), p. 52, n. 3.
3. Homer, *The Odyssey* XII: 185–191, new verse trans. by Albert Cook (New York: W. W. Norton, 1967), p. 166.
4. I Enoch 32:3: tree of knowledge; I Enoch 24–25: tree of life. Eve is mentioned in 69:6, but that represents a different stratum. I Enoch 6–11, 54–55:2, 60, 65–69:25, and 106–107 are fragments of the lost Book of Noah mentioned in Jubilees 10:13 and 21:10. For a discussion of these textual intricacies refer to R. H. Charles's

introduction to "The Book of Enoch," in the collection edited by him, *The Apocrypha and Pseudepigrapha of the Old Testament in English: II, Pseudepigrapha* (Oxford: Clarendon Press, 1969; reprint of 1913 ed.), 168–170. (All citations of the pseudepigraphal works are from this collection—hereafter referred to as "Charles." I Enoch was originally written in Aramaic but is extant only in an Ethiopic text translated from a Greek version. Its earliest part dates from around 170 or 164 B.C. See D. S. Russell, *The Method and Message of Jewish Apocalyptic* (Philadelphia: Westminster Press, 1964), p. 51.

5. The watchers are "the holy angels who watch" and who do not sleep (I Enoch 20:1, 39:12–13, 40:2, 61:12, 71:7). The title first appears in Dan. 4:13, 17, 23. We provide the following passage from I Enoch 6:1–5 so that the reader may compare it with Gen. 6:1–4, cited above:

> And it came to pass when the children of men had multiplied that in those days were born unto them beautiful and comely daughters. And the angels, the children of the heaven, saw and lusted after them, and said to one another: "Come, let us choose us wives from among the children of men and beget us children." And Semjaza, who was their leader, said unto them: "I fear ye will not indeed agree to do this deed, and I alone shall have to pay the penalty of a great sin." And they all answered him and said: "Let us all swear an oath, and all bind ourselves by mutual imprecations not to abandon this plan but to do this thing."

I Enoch 86–89 tell the entire story in symbolic dream visions written by another hand.

6. Other lists of the secrets revealed are found in 65:6–8 and 69:6–12. (As a result of the interwoven traditions, both Semjaza and Azazel are named as leaders in different passages.)

7. Syrian Apoc. Baruch 10:8 and 56:10–15.

8. See Jub. 4:22, 5:1–11, 7:20–25. Jubilees probably dates from around the middle or the end of the second century B.C. See Charles, p. 6; H. H. Rowley, *The Relevance of Apocalyptic* (London: Lutterworth Press, 1944), pp. 58 and 81 ff.; and Russell, *Method and Message of Jewish Apocalyptic*, p. 54. J. T. Milik thinks that Jubilees may have been composed by a member of the Qumran Community: see D. Barthelemy and J. T. Milik, *Discoveries in the Judaean Desert*, I (Oxford: Clarendon Press, 1955), 32.

9. In 7:21 the specific reasons for the Flood are given.

10. Jub. 7:20–39 and ch. 10 are probably fragments from the lost Book of Noah referred to in Jub. 10:13 and 21:10. See Charles, p. 24.

11. Here we have a preview of the demonology reflected by the

gospels, where devils are likewise connected with sickness and disease.

12. Tennant (*Sources of the Doctrine of the Fall*, p. 192) and Norman Powell Williams (*The Ideas of the Fall and of Original Sin: A Historical and Critical Study* [London and New York: Longmans, Green, 1927], p. 28) note that Jub. 7:26–39 and 10:1–15, which attribute the post-Noachian wickedness to the demons who rose from the dying giants, are interpolations from the lost Book of Noah. Williams further maintains that the original author of Jubilees had already abandoned the watcher legend and drew his Fall story from the Paradise narrative. Charles (p. 9) and Tennant (p. 193) believe that Jubilees does not give much weight to the Paradise story as an explanation of the sinfulness of Adam and Eve's descendants. The watchers are the primary causes of the corruption before the Flood; the demons afterward.

13. The watcher legend overwhelms the impact of the Paradise-Fall story as an explanation for the continued influence of evil. See n. 12.

14. Both the source and the date of the Testaments are highly problematic. Charles (pp. 282 and 289–290) suggests 109–107 B.C. as the *terminus a quo*. Dating depends on whether one views the work as primarily Jewish, Essene, or Christian. Russell (*Method and Message of Jewish Apocalyptic*, pp. 56–57) provides an excellent review of the opinions. (References to the watchers and their sin are also found in the Testaments of Dan 5:5–6 and Naphtali 3:5.)

15. See chs. 15–30. L. S. A. Wells ("The Books of Adam and Eve," in Charles, pp. 124, 126–127, 129) believes that the original version of the *Life of Adam and Eve* (erroneously called the Apocalypse of Moses) was written in Greek by a Jew of the Dispersion, perhaps in Alexandria, not earlier than the first century A.D. and not later than the fourth century (more specifically, between 60 and 300 A.D.). Its content renders the earlier date more probable. He maintains that the earlier work represented, by the Apocalypse of Moses, was later embellished and translated; such is the origin of the Latin *Life of Adam and Eve*. Russell (*Method and Message of Jewish Apocalyptic*, p. 59) maintains that the *Life of Adam and Eve* was originally written in Aramaic, probably some time before 70 A.D., since the temple is apparently still standing (*Vita* 29:6).

16. There are inconsistencies in the text, since Satan also appears in the form of an angel who sings: cf. Apoc. 17:1, and likewise *Vita Adae et Evae* 9 (compared with II Enoch 18:9). In his note on Apoc. Moses 17:1 Wells says that it points to the old idea of a literal seduction and refers to II Cor. 11:14, Gen. 6:1–6, I Enoch 6–12 and 88–110. On pp. 126 and 130 of his introduction to the

work Wells notes that II Cor. 11:14 reads like a citation from Apoc. Moses 17 or its prototype.

17. Adam's account of the Fall is found in Apoc. Moses 7:1–3 and *Vita Adae et Evae* 32–33.

18. *Vita Adae et Evae* 20:1, where Eve cries out before giving birth to Cain.

19. *Vita* 12–17. Chapter 15:1 is the sole reference to the fallen angels who follow Satan. Wells remarks ("The Books of Adam and Eve," in Charles, p. 126) that the demonology of *Vita* 13–17 is not distinctively pre-Christian.

20. Apoc. Moses 9:2, 10:2, 32:1–2; *Vita* 5:3, 35:2–3, 37:2–3.

21. *Vita* 3:2–3; Slavonic *Life* 29:2.

22. Originally written in Greek, possibly at Alexandria, this book is now extant only in Slavonic. W. R. Morfill and R. H. Charles assign it to 1–50 A.D. (Charles, *Pseudepigrapha*, pp. 426 and 429). Russell (*Method and Message of Jewish Apocalyptic*, p. 61) notes that such an early date is greatly challenged, especially since the calendar that is provided forms part of the Easter computation developed in the *seventh* century.

23. See Charles's note on II Enoch 18:3 (pp. 439–440), in which he discusses the complexity involved both in distinguishing the various types of fallen angels and in determining the sequence of their corruptive activities. He also notes that the Similitudes, a later addition to I Enoch (chs. 37–70), similarly places the fall of the angels before the Fall of Adam. They also sinned by becoming subject to Satan: see I Enoch 54:6, 40:7, 64:1–2 and 69:6.

24. See Henry St. John Thackeray, *The Relation of St. Paul to Contemporary Jewish Thought* (London: Macmillan, 1900), pp. 50–57; also see Tennant, *Sources of the Doctrine of the Fall*, pp. 208–209. Both authors suggest our interpretation.

25. Apoc. Abraham, 14 and 23–24; for English text see George H. Box, *The Apocalypse of Abraham*, edited with a translation from the Slavonic (London: S.P.C.K., 1918). The original work is dated between 70 and 120 A.D. It appears to have been primarily of Jewish authorship but ultimately reworked by a Christian editor after many Christian interpolations had been introduced. Some find a gnostic tone in its positions. It is extant only in a Slavonic translation from Greek. See Box, pp. x, xxi ff., and Russell, *Method and Message of Jewish Apocalyptic*, p. 60. Gregory of Nyssa in his earlier work, *On the Making of Man*, held a position resembling that of this Apocalypse. He rejected it in the later *Catechetical Oration*.

26. In II Bar. 56:10–15 Adam seems in some way responsible for the watchers' fall. The work is dated either late first century or second century A.D. It was originally written in Aramaic but is extant

only in a Syriac version made from a previous Greek translation (see Russell, *Method and Message of Jewish Apocalyptic*, pp. 64–65).

27. Sir. 25:24–26. The Alexandrian Greek translation is dated after 132 B.C. The original Hebrew version was written in Palestine about 190 or 180 B.C.

28. Wis. 2:23–24; written sometime during the last half of the first century B.C.

29. See Tennant, *Sources of the Doctrine of the Fall*, pp. 145–176; W. D. Davies, *Paul and Rabbinic Judaism* (New York: Harper & Row Torchbooks, 1948), pp. 9–11; Robin Scroggs, *The Last Adam: A Study in Pauline Anthropology* (Philadelphia: Fortress Press, 1966), pp. 16–22 and 38–39.

30. Solomon Schechter notes that the rabbis identified the *evil yetzer* with Satan and lust (*Aspects of Rabbinic Theology* [New York: Schocken Paperbacks, 1969; orig. ed. 1909], pp. 246–263).

31. Regarding demonology, see Matt. 4:1–12, 8:29, 12:24–28 and 43–45; Mark 3:22, Luke 11:18 and 24–26, 22:31. Regarding Jesus' attitudes toward women see Leonard Swidler, "Jesus was a Feminist," in *Catholic World*, CCXII, No. 1,270 (Jan. 1971), 177–183.

32. Another passage reflecting a positive viewpoint is the parenthesis of I Cor. 11:11–12. Ephesians 5:25–30, whose Pauline authorship is disputed, is also somewhat positive in its command that husbands *love* their wives. Joachim Jeremias' description of the Jewish woman's position before her husband shows the uniqueness of such a command (*Jerusalem in the Time of Jesus*, trans. F. H. Cave et al. [Philadelphia: Fortress Press, 1969], pp. 359–376).

33. Joseph A. Fitzmyer lists the proponents and discusses the problems of such an interpretation in "A Feature of Qumran Angelology and the Angels of I Cor. 11:10," in *Paul and Qumran: Studies in New Testament Exegesis*, ed. Jerome Murphy-O'Connor (Chicago: Priory Press, 1968), pp. 34–36. The entire article (pp. 31–47) discusses many other difficulties concerning this passage. The article was originally published in *New Testament Studies*, IV, No. 1 (Oct. 1957), pp. 48–58.

Annie Jaubert interprets *exousia* in an active sense: it is a sign of woman's capacity and right to worship. But in actively fulfilling that obligation, Paul insists that women must conform to the order of creation where men have priority at worship. Jaubert believes that Paul renders the context positive by his observation that the two sexes are interdependent in the Lord. She suggests that I Cor. 14:34–35 is an interpolation from the Pastorals ("Le voile des femmes [I Cor. XI. 2–16]," *New Testament Studies*, XVIII, No. 4 [July 1972], 428–430). In "Authority on Her Head: An Examination of I Cor. XI, 10," *New Testament Studies*, X, No. 3 (April 1964), 410–416, M. D. Hooker likewise interprets *exousia* in an active sense: it is woman's power to reflect the glory of God in prayer and prophecy. Man is uncovered lest he who is God's image hide the glory of God. Woman is covered lest she who is from man distract the angels at worship by reflecting man's glory. Hooker feels that Paul contrived such theological reasoning to solve a practical problem at worship where men rather than angels were distracted by women's hair. God was not to be rivaled by anyone.

34. Gerhard Kittel, "Die *Macht* auf dem Haupte I Kor. 11, 10," *Rabbinica, Arbeiten zur Religionsgeschichte des Urchristentums,* Bd. I, Heft 3 (Leipzig: J. C. Hinrichs, 1920), pp. 17–31. To the ancient Palestinians an uncovered head symbolized freedom. A covered head was the sign of respect for the power of another. Jewish women *covered* their heads by means of a complicated coiffure with plaited hair, ribbons, bands, and cloth. A bride uncovered her head as a proof of virginity. Her head was then covered to indicate that she was now placed under the husband's authority. The rabbis had a number of reasons why women should have their heads covered: out of respect for the angels who keep the order of creation, in which women were subject beings; lest evil spirits infest homes, attracted by a woman's uncovered hair. All these points are discussed in H. L. Strack–P. Billerbeck, *Kommentar zum Neuen Testament aus Talmud und Midrash:* Bd. III, *Die Briefe des Neuen Testaments und die Offenbarung Johannis* (München: C. H. Beck'sche Verlagsbuchhandlung, 1965; reprint of the 4th ed. 1926), pp. 423–440.

35. Hans Lietzmann, *An die Korinther I–II,* 4 Aufl., Bd. 9, in *Handbuch zum Neuen Testament* (Tübingen: J. C. B. Mohr, 1949), p. 55.

36. "A Feature of Qumran Angelology," pp. 40–41.

37. Ibid., pp. 41–45. See also Matthew Black, *The Scrolls and Christian Origins: Studies in the Jewish Background of the New Testament* (London and New York: Thomas Nelson, 1961), p. 30.

38. Henry J. Cadbury, "A Qumran Parallel to Paul," *Harvard Theological Review,* LI, No. 1 (Jan. 1958), 1–2.

39. Annie Jaubert ("Le voile des femmes," p. 419) notes that the *traditions* to which Paul refers probably come from the more ancient Churches of God in Palestine and Syria. To explain the requirement of head covering for women she turns to rabbinic literature (pp. 424–427). She admits that Paul's reference to the angels comes from a Jewish milieu (pp. 427–428). But the influence of the Pseudepigrapha is neglected, because Jaubert, like Fitzmyer, believes that Paul refers only to good angels who are no longer susceptible to seduction. We agree on the matter of angelic incorruptibility, but unlike Fitzmyer and Jaubert, admit a

much more subtle influence of pseudepigraphal motifs. Tertullian, who is wrongly cited by Jaubert (p. 429), as if he supported Lietzmann, does not say women must be veiled lest they again seduce the angels, but rather because they once did so. For him the veil is a brand of shame. Our treatment of Tertullian below will cite passages from *Adversus Marcionem* 5,8 and *De virginibus velandis* 7 in support of that position. At this point we cite the Midrash on Genesis, which received its final form just after the fifth century: "Why does a man go out bareheaded while a woman goes out with her head covered? She is like one who has done wrong and is ashamed of people; therefore she goes out with her head covered" (Genesis Bereshith 17:18, *Midrash*, I [London: Soncino Press, 1961, orig ed. 1939], 139). The influence of the watcher myth upon the Qumran community is known from *The Zadokite Document* (2:14–3:12); see Theodor H. Gaster, *The Dead Sea Scriptures* (New York: Doubleday Anchor Books, 1964), pp. 73–74.

40. Thackeray (*The Relation of St. Paul to Contemporary Jewish Thought*, pp. 50–57) sees a relationship between the sexual motifs found in Apoc. Moses 19 and II Enoch 31:6, and the ideas expressed in I Cor. 11:10, II Cor. 11:3, and I Tim. 2:13–15. Scroggs (*The Last Adam*, p. 76) rejects any interpretation of II Cor. 11:3 as a literal seduction. He maintains that Paul knew the rabbinic Haggada about Eve, but he does not use it for the purpose of making her the originator of sin, as did some rabbis. To a degree we must concur; Rom. 5 does overshadow all our texts. Nevertheless the application of the Haggada within the Pauline literature calling for subjection is equivalent to a practical indictment of women.

41. Italics are mine. Adam was not even deceived: ἠπατήθη; the woman was thoroughly deceived: ἐξαπατηθεῖσα. Interestingly enough, even modern translations might reflect the prejudices of pseudepigraphal myths. In the New English Bible and in the Jerusalem Bible the "serpent seduced . . . Eve" (II Cor. 11:3), but when Adam is involved the same Greek verb is rendered as "deceived" or "led astray" (I Tim. 2:14). (Davies *Paul and Rabbinic Judaism*, p. 32) maintains that the presence of the same verb (ἐξαπατάω) in Rom. 7:11, where Paul says that sin seduced or deceived him, connects that passage with II Cor. 11:3.

42. See also I *Apol.* 5:2 and II *Apol.* 7:2 ff. Unless otherwise noted, citations of the Fathers will be from the English translation, eds. Alexander Roberts and James Donaldson, *The Ante-Nicene Fathers* (1885–1897 American reprint of Edinburgh ed., 1867–1880), revised by A. Cleveland Coxe (New York: Charles Scribner's Sons, 1899).

43. *Dialogue with Trypho*, ch. 100; see also chs. 79, 124, 103 and 88. (Rendition is mine.)
44. See *Adversus Haereses* 4, 36, 4; 4, 16, 2; 1, 15, 6; 5, 28, 2; *Proof of the Apostolic Preaching* 10; 18; 27 and 85 and compare with *Adv. Haer.* 5, 23, 1 and 2; 5, 16, 3; 5, 5, 1 and *Proof* 15 and 34. Chapter 18 of the *Proof* reads as follows:

> And wickedness very long continued and widespread pervaded all the race of men, until very little seed of justice was in them. For unlawful unions came about on earth, as angels linked themselves with offspring of the daughters of men, who bore to them sons, who on account of their exceeding great size were called Giants. The angels, then, brought to their wives as gifts teachings of evil, for they taught them the virtues of roots and herbs, and dyeing and cosmetics and discoveries of precious materials, love-philtres, hatreds, amours, passions, constraints of love, the bonds of witchcraft, every sorcery and idolatry, hateful to God; and when this was come into the world, the affairs of wickedness were propagated to overflowing, and those of justice dwindled to very little.

See J. Quasten and J. C. Plumpe, eds. *Ancient Christian Writers*, Vol. XVI, trans. Joseph P. Smith (Westminster, Md.: Newman Press, and London: Longmans, Green, 1952), p. 58.
45. "He (Satan) was envious of God's workmanship, and took in hand to render this (workmanship) an enmity with God" (*Adv. Haer.* 4, 40, 3). The same idea is developed in *Adv. Haer.* 5, 24, 4 and *Proof* 11; 12; 16. Satan wanted man to adore him as a god (*Adv. Haer.* 5, 24, 3).
46. "For it was by means of a woman that he got the advantage over man at first, setting himself up as man's opponent" (*Adv. Haer.* 5, 21, 1). Adam was caught in the crossfire of a battle between the serpent (Satan) and God. Through Christ, God conquers Satan, restores man to His image and likeness, and recapitulates all creation (see *Adv. Haer.* 3, 16, 6; 3, 23, 1 and 2; 5, 21, 1 and 2; 4, 40, 1; and *Proof* 32). Christ placed Satan under the power of man (*Adv. Haer.* 5, 24, 4).
47. *Adv. Haer.* 4, Preface, 4; 5, 19, 1; 5, 23, 1; and *Proof* 16.
48. *Adv. Haer.* 3, 22, 4 and 5, 19, 1.
49. *Proof* 14; cf. *Adv. Haer.* 3, 22, 4.
50. Adam's childlike innocence is established in the following texts: *Proof* 12; 14; 16; *Adv. Haer.* 3, 22, 4; 3, 23, 5; 4, 38, 1–4; 4, 39, 2. See also Theophilus of Antioch, *To Autolycus* 2, 25, and Clement of Alexandria, *Protrepticus*, ch. 11.
51. I wish to acknowledge the many insights I received about

Irenaeus from discussions with my colleague Donald R. Schulz. His unpub. doctoral dissertation, "The Origin of Sin in Irenaeus and Jewish Apocalyptic Literature" (McMaster University, Ontario), goes far beyond our glance at Irenaeus' thinking.

52. *Adv. Haer.* 3, 23, 5.
53. *Adv. Haer.* 4, 40, 3 and 3, 23, 3 and 5.
54. See *Adv. Haer.* 5, 19, 1; 5, 21, 1; 3, 22, 4; 3, 23, 7; 3, 21, 10; and *Proof* 33.
55. *Paedagogus* 3, 2 and *Stromateis* 5, 1.
56. *Paed.* 2, 12. See J. Defferrari *et al.*, eds., *The Fathers of the Church*, Vol. 23: *Christ the Educator*, trans. Simon P. Wood (New York: Fathers of the Church, Inc., 1954), p. 195).
57. *Strom.* 3, 14–17 (esp. 3, 15), as well as *Protrepticus* 11.
58. See *Ideas of the Fall*, p. 204, n. 2.
59. *Strom.* 3, 16. Solomon Schechter mentions "Rabbi Acha who, with reference to Ps. 51:7, expressed himself to the effect that in sexual intercourse even the saint of saints cannot well escape a certain taint of sin, the act of cohabitation being performed more with the purpose of satisfying one's animal appetite [evil yetzer] than with the intention of perpetuating the human species (Lev. R., 14, 5)" (*Aspects of Rabbinic Theology*, p. 253). Compare such a position with *Paed.* 2, 10.
60. *Paed.* 2, 10 (11 in Roberts and Donaldson, *Ante-Nicene Fathers*).
61. *In Leviticum homiliae* 12:4 and 8:3, as well as *in Lucam homiliae* 14, and *Contra Celsum* 7, 50.
62. Origen knows I Enoch, but does not treat it as inspired scripture; see *De Principiis* 1, 3, 3; 4, 35 (4, 4, 8); *In Ioannem* 6:25, *Contra Celsum* 5, 54; *in Numeros homiliae* 28:2.
63. In *Contra Celsum* 4, 40 the curse spoken against Eve is said to apply to every woman. However, this does not seem to be especially significant, since Origen notes the same is true regarding the curse against man.
64. *De Oratione*, chs. 20–22; *De Virginibus Velandis*, chs. 4–11 (esp. ch. 7); *Adversus Marcionem*, 5, 18; and *Apologeticus* 22. To reconstruct Tertullian's demonology, compare *Apol.* 22 with I Enoch 15:8–9 and *De Spectaculis*, chs. 10, 12, 13, and 23.
65. *De Cultu Feminarum* 2, 10 and 1, 2 and 4 (cf. I Enoch 8:1). In a discussion of astrology Tertullian writes: "One proposition I lay down: that those angels, the deserters from God, the lovers of women, were likewise the discoverers of this curious art . . ." (*De Idololatria* 9; cf. I Enoch 8:3).
66. *De Cultu Fem.* 1, 3; De Idol. 4 and 15 (cf. I Enoch 19:1 and 99:6–7).
67. *De Spectaculis* 2; *De Testimonio Animae* 3; *De Carnis Resurrectione* 34; *De Carne Christi* 14.
68. *De peccatorum meritis et remissione* 1, 57; *Contra Iulianum* 5, 52

and 3, 57; *De nupt. et concup.* 1, 29 and also 20; 21; 25 and 28. For further references see J. N. D. Kelly, *Early Christian Doctrines*, 2d ed. (New York: Harper & Row, 1960), pp. 364–366. Perhaps Augustine reflects his friend and mentor Ambrose (see *Apol. David* 11), who in turn reflects Origen. Gregory of Nyssa in his earlier *De Opificio hominis*, 16–17, held that all sexual distinction and generation originated from the Fall (see also *De Virginitate* 3). He retreated from that position in his later *Catechetical Oration*.

69. In an article entitled "The Symbol of Virginity" (*The Religious Situation: 1969*, ed. Donald R. Cutler [Boston: Beacon Press, 1969], pp. 775–811) Herbert Richardson maintains that theologians have not given sufficient attention to the way sexual behavior functions within a specific social system. The patriarchal system of the Hebrews and the Greek city-state had to *exclude* women so that men could establish their dominance. Monastic virginity excluded sex so that persons of both sexes might establish mutual nonsexual (i.e., nongenital) relationships of love with one another. This was an important step closer to the modern discovery that sex should ideally be exercised only within the situation of love that flows from a caring personal relationship. Richardson observes that the Second Vatican Council's (1962–1965) recognition (*Pastoral Constitution on the Church in the Modern World*, sections 49–50. See *The Documents of Vatican II*, Walter M. Abbott, ed. [New York: Guild Press—American Press—Association Press, 1966], pp. 252–255) that mutual love is as important an end of marriage as procreation reflects this new functionality for sex.

The Theology and Leadership
of Women in
the New Testament

CONSTANCE F. PARVEY

Christianity grew out of the rich intellectual and spiritual soil of Judaism—of Jewish Palestine and Jews living throughout the Roman Empire. However, as the Church was separated from the synagogue and gained its own independent foothold, it also incorporated ideas from the many diverse cultures present in the Hellenized Roman world and from the mystery religions popular throughout the empire at that time. Within both Judaism and Greco-Roman culture women played a crucial role. It is in front of this historical backdrop that attitudes toward women and levels of their participation in the early Church will be examined.

Most discussions of women in the New Testament revolve around Jesus' attitudes toward women. Unlike them, this chapter revolves around the attitudes of the primitive Church itself as seen through the New Testament. It explores the theology of Paul in relation to women, the parables and stories of Jesus referring to women, and the descriptions of New Testament writers themselves about the participation of women. The primary concern of the chapter is not Jesus' attitudes but how the early Church embodied

117

theologically and socially different attitudes toward women as a consequence of Jesus' coming.

THE HELLENISTIC AND JEWISH BACKGROUND

Within the Roman Empire in the first century A.D. many women were educated, and some were highly influential and exercised great freedom in public life. By contrast, although the evidence is not conclusive, Jewish women seem to have been little affected by the relatively emancipated status of their Roman counterparts.

In Rome, both Stoic and Epicurean philosophers encouraged the public education of women and advocated egalitarian women-men relationships. The support of this intellectual elite not only contributed to making changes in the legal status of women but also helped make it possible for at least some upper-class women to achieve vocational recognition as poets, writers and historians—and there is even on record one woman engineer.[1] That some women made a lasting contribution to the intellectual life of Rome is seen in the fact that the works of the poetess Sulpicia were still read in Gaul in the fifth century A.D., and the *Memoirs of Agrippina* were used as a basic reference by Tacitus, the Roman historian.[2]

The Stoic philosophers—Seneca, Musonius Rufus, and Epictetus—all stressed the dignity of women-men relationships. Seneca stated that women have the "same inner force, and the same capacity for nobleness as men."[3] Yet most of these men qualified their views, seeing women exercising their equality primarily within traditional family roles. Typical is the comment of Musonius, who, in advocating the education of women, used the rationale that "Only a woman trained in philosophy is capable of being a good housewife."[4]

Most women were under the financial and legal guardianship of a father or husband. After the Second Punic War, with the rise of a middle class in Rome, dowry rights were kept under the control of the father rather than relinquished at marriage to the husband. This was aimed at keeping family estates intact, but it had the side effect of giving women more control over their property and more independence in the marriage relationship. As a result of this change in family law it became possible for a woman to divorce her husband, but it did not entirely free her from male domination. Though she could divorce, and often did, she was still legally under her father's guardianship, and if her father died, she was under the care of his appointed agent.[5] In spite of this legal subordination, some women obtained considerable power over their property and managed large concentrations of wealth. Legally, women could inherit, be partners in legal contracts, make wills and initiate divorce.[6] During the reign of Claudius there were evidently even women shipbuilders living in Italy outside of Rome. Claudius requests their aid and offers them special rewards if they will cooperate in his shipbuilding program.[7] No doubt there were women who had attained substantial power through family inheritance and through increasing exercise of their legal independence. The impact of such powerful and influential women is reflected in a response of Martial's. When asked why he would not consider marrying a rich woman he replied, "Because I have no wish to become the wife of my wife."[8]

In spite of the legal problems of guardianship and the fact that women were never given the right to vote, women in the Roman Empire achieved a much higher legal status than women in Greece or in the East, and they were at liberty to appear independently and without a male escort at such public events as the theater, banquets and the Roman games. There was evidently a trend toward women's emancipation in the empire, but it was not met entirely with favor; in fact, it was severely criticized by most popular writers of the time.[9] In their eyes this freedom of women was associated with libertinism, female domination and a breakdown in the general moral standards. Little that was positive was said about it, and much that was negative has been written. Typical are the writings of the satirist Juvenal. In a long poem entirely devoted to female faults, written in about 116 A.D., he criticizes women's education, which had contributed to their insubordination in marriage: "I hate her who is skilled in antiquarian lore, quotes verses I never knew, and corrects the phrases of her husband as old-fashioned."[10]

Even as early as the second century B.C. women's emancipation seems to have been a problem. Cato the Elder, writing in 195 B.C., predicted disaster should wives receive more rights that would loosen them from their subordinated status. Objecting to changes in the legal status of wives, he says:

> Review all the laws with which your forefathers restrained their licence and made them subject to their husbands; even with all these bonds you can scarcely control them. What of this? If you suffer them to seize these bonds one by one and wrench themselves free . . . do you think that you will be able to endure them: the moment they begin to be your equals, they will be your superiors.[11]

How much the freedom of Roman women influenced the Jewish women who were among the first adherents to the Christian Church is, however, quite another question. Though Jewish women lived in the cosmopolitan Hellenistic cities of Italy, Greece, Egypt and Asia Minor, given the central importance of family life within the religious and cultural context of Judaism, they were very confined. Within the family Jewish women had a distinct and decisive role, but it was limited to the sphere of what we today would call the private life—care of children and husband and performance of domestic duties. In the Talmud the purpose of marriage is to "grind corn, suckle children, be a beautiful wife and bear children."[12] Not only were women's domestic obligations restricting, but they were doubly confined because of the complex laws and rituals surrounding menstruation and childbearing.[13] Legally, in the home the adult Jewish woman was under the domination of her husband, and spiritually, within the public life of the religious community, she had essentially no role.[14] The study of the scriptures and the practice of worship were totally the work of men.[15]

Within the Jewish family the woman was the conservator of tradition and bound to the regulations and restrictions that served to keep the Jewish family a closely knit unit capable of resisting outside pressures to conform to the mores of the mainstream of Hellenistic society. Though in commercial and legal spheres Jews followed the customs and laws of the empire, in the sphere of the family and religious life they maintained their own separated, particularistic identity, and the confined role of the woman was critical to maintaining this separateness. The Books of Esther and Judith, popular in the Jewish piety of the time, whose heroines rescued Israel from the contamination of pagan religions, were used as models for Jewish women to stay within the tradition, resist social contact and marriage with non-Jews, and be a bulwark against outside incursions into Jewish family and religious life.[16]

Though there is evidence of intermarriage between upper-class Gentiles and Jews, and in Alexandria, which contained the largest Jewish population of the ancient world, divorce proceedings among Jews were conducted in Roman rather than in Jewish courts,[17] it does appear that Hellenistic women throughout the empire achieved a far greater degree of legal and social independence and freedom of movement than did Jewish women. No doubt, in large urban areas such as Alexandria, Hellenistic culture did make its impact on the life styles of Jewish women as well, but basically their lives appear to have been well circumscribed and protected by family and female obligations and by their subordinated status.

In contrast to Judaism, the Greco-Roman religions were more open to the participation of women. In addition to the prominence of the vestal virgins of Rome in the national cultic life, there were specific religions such as the cult of Isis, to which Cleopatra gave allegiance and into which many women were initiated. The influence of women, however, both in leadership and in numbers, was most noticeable among the gnosticized religions. Unlike the Hellenistic mystery cults, gnosticism was not a specific religious sect but a radical pneumatic religious disposition that was diffused throughout the religions of the Near East. It was syncretistic, picking up insights, myths and information from many sources, and at the same time penetrating all religious sects and movements, including the Judaism of the pre-Christian times. Gnostic spirituality was part of the religious environment in which early Christianity settled and to which it had to respond. By the second century A.D., Gnostic thought and Christianity were so intertwined that there were large Gnostic Christian sects established all over the empire, and Gnostic thought found inroads into many Christian congregations. Though Gnostic Christian communities were modeled after the early Church to the point of having their own Gnostic gospels, Gnostic beliefs were basically antithetical to those expressed in the canonical gospels.[18] The Gnostics believed that the world was beyond redemption and under the control of the forces of evil.

Because the world was irredeemable, they believed that a person could be saved only by finding a way to set free the divine spirit imprisoned inside himself. They believed that once this spirit was unleashed, the person was no longer demon- but spirit-possessed, and he was transported into an otherworldly spiritual reality over which the forces of the demon had no control.[19] In the second century, though both the early Church and the Gnostic Christians drew on the same basic material about Jesus, the Gnostics negated this world, while the early Church lived in the hope and promise that this world would be redeemed. Many women in the primitive Church were participants in this radically spiritualized movement. In particular, it is knowledge of Gnostic influences and tensions in the Church in Corinth that has helped to shed new light on conventional interpretations of women in Saint Paul's letter to that congregation.

Awareness of the Gnostic movement as part of the New Testament milieu is vital in exploring the problem of attitudes toward women. In the formative period of the New Testament, although the Jewish traditions and religious laws kept women confined, the Greco-Roman culture and law gave ample indication that there were many cultural, social and spiritual factors at work in the Roman Empire pointing favorably toward a new definition of women's status. But it is impossible to jump directly from these historical references to a new definition of women's status in the early Church without adding the essential ingredient of the powerful, explosive, disruptive thought of the New Testament itself. There can be no understanding of women's role in the New Testament without capturing this revolutionary force of the beliefs of early Christians, including among them women who were both Jew and Gentile in background. The people of the primitive Church felt that they were living in the days of the final perfection of history. Both Jews and Hellenists among the early Christians thought that the world was being redeemed and that they were already living in the last days. In accordance with Jewish expectations of the end times, they believed that God had already begun to inaugurate a new order and ethics of humankind that would imminently be consummated. More than anything else, it was this belief that the victory over evil had been won and the end times were near that established an eschatological fervor within the community of the New Testament itself, which in turn gave an unprecedented position to women. As Jewish culture held onto its traditions regarding women, and as Hellenistic culture was carving out new definitions, these converged into a new configuration in the primitive Church. Because of this sense of the urgency of the end times, a new and radically equivalent role of women and men together in Christ was forged. Examination of the Pauline epistles and the gospel opens up the theological and social dynamics of this significant breakthrough.

SAINT PAUL AND WOMEN

At first glance, Paul does not seem a very hopeful candidate for the role of emancipator of women. Though a gifted visionary, theologian, teacher and organizer, he was not a social reformer in the modern sense. Like many other men of genius, he found it difficult to adapt his social thought to conform with his radically new theology. This is precisely the problem he is up against in relation to women in the Corinthian congregation.

The congregation, like the city itself, capital of the province of Achaia and a wealthy trading and shipping center, seemed to be plagued with the sins of success, excess extravagance and dissipation. Also like the city, the congregation was cosmopolitan, a mixture of Greeks, Romans and Jews,[20] and it was probably influenced as much by the new gnosticizing religious movement as it was by Judaism.

The most frequently cited passages reflecting Paul's attitude toward women are found in chapters 11 and 14 of his first Corinthian letter. In these passages Paul responds to problems created by some women's causing disruption in the public worship. According to the then-current Jewish customs governing the conduct of women in the worship of the congregation, women had no duties or rights. They were to remain silent and within a segregated section of the synagogue—unheard and unseen.[21] In contrast to these Jewish customs, Christian women in the Corinthian congregation were quite visible and were making themselves heard. They were allowed to offer prayers and prophecies, but some women seem to have overstepped the boundaries of their new role. First, they were not behaving as pious Jewish women were expected to do—keeping their heads covered—and second, they were not keeping their mouths shut, but were participating beyond the role ascribed to them. Paul reprimands them for this misconduct twice in the same letter:

> Any man who prays or prophesies with his head covered dishonors his head, but any woman who prays or prophesies with her head unveiled dishonors her head—it is the same as if her head were shaven. (I Cor. 11:4–5)

> As in all the churches of the saints, the women should keep silence in the churches. For they are not permitted to speak, but should be subordinate, as even the law says. (I Cor. 14:34–35)

The Church's interpretation of its attitudes toward women has traditionally centered on these two Corinthian outbursts. However, earlier chapters in the same letter indicate that Paul's concern with the Corinthians is not so much with women as such as with a whole cluster of difficulties in the congregation, all of which show signs that gnosticized, pneumatic believers had penetrated its midst, disregarded established customs, and among other problems they had created, had also influenced some of the women. The Gnostics in the Corinthian congregation, both men and women, give evidence of acting like spiritual libertines. They considered themselves carried away by a higher loyalty and were preoccupied with their own private ecstasies. Because they believed they were acting on the instructions directed by the divine spirit-possession within them, they considered themselves superior to others, and thus considered their action independent of any human judgments, criticisms or control.[22] The disorderly conduct of the women fits into a general picture of turmoil and breakdown in the congregation. There were problems of prostitution (I Cor. 6:9–20), of unacceptable sexual involvements practiced openly by members without congregational censure (I Cor. 5:1–2), and there were quarrels that normally would have been reconciled in the congregation which were being taken to the pagan Roman courts for settlement (I Cor. 6:1–4). The Corinthian congregation was in disarray, and the troubles with the women were only one part of this larger gnosticizing problem.

It is against the background of this struggle with Gnostic heterodoxy that Paul issues his two above-cited dicta against women. These passages have not only had an impact on the later epistles within the New Testament but they have provided the shape for the fundamental religious and social attitudes toward women in both the Eastern and Western churches to the present day. These references have been used as proof texts for explaining why women should be prohibited from priestly and liturgical roles, and they still constitute today a major justification for maintaining women in a subordinated role in the Church and in society at large. An exploration of the context and intention of these dicta is fundamental to opening up a better understanding of the role of women in the churches of the New Testament period.

I Corinthians 11

In chapter 11, with regard to the mandate that women keep their heads covered, Paul clearly appears to be arguing against the influence of radical Gnostic ecstatics, who were said to have an aversion to women covering their heads,[23] and he attempts to confront them with reasons why they should maintain the traditional Jewish custom. Theoretically, he says, women should keep their heads covered as a sign of subordination to men: "But I want you to understand that the head of every man is Christ, the head of a woman is her husband, and the head of Christ is God" (I Cor. 11:3). This pattern of argument fits into the Jewish tradition of the time, which considered a woman's head covering a sign of the subordinate status to which she had been subject since the beginning of creation because of the sin of Eve. Because all women shared Eve's misfortune, it was believed that for a woman to exhibit her head uncovered was like exposing a physical deformity. To buttress his theoretical argument of subordination Paul adds a practical consideration, asserting that it just isn't becoming for a woman to pray without a head covering. A parallel statement from the Talmudic literature of Paul's time is illustrative of this attitude; it asserts that it is not only unattractive but shameful for a woman to appear unveiled: "Why does a man go about bareheaded while a woman goes out with her head covered? She is like one who has done wrong and is ashamed of people: therefore she goes out with her head covered" (Gen. Ber. XVII. 8).

Building on these statements, Paul further enlarges his argument, declaring that women should keep their heads covered "because of the angels." In the Jewish apocalyptic literature of the period the head covering of a woman was considered necessary to give power to her head so that she might ward off the attack of evil spirits,[24] protect herself against her own natural female weakness in the face of evil, and avoid being seduced by fallen angels. How much inclined to weakness women were considered to be in first-century Judaism is clearly reflected in the writings of Philo, the most universally read Jewish philosopher of the time. In his discussion of the soul he characterizes the differences between male and female traits:

> The soul has, as it were, a dwelling, partly men's quarters, partly women's quarters. Now for the men there is a place where properly dwell the masculine thoughts [these are] wise, sound, just, prudent, pious, filled with freedom and boldness, and kin to wisdom. And the women's quarters are a place where women's opinions go about and dwell being followers of the female sex. And the female sex is irrational and akin to bestial passions, fear, sorrow, pleasure and desire from which ensue incurable weakness and indescribable diseases.[25]

Paul—through his assertion that women need protection against the angels—reflects with Philo the thought of his time. His "protection against the angels" argument is his way of stating his own anxiety about a woman's ability to remain steadfast. Like other rabbis of his time, Paul felt that women needed a kind of armoring, a kind of shield, a veil over their heads that could sustain them against evil forces. In brief, Paul is saying that by nature women are weak and need protection. Therefore these women in Corinth are acting in a way disrespectful to their own nature by not recognizing their need for the protection of a head covering while they are in the congregation.

However, having set forth this high-powered argument based on religious assumptions about women's subordinated status under the law (II Cor. 11:3) and women's weakness because of the angels, Paul does not close the issue. On the contrary, he makes a surprising about-face, and in so doing contradicts his basic assumptions in such a way as to raise doubts about the validity of his entire previous argument. He radically alters what he has just implied about women as the subordinated sex, inserting a statement about their new equality and reciprocity in Christ: "(Nevertheless, in the Lord woman is not independent of man nor man of woman; for as woman was made from man, so man is now born of woman. And all things are from God)" (I Cor. 11:11-12).

This is not to be understood solely as a reference to a physical, biological relationship. It reflects a new sense of the interdependence of the body in Christ as later described in Cor. 12, where no part of the body is subordinated to any other and each is essential to the whole: "If one member suffers, all suffer together; if one member is honored, all rejoice together. Now you are the body of Christ and individually members of it" (I Cor. 12:26-27). The new structures of the body that follow in I Cor. 12 are not sex-related but "gift-task-function"-related. "And God has appointed in the church first apostles, second prophets, third teachers, then workers of miracles, then healers, helpers, administrators, speakers in various kinds of tongues, etc." (I Cor. 12:28).

The general lines of Paul's argument in I Cor. 11 follow the religious presuppositions of the Judaism of the time. The weight of his argument is determined by the cultural and religious situation in which he was brought up, but with one exception. By inserting verses 11 and 12 he points toward a new set of assumptions about how differentiations are made in the body of Christ.

Having projected the seeds of the new vision and sketched its broad strokes, Paul remained however, still socially a product of his time. This is clearly evidenced by the way he ends this discourse. It is Paul the conservative rather than Paul the innovator who is now speaking: "If any one is disposed to be contentious, we recognize no other practice, nor do the churches of God" (I Cor. 11:16). Even with his vision of the new personhood of women and men in Christ, in the end it is not theology but established custom that seems to have won the day. This falling back and resting his argument on custom is a significant insight into Paul's development. It indicates that at this early point in his missionary experience he had not yet come to grips with the implications for changes in social customs and traditions implicit in his newly forming theology. On the theological level, by envisioning the new interdependence of men and women in Christ, Paul makes a fundamental breakthrough in new images for women, but on the cultural, social level, he clearly identifies himself as a first-century Jewish teacher for whom arguments from custom have authority and validity of their own.

I Corinthians 14

In chapter 14 Paul follows a style of argument with regard to the second mandate against women similar to that used in chapter 11. This time his dictum is against women speaking out in the public worship of the congregation. Paul obviously approved of the participation of women in prayers and prophecies in chapter 11 as long as their heads were covered, but in chapter 14 some kind of disruption related to women's participation provokes him to instruct women to keep silent. Though the source of the irritation is not clear, the context implies that women have been asking questions, and in so doing, acting out of step with the established congregational order. The precise problem is unknown. All we have is Paul's reply to a troublesome situation.

He begins with an appeal to the Torah, arguing that according to the law, women have no license to speak. This would certainly be a difficult point for any of Paul's adversaries to argue against were it not for the fact that Paul himself in his later epistles argues against the validity of the law now that the age of the spirit has come. In Gal. 3:17–19 Paul states that the law was a temporary measure. It was added to make wrongdoing a legal offense. It was a temporary measure pending the arrival of the "issue" to whom the promise was made.[26] Whether or not Paul fully realized this weakness in his argument or whether he had not yet clearly developed his thinking about the new Torah of Christ, it is significant that he does not choose to dwell on this argument from the law, but follows rather closely the outline of his previous argument in chapter 11. Rather than expanding on the theoretical implications of the Torah, he switches his disputation to the practical level, suggesting that the problem could be solved if women would only reserve their comments and ask their husbands at home.

On the surface, this could conceivably solve the problem; however, it assumes that all of the women addressed have husbands. Given the discussion in chapter 7 on celibacy, this is highly unlikely. It is more probable that among the women who are disturbing the worship are some who have chosen the vocation of celibacy. Presumably, then, having to deal with a situation that includes both married and celibate women, Paul is finally forced to revert once more to an argument from custom, saying: "For it is shameful for a woman to speak in church" (I Cor. 14:35b). This outburst again reflects current religious attitudes. In the rabbinic literature at that time many explanations existed as to why women were forbidden to speak out in the congregations, all tending to revolve around women as objects of sexual pleasure and the masculine sensibility that a woman's voice or her appearance was too sexually provocative for the men. A typical Talmudic illustration of this is the following: "A woman's voice is a sexual excitement, as it says . . . for sweet is thy voice and thy countenance is comely" (Ber. 24a). Since the voice of a woman would shock and distract the men from their prayers, women were required to keep silent, according to the Talmud, "out of respect for the congregation" (Meg. 23a). This meant implicitly the congregation of men, since within the synagogue women would not have been considered congregational members.

This disturbance of the women cited in I Cor. 14 puts Paul in an entirely new situation on several levels: the old law is no longer valid; he is probably addressing both married and celibate women; he has no "word from the Lord" on this subject. Paul has no established norms to deal with this. It is clear from chapter 11 that women have the privileges of participation in prayers and prophecies, but in this case their participation seems to have gone beyond what were considered established boundaries. In what is an obviously problematic situation, and with no clear authoritative right or wrong, Paul finally winds his way around this argument by throwing the problem back on the congregation. He calls its ecstatic prophets into accountability, and in so doing he not only challenges the genuineness of their prophetic and spiritual gifts of discernment but he puts his own authority as an interpreter to the test:

> *What! Did the word of God originate with you, or are you the only ones it has reached? If any one thinks that he is a prophet, or spiritual, he should acknowledge that what I am writing to you is a command of the Lord. If anyone does not recognize this, he is not recognized.* (I Cor. 14:36–38)

The context shows that Paul is certainly not in favor of these women addressing the congregation, but at the same time he does not want to withhold genuine ecstatic gifts (I Cor. 12:4–11). By challenging the congregation's spiritual capacities for discernment, he turns the whole problem of ecstatic behavior back on the Corinthian congregation itself. That, however, is not the end of it. As a good rabbi, he does not leave them without giving them some practical pastoral advice about how to handle their problems with ecstatics: "So, my brethren, earnestly desire to prophesy, and do not forbid speaking in tongues; but all things should be done decently and in order" (I Cor. 14:39–40).

His final word is not "Let all be done according to the law," which would totally cut out the women, but his emphasis is on decency and order, which would include them.[27] This "decency and order" argument of Paul's is very symbolic. It reflects both Paul's training as a rabbi and his difficulties with the Gnostics. That matters of the spirit can be handled with decency and order reflects the ethics of the rabbinic tradition wherein ethical and moral problems are never solely an individual matter, but individual ethics are derived from the ethic that best benefits the whole community. Consequently a chief concern of a rabbi must always be to maintain communal order out of consideration for each individual, and particularly out of consideration for weaker members, who may be harmed by the evil influences of those who appear to be stronger, but whose leadership may be destructive to the community's common life.

Gnosticism by its very nature was antithetical to this rabbinic concern. In contrast to the structures of rabbinic Judaism, much of the movement seemed like a model of religious anarchy. While in

Judaism the spirit was considered a gift to the community, in gnosticism the individual divine spark in itself had divine authority, with no regard for the influence of one's actions on another, and no human means for judgment. Paul's whole approach to ethical and moral problems in the congregation was from the point of view of building up the Body of Christ, and his negative dicta to these spirits in Corinth were largely measured by whether or not they contributed to or undermined the congregation's corporate life.

Confused, and plagued with the dangers of ecstatic arrogance, the Church in Corinth was full of problems. It was not at all like the idealized picture most Christians have of the early Church. The thrust of Paul's response to this crisis is an appeal to the congregation's corporate life in Christ—he appeals to them to see their identity not as an aggregate of individualistic Gnostic spirit but as recipients of a common spirit that is the basis of their life together:

> For just as the body is one and has many members, and all the members of the body, though many, are one body, so it is with Christ. For by one Spirit we were all baptized into one body— Jews or Greeks, slaves or free—and all were made to drink of one Spirit. (I Cor. 12:12–13)

In I Cor. 14, Paul refutes all attempts to establish a Church on any other basis than that of the shared corporate gifts of the congregation, which flow out of their unified gift of membership in Christ's fellowship.[28] Paul was hardly an advocate of individual freedom of expression in the Corinthian congregation; but even given all the turmoil, he did admit a public role for women in worship that had not previously existed in Jewish tradition or customs.

The Corinthian congregation was obviously a lively place. We know little of what it did well and much of what it did badly. It is entirely possible that Paul's negative dicta against women are evidence of the fact that women played a vital role in the congregation. It was a woman, Chloe, who was Paul's major source of information about the abuses in Corinth (I Cor. 1:11), and we know from other references in the New Testament that Paul maintained a continuing fellowship with Priscilla and Aquila, a husband-wife team who are mentioned in other references to the Corinthian ministry.[29] There was also Phoebe, mentioned in Rom. 16, whom Paul refers to as a fellow worker and patronness of the Church. And though we know nothing about the role, or influence, of the celibate partners in the Corinthian Church, we do know that they existed and contributed to the total life of the congregation. Finally, if women could prophesy, they could play not only a vital but a prominent role in the congregation. In the ordering of gifts that Paul himself lists, the prophets are listed next to the apostles as the most valuable members of the fellowship: "Now you are the body of Christ and individually members of it. And God has appointed in the church first apostles, second prophets, third teachers . . ." (I Cor. 12:27–28). Within the framework of his ethics of "decency and order" Paul, unlike his rabbinic contemporaries, did allow a primary place for the participation of women.

Galatians 3:28: Ethics of the Inter-time and Its Effect on Women

Paul's primary witness was that the old law was being surpassed, and a new age of promise—in terms of women, the time of Mary rather than of Eve—was coming into existence. He did not, however, at the time of the writing of I Corinthians yet fully grasp its implications for fundamental social change. Called upon to deal with the perilous state of that congregation, he attempted to use the norms of the old religious and social order as staying power for this transitional period. He appealed to established customs while at the same time acknowledging that in the final times the theological validity of the old order was in the process of being erased and replaced by a new and perfected order of God's relationship with his creation and with his male and female creatures. This sense of the imminent approach of the end times is the driving force of Paul's theology, and it is in the midst of the enormous religious and social flux it caused that Paul formulated his basic Christian ethics.

To help ward off the dangers of the dissolution of corporate life, as it struggled to find its equilibrium in this transitional situation, Paul set forth the dynamics of what he sees as an appropriate ethics. First described in I Corinthians, it is this that constitutes the basis for his future-oriented ethics of the inter-time.

> I mean, brethren, the appointed time has grown very short; from now on, let those who have wives live as though they had none, and those who mourn as though they were not mourning, and those who rejoice as though they were not rejoicing, and those who buy as though they had no goods, and those who deal with the world as though they had no dealings with it. For the form of this world is passing away. (I Cor. 7:29–31)

By the time of the letter to the Galatians, Paul had further developed this inter-time ethics and had shaped a new synthesis of his thought. In Galatians he expresses his theology of a new mankind in which the old religious obstructions of racial laws, economics and sex have been broken down.[30] In the ethics of the inter-time there is no room for artificial religious and social hindrances. The three conditions of humankind that previously lived in separation under the Jewish law are now incorporated into the unity of one fellowship of Christ: "There is neither Jew nor Greek, there is neither slave nor free, there is neither male nor female; for you are all one in Christ Jesus" (Gal. 3:28).[31]

In terms of the ethics of the imminence of the Kingdom, the laws and regulations for Jews and non-Jews, freemen and slaves, and men and women have all been voided and emptied of meaning. All people now live under the same expectancy and the same promise of the future. In relation to women, this new ethics resulted in dramatic changes in traditional religious institutions in which long-established traditions had given the most privileged positions to men.

In Galatians, Paul is not only clearly aware of the presence and imminence of the new creation but he is also aware that it will demand changes in customs. People who previously had been subordinated by the law will now live in cooperation and reciprocity. Paul is confident that in the new age, relationships between men and women will usher in a totally new religious and human spirit,[32] and not merely mirror the pre-Fall images of Adam and Eve. "Therefore, if anyone is in Christ," says Paul, "he is a new

creation" (II Cor. 5:17); and in Galatians he explicitly states that
both men and women are heirs of the promise (Gal. 3:29) and
coheirs with Christ.

The new age will have social implications. In it there will be
no discriminating laws. The coming of Christ rules out the need
for religious, economic and sexually designated subordinating roles.
In speaking to the issue of Gentile circumcision, Paul makes it clear
that "neither circumcision nor uncircumcision is of any avail, but
faith working through love" (Gal. 5:6). This means that the practice of Jewish circumcision in the older order, both as a mark of
man's status before God and his relationship with others, is now
totally without function. In Christ, Jews and Gentiles are no longer
set apart by theological, social and racial differentiations. Through
the same baptism they are one in Christ. There are no economic
differentiations between slaves and free and no sexually determined
discriminating boundaries between men and women.

Though the ethics of the end-times clearly introduced the concept of the equivalence of men and women, it did not carry with
it the denial of their sexual identity as males and females. Some
Gnostics believed that in the perfect spiritual world men and
women would become androgynous and sexual identity would be
dissolved. According to certain noncanonical Gnostic gospels, equivalence between men and women could be achieved only when
women were changed into men. An example of this is found in the
Gnostic gospel of Mary, Coptic, second century:

> Mary stood up and greeted all of them and said to her brethren,
> "Do not mourn or grieve or be irresolute, for his grace will be
> with you all and will defend you. Let us rather praise his great-
> ness, for he prepared us and made us into men." When Mary
> said this, then their hearts changed for the better and they began
> to discuss the words of the [Saviour].[33]

According to Paul, the sexuality of men and women is not
erased with membership in Christ. What is changed is that the
sexually determined barriers that once kept women and men from
being a community of equals in the religious life have been elimi-
nated. The Gnostics tried to resolve the imbalance caused by the
subordination of women by projecting the biological miracle of

androgeny, while Paul's "one in Christ" moved to correct the root problem of the sexual inequity in fundamental religious attitudes.

While at times Paul tried to maintain that the pattern of life in the new age begins with one's status in the social structure—for example, slaves remain slaves and Jewish Christians are still permitted to practice circumcision—he also presented the people with new social alternatives. In the case of women and men this was possible through celibacy. Either could renounce marriage for the sake of the Kingdom. For women, celibacy was revolutionary. It legitimatized for them an independent vocational status. They could choose not to raise families and have husbands.[34] They could choose from a variety of leadership positions within the Christian community and yet remain celibate. In the light of the urgency of the end times, Paul himself felt celibacy to be the most desirable choice. Because Paul had no "word of the Lord" on the position of celibate women, it meant that their subordinated position—as was customary in marriage—would not be assumed in celibacy. In a community of celibate women and men subordination as traditionally known in marriage had no social meaning. The mere possibility of an image for women that was not biologically determined, but was determined by being "in Christ," had already planted the seeds for a new translation and transformation of the identities of women and men which affected not only the Church but also family life.

Though to modern ears Paul's new theology of men and women in Corinthians and in Galatians may sound like that of a typical male chauvinist—"equality in the abstract only"—within the context of the first century A.D. it was without precedent. Paul was struggling to find his way through the crisis of early Christianity—living in the tension between what had been in the tradition, what was happening at the moment and what was believed to be imminent. Though in Corinthians he had difficulty acknowledging, understanding and handling the problems of women as participants in worship, in Galatians Paul provided the radical theological underpinnings for the development of a mutuality of status "in Christ" which opened up an absolutely new arena to the human psyche. The inter-time ethics of Paul was no mere accommodation, or coping device, to deal with an extraordinary circumstance. It was a projection of a new vision of the once segregated human family now united in the common promise and future of Christ's community.

Women in the Later Epistles

No writing on Paul and women would be complete without reflecting on the third generation of Christians and their attitudes toward woman's place in the life of the congregation.

In what are known as the Pastoral Epistles, written near the end of the first century A.D. and the turn of the second, the intertime ethics of Paul has disappeared. The eschaton, the fulfillment of the end times, had not come. Both the disruptions of the spirit, which had caused the original conflicts of Corinth, and the problems of reconciliations in Galatians had subsided. It is in this context that I Timothy is written. Here the position of women is very restricted. Prayers must be said only by men. Women must dress modestly and act soberly. They must listen quietly and always be learners, and they must fill all of their hours with good deeds. Specifically, women must be quiet and must not domineer over their husbands. As if this were not enough, women were no longer mentioned as being saved by incorporation into Christ and by life in the new creation, but women are mentioned only as "saved through motherhood" (I Tim. 2:15).

The reasons for this hardening of attitudes toward women remain unknown. It certainly was in part related to the realization that the end times were not soon to come. This probably took the edge off the ethical imperatives and led to a kind of spiritual slowdown. In addition, the fact that ecstatic groups such as those in Corinth got out of control and still lived on in later Gnostic groups (e.g., the Montanists) led the Church to be cautious and more conservative. Both II Timothy and Titus make reference to the Gnostic teachers who have gotten into families and homes and who "capture weak women, burdened with sins and swayed by various impulses, who will listen to anybody and can never arrive at a knowledge of the truth" (II Tim. 3:6–7). These Gnostics, reports Titus, "must be silenced, since they are upsetting whole families by teaching for base gain what they have no right to teach . . ." (Titus 1:11).

The later Church no longer felt the spiritual problems of Paul and no longer shared his struggles. The substance of Paul's theology was still there, but the power that had provoked it had been weakened. This meant that along with concern for the new status of slaves and a new unity between Jews and Gentiles, the new equivalence between men and women also suffered from spiritual atrophy. The theology and forceful vision of Paul were obscured. As a result the later epistles accepted Paul's external statements about customs at face value and overlooked their underlying and radically new theology. The dicta of Paul in I Corinthians, intended as temporary measures, became frozen and transmitted as carbon-copy guidelines for use in the later churches.

The Pastoral Epistles absolutized Paul's ethics of the intertime, determined by the customs and mores of the old order, and spiritualized his ethics of the new creation. This freezing of ethics meant that there was no longer a theological vehicle for the transformation of ethics from the old traditions of the past to the new promise of the future. As a consequence, the later epistles are almost a rerun of social relationships between men and women in the rabbinic communities of the pre-Christian period.

The subordinated role of women in the Christian tradition is not so much a problem caused by Paul as it is a problem of how the Christian tradition has since chosen to interpret Paul. By using his dicta against women as a justification for maintaining the status quo, the Church has overlooked the new theology of men and women in Christ that was envisioned, and neglected these uniquely new theological formulations of I Cor. 11:11–12 and Gal. 3:28. With this neglect it lost its means for the continual transformation of itself from the old to the new creation.

THE PROMINENCE OF WOMEN IN THE PRIMITIVE CHURCH

There is ample evidence in the gospels and in Acts of a dramatic new role for women. Most of the twentieth-century literature about women in the New Testament looks at the subject from the point of view of Jesus' treatment of women, and recent publications of this type show Jesus had a much more liberated attitude toward women than other rabbis of his time; indeed, he may have been history's first "feminist."[35]

Though it is true that the parables of Jesus and stories about his life reflect the context in which they occurred—that of a rabbi teaching in Palestine—they also reflect the successive settings in which they were written down and finally shaped by their various editors—Luke, Matthew, Mark and John—into the gospels as we now know them. It is from this perspective that the question of women in the gospels will be approached. The focus will not be primarily on Jesus' relationships with women but on what the gospels themselves reflect about the social status of women in the worship, teaching and missionary life of the Church at the end of the first century of the Christian era. Having explored the radical theology of Paul in relation to women, this will be a brief look at what women were actually doing in the primitive Church as seen by other New Testament writers.

Rather than cover everything, we will concentrate on Luke and Acts. Though they are probably written by the same author, we will explore Luke from the point of view of a catechism for new Christian converts at the end of the first century A.D., and consider Acts as a chronicle of events of the first Christian community.

Luke and the Education of Women

Luke is especially interesting because it has many more stories that include women than do Mark and Matthew. Though all three draw on common material about Jesus, Luke appears to be addressing his gospel to a setting in which there were a substantial number of women present either as students of the primitive catechism or as potential converts to the early missionary churches. Since the literary style of both Luke and Acts shares many similarities with the missionary literature of Hellenistic Judaism, both of these works may have been compiled in a Hellenistic setting and may well reflect the more emancipated attitudes toward women in that setting.

The stories surrounding Jesus' life and his parables were used to correct and instruct their listening audiences. Luke's gathering of the material, unlike parallel Jewish literature and unlike the other gospels, shows an extreme sensitivity to its listeners as including women as well as men. The most striking example of this is in what are called the "pairing parables."[36] Luke not only incorporates some of the "pairing" parables shared by Matthew and Mark but he adds several new pairings of stories of his own. In the description of Jesus' ministry of healing, Luke juxtaposes the healing of a man (the centurion slave: 7:2–10) with the healing of a woman (raising from the dead of a widow's son: 7:11–12). Later on, the parable of the Good Samaritan is directed toward men (10:29–37), and juxtaposed to the story about Mary and Martha, directed toward women (10:38–42). Also, in the parables, Luke couples the parable of the man and the lost sheep (15:3–7) with that of the woman and the lost coin (15:8–10).[37] In each case of male-female pairing, both illustrations make the same point about the nature of the Kingdom and both carry the same message about the openness of the Kingdom to previously excluded groups. Other than as a pedagogical device for repetition, there is no apparent reason for stating the same message twice except to choose examples that would make the message clearly understandable to different groups—the female and the male listeners.

Luke also couples male and female illustrations to describe what it requires to come to terms with the meaning of discipleship: the example of the king in battle (14:31–33), which men would appropriate as referring to them, and the example of the salt used in cooking (14:34–35), which women would immediately grasp. The parables of Jesus were directed to real-life situations, and correspondingly, in their written form they are addressed to another social reality in the real-life situations in the primitive churches. They not only reflect the daily life of Palestine but they also reflect the audience, the important constituencies of women and men who shaped the missionary and catechetical movement of the primitive Christian congregations.

The most obvious evidence of the existence of the two audiences—male and female—is the story of Jesus' reprimand by the Pharisees for his healing on the Sabbath. The very same story is mentioned twice. In each case Jesus accuses the Pharisees of being more helpful to a work animal on the Sabbath than to a human being. The only difference in the two accounts is that in one case the person is a crippled old woman (Luke 13:10–16) and in the other it is a man afflicted with dropsy (Luke 14:2–6). Though the stories carry identical messages, each rendering is designed to appeal to different audiences of learners—one to men, the other to women.

This focus on Luke should, however, not lead to misunderstanding. Luke is not the only gospel to address itself to both a male and a female audience. That women were significant in the teaching and learning life of the primitive Church is also shown in the common sources from which both Matthew and Luke draw. For example, both Matthew and Luke pick up those sayings of Jesus that point out that the coming of the Kingdom will bring about a crisis destined to affect men and women equally. It is imminent. It will catch both men and women in the course of their daily lives: "I tell you, in that night there will be two men in one bed; one will be taken and the other left. There will be two women grinding together; one will be taken and the other left" (Luke 17:34–36).[38]

In addition, both Matthew and Luke pick up the vocationally oriented metaphors for the Kingdom, making reference to both men and women:

> He said therefore, "What is the kingdom of God like? And to what shall I compare it? It is like a grain of mustard seed which a man took and sowed in his garden; and it grew and became a tree, and the birds of the air made nests in its branches." And again he said, "To what shall I compare the kingdom of God? It is like leaven which a woman took and hid in three measures of meal, till it was all leavened." (Luke 13:18–21)[39]

The wonders of a mustard seed are familiar to the farmer. The insignificant amount of leaven needed to create a whole mass of dough is known to every housewife. Both stories illustrate the identical message: the Kingdom begins insignificantly—almost unnoticed—but in its final stage it will be like an enormous mustard tree or a massive leavened loaf.[40]

Though the other gospels also include many references to women in relation to the life and teachings of Jesus, the Gospel of Luke gives the richest evidence of being shaped by a social context in which there were large numbers of women present who were schooled in the scriptures. The most convincing internal documentation of this is the story of the encounter of Mary and Martha with Jesus, a story appearing only in Luke's gospel (10:38–42). It is this illustration that puts to the test the traditional roles of women as domestic servants and deliverers of hospitality. Mary, rather than helping her sister as she busies herself with domestic duties to accommodate their guest, seats herself at the feet of Jesus to be attentive to what he has to say. In a typical Jewish setting of that time women would not have been allowed to sit at the feet of a rabbi. With a few rare exceptions of rabbis' daughters, it was not considered worth while to waste time educating young women. Martha, irritated by her sister's behavior, asks Jesus to reprimand her. But to Martha's surprise Jesus comes to Mary's aid and rebukes Martha instead, saying: "Mary has chosen the good portion, which shall not be taken away from her" (10:42). The inclusion of this story about Jesus, unique to Luke's gospel, is the keystone of the changed status of women that it reflects. While previously the learning of scriptures was limited to men, now it is opened to women. The story of Mary and Martha enabled women to choose. Mary departed from her ascribed role and was commended by Jesus for so doing. This meant that other women were encouraged to choose this new alternative: to be allowed, as were the young men, to learn the scriptures at the feet of a rabbi.

There are indications within the parables themselves, however, that women's participation was still problematic. The account in Matthew of the wise and foolish virgins is one such example (Matt. 25:1–13). Here the kingdom of heaven is compared to ten maidens —five wise and five foolish—who await the bridegroom. The foolish virgins, however, did not prepare for a delay in the bridegroom's coming, and they ran out of oil. While they were out fetching a new supply the bridegroom arrived, and since they were not present at the critical moment, they were locked out of the feast, while the wise virgins, who had come prepared in the beginning, were let in. Looked at from within the social context, the implication of this parable could be that though the Kingdom is open to women, not all of them will enter, because not all of them will be capable of being prepared. Whatever Matthew's intention might have been, he has chosen a metaphor relating to women to make his point about who is likely to make it into the Kingdom and who isn't.

Though Luke's gospel expresses much male-female balance in its structure, it also alludes to the difficulties of women gaining access to the Kingdom. The parable of the woman and the unjust judge is one such example (Luke 18:2–8). Considering the unjust judge to be the principal character, the parable is a metaphor of the Lord's forgiveness. If the unrighteous judge will give in to the nagging, pestering requests of this old woman, how much more will he give in to the persistent prayers and cries of any needy Christian. Widows, particularly in the early Christian congregations, because they were most often dependent on the Church for financial support, had difficulty gaining acceptance. In this case Jesus takes the most extreme example of need, the widow, and illustrates by this parable that even this old woman will be heard in the court of the Lord if she persists day and night. If it is possible for even the most unlikely candidate—an annoying and troublesome old woman—to gain access to the Kingdom, it is certainly possible for anyone.

Though women are perceived as an essential part of the learning audience of the gospels, particularly in Luke, it is obvious that the gospels still reflect the social fabric of the early Church. In this setting women still had to overcome cultural, religious and legal impediments as they moved into a new religious and social position. In contrast to rabbinic Judaism, the pedagogical structure of Luke clearly indicates that it is essential to educate both women and men. In choosing illustrations as familiar to women's lives as to men's, all of the central religious issues are as clearly available for the education of women as of men.

Acts and the Leadership of Women

On the basis of what we now know about the status of women in other parts of the New Testament and about Jewish women and other women in the Greco-Roman world, Acts becomes the best source of information in the New Testament on the prominent role of women in the primitive Church. Written to convince inquiring audiences of the validity of the Christian message, its intention was to show that through the intervention of the Holy Spirit, God was guiding the salvation of mankind and would inevitably lead it to its final destiny. To the writer of Acts the gifts of prophecy and the miracles were the first sign of the unfolding messianic times, and both women and men were its recipients. One possible reason for so much emphasis on women in Acts is that the early Church had more success among women, especially in the middle and upper classes.

The first clue in Acts about the significance of women in the primitive congregations is that Saul (the name of Paul before his conversion), in applying to the synagogue in Damascus for permission to arrest members of the Church whom he found there, especially requested permission to arrest women as well as men (Acts 9:1–2). If the women were safely under the domination of their husbands in private and silenced in the churches in public, it would hardly have seemed necessary for him to make a point of persecuting women. Punishing and imprisoning the men should have been sufficient (8:3, 9:2, 22:4).

That women were very active participants in the primitive Church is attested by numerous references to influential women in the congregations (13:50, 17:4 and 13). In Antioch, for example, Paul and Barnabas were forced to leave town because Judaizing Christians won the support of "women of standing" in the congregation and stirred up so much dissent among the worshippers and leading men of the city that their missionary intentions proved hopeless. The extent of these influential women is not known, but that they could wield considerable power is apparent.

Acts provides some glimpses of how prominent some of these women might have been. One example is the story of the conversion of Lydia from Thyatira, a dealer in purple dye (16:14–16). Not only does she appear to be a woman established in the commerce of a city known for its trade guilds—tanners, linen workers, leatherworkers, dyers—but also, with her conversion, Acts states that her whole household became followers of "the new way." Lydia appears to be a woman of means who could compete in the commercial world and also be head of a large household, probably including servants and slaves. She is a woman whose position seems to be in marked contrast to that of the servile Jewish women recounted in the gospels, but not too dissimilar from her Hellenistic counterparts. This contrast between the status of Lydia and that of women in the gospels probably reflects the fact that the gospels have their genesis in the predominantly rural Jewish environment of Palestine, while Acts reflects contact with the urban (commercial) environment of the Hellenistic cities.

The status of Hellenistic women is part of the historical complexity that affects any exploration of the status of women in the primitive congregations. The women mentioned in Acts were, for the most part, not living in Palestine, but in the cities of Asia Minor, Egypt and Greece, which were subject to Roman law and were coming under its cultural ascendancy while still maintaining their diversity. Though the majority of women mentioned in Acts are probably Jewish women, converts from the Diaspora synagogues, and not Gentile women, the emancipation and independence of Hellenistic women probably had an impact on them.

Not only were there "devout women of high standing," women with some political muscle, and women with independent resources in the primitive Church, but there were also women who were students of scripture following the "Mary" rather than the "Martha" model. Acts makes special reference to the fact that in Beroea, a Macedonian city, both men and women "received the word with all eagerness, examining the scriptures daily to see if these things were so" (17:11–12).

There were also women with emancipated roles among the husband-wife teams with whom Paul worked. The most frequently mentioned couple is Priscilla and Aquilla, who were teachers and tentmakers with Paul, and Christians of Jewish origin, whom Paul had met in Corinth after they had been expelled from Rome in the Jewish persecutions of the Emperor Claudius. Gatherings for worship were also held in the homes of women. The house of Mary, the mother of John Mark, was used in this way (Acts 12:12), as were the houses of Lydia and Dorcas. A woman who provided such shelter and hospitality to the early Christians had a specially designated status as "patronness" of the congregation.

There were also other women with special status, including one who was referred to as a "disciple"—a Jewish woman of independent means, a seamstress living in the Jewish city of Joppa, who was called Tabitha (also referred to as Dorcas) (Acts 9:36–43). Tabitha was evidently well known and admired for her charitable work, her fine craftsmanship as a seamstress and her graceful manner (Tabitha means "gazelle"). Like Paul and Barnabas, she was never named with "the Twelve." Unlike them, her designation as "disciple" has been minimized by the Church. Contrary to popular belief, there is no agreement in the New Testament itself as to how many disciples there actually were, or who they were. The term can imply one who is merely a follower, or it may refer to one who is under the instruction of a specific rabbi or teacher and part of a small elite group of his adherents. Whatever the specific significance of the title "disciple" as applied to Tabitha, she was felt to be so valuable to the Christian community in Joppa that many widows wept at her death and Peter rushed to her side from a neighboring town to raise her from the dead—the first such miracle performed by an apostle. To be recorded as raised from the dead, and to be the focus of the first such miracle by a fellow disciple, she must have been considered indispensable to the congregation. Her exact status remains unknown, but that she was much more than merely one of the many followers is clear from the story about her.

In Acts women are also designated as prophets. As prophets they were given authority to address themselves to central meanings of the faith: to inspire, clarify, and bring new insights. The four unmarried daughters of Philip, one of the Seven, were among these first-generation prophetesses. Though prophecy was a characteristic mark of the primitive Church, it was not the possession of all, but the gift of a few. The daughters of Philip were probably also among the first women celibates who decided not to marry for the sake of the Kingdom. Given their high status as prophets, it is probably no coincidence that Philip's daughters were Greek—either Greek-speaking Jews or Hellenists. Their special status may reflect the fact that they were products of the less restricted, more self-reliant pattern of life possible for women within Hellenistic society.

Acts begins with the signs of the end times, seeing the primitive Church in Jerusalem as the beginning of the fulfillment prophesied by Joel: "I will pour out my Spirit upon all flesh, and your sons and your daughters shall prophesy" (2:17). And it ends with Paul in Rome and the opening up of the mission to the Gentiles. Writing about the things that have been accomplished in the first Christian community, Acts reports a great deal about the important participation of women, a fact that was no doubt significant in attracting women into early congregations. Though at the end of the first century members of the Church were drawn largely from the lower classes, this was less true of women than of men. As sources outside the New Testament report, and as Acts amply illustrates, women from all social levels were drawn into participation in the first-century churches. In worship, teaching, institutional and missionary life the Spirit, indeed, was poured out on both "sons and daughters."

SUMMARY

The New Testament discloses to us that women were educated in the scriptures and that they assumed leadership roles of sufficient magnitude to attract many women into Christian congregations. Their participation was, however, not without problems. Although attitudes toward women in the New Testament reflect both theologically and socially a first-century Jewish religious and cultural cast, Paul's theology of equivalence in Christ provided a vehicle for building a new religious and social basis for women-men relationships in the future. This radically new theology of women, however, became obscured in the later epistles. What Paul had understood as a kind of temporary status-quo ethics—in the context of the imminent end times—became translated two generations later into moral guidelines for keeping things as they are forever.

The later Church, when it lost the vision that the Kingdom was coming, also lost the theology that enabled it to live as though the Kingdom were at hand. As a consequence, it inherited two seemingly widely divergent messages: the theology of equivalence in Christ; the practice of women's subordination. In attempting to reconcile them, it maintained a status-quo ethics on the social level through the subordination of women, and it affirmed the vision of equivalence on the spiritual level by projecting it as an otherworldly reality. Throughout the history of the Church this has led to complex and confused theological arguments, with their consequent social distortions, the sum of which is that men belong to this world and do the work of the Church, while women belong to the next world and act in the Church only as hidden helpers and servants to men. Men are of this world, but women are of the Spirit. The net effect of this piety, which in its dualism is much closer to gnosticism than to Christianity, has been that women have been effectively removed from public influence in the Church. One might on rare occasion become a saint, but certainly not a priest; one might become a teacher, but certainly not a theologian or bishop. The consequence of this distorted spirituality and skewed social reality has been that women have been precluded from receiving or ever developing fully responsible and equal roles in the Church's spiritual, theological and institutional life.

The present-day church, in order to recover its kinship with the primitive Christian message, will have to overcome this sexist dualism and dare to live out in all areas of its institutional and spiritual life this first-generation formula of "neither male nor female" in Christ. Not until the Church overcomes this spiritual dualism and social negation of women by again recovering the theological vision of itself as a people of promise, unfolding the new creation, will it again discover the absolutely unique theological insight and profound social meaning of Paul's "neither male nor female" in Christ. It was neither social reality alone nor spirituality alone to which Paul gave new definition. To be "in Christ" was to be party to the ushering in of an entirely new mode of human existence.

NOTES

1. Peter Ketter, *Christ and Womankind* (Westminster, Md.: Newman Press, 1952), p. 21.
2. Samuel Dill, *Roman Society from Nero to Marcus Aurelius* (New York: Macmillan and Co., 1905), p. 79.
3. Ibid., p. 329.
4. Ketter, *Christ and Womankind*, pp. 21–24.
5. Until the reign of Justinian a woman could not be appointed a guardian, even over her own children. See J. P. V. D. Balsdon, *Roman Women; Their History and Habits* (London: Bodley Head, 1962), p. 275.
6. Rome had a much larger concept of subordination than simply that of subordination of women to men. A man was unimportant in comparison with his family, a citizen unimportant in comparison to the body of citizens. Persons were subordinated to the group, and because of this social structure some women in powerful families achieved very-high-status positions.
7. Balsdon, *Roman Women*, p. 276.

8. Ketter, *Christ and Womankind*, p. 20.
9. Roman literature is full of criticism of wives, but not of husbands. See S. W. Baron, *A Social and Religious History of the Jews* (New York: Columbia University Press, 1937), I, 214.
10. Morton M. Hunt, *The Natural History of Love* (New York: Minerva Press, 1967), p. 83.
11. Ibid., p. 65 (from Livy, *Roman History*, Bk. XXXIV sec. iii).
12. Babylonian Talmud, Ketubot 56b.
13. Victor Tcherikover, *Hellenistic Civilization and the Jews* (Philadelphia: Jewish Publication Society of America, 1959), pp. 355–357. Also see George Foot Moore, *Judaism in the First Centuries of the Christian Era; The Age of the Tannaim* (Cambridge, Mass.: Harvard University Press, 1950), I, 126.
14. A wife was obliged to be faithful in marriage, but not a husband. A husband could divorce his wife, but a wife had no legal grounds to leave her husband. See Baron, *A Social and Religious History of the Jews*, I, 264 ff, and also Isidore Singer, ed. *The Jewish Encyclopedia* (New York: Funk & Wagnalls, 1906), XII, 556–558.
15. Baron, *A Social and Religious History of the Jews*, I, 271.
16. Tcherikover, *Hellenistic Civilization and the Jews*, pp. 355–357, speaks of the noncompromising spirit of the Books of Esther and Judith as opposed to the assimilating attitudes of Philo and Aristeas.
17. Ibid., p. 349.
18. See Hans Jonas, *The Gnostic Religion* (Boston: Beacon Press, 1958), p. 46. He demonstrates how the spiritual mentality of the Gnostics is determined by their "hostility toward the world and contempt for all mundane ties."
19. Robert M. Grant, *Gnosticism* (New York: Harper & Row, 1961), p. 15.
20. See Acts 18 (R.S.V.).
21. Recent excavations of Palestinian synagogues have uncovered galleries for women. See Baron, *A Social and Religious History of the Jews*, I, 271.
22. Jonas demonstrates how the Gnostics, starting from a moral point of view, moved in one of two directions: either total asceticism or total libertinism. In the first instance, the Gnostic cuts himself off from society by avoiding contact with it and contamination by it; in the second, he deliberately flaunts the norms as a way of expressing his total freedom from established moral laws. See Jonas, *The Gnostic Religion*, p. 46.
23. Werner Georg Kümmel, *Introduction to the New Testament* (London: SCM Press, 1966), p. 202.
24. H. J. Schoeps, *Paul: The Theology of the Apostles in the Light of Jewish Religious History* (London: Lutterworth Press, 1961), p. 39. Schoeps draws attention to parallel references in rabbinic

literature, in the history of religion, and in the Haggada tradition of Judaism, pointing out that this tradition is difficult for modern man to understand.

25. Philo Judaeus, *Questions and Answers on Genesis*, trans. R. Marcus (Cambridge, Mass.: Harvard University Press, 1953).

26. Also see Rom. 4:13 and discussion in Schoeps, *Paul*, pp. 199 ff., about Paul's attitude toward the law in an age of transition.

27. For a parallel view of the role of order and discipline in the Judaism of the time, see Helmer Ringgren, *The Faith of Qumran*, trans. Emilie T. Sander (Philadelphia: Fortress Press, 1963), pp. 212 ff. Though the Essenes were more rigorous in their organizational structures than the primitive Church, their punishment of offenders for laughing or falling asleep during a congregational meeting gives some flavor of the mores of that time.

28. For a discussion of the paramount importance of community life in relationship to the Corinthian correspondence see Arthur Darby Nock, *St. Paul* (New York: Harper & Row Torchbooks, 1963), pp. 168–170.

29. See Acts 18:18, 26 and I Cor. 16:19.

30. See discussion by Amos N. Wilder, "Kerygma, Eschatology and Social Ethics" in W. D. Davis and D. Daube, eds. *The Background of the New Testament and Its Eschatology* (New York: Columbia University Press, 1956), pp. 525–535.

31. See discussion on the human unity of the Body of Christ, with special reference to Gal 3:28, in Ernst Käsemann, *Essays on New Testament Themes* (Naperville, Ill.: Allenson, Inc., 1964), p. 69.

32. See Kümmel, *Introduction to the New Testament*, p. 140. Here he discusses the life in the new age as resulting from incorporation into a new humanity in Christ that is the result of a totally "new impulse."

33. Grant, *Gnosticism*, p. 66.

34. Not only had celibacy never been an option for Jewish women but there were laws in the Roman world that prohibited women from remaining single and made it mandatory for them to remarry after divorce or widowhood. It was only through Christianity that celibacy for women became a socially acceptable status for them.

35. Leonard Swidler, "Jesus Was a Feminist," in *Catholic World* (Jan. 1971), pp. 177–183.

36. Joachim Jeremias, *The Parables of Jesus* (New York: Charles Scribner's Sons, 1955), pp. 70–74.

37. These two parables also appear in Matthew, but they are separated and refer to different contexts.

38. See also Matt. 24:40.

39. See also Matt. 13:31–33.

40. Jeremias (*The Parables of Jesus*) recognizes the similarities of the stories, but he does not suggest that their differences are due to different audiences of women and men.

Misogynism and Virginal Feminism in the Fathers of the Church

ROSEMARY RADFORD RUETHER

The usual image of the Fathers of the Church, especially among those promoting women's liberation, is that of fanatical ascetics and woman haters. Hatred of sex and hatred of women are identified.[1] But this view tends to ignore the high praise of women, in their new role as "virgins," in patristic theology. It also fails to explain the rise of that veneration of Mary that is characteristic of patristic thought in the fourth century A.D. In this chapter I wish to show that this ambivalence between misogynism and the praise of the virginal woman is not accidental. One view is not more "characteristic" than the other. Both stand together as two sides of a dualistic psychology that was the basis of the patristic doctrine of man.

The rise of an alienated experience of bodily reality in late antiquity is one of the puzzles of the history of consciousness which would bear much more study from a worldwide comparative-religions perspective. Contemporary Christians, embarrassed by classical Christian asceticism, are wont to stress the naturalism of the Old Testament and to condemn body-soul dualism as Hellenistic and unbiblical. This procedure fits in with the Protestant quest for an original point of unblemished integrity in the Bible which marks all unpalatable Christian doctrines as due to some later accretion of unbiblical views, usually seen as derived from "Hellenism."[2]

But this thesis is misleading as a historical account of the development of that dualism in antiquity that became the cultural mould within which Christianity was formed. The fact is that every religion in antiquity—Babylonian, Canaanite, Persian, Greek and Jewish—passed from a naturalistic to an otherworldly religious hope in the period from approximately the sixth to the second centuries B.C. Egyptian religion made this transition even earlier, as it changed from the life-affirming religion of the early Kingdom to the death-centered religion of the imperial New Kingdom.[3] Greek religion was transformed from the Apollonian celebration of the body of the Hellenic world to a Platonic flight from the body, after the *polis* lost its freedom and was absorbed into the empire of Alexander the Great. Judaism also was changed from a naturalistic religion of this-worldly hope to one of apocalyptic despair as it lost its national autonomy and passed under the yoke of the Persian, Greek and Roman empires. After the fall of Jerusalem, in 70 A.D., apocalypticism changed into an esoteric subculture of Jewish gnosticism and mysticism.[4] Even the ancient cults of the Earth Mother, with her rain-and-vegetation consort, such as Baalism and its counterparts in the worship of Astarte, Magna Mater and Isis, moved from naturalistic celebrations of the renewal of bodily fecundity to eschatological religions of the salvation of the soul after death. Christianity, born in Jewish apocalypticism and nurtured in the world of Hellenistic syncretism, drew together all the streams of religious consciousness from antiquity, Greek, Jewish and Oriental, but precisely in their *alienated, anticosmic stage of development!*[5]

This alienated experience of reality was expressed in a dualistic doctrine of being. This created a conflict between the biblical view of the goodness of physical creation (derived from the world-affirming religion of earlier Judaism) and the alienated, world-fleeing view of redemption which expressed a pessimism about the world and its possibilities of the later imperial period. This latent conflict in the foundations of Christianity was brought out in the open in the clash between the mainstream Church and left-wing Gnostics in the second century A.D. Gnosticism tried to reconcile the doctrines of creation and redemption by reading an other-

worldly doctrine of redemption back into a fallen doctrine of creation. The Gnostics believed that the world was created through an
error by an evil Demiurge, while man's original and final home was
an otherworldly, spiritual realm far removed from this evil material
world. Christianity rejected this solution. Instead it affirmed a unity
between the Father of Jesus Christ and the Creator God of the Old
Testament and a continuity between Israel and the Church. This
unity between creation and redemption was expressed in the appearance of a "cosmological Christology," in which the Christ of
the world-to-come was identified with the Word of God, through
whom the physical world was made.[6] Yet this affirmation of the
unity of the Christ of the end with the Creator of the beginning
did not substantially modify Christianity's commitment to an
otherworldly, spiritualist view of redemption. So the two doctrines
remained (and still remain) in conflict, each modifying the other
in strange and incompletely defined ways.

Origen (the Greek theologian of the early third century A.D.)
tried to reconcile the two by spiritualizing creation. First there was
a heavenly spiritual creation, and then a material creation appeared
as a result of the fall of the souls. It was this first creation that was
man's true home, to which he returned through redemption.[7] But
the Church condemned this view as too much like gnosticism.
Nevertheless the orthodox Greek theologians of the fourth century
A.D. followed a modified Origenism that saw the original creation
and humanity as spiritual and unitary, in contrast to a secondary,
more grossly bodily, bisexual form. It was this spiritual creation
that was their cosmogonic point of reference for redemption.
Origen developed the Pauline doctrine of the "spiritual body" of
the resurrection to suggest an original creation that was a "non-
bodily sort of body," in which the substance of man was absorbed
into his soul in a way that made this original creation "spiritual."
In this way he modified the conflict between the Jewish bodily
creation and the Greek spiritualist redemption. This allowed Christianity to claim the Jewish doctrine of the resurrection of the body,
but with a Platonic spirituality. Second-century Western thinkers,
such as Justin, Tertullian and Irenaeus, affirmed more vigorously
the original physical creation. But this lent itself to a sensual mil-
lenarianism that was offensive to the Eastern tradition.[8] The later
Church Fathers compromised by affirming an original bodily crea-

tion that wasn't quite sensual and the resurrection of a body that wasn't quite bodily but had been transformed into a "spiritual body." But even this modification of both creation and redemption could only obscure, but could not resolve the contradiction. Despite its body-affirming doctrine of creation, both Greek and Latin Christianity remained committed to a Platonized spirituality and eschatology that defined redemption as the rejection of the body and the flight of the soul from material, sensual nature. The patristic view of woman fell between the two stools of this ambivalence about the goodness of the body and sexuality.

A comparison of the doctrine of creation of the fourth century A.D. Greek Church Father, Gregory of Nyssa, with that of the great Latin Father, Augustine, will illustrate the similarity, but also the difference of emphasis, that remained between the two traditions. The crucial biblical text for the creation of man was Genesis 1:27: "God created man in His own image; in the image of God he created him; male and female He created them." If the Fathers could have had the first part of the text without the final phrase, they would have been happier. Indeed, they often quote only the first part of this text without alluding to the second[9] About the character of the image of God in man they had no doubts. This referred to man's soul or reason. The Hellenistic Jew Philo had already established this interpretation by the first century A.D.[10] The problem came with reconciling this spiritual interpretation of the image of God with the subsequent reference to bisexuality, which they saw as a bodily characteristic. Since God was wholly spiritual and noncorporeal, this appeared to mix contraries and imply either a sexed spirituality or a bodily God. Since it was anathema to think of God as bodily, with male and female characteristics, the two parts of the text must be separated so that the "image" could be defined in a monistic, spiritual way, and bisexuality could refer to something other than the nature of God as reflected in man.

For Greek thought it was axiomatic that spiritual reality was unitary (*monistic,* from which the words "monk" and "monastic" derive). Duality appears only with matter. So God cannot be dual, nor can man's spiritual image be bisexual. This does not mean an "androgynous" view of God and the original humanity, as some recent commentators have thought. The guiding view of the Fathers was not an androgyny that preserved bisexuality on a psychic level, but rather that monism which, alone, is appropriate to spirit.[11] This could be stated by identifying maleness with monism, making femaleness secondary, or else by a nonsexual monism, but not by a true androgyny. Gregory Nyssa chose the latter course, and Augustine the former.

For Gregory Nyssa the image of God is purely spiritual. It reflects the unitary, spiritual nature of the Divine Word, which is, in turn, the image of the transcendent Father. The reference to bisexuality in the second part of the verse does not refer to the image of God in man at all, but to that bodily nature, foreign to God, that was added to man with a view to the Fall.[12] But that spiritual, or "angelic," nature, to which man is restored in redemption, does not preserve this bisexuality, but, like Christ, resurrected man is "neither male nor female" (Gal. 3:28). Thus creation and redemption are coordinated in the monism of the soul, which mirrors its divine Archetype. The virgin or monk (*monos*) is the soul redeemed from the duality of bodiliness to return to that monism of the heavenly world. Thus Nyssa must modify the bisexual character of bodily creation by making it subsequent to an original monistic spiritual creation.

> "In the image of God he created him." There was an end of the creation of that which was made "in the image." Then it makes a resumption of the account of creation, and says "male and female created He them." I presume that everyone knows that this is a departure from the Archetype, for "in Christ," as the apostle says, "there is neither male nor female."[13]

Nyssa takes it for granted that the "image" must be monistic, and bisexuality must refer to something else, namely, to man's bodily nature, which is not made in God's image, but appears only with a view to the fall of soul into carnality, sin and death. Man is a compound of the divine incorporeal nature, to which his soul corresponds, and the irrational, material nature of brutes, toward which his body tends. The two parts of the text refer to this dual nature of man. But only the first part belongs to the divine "image," whereas the second half refers to man's bodily nature, which does not correspond to the divine Archetype.

Nyssa then tries to qualify this identification of the soul with the divine nature and relate it to the dualism of the body, lest he be accused of gnosticism. The nature of the soul is only "like," not identical, with that of God. It is separated from the uncreated divine nature as the mutable from the Immutable. If man, through his spiritual nature, had adhered to the immutable nature of God, through the Divine Word in whose image his soul was made, he would have been immortal. His physical substance would have remained absorbed into his spiritual being in a way that would have rendered him "changeless." But man has a second principle of mutability that reflects his created status. This does not derive from God, but from that "nothingness" from which the world was made. Nyssa does not want to accept the gnostic view of a primordial evil "matter," but he sublimates this idea by taking it back a step farther and calling it "mutability" rather than matter. Matter, created by God, is good, but it has a negative possibility, derived from that nothingness that God overcame in creating the world which expresses itself in "mutability"—that is, a tendency to fall away from being back into nothingness. If man had been obedient to God, his body would have been held by the divine immutability and would have remained undying. But when man turned from God to that mixed reality of the body that tends toward nothingness, his material principle becomes mutable and mortal. It is with a view to this fall into mortality that God created man's bisexuality, so that when man had fallen from immutability to mutability and had become subject to death, he would have a remedy for this in procreation.[14]

Nyssa is not quite sure whether there would have been any marriage in Paradise. Perhaps the original Adam, remaining unfallen, would have been the sole expression of a unitary humanity. Nyssa suggests that there might have been some angelic way of procreating that would have created a multiplicity of souls, just as there is a multiplicity of angels, but without bisexuality or marriage. Origen had solved this problem earlier by making the original spiritual humanity a multiplicity of single souls in the community of the pleroma. Thus, for Nyssa, man's image is spiritual and monistic. Bisexuality pertains to that lower nature which both drags man down to sin and death and provides a remedy in procreation, but redemption is return to the monistic nature of the angels.

In Augustine this same story is told with a somewhat different emphasis, which makes bisexuality more intrinsic to creation, but in a way that makes the "image" itself more androcentric. In other words, Augustine assimilates maleness into monism, and this makes femaleness rather than bisexuality the image of the lower, corporeal nature. For Augustine, man as the image of God was summed up in Adam, the unitary ancestor of humanity. But Adam is compound, containing both male spirit and female corporeality. When Eve is taken from Adam's side, she symbolizes this corporeal side of man, taken from him in order to be his helpmeet. But she is a helpmeet solely for the corporeal task of procreation, for which alone she is indispensable.[15] For any spiritual task another male would be more suitable than a female as a helpmeet.

Inexplicably, Augustine must also affirm that Eve, too, has a rational nature, being likewise a compound of spirit and body. Yet in relation to man she stands for body *vis-à-vis* male spirit.[16] Moreover, Augustine persists in calling this latter her "nature," not only with a view to sin but in the order of nature as well. Augustine defines the male as, alone, the full image of God. Woman, by herself, is not this image, but only when taken together with the male, who is her "head." Augustine justifies this view by fusing the Genesis text with I Corinthians 11:3–12.

How then did the apostle tell us that the man is the image of God and therefore he is forbidden to cover his head, but that the woman is not so, and therefore she is commanded to cover hers? Unless forsooth according to that which I have said already, when I was treating of the nature of the human mind, that the woman, together with her own husband, is the image of God, so that the whole substance may be one image, but when she is referred to separately in her quality as a helpmeet, which regards the woman alone, then she is not the image of God, but, as regards the man alone, he is the image of God as fully and completely as when the woman too is joined with him in one.[17]

This assimilation of male-female dualism into soul-body dualism in patristic theology conditions basically the definition of woman, both in terms of her subordination to the male in the order of nature and her "carnality" in the disorder of sin. The result of this assimilation is that woman is not really seen as a self-sufficient, whole person with equal honor, as the image of God in her own right, but is seen, ethically, as dangerous to the male. Augustine works this out explicitly, but patristic theology makes use of the same assumptions of woman's subordination to man in the order of nature, and her special "carnality" in the disorder of sin, which imply the same attitudes, however unjustified by the contrary assumption of the equivalence of male and female in the original creation. This definition of femaleness as body decrees a natural subordination of female to male, *as flesh must be subject to spirit in the right ordering of nature.*[18] It also makes her peculiarly the symbol of the Fall and sin, since sin is defined as the disordering of the original justice wherein the bodily principle revolts against its ruling spirit and draws the reason down to its lower dictates.

This double definition of woman, as submissive body in the order of nature and "revolting" body in the disorder of sin, allows the Fathers to slide somewhat inconsistently from the second to the first and attribute woman's inferiority first to sin and then to nature. In Augustine the stress falls decidedly on the side of woman's natural inferiority as body in relation to mind in the right ordering of nature, and thus he is somewhat temperate in his polemics against Eve as the original cause of the Fall. For him, the Fall could only occur, not when the body tempts, but when the male ruling principle agrees to "go along." This, however, does not imply a milder view of sin, only a more contemptuous view of Eve's capacity to cause the Fall "by herself."[19] In other Fathers, such as Tertullian, Eve is made to sound as though she bore the primary responsibility. Tertullian demands an abasement of woman and the covering of her shameful female nature as the consequence of her continuing imaging of this guilty nature of Eve.

> You are the Devil's gateway. You are the unsealer of that forbidden tree. You are the first deserter of the divine Law. You are she who persuaded him whom the Devil was not valiant enough to attack. You destroyed so easily God's image man. On account of your desert, that is death, even the Son of God had to die.[20]

Even the mild Clement of Alexandria, who defends more generously than some of the other Fathers, the spiritual equivalence of woman with man and the dignity of marriage as a relationship, speaks of woman as having to blush for shame "when you think of what nature you are."[21]

This assimilation of woman into bodiliness allows Augustine to explain why woman's subjugation is "natural" within the order of creation, but it makes for some contradiction when it comes time to defend woman's redeemability and her ability, like that of the man, to become "virgin" and return to the monistic incorporeal nature. This conflict does not appear in Nyssa in the same way, because he makes bisexuality, rather than femaleness, the symbol of corporeality, and thus makes woman and man equivalent, both in their spiritual natures and in their sexed bodily natures. But, then, the Greeks had the corresponding conflict of an inexplicable use of language which suggested that woman was subordinate to man in nature and peculiarly identified with "carnality"—a language to which they, too, were addicted.

Augustine attempts to explain this contradiction by distinguishing between what woman is, as a rational spirit (in which she is equivalent to the male), and what she "symbolizes" in her bodily nature, where she stands for the subjection of body to spirit in nature and that debasing carnality that draws the male mind down from its heavenly heights. But he thinks that what she thus symbolizes, in the eye of male perception, is also what she "is" in her female nature! It never occurs to him that defining woman as something other than what she is, and placing her in subjugation in the order of nature *from the perspective of the male visual impression of her as a "body"* is nothing else than an expression, in the male himself, of that disorder of sin, and thus, in no way a stance for the definition of woman's nature! For Augustine, however, this androcentric perspective is never questioned, but presupposed. Yet he, too, must admit that woman has "another" possibility beyond this androcentrically conceived bodiliness. She, too, has a rational nature and can be saved by overcoming the body and living according to the spirit. Augustine cannot deny this since he, along with all the Church Fathers, believes that woman can become "virgin" and live the monistic, angelic life.

There is a parallel tradition in the Church Fathers, however, according to which the doctrine of Eve's role in sin is interpreted as a possibility of her liberation from sexual oppression and male domination under the gospel. This view assumed the equivalence of male and female in creation and interprets woman's subordination as the effects of sin, whereby Eve was cursed to bear children in sorrow and to be under the power of her husband (Gen. 3:16). Virginity, then, is interpreted as the resurrected life of the gospel whereby woman is freed from this twofold curse on Eve of the sorrows of childbearing and male domination. Thus, for example, Cyprian, the great African doctor, says to the virgin: "You do not fear the sorrows of woman or their groans. You have no fear of the birth of children. Nor is your husband your master, but your Master and Head is Christ, in the likeness and in the place of man."[22] This sentiment is voiced by many other ascetic writers, yet, contradictorily, they also speak of this liberation as freeing woman from those "natural" inferiorities of bodily weakness and pettiness, maliciousness and sensuality of mind which are typically feminine, whereas all the virtues that are associated with salvation —chastity, patience, wisdom, temperance, fortitude and justice— are distinctively masculine.[23] Thus Leander of Seville speaks of virginity as freeing woman from the sexual oppression and male domination of the curse of Eve, yet nevertheless speaks of all the weak traits of mind and body, which are contrary to salvation, as feminine *by nature*. The virgin, by contrast, "forgetful of her natural feminine weakness, she lives in manly vigor and has used virtue to give strength to her weak sex, nor has she become a slave to her body, which, by natural law, should have been subservient to a man."[24]

By thus slipping back from what is the consequence of sin to what is natural, and attributing the effects of sin to woman's "nature," the Church Fathers can simultaneously laud virginity as a liberation from sin, and yet, where women are concerned, prevent that from in any way being interpreted as a liberation for a boldness, integrity, or independence unfitting the "nature of a woman." This evidently came up as a very real pastoral problem in the fourth century, when many women were taking literally the Church's ascetic preaching as a mandate for woman's liberation. Thus, for example, we find Augustine writing to a certain self-willed African matron, Ecducia, who had exacted a vow of continence from her husband and had begun to act with that liberty to dispose of her person and property autonomously befitting one whom the converted life had restored to equivalency with the male! Augustine begins the letter by defining the essential subjugation of woman to man as natural law, and decreeing that the woman has no right to dispose of her own body without male permission: "It is a sin to refuse the debt of your body to your husband." Since her husband had once consented, Augustine gives permission for her to continue in the life of continence, but reproves her severely for acting with independence in the disposal of her property and her personal conduct of life, which is incompatible with the nature of a woman, who does not have her own "head" but belongs to her husband, who is her "head."[25]

This slippage between woman's nature as a consequence of sin and the characterizing of these lower traits of mind and body as feminine by nature caused a confusion in patristic thought over the sexual character of the risen body. If woman was essentially body and had sensual and depraved characteristics of mind, then it followed (according to a dualistic view of redemption) that either she was irredeemable or else she was redeemed only by transcending the female nature and being transformed into a male. This is in sharp contrast to the male ascetics, where virginity is seen as restoring men to all those natural traits of nobility of mind and transcendence to the body that are masculine *by nature*. Since it was normal to speak of the virgin who lived the "angelic life" as having transcended her female nature and having become "male" (*vir*),[26] this led to a belief that in the Resurrection there would be only male bodies, all females having been changed into males. Both Augustine and Jerome must inconsistently deny this conclusion, insisting that humanity will rise as "male and female," but in some incomprehensible way that will spiritualize the body so that it is no longer sensual or feels any libido linking the sexes with each other (i.e., having become monistic). And there will be a transformation of the female bodily characteristics so that they are no longer suited to intercourse and childbearing, but are fitted now "to glory rather than to shame."[27]

What all this is supposed to mean is anyone's guess, but it points up clearly the dilemma of patristic anthropology. The Fathers wish to affirm a doctrine of redemption that coheres with the original bisexual creation that God had declared "very good." But since *they* have declared this to be "very bad," and see redemption as the rejection of body, bisexual relations and female "nature," they can only affirm this continuity by peculiarly mutilating these characteristics in their view of both creation and redemption. That woman has a rational mind equivalent to man's is never entirely denied, and indeed is assumed by the view that allows her to lead the monastic life. But since she is somehow made peculiarly the symbol of "body" in relation to the male (i.e., in a male visual perspective), and is associated with all the sensual and depraved characteristics of mind through this peculiar "corporeality," her salvation must be seen not as an affirmation of her nature but a negation of her nature, both physically and mentally, and a transformation into a possibility beyond her natural capacities.

The redeemed woman becomes "unnatural" and "virile" in a way contrary to nature. Such a view not only forces upon the female ascetic a doubled self-subjection of her body and personality but also the duty of that abasement of her "visual image," so that she will in no way appear in the body as a woman before the eyes of the male. It is from this obsession with blotting out the female bodily image that we find that peculiar involvement in the Fathers with questions of female dress, adornment and physical appearance. The woman must be stripped of all adornment. She must wear unshapely dress and a veil that conceals her face and limbs. Finally, she must virtually destroy her physical appearance so that she becomes unsightly.[28] This induces a literal schizophrenia in the relation of the male to the woman; he is exhorted to love her as redeemable "soul," but in a way that totally despises her in all her bodily functions as a woman and identifies all depraved psychic characteristics with femininity. Thus, in Augustine's words:

> A good Christian is found in one and the same woman to love the creature of God whom he desires to be transformed and renewed, but to hate in her the corruptible and mortal conjugal connection, sexual intercourse and all that pertains to her as a wife.[29]

Augustine goes on to compare the relation of the Christian husband to his wife as comparable to the mandate to "love our enemies."

In contrast to Nyssa, Augustine defended the bisexual character of the original creation, defining woman as the original material principle in relation to spirit. What was lacking in original creation was not bisexuality but sexual libido—that is, instead of making the original creation nonsexual, he makes it nonsensual. This view leads to Augustine's belief that in Paradise man would have "used" woman in a completely "unfeeling" way, just as he moves his hand or his foot dispassionately and in a way that is totally under control of the rational will. Specifically, the male would have been innocent of that "hideous" erection of his sexual organ and that rush of sensual feeling that defies rational control in his response to the visual image of woman. With the same rationality and dispassion that a farmer sows his seed in the furrow of a field, the man would have sowed his seed in the woman.[30] Procreation, indeed, is the only purpose for the existence of a female as distinct from a male body. In Augustine's view, then, rightly ordered sex is properly such as to be depersonalized, unfeeling and totally instrumental. It relates to the female solely as a body to be used for procreation—that is, literally a "baby-making machine." When, however, man loses this original justice and succumbs to the body, then sinful carnality, signifying the revolt of the bodily against the intellectual principle, enters in. Then man loses control of his own bodily members and finds his sexual organ responding with an irrational "will of its own" to the female bodily presence, the *sole purpose of which is sensual pleasure*. Thus in the sinful relation woman is likewise totally depersonalized, but now in a masturbatory rather than in an instrumental way. At no time, for Augustine, do bodily relations appear as a vehicle for personal relationships.

Augustine believes that the seat of this disordered affection due to sin is the male penis, whose spontaneous tumescence, in response to sensual stimuli and independent of consciousness, is the literal embodiment of that "law in the members that wars against the law of the minds."[31] Augustine's horrified description of the male erection and its key role in his doctrine of sin and the transmission of original sin usually brings embarrassed laughter from historians of doctrine, if they have the temerity to refer to this view in explicit terms at all. It is usually supposed to reflect some personal sexual hang-up of Augustine's resulting from obsessions caused by his illicit sexual experiences, and thus not to reflect on these doctrines themselves.[32] A personal obsession it may well have been, but one that reflected a collective obsession of Augustine's religious culture. Such a pointing to the erection of the penis as the essence of sin was a bit graphic, but nevertheless a perfectly consistent expression of that view of man and redemption that we have been discussing. Thus there is no way to criticize this particular conclusion in Augustine's thought without finally entering into a fundamental reconstruction of this entire system of theological anthropology of which it was an expression.

But if the male erection was the essence of sin, woman, as its source, became peculiarly the cause, object and extension of it. This, as we have noted, results in an essentially depersonalized view of the relationship to woman. She becomes literally an extension of the male body, to be used either in a masturbatory way for "carnal pleasure," or, in a right ordering of the male body in relation to its "head," in an instrumental way as a mechanism under male control for impregnation and incubation of the fetus. In neither case does she appear as a true "other" or "thou" to which the male relates as a person. Such a depersonalization of woman must be seen as a necessary consequence of the assimilation of the male-female relationship into the soul-body relationship, which implies a subject-object relationship between man and woman. The soul-body or subject-object relationship between the self and the "other," as visually perceived object, essentially abolishes the "other" as a "thou" or a person to be related to with a mutuality due to the meeting of person with person in and through the body. The very soul-body dualism of the Fathers blotted out the possibility of such a personal relationship through the body, and made the relationship of man to woman essentially a subject-object relationship, in which the woman as "sex object" was to be either wrongly abused for carnal pleasure or "rightly used" in a dispassionate and objective (even clinical!) way as a material means or "machine" for the achievement of a further objective, that is, the building up of the implanted male seed into a child.

This depersonalized view of sexual relations gives three basic images of the possibilities of woman in the Church Fathers: woman as whore, woman as wife, and woman as virgin. As whore, woman is wholly the image of that "revolting carnality" that entices the rational mind down from its heavenly seat to "wallow" in the flesh. Here woman is depicted as the painted strumpet, strutting forth with all her natural and artificial allures, the very incarnation of that "fleshly" principle in revolt against its "head" which subverts all right ordering between mind and sense. As wife, woman is also essentially body, but now the image of that totally submissive body, obedient to her "head," which serves the male without a murmur even under harsh and unjust treatment. Such a woman has no personal rights over her own body, but must surrender her body to her husband on command, receiving from such use no personal pleasure, but allowing herself to be used solely as an instrument of procreation.[33] This definition of the wife allowed Augustine even to rationalize patriarchal polygamy, since this was done out of no lust on the part of the biblical worthies, nor did their wives derive any sensual gratification therefrom, but they gave themselves to this excessive "marrying and giving in marriage" only in obedience to God's accelerated command to "increase and multiply" in order to make up that whole of the people of Israel from whom Christ was to be born.[34] But under the dispensation of the Resurrection there is now a third possibility for woman—as virgin. Here alone woman rises to spirituality, personhood and equality with the male, but only at the expense of crushing out of her being all vestiges of her bodily and her female "nature."

However, since man no longer exists in Paradise, where a right ordering of spirit to body in marriage is possible, totally sinless procreation is no longer available. Here again we see the dominance of an antibodily view of redemption over a bodily view of creation in the Fathers. The converted life is not interpreted as giving a new possibility of integrity within marriage or "Christian marriage," but rather it is seen simply as rejection of body. To marry at all is seen as choosing the lower course, not really living in the resurrected order, and hence being under that dispensation of sin which makes sexual relations intrinsically debasing to the mind. Marriage, then, is seen as intrinsically inferior to virginity. It is not debased entirely, since it has the honor due to its instrumental purpose of procreation. But the sex act is only forgiven and not redeemed thereby, and so marriage is seen as bringing forth only the thirtyfold of virtue, in contrast to the sixtyfold of widowhood

and the one hundredfold of virginity.[35] Only continence corresponds authentically to the redeemed life. Many would allow no
second marriage, while those who allow it see it justified only as a
remedy for concupiscence, bringing forth no virtue at all.[36] The
married, moreover, are exhorted to be totally continent except
when about the intentional work of procreation, and even better,
to abjure procreation for a vow of total continence.[37]

The marital act is seen as intrinsically debasing to a woman,
and she is consoled for her loss of "integrity" only by dedicating
her daughters to virginity and thus regaining in them what she has
lost in herself.[38] If she must sink to the lowest position short of
outright evil and become a "mere wife," she is exhorted to be
totally meek and to submit herself, mind and body, totally to her
husband, who is her "head" and has complete proprietary rights
over her body, even to the point of physical abuse or death. The
husband is exhorted, of course, to love his wife, but to love her
"as he would his own body." But this is because it demeans his
own dignity as the "head" to do otherwise, and not because the
wife has an intrinsic dignity as a person or rights over her own
body.[39] Such a theory of the married woman in Christianity not
only did not lift up the position of woman beyond what it had
been in antiquity but even fell below those legal rights to personal
and economic autonomy which the married woman had been
winning in late antique society. Thus the frequent claim that
Christianity elevated the position of woman must be denied. It
actually lowered the position of woman compared to more enlightened legislation in later Roman society as far as the *married
woman* was concerned, and elevated woman only in her new "unnatural" and antifemale role as "virgin."

However, even the total submissiveness of the wife in the
marital relationship does not succeed in restoring the marital act
to that sinless instrumentality of Paradise, according to Augustine.
In the disorder of the bodily nature due to the Fall, however much
the couple intends to perform the act in a totally dispassionate and
instrumental way, the disorder of the bodily members inevitably
produces an involuntary "side-effect" of "filthy" carnal pleasure.
This is forgiven in the couple themselves if it is totally involuntary,
unintentional and despised, their only conscious intent being procreation.[40] However, this cannot remedy the fact that the act, al-

though good in its intent and end, is now inherently sinful in its means. This results in a corruption of its object as well, in the form of a child who is born "tainted" by original sin.[41] Moreover, if the couple intends to enjoy carnal pleasure as well, although not impeding procreation, the act becomes venially sinful, although forgiven under that secondary apostolic concession as a remedy for illicit fornication—namely, because "it is better to marry than to burn." But the Fathers endlessly stress the fact that this "remedy for concupiscence" is only a concession to weakness, and never a good in itself. As Jerome, with his strict logic would put it, "If it is good not to touch a woman, then it is bad to touch a woman" always and in every case.[42] Finally, if the couple intends only carnal pleasure and impedes procreation (and this would include all methods making use of the natural infertility of the woman's body during menstruation, pregnancy, lactation or menopause), then the act is wholly sinful and equivalent to fornication.[43]

Sex is thereby conceived of as narrowly as possible, as either impersonally instrumental or carnally masturbatory, with no role left for the expression of a personal love relationship as a legitimate purpose of sex. Of Augustine's oft-quoted three purposes of marriage—procreation, remedy for concupiscence and "symbol of unity"[44]—only the third falls within a possible definition as a personal relationship. Recent Catholic authors have tried to build such a view out of this "third purpose" of marriage, but Augustine himself never developed this idea of "symbol" as meaning that the sex relationship had as a legitimate purpose the expression of personal love. Rather, the idea remained vague and underdeveloped in his thought as an abstract symbol of the unity between God and the soul, or Christ and the Church. This lack of any development of the sex relationship as a personal love relationship, then, committed patristic thought to a puritan-prurient ambivalence toward sex as either "dirty" or objectively instrumental. Woman in both cases is "used" as a sexual object, not loved through the body as a person.

This same puritan-prurient ambivalence, needless to say, still continues to condition post-Christian society today, even as it revolts against the puritan side of the ambivalence to embrace the prurient instead. However, this new "sexual liberation," as much as the older sexual puritanism, does not liberate but confirms woman as the object of sexual oppression, for in this case, too, woman appears essentially as "body" rather than as a person. Moreover, it is common for the Fathers to regard the sexual act as so inherently "polluting" that even the married who have recently indulged in it are advised not to approach the church or the sacraments. For Jerome and others it is axiomatic that one cannot pray if one is living in carnal union. Either temporary or permanent vows of continence are the prerequisite for prayer, and so the priest, who must pray constantly, should be wholly continent.[45]

With such a view, it is no wonder that the Fathers regard the sexual act, even in marriage, with a constantly anxious eye and exhibit an inordinate compulsion to persuade couples to have as little of it as possible. They hope for that dispassionate sex used solely for procreation, but obsessively imagine to themselves those "inordinate and excessive embraces" in which the couples are doubtlessly indulging themselves under cover of the decency of marriage.[46] They expect the slightest encouragement to pleasure for its own sake to lead on endlessly to riotous, all-consuming rut. In their excessive repressiveness toward sensual libido of any kind (this includes all pleasurable experiences of the body, with sex as only the "worst" of these), they magnify its power to gigantic proportions and image it as a "beast in the belly," which, given an inch, will immediately take a mile. Only the ever-vigilant and total effort to keep this beast chained down to the slightest twitching of its tail will suffice to contain its fierce, mind-consuming energy.[47] Modern Freudian psychology can well explain why such a mechanism of repression was bound to be self-defeating and always to produce its own opposite in obsession with sexual fantasies. Unable to contain this result, asceticism dealt with it in two ways: first, by a pruriency that exercised a perverted sexual libido through constant excoriations of sensuality in ascetic literature; second, by a sublimation of sexual libido that rejected it on the level of physical experience, but allowed it to flourish on the level of fantasy elevated to represent the ecstatic nuptials of the bridal soul with Christ. That spiritualizing of the Song of Songs, to represent the marriage of the virgin soul with Christ, allowed the ascetic imagination to dwell in the most pictorial detail upon the sensations of the sexual act while fantasizing this as a spiritual relationship. Thus Leander of Seville, in a treatise on the training of nuns, speaks of the virgin's mystical communion with Christ as "lying on the chaste couch with the bridegroom, while he encircles your head with his left hand and fondles you with his right."[48]

Even though Augustine's definition of original sin, as transmitted through an inherently sinful character of sexual libido, only brought to definitional form the emotional prejudices of the Church Fathers generally, this view was shocking to many in its apparent debasement of the goodness of marriage and the blessings of progeny, so contrary to the Old Testament view. Jerome and Augustine endlessly defend themselves against the charge of Manichaeanism by arguing that marriage is honorable because of its *good end* in procreation, even though the *means* are debasing. Children remain a good end, even though intrinsically *tainted* by these debased means, so that, without spiritual rebirth, they are not children of God and are doomed to damnation. Moreover, in these latter days God's command to increase and multiply has been rescinded. There is no more need for children, even though they are still "allowed."

It is obvious that such a defense of the goodness of marriage and children, after all these qualifications, became, in the popular mind, indistinguishable from outright condemnation. To the charge that Christians wished to bring the human race to an end in one generation Jerome replies testily that, continence being such a heroic path, possible for only a few, there is no danger of such a result. Both he and Augustine agree, moreover, that the Old Testament blessing on fecundity has now been rescinded by God.[49] This command to increase and multiply was given only to the Jews, the type of the "carnal" people (an interesting correlation here between patristic misogyny and anti-Semitism), to create the physical people of God from whom the Messiah was to be born in his bodily nature. Indeed, God, in this earlier dispensation, even allowed polygamy in order to hurry up the process, although Augustine argues against polyandry on these some grounds, since one man can impregnate many women, but one woman cannot be impregnated simultaneously by many men. Polyandry is also ruled out on the basis of the nature of the man-woman relationship, since "nature allows multiplicity in subjugations, but demands singularity in dominations"; as many members can be subject to one head, and many slaves to one master, but not *vice versa*.[50]

Here we see how intrinsic to Augustine was that assimilation of the man-woman relationship into the subject-object relationship—one of domination and subjugation.

However, now that Christ has been born from Israel and has brought about the reborn life of the Resurrection, the need for physical progeny is fast coming to an end. The pagans, indeed, create sufficient offspring to provide the raw material for spiritual rebirth, and so it would be well for Christians to abjure the first entirely, in order to concentrate all their attention on the second, which is their proper task. Such a strange divorce of physical nurture from spiritual birth in Augustine was doubtless a cause of that almost complete lack of any genuine model of Christian marriage as itself a "school of the soul," such as might have been expected by the New Testament modeling of the Church upon the family. The charge that this view would bring the human race to an end does not discomfit Augustine at all. He declares that there have already been enough souls to fill heaven, and if only all men would follow the Christian example and refrain from the obsolete command to increase and multiply, and rise to the angelic life where there is no more "marrying and giving in marriage," the end of the world would be hastened and the time of blessedness, when the physical cosmos would be transformed into the spiritual New Creation, would dawn all the sooner.[51] Such views in the Fathers show clearly not only a continuation of early Christian apocalypticism but also its linkage with a *fin de siècle* mentality in late antiquity at the time of the fall of civilization.

Viewing virginity as the shortest route to heaven, not only for man but for the cosmos, it is not surprising that the Fathers were assiduous in their urgings of the superiority of virginity to marriage, and dedicated both treatises and personal letters to the task of persuading Christians to renounce marriage for continence. Jerome was the most indefatigable champion of this particular task. One has only to read through his collected letters to be astonished at the number of these addressed to women and which have as their main purpose the dissuasion of marriage and the exhortation to continence. During his years in Rome as secretary to Pope Damasus, Jerome was intimate with the highest Roman aristocratic circles and became the counselor of a coterie of women from these families who cultivated the ascetic life in the privacy of their

mansions. Scarcely was a mother or daughter bereft of her husband
but Jerome had pen in hand to spell out the horrors of marriage,
the disgust of childbearing, and the glories of the new continence of
widowhood that was now within their grasp. They had lost, to be
sure, the first glory of virginity, but the second glory of widowhood
was now open to them.[52] (Jerome, like Augustine, was incontinent
in his youth.)[53] If a mother decides to dedicate her daughter to
virginity, Jerome is prepared to prescribe an entire course of education for the newborn girl.[54] He will be her *paedagogus*, as Aristotle was for Alexander. The child must be kept secluded and never
allowed to stir from her mother's side, so that all independence
becomes foreign to her mind. She must not go to the baths with
eunuch servants (as was customary), because these men, although
they have lost the power for the act, still retain the lewd desire.
Nor should she be allowed to bathe with married women, for the
pregnant bodies of women are utterly disgusting and will arouse in
the girl thoughts about the potential of her own body injurious to
her vocation. After she grows older she should shun the company
of married women altogether and should forswear all bathing, for
she should blush for shame at the very idea of seeing her own
unclothed body. She should be trained in vigils and fasts, and by
"cold chastity" put out the flames of lust. Any food or drink that
will arouse the natural bodily heats should be avoided. Squalid
dress and neglect of hygiene will spoil her natural good looks and
keep her from becoming an object of desire. For Jerome a "clean
body signifies a dirty mind." The girl should not busy herself with
secular learning or cultivated ways, but should cling only to the
scriptures and make the writings of the Church Fathers her only
literature. Banqueting, the bustle of the streets, the sight of
fashionably dressed women or curled and perfumed fops, the social
rounds of high Roman society—all this is anathema. Finally,
Jerome despairs of the child's receiving this proper upbringing
among the myriad temptations of the great city and urges the
young mother to send the infant to him and her grandmother
Paula, so she can be trained in the "angelic life," which, "while in
the body lives as though it were without flesh" in a suitable
environment.

Jerome is quick to transmit the gospel of virginity and abhor-
rence of marriage not only to his intimates but also to recently

widowed women with whom he has only a hearsay acquaintance. His vivid descriptions of the lusts of the eye and the burnings of inner bodily cravings are lavished with as much intimate detail in letters to women whom he has never met as in those to women for whom he has been a personal counselor.[55] Therefore, it is a mistake for the reader to suppose that this detail indicates either such intimate relations with the women thus addressed or frustrated personal sexual desires toward them. The frustration is generic rather than personal, and the detailed prurient language comes forth on any and all occasions as the rhetorical *topoi* of the overheated ascetic imagination. Thus to the wealthy, recently widowed Roman aristocrat Salvina, whom Jerome had never met and who has in no way communicated with him, he addresses this unbidden advice:

> Never let pheasants be seen on your table . . . nor fancy that you eschew meat diet when you reject . . . the savory flesh of other quadrupeds. It is not the number of feet but the delicacy of flavor that makes the difference [i.e., fowl are also to be prohibited]. . . . Let those who feed on flesh serve the flesh, whose bodies boil with desire, who are tied to their husbands and who set their hearts on having offspring. Let those whose wombs are burdened cram their stomachs with flesh. But you have buried every indulgence in your husband's tomb . . . Let paleness and squalor be henceforth your jewels. Do not pamper your youthful limbs with bed of down or kindle your young blood with hot baths . . . Take no well curled steward to walk with you, no effeminate actor, no devilish singer of poisoned sweetness, no spruce and well shorn youth . . . Keep with you bands of widows and virgins . . . Let the divine Scriptures be always in your hands and give yourself frequently to prayer that such shafts of evil thoughts as ever assail the young may find thereby a shield to repel them.[56]

To a young ascetic woman in Gaul, living in spiritual marriage with a priest, who has quarreled with her mother but whom Jerome has no reason to suspect of other wrongdoing, he addresses a letter filled with vivid descriptions of her mincing gait, her pretended ascetic dress, carefully ripped to display the white flesh beneath; her shawl, which she allows to slip and quickly replaces to reveal her curving neck; the enticements of the table and youthful gallants, which she pretends to avoid but actually seeks out; her sexual fantasies and probable fornications with the priest, whom she pretends to have only as spiritual counselor. All this is pure fantasy, since Jerome has never met the woman![57]

Descriptions such as these, which fill Jerome's letters, leave the reader with a dilemma as to how to understand such ascetic enthusiasm that compels such remarkable pruriency toward women, known and unknown alike. This most probably should be taken as the by-product of violent libidinal repression that generates its own opposite in vivid sensual fantasizing under the guise of antisensual polemics. In this his views and psychology do not differ essentially from those of other Church Fathers, although he was more skilled than most in their rhetorical expression. But Jerome may also be seen as having found a somewhat better outlet for this frustration than some others, for he sublimated the repression of physical relations with women into a sincere and deep spiritual companionship with several women friends (unlike Augustine, whose rejection of physical concourse with women was sublimated only into an odd love-hate relationship with his mother, and who saw his conversion as the discarding of any relationships with other women, expressing otherwise only contempt for the possibilities of women as spiritual companions of men). Jerome, however, cultivated a close spiritual friendship with a group of ascetic women whom he regarded genuinely as his companions in the pursuit of the higher life. Although many were quick to accuse him of less honorable designs (and he was ready to return the compliment toward other monks intimate with women), there is no doubt that his love for these women was both authentic and yet platonic, especially toward Paula, who joined him as his companion to build the monastic life in Palestine. As Jerome leaves Rome for Jerusalem, with Paula soon to follow, he writes of this to Ascella, another intimate of the ascetic circle:

It often happened that I found myself surrounded with virgins, and to some of these I expounded the divine books as best I could. Our studies brought about constant intercourse; this soon ripened into intimacy, and this, in turn, produced mutual confidence. If they have ever seen anything in my conduct unbecoming a Christian, let them say so! . . . No; my sex was my one crime, and even on this score I am not assailed save when there is talk of Paula coming to Jerusalem . . . Of all the ladies in Rome, but one had power to subdue me and that one was Paula. She mourned and she fasted. She was squalid with dirt; her eyes were dim with weeping. . . . The Psalms were her only songs; the gospel her whole speech; continence her one indulgence; fasting the staple of her life. The only woman who took my fancy was one whom I had not so much as seen at table. But when I began to revere, respect and venerate her as her conspicuous chastity deserved, all my former virtues forsook me on the spot [his reputation as such in Rome]. . . . I write this in haste, dear Lady Ascella, as I go on board, overwhelmed with grief and tears. Yet I thank God that I am counted worthy of the world's hatred. . . . Salute Paula and Eustochium, who, whatever the world may think, are always mine in Christ. Salute Albina, your mother and Marcella, your sister; Marcellina also and the holy Felicitas; and say to them all: "We must all stand before the judgement seat of Christ" and there shall be revealed the principle by which each has lived. And now, illustrious model of chastity and virginity, remember me, I beseech you, in your prayers, and by your intercessions calm the waves of the sea.[58]

Jerome is generous to the point of extravagance in his praise of these ascetic women. His encomium on Paula, written to her daughter Eustochium after her death, gives us a sketch of Jerome's ideal of the spiritual woman as both ascetic and "mother of virgins," in the double sense of training her own daughters in this ideal of life and becoming the prioress of a community of virgins, next to Jerome's community of monks (for whose physical support she provided her fortune).[59] For Jerome these women are not merely disciples, but they, especially Paula, are in the fullest sense spiritual comrades in the ascetic battle, whom he is happy to regard as peers and even his teachers.

Women in Jerome appear in three roles, the strumpet, the wife and the virgin, but the image of the wife has almost disappeared between the two contraries, the strumpet and the virgin. Marriage he regards as inherently polluting, and childbearing disgusting. He turns warm toward infants only when he can imagine them, not as the verminous offspring of defiling sex, but as candidates for virginity. He can see no reason for anyone to marry except lust or covetousness. To the widow Furis he writes: "Confess the shameful truth. No woman marries to avoid cohabiting with a husband. At least if passion is not your motive [for wanting to remarry], it is mere madness to play the harlot just to increase your wealth."[60] Toward the desire for progeny he expresses a similar asperity. Once having experienced disgusting intercourse, the heaving stomach, the vomits of pregnancy, any woman who would wish to try this again is like a dog that returns to its vomit.

> Do you fear the extinction of the line of Camillus, if you do not present your father with some little fellow to crawl upon his breast and slobber on his neck? . . . Your father will be sorry, but Christ will be glad . . . Let your father do what he likes with what is his own. You are not his to whom you have been born, but His to whom you have been born again.[60]

If the wife is not on her way to continence in widowhood, she is on her way down to harlotry. The image of the "good wife," even in the sense of the submissive wife, is largely absent from Jerome, who paints the wife under the rubric of the nagging, whining bitch of Greek satiric misogynism.[61]

Jerome waxes warm only when describing the virgin and her contrary, the strumpet. The image of the "sensual woman" haunted his imagination even in the midst of his most violent ascetic rigors. To Eustochium he describes his period of severest asceticism in the desert thus:

> Although in my fear of hell I had consigned myself to this prison where I had no companions but scorpions and wild beasts, I often found myself amid bevies of girls. My face was pale and my frame chilled with fasting, yet my mind was burning with desire and the fires of lust kept bubbling up before me when my flesh was as good as dead.[62]

In his violent excoriations of sensuality Jerome can conjure up the most vivid word pictures of all the typologies of the sensual life. First of all, there is the wanton woman herself, with painted face, artificial allurements of ornament and coiffure, her dress carefully draped to reveal her figure, her flashing eyes and coquettish airs. But around her are all the other types of fleshly society; the arrogant matron surrounded with a troop of eunuchs; the effeminate curled and perfumed fop; and also the types of depraved pseudo-religiosity—the false virgin who plays the wanton beneath her dark dress of feigned modesty; the avaricious priest who haunts the homes of wealthy widows; the lusty monk who, under the pretense of spiritual counsel, pushes his way into the very bedrooms of high-born women.[63] In Jerome the acid of Christian asceticism has sharpened the pen of that tradition of Roman satire that was always ready to depict depraved lust and hidden vice in purple prose.[64]

But once women have set their feet firmly on the path of continence, Jerome is filled with warm affection for them. All of his rhetorical skill in depicting the temptations of the flesh and the hidden devices of the mind, by which sensuality breaks out in new forms, is brought to bear upon their spiritual counseling. Jerome turns an ever-anxious eye upon the temptations that beset their spiritual combat, but he is also warm in praise of their virtues. Not only do his ascetic sisters learn Greek and Hebrew more quickly than he, but they speak these languages, which he himself has struggled so hard to master, fluently and without accent. Their exegetical skills match his own, and when he departs for Jerusalem, Marcella takes his place as the leading scripture authority in Rome, to whom laity, priests and bishops turn for explanations of difficult passages.[65] Jerome, however, never allows it to be suggested that even such abilities cancel out the apostle's prohibition against women teaching in the Church. They exercise their learning only with the modesty and concealment befitting a woman.[66]

Their ascetic prowess also matches or surpasses his own. If he has given much to the poor, Paula has given all and has exhausted her fortune in almsgiving and support of the monks. If he has fasted to the point of paleness, she has fasted to the point of death. Indeed, in his encomium on Paula, Jerome paints himself in the role of the moderate, ever fearful for her health and financial security, while she, with far greater faith and commitment, throws all restraint to the winds and puts his pusillanimity to shame.[67] In other words, in those very areas in which Jerome most prized his own accomplishments he is willing to depict his spiritual sisters as his peers and even his teachers.

Not least does he praise these women for their "unnatural-

ness." The virgin woman is seen as rising to a "virility" that conquers the fickle mind and feeble flesh intrinsic to woman. The
angelic life demands the male to rise above his body, but it demands that woman rise above her "nature," crushing out from herself all that pertains to her "femaleness." To Demetrias, an aristocratic lady who has chosen virginity, Jerome writes a letter of praise
in which he says:

> You must act against nature or rather above nature if you are to
> forswear your natural functions, to cut off your own root, to cull
> no fruit but that of virginity, to abjure the marriage bed, to shun
> intercourse with men and, while in the body, to live as though out
> of it.[68]

Moreover, this unnaturalness can include defying the wills of their
fathers, abandoning the responsibilities of their households—the
supervision of wealth, estates and servants which was the economic
sphere of the Roman matron—and even turning their backs on
their children to seek the "higher life." In his encomium on Paula,
Jerome describes admiringly how she left behind her house, children, servants and property in Rome, to the great outcry of worldly
society. As her ship departs from the dock her infant son, Toxotius,
stretches forth his hands and her older daughter, Rufina, sobs
silently on the pier, but, "overcoming her love for her children with
her love for God," and turning her eyes heavenward, she sails out
to sea, with never a backward glance, into the glorious virginal
horizon to join Jerome in monastic rigors in the East.[69] Jerome
even regards an occasional outburst of grief on the death of parents
or children as backsliding into that "lower female nature" that the
woman must crush from her being in order to rise to the angelic
life—understandable, but nevertheless to be reproved.[70]

Jerome's view of marriage and virginity differs in emphasis
from that found in Greek Fathers such as Gregory of Nyssa. The
Greeks are likely to stress more the transience of the goods of
marriage than the defiling character of sex. This fits in with Nyssa's
stress on mutability rather than sexuality as the essence of the
lower nature. Nyssa, in his treatise on virginity, inveighs against
marriage, not by making sex dirty, but by speaking sadly of the
mutability of all worldly loves. Sentimentally he depicts the hand-

some young husband who dies, the beloved child who goes to an early grave. These things are not made to sound depraved, but are merely seen as passing goods. Those who fix their affections on these finite relationships are doomed to tragedy and loss. Better, then, not to place one's heart on passing goods but to look to heavenly things that do not pass away.[71]

Nyssa has a much more positive outlook on married life than do Augustine and Jerome; he was probably himself married and lived in a positive context of Christian homelife in his own family and those of his friends, such as Gregory Nazianzus. Both of these Greek writers tend to view the forum and the marketplace, the entanglements of economic and political life, as much more symbols of "worldliness" than sex; they speak positively of the married household as the place where the woman particularly can practice the "philosophical life" without denying her role as wife or mother.[72] For Gregory Nyssa "virginity" comes close to being a metaphor for an inner attitude of detachment and spiritual uplifting of the mind, rather than being fixed upon the question of lack of sexual union. He can readily imagine the married woman living this "virgin" life in the semiseclusion of the Greek household, without denying her marital and maternal duties, but rather discharging these simply and without overmuch absorption while giving her full affection to the life of vigils, fasting and prayer. In this he had the examples of such notable women of his own family and acquaintance as his own mother and sister and the mother and sister of Gregory of Nazianzus.[73]

Nyssa, indeed, even believes that the person who can combine both the lower and the higher goods in a right ordering in this fashion has the first rank of virtue, whereas only he who is weak of will, and for whom the presence of these lower things will lead to a disordered affection for them, should be advised to shun marriage for celibacy. Celibacy thus becomes second in rank to the ideal state, which would combine the active and the contemplative life in a right harmony. Nevertheless Nyssa believes that such a combination is so difficult that it is in practice impossible for most people. Therefore, those who wish to live the life of detachment and contemplation usually must purchase it by headlong flight from the body, the woman and the world.[74]

One finds in other Greek writers, of course, the more contemptuous view of marriage and the wife, the horror of sex and sensuality found in the Latins. But, in general, the shift of empha- sis from sex to mutability as the source of danger causes less of the obsession with sex as the chief symbol of sin in the Greek ascetic writers of this period, who keep some sense of the Platonic ideal of life as a harmony of goods. In the Greeks, too, we find the portrait of the ascetic woman and encomiums of praise on the new Christian spiritual woman, but unlike Jerome's, these women are their own married sisters and mothers, rather than women who must be wrenched from their context in the home in order to rise to the "angelic life." The Greeks, moreover, generally sided with Pelagius and Julian in their suspicion of Augustine's view of origi- nal sin, and found his excessive emphasis on the sinfulness of even marital sexuality and the transmission of sin thereby unpalatable.

In this twilight period of antiquity, we see, then, the image of the virginal woman appearing as a new cultural ideal, raising up the possibility of woman as capable of the highest spiritual develop- ment, which could lead to the *summum bonum* of communion with the divine, intellectual nature of the Divine itself. Such heights had previously been reserved for men in antiquity, although the twilight of Neoplatonism also boasted a woman sage, Hypatia. Many streams of imagery flowed together to make up the portrait of this "spiritual woman." The Song of Songs, which had been adapted as a Hebrew marriage hymn from the Ba'alistic cult of fecundity, was spiritualized by Origen and made into an allegory of the nuptials of the soul with the Logos, or the Church with Christ.[75] The soul, although masculine in relation to the body, was depicted as feminine in relation to the divine Logos. This feminine character of the soul lent itself to a sublimated erotic imagery that described the lovemaking of the Virgin Psyche with Christ. An- other feminine image was derived from that of Israel as Bride of Yahweh in the Covenant. The Church inherited this image in its eschatological form as the Bride of Christ in the Resurrection (Rev. 21:2 and 9). The Church can also be depicted in the colors of the Sibyl, or muse—that wise old woman who is as old as creation, and who guides the soul on its spiritual path. Here the Church is the mother of reborn souls and the "wise counselor" who instructs the seer in the Shepherd of Hermes. Finally, there is the image of Sophia, who, like Athena, springs from the head of Zeus. She is the Wisdom of God, the daughter of Yahweh, who sits at his right hand and is the mediatrix of all redeeming knowledge (Sir. 14:20–15:8; Wis. 8:2 ff. *et passim*).

All these traditions of feminine spiritual imagery were gathered together into Mariology, which began to emerge in the fourth century A.D. This new praise of Mary, as the epitome of all these images of spiritual womanhood, soon succeeded in restoring to Mary the ancient titles of Queen of Heaven and Mother of God of the ancient Mediterranean Earth Goddess, crowning her with the moon and the stars of Isis, the turret crown of Magna Mater, placing her enthroned with the divine child on her lap in an ancient image derived from the iconography of Isis and Horus, rededicating ancient temples of these Earth goddesses to Mary,[76] and finally escorting her to the very Throne of God to take her seat beside the Jewish Ancient of Days and his son Messiah, who had once ruled the heavens in exclusive patriarchal splendor. The doctrine of Mary's assumption waited for official declaration until the peculiarities of twentieth-century ultramontane Roman Catholicism, but it had already emerged in popular piety in Egypt by the early fifth century A.D. and from there, spread rapidly north and west.[77] Virginal woman was thus bound for heaven, and her male ascetic devotees would stop at nothing short of this prize for her. But they paid the price of despising all real physical women, sex and fecundity, and wholly etherealizing women into incorporeal phantasms in order to provide love objects for the sublimated libido and guard against turning back to any physical expression of love with the dangerous daughters of Eve.

Perhaps the task of Christians today, as they take stock of this tradition and its defects, is not merely to vilify its inhumanity but rather to cherish the hard-won fruits of transcendence and spiritual personhood, won at such a terrible price of the natural affections of men and the natural humanity of women. Without discarding these achievements, we must rather find out how to pour them back into a full-bodied Hebrew sense of creation and incarnation, as male and female, but who can now be fully personalized autonomous selves and also persons in relation to each other, not against the body, but in and through the body.

NOTES

1. William Phipps, *Was Jesus Married?* (New York: Harper & Row, 1970), pp. 142–163.
2. Ibid., pp. 120–124. This view was popularized by the great Church Historian, A. Harnack, writing at the turn of the century.
3. Franz Cumont, *Oriental Religions in Roman Paganism* (New York: Dover, 1956); see also S. Dill, *Roman Society from Nero to Marcus Aurelius* (New York: Meridian Books, 1956), pp. 547–626.
4. G. Scholem, *Major Trends in Jewish Mysticism* (Jerusalem: Schocken Books, 1941), chap. 1 and *passim*.
5. I have worked out this thesis in detail in an unpublished study of the origins of Christology, entitled *Messiah of Israel and the Cosmic Christ.*
6. The Synoptics are innocent of cosmological Christology. It probably appeared first in Hellenistic Jewish synagogues familiar with Philonic Logos speculation by the second decade after the death of Jesus, being taken from this source by Paul in Col. 1:12–20. It appears also in Eph. 1:20–23, Heb. 1:2–4 and John 1:1–13.
7. Origen, *De Principiis* 2, 8, 1.
8. Justin Martyr, *Dial.* 80 ff.; Tertullian, *Adv. Marcion.* 3, 24; *De Spec.* 30; Irenaeus, *Adv. Haer.* 5, 32, 1.
9. For example, Athanasius' *De Incarnatione* and Origen's *De Principiis* develop an anthropology built on the doctrine of the "image" without any mention of bisexuality.
10. Philo, *Leg. All.* I, 31–32; *De Conf.* 62–63; also see *De Migr. Abr.* 174.
11. M. N. Maxey, "Beyond Eve and Mary," *Dialog.* X (Spring 1971), 112 ff.
12. Gregory Nyssa, *De Opif. Hom.* 16.
13. Ibid., 16.7.
14. Ibid., 16.14; 17.1.
15. Augustine, *De Grat. Ch. et de Pecc. Orig.* II, 40.; *De Genesi ad Lit.* 9.5.
16. Augustine, *Confessiones* 13.32; *De Opere Monach.* 40.
17. Augustine, *De Trinitate* 7.7, 10.
18. Augustine, *De Contin.* I.23; Augustine parallels the supra- and subordinations of Christ and the Church; man and woman and the soul and the body. On the ambivalence between an equivalent and a subordinate view of women in the Fathers, especially Augustine, see Kari Elizabeth Børresen, *Subordination et Équivalence; Nature et rôle de la femme d'après Augustin et Thomas d'Aquin* (Oslo: Universitets-forlaget, 1968).

19. Augustine, *De Civitate Dei* 14, 11; *De Genesi ad Lit.* 11, 42.
20. Tertullian, *De Cultu Fem.* 1, 1.
21. Clem. Alex., *Paedagogus* 1, 4; 3, 1–2; *Stromata* 2, 23; 3; 4, 8 and 19; cf. *Paedagogus* 2, 2.
22. Cyprian, *De habitu Virg.* 22; Jerome, *Ep.* 130, 8.
23. Ambrose, *De Cain et Abel* 1, 4; see also Jerome, *Ep.* 130, 17.
24. Leander of Seville, *De Instit. Virg.*, preface.
25. Augustine, *Ep.* 262, to Ecducia.
26. Leander of Seville, *De Instit. Virg.*, preface; also Jerome, *Comm. in Epist. ad Ephes.* 3.5; and *Adv. Helvid.* 22.
27. Augustine, *De Civitate Dei* 22.17; Jerome, *Ep.* 108, 23, to Paula.
28. Tertullian, *De Cultu Fem.* 2, 2.
29. Augustine, *De Sermone Dom. in Monte*, 41.
30. Augustine, *De Civitate Dei* 14, 26; *Contra Iulian.* 3, 13, 27; *De Grat. Chr. et de Pecc. Orig.* 2, 40.
31. *De Civitate Dei*, 14, 24; *De Grat. Chr. et de Pecc. Orig.* 2, 41; *De Nupt. et Concup.* I, 6–7, 21, 33.
32. D. S. Bailey, *The Man-Woman Relation in Christian Thought* (London: Longmans, Green, 1959), pp. 55–58.
33. See Augustine's description of his mother as the perfectly submissive wife even under unjust treatment (*Confessions* 9); also see John Chrysostom, *Epist. ad Eph.*, hom. 13; hom. 22; hom. 26, 8.
34. Augustine, *De Nupt. et Concup.* 9–10; *De Bono Viduit.* 10.
35. Mark 4:20; Cyprian, *De Habitu. Virg.* 21; Athanasius, *Ep.* 48.2; Tertullian, *De Exhort. Cast.* 1; *Adv. Marcion.* 5, 15; Jerome, *Eps.* 22, 15; 48, 3; 66, 2; 120, 1, 9; *Adv. Jov.* 1, 3; Augustine, *De Sancta Virg.* 45; Ambrose, *De Virg.* 1, 60.
36. Hermas, *Mand.* 4, 4; Tertullian, *Ad. Uxor.* 1, 7; *De Exhort Cast.* Cyril of Jerusalem, *Cat.* 4, 26; Minucius Felix, *Oct.* 31; John Chrysostom, *In Epist. ad Tim.* 7, 4; *In Epist. ad Tit.* 2, 1; Ambrose, *De Offic.* 2, 27; *De Vid.* 12, 89, 58; Augustine, *De Bono Viduit.* 6; *De Bono Conj.* 21; Epiphanius, *Haer.* 59, 6; Gregory Nazianzus, *Orat.* 37, 8; Basil, *Ep.* 99, 50; Jerome, *Eps.* 48, 8; 79, 10; 123, 9; *Ad. Jov.* 1, 15, 16.
37. Leo I, *Epist.* 14, 5; 167, 2; Augustine, *Adv. Iulian.* 5, 16; *Eps.* 188, 1 and 220; *De Bono Conj.* 3; *De Sermone Dom. in Monte.* 1, 14; *De Consensu. Evang.* 2, 2; *C. Faust. Manich.* 23, 8; *De Nupt. et Concup.* 1, 12.
38. Augustine, *De Bono Conj.* 3, 15; *De Bono Viduit.* 8, and 11; Jerome, *Ep.* 107, 13, to Laeta.
39. John Chrysostom, *Epist. ad Eph.* hom. 26, 8; Augustine, *De Conj. Adult.* 2, 15.
40. Augustine, *De Grat. Chr. et de Pecc. Orig.* 2, 38, 42; *De Nupt. et Concup.* I, 8–9, 19, 25–26; *De Bono Conj.* 10; *Duas Epist. Pelag.* 1, 27, 30.
41. Augustine, *De Pecc. Merit. et Remiss.* 1, 29; *De Grat. Chr. et de*

Pecc. Orig. 1, 27; 2, 41–44; *De Nupt. et Concup.* 1, 13, 22; *Adv. Iulian.* 3, 7; 5, 14.

42. Jerome, *Ep.* 48, 14; Augustine, *De Nupt. et Concup.* 1, 16; *De Bono. Conj.* 6, 11.

43. Augustine, *De Nupt. et Concup.* 1, 17; *De Bono Conj.* 10, 11; *De Conj. Adult.* 2, 12.

44. Augustine, *De Grat. Chr. et de Pecc. Orig.* 2, 39; *De Nupt. et Concup.* 1, 19; *De Bono Conj.* 17; *De Genesi ad Lit.* 9, 7.

45. Ambrose, *De Poenit.* 2, 10; *De Elias* 7, 9; *De Offic.* 1, 50; Pseud-Clement, *Hom.* 11, 28, 30; *Recog.* 6, 10, 11; Augustine, *De Fid. et Op.* 6; Tertullian, *De Exhort. Cast.* 11; Jerome, *Eps.* 22, 22; 48, 15; *Adv. Helvid.* 22; *Adv. Jov.* 1, 7, 34.

46. Jerome. *Hom.* 80; Methodius, *Conviv.* 9, 4; Augustine, *De Bono Conj.* 11.

47. Jerome, *Eps.* 22, 11; 123, 9; 54, 9.

48. Leander of Seville, *De Instit. Virg.*; Jerome, *Eps.* 22, 6; 19, 25; 53, 7–9; 48, 10; 123, 13.

49. Jerome, *Adv. Jov.* 1, 36; Augustine, *De Nupt. et Concup.* 1, 14–15; *De Bono Conj.* 13; *De Bono Viduit.* 8, 11; *De Sancta Virg.* 9, 9, 16.

50. Augustine, *De Bono Conj.* 17–20; *De Nupt. et Concup.* 1, 9–10.

51. Augustine, *De Bono Conj.* 10; *De Bono Viduit.* 9–11, 23–28; Jerome, *Eps.* 123, 17; *Adv. Jov.* 1, 16, 29; *Adv. Helvid.* 22.

52. Jerome, *Eps.* 38, to Marcella; 54, to Furia; 79, to Salvinia; 123, to Ageruchia; 74, to Rufinus. A third of Jerome's letters and many of his longest letters are to women.

53. *Ep.* 48, 20.

54. *Ep.* 107, to Laeta.

55. *Ep.* 79, to Salvina.

56. *Ep.* 79, 7–9.

57. *Ep.* 117.

58. *Ep.* 45, 2–7.

59. *Ep.* 108.

60. *Ep.* 54, 4.

61. *Adv. Jov.* 1, 41–47, quoting Theophrastus.

62. *Ep.* 22, 7.

63. Jerome, *Eps.* 13, 24–29; 22, 16; 52, 5; 54, 7, 13; 107, 8; 108, 15; 117, 6, 7; 125, 16; 127, 3.

64. S. Dill, *Roman Society in the Last Century of the Western Empire* (New York: Meridian Books, 1958), pp. 125–136.

65. *Eps.* 127, to Marcella; 39, on Blesilla.

66. *Ep.* 127, 7.

67. *Ep.* 108, on Paula to Eustochium.

68. *Ep.* 130, 10.

69. *Ep.* 108, 6.

70. *Ep.* 39, 6.

71. Gregory Nyssa, *De Virg.* 2.
72. Gregory Nyssa, *De Virg.* 8; Gregory Nazianzus, *Orat.* 8, 8, on Gorgonia.
73. Gregory Nyssa, *Dial. de Anima et Resurrect.*, to Macrina; Gregory Nazianzus, *Orat.* 8, on Gorgonia; *Orat.* 7, on Caesarius; *Orat.* 43, on Basil (the brother of Gregory Nyssa).
74. Gregory Nyssa, *De Virg.* 8.
75. Origen, *Comm. on the Canticle of Canticles*; Jerome, *Adv. Jov.* 1, 30.
76. See text and notes in G. Miegge, *The Virgin Mary* (Philadelphia: Westminster Press, 1955).
77. Ibid., pp. 83–106.

Images of Women
in the Talmud

JUDITH HAUPTMAN

INTRODUCTION

The Talmud is a sixty-three volume explanation and amplification of the Torah, which Jews have been passionately studying, probing the depths of, and commenting on for the last 1500 years. It is unique in that it defies literary classification. The Talmud is not exclusively a law code, a biblical commentary, or a collection of courtroom decisions. It does include commentaries on the verses of the Bible, development of legal concepts and their application to contemporary living, anecdotes from the lives of the rabbis, dialogues with non-Jews, scientific theory, medical advice, and individual opinions on a variety of subjects, such as the nature of man, marriage, the world-to-come, dream interpretation, and many other areas of interest.

The Mishnah, the six-tome code of law that forms the superstructure of the Talmud, was published, perhaps orally, around 200 c.e., and included all the legal development from the time of the Torah. In succeeding generations Jewish scholars, rabbis, began studying this code intensively, explaining the underlying legal principles and applying these laws to new situations as they arose.

In the many academies in Babylonia and Israel, notes and questions and answers were appended to the individual laws, and in time this material—the Mishnah together with the explanatory matter, relevant anecdotes, and abstracts of philosophical and theological discussions—coalesced into a work called the Talmud, literally, "the teachings."

The Talmud represents the thinking and legislation worked out over a millennium by brilliant and incisive minds, with the goal of fashioning a community of God-fearing and socially sensitive human beings; it lies at the core of Jewish practices today. An attempt will therefore be made to elicit from this material the rabbinic attitudes toward women, their legal and social status, their role in life, and their most common characteristics.

One approach to the study of the legal status of the Jewish woman in Talmudic times is by analyzing marital law.

BETROTHAL

According to the Talmud, Jewish marriage is effected in two stages: the betrothal, and a year later the marriage ceremony. A man betroths a woman by presenting her with any object minimally valued at a penny and by making a declaration of betrothal. There are two other means of betrothal: by a document, and by sexual intercourse (Kiddushin 2a).[1] Since the three methods of acquiring fields—by money, document, or taking possession (26a) —are so similar to those for marriage, some scholars view marriage as the purchase of a woman, who then becomes her husband's property.

Although the form of acquisition is admittedly similar to a purchase and is probably a relic of the ancient Near Eastern custom of buying a bride, certain other elements of the marital arrangement make it distinctly different. First, property is sold solely at the discretion of the owner, whereas the consent of the woman must be obtained before betrothal may take place (2b). Second, the Talmud explicitly instructs a father not to arrange a marriage for his daughter while she is still a child, but to wait until she matures and points out to him the man she wants to marry (41a).

Third, the Talmud warns against a hasty decision to marry without prior discussion of the relationship, thereby showing concern for the stability of the marriage (12b).

Furthermore, the rabbis provided for a woman's emotional, social, and sexual satisfaction in marriage. Bigamy was permitted, but it was not practiced. A man was not to betroth a woman unless he had first seen her, for fear that he would first betroth her and then find her repulsive (41a). Stipulations to a marriage could be made, but never the stipulation that a man deny his wife her conjugal rights, because that would be violating the essential marital relationship as defined in the Torah (19b). These laws indicate that the rabbis viewed marriage as a relationship between two human beings, each with his or her own set of needs, and not just a way for a man to arrange for his own pleasure and comfort.

It would, therefore, be incorrect to determine that marriage in Talmudic times was merely the acquisition of a wife. Neither could it be said that the rabbis equalized woman's status with man's. It was the husband who betrothed the wife to him, who set her aside for himself, and not she who betrothed him to her. Women were protected by the rabbis from exploitation and had their basic rights safeguarded; men still occupied the dominant position.

THE MARRIAGE DOCUMENT—THE KETUBAH

Before the wedding ceremony takes place the groom presents the bride with a document called the ketubah, an outline of the husband's obligations to his wife. The primary obligation is an outright grant to the wife in the event of divorce or the husband's death. He or his estate is to pay her two hundred zuzim if he married her while she was still a virgin, or one hundred zuzim if she was not a virgin at the time of marriage (Ketubot 10a).[2] Since these sums were not very considerable, it became customary to write in additional amounts. These sums represented the entire claim that the wife had upon the husband's estate.

The husband's other obligations, not usually spelled out in the ketubah, include support, conjugal rights, medical care, ransom— even at the expense of all of his property—and burial. Provisions are also made for the support of a woman's daughters after her husband's death. After the widow's death her sons inherit all the property that she brought into the marriage, plus the *ketubah* money due her from her husband's estate, over and above the inheritance that they share with any half brothers (64b, 61b, 51a, 46b, 52b).

The Talmud also lists a wife's obligations to her husband. The services a woman is to perform in the home are determined by local custom. In some places, in addition to child rearing and housework, she is obligated to spin, weave, and sew clothes for the family. Even if a man can provide his wife with servants to perform all these duties for her, he is not to let her sit by idly, because idleness leads to boredom, and boredom to promiscuity (59b).

Any income the wife derives from the sale of handicraft belongs to her husband, as does anything of value that she finds. All of a woman's assets are managed by her husband for the duration of the marriage; although she retains continuous ownership, all income from them accrues to her husband. Should the wife predecease the husband, he inherits all the property that she owned at the time of the marriage, and any that she acquired subsequently (65b, 78a, 48b).

Another category of the wife's duties are of a more personal nature. She is expected to wash her husband's face, hands, and feet, make his bed, and pour his wine (61a, and Rashi *ad locum*).

These lists of mutual obligations make the legal status of a married woman very clear. To begin with, satisfaction of her daily needs is guaranteed for the duration of the marriage. She is also protected in the case of practically any eventuality, including divorce and even kidnapping. Not only is she promised no loss of status after her husband's death but even her sons and daughters enjoy certain privileges of inheritance.

In exchange for all the husband's obligations to his wife she had to perform services for him, some because she was so bound, and others because she wanted to endear herself to him.

The very fact that it is the wife who needs the *ketubah* highlights her total dependence on her husband. It is he who has all the means of support at his disposal. Even if the wife had independent sources of income when they married, they are taken over by the husband for the duration of the marriage, unless otherwise stipulated. It is the husband who makes all the decisions regarding their life together and who determines the fashion in which he will satisfy his wife's needs. The only restrictions placed upon him by the *ketubah* are that he must maintain minimal levels of support.

Assuming that in Talmudic times, as a result of social structures and conditioning, a woman was eager for a man to take full responsibility for her care, protection, and support, and did not want to make important decisions regarding her own life, or seek fulfillment outside the home, this marriage document, together with all the laws surrounding it, provided a supremely ethical guide to the treatment of wives. If both husband and wife lived according to this set of rules, they would establish a satisfactory relationship: the woman, helpless and dependent, because she would find security and kind treatment, and the husband, protective and domineering, because he would have a wife to take care of his needs.

THE MARRIAGE CEREMONY

While the bride and groom stand under the wedding canopy—a symbolic representation of the bride's entry into her husband's home—seven blessings are recited. They illustrate how the individual Jew, through ritual, links himself up with universal Jewish concepts and values—in this case, theological, historical, and eschatological.

The first four blessings mention God as Creator of the world, of man, and of woman. Another refers to the harmony in the Garden of Eden at the beginning of history, and two more are prayers for a recreation of that harmony in the near future (8a).

These blessings set up a parallel between the rejoicing of one couple in the embrace of the Jewish community, and Zion, the grieving mother, waiting to embrace her children once more. They express hope that the rejoicing of this couple will be repeated again and again by other couples celebrating their weddings in Israel. It was the wedding ceremony celebrating the joining together of two individuals which caught hold of the Jewish imagination and aroused longings for the coming together of other disparate parts— the Jewish people and the land of Israel.

The great outpouring of joy that characterizes these blessings stands in sharp contrast to the emphasis above on the legal aspects of marriage. They capture the rabbis' intensely emotional response to marriage and complement the legal framework by describing marriage as a relationship that generates love and happiness for the couple and the community.

DIVORCE LAW

Talmudic divorce proceedings offer a good example of the dynamic nature of Jewish law. Divorce law is based on the verse in Deuteronomy (24:1): "A man takes a wife and possesses her. She fails to please him because he finds something obnoxious about her, and he writes her a bill of divorce, hands it to her, and sends her away from his house." These words clearly indicate that one partner only may terminate the marriage, namely the husband, on the grounds of any conceivable pretext. The implicit discrimination against women in this legal proceeding is overwhelming. It can perhaps be rationalized somewhat by remarking that women in those days preferred to remain married unhappily rather than seek divorce, because life alone was worse than an unhappy marriage.[3]

The rabbis of the succeeding generations sensed that this biblical law was incompatible with the social situations of their day. Ways had to be found to circumvent this law, since women in certain instances did want to divorce their husbands. Outright abrogation of a divine law was impossible. With this in mind, the rabbis devised a way for the Jewish courts to compel a man to say that he would voluntarily divorce his wife. According to one view, if a woman said "I find him repulsive," the court could come to her aid.[4] Other rabbis felt that this method should be limited to cases based on reasonable grounds, such as denial of conjugal rights, cruel treatment, and the husband's affliction with a skin disease.[5] However, the fact that a woman was given the opportunity to seek a divorce with the aid of the court, even if, according to the second view, she was given less latitude in doing so, was a very significant step in the direction of promoting social justice in this area.

Also reflected in the divorce laws is concern for a divorced woman's privilege of remarriage. Since a divorcée who wishes to remarry must present a proof of divorce, called a *get*, the rabbis made provisions to help keep the *get* valid. For instance, a woman may not be divorced unless she is made aware of the necessity of preserving her *get*, and the *get* must be written in indelible ink.[6]

Underlying the divorce laws is a trend toward discouraging divorce. Ways are provided for forcing the husband to reconsider his perhaps hasty decision to divorce his wife. For instance, he must prepare a document expressly for her at the time he makes the decision to divorce her.[7] This document, which must meet many detailed criteria, takes time to prepare, giving the husband ample time to change his mind.

Discouraging divorce liberated the wife. She no longer had to give in to every whim of her husband for fear of losing him, and was free to maintain her dignity as a human being of value.

The leniency of the laws concerning the "anchored" woman— one whose husband had disappeared and yet could not be proved dead—serve as another example of the rabbinic efforts to circumvent existing law in order to protect rights of women. Ordinarily two male adult witnesses who undergo thorough investigation are required to establish any piece of evidence. However, in order to verify a man's death, any testimony is accepted, including a woman's, and even a child's inadvertent admission.[8] No thorough investigation of the witnesses is required. These special provisions did succeed in greatly reducing the number of women who found themselves in such difficult circumstances, but did not solve the problem completely.[9]

WOMEN AND COMMANDMENTS

The over-all aim of Jewish observances is to make man more sensitive to the ethical and religious dimensions of life. One way to gain further insight into woman's position in Talmudic times is to measure the extent of her participation in these observances and to see what value is placed on her developing these sensitivities.

For the purpose of setting up some general rules relating to women and the commandments, the Talmud makes the following distinctions: First it divides the commandments into two categories, the active and the passive, or the positive and the negative. Each of these categories is further divided into time-bound and nontime-bound commandments. The rules state that women are obligated, in exactly the same way that men are, to abide by all the negative commandments, time-bound or not. For instance, no one, male or female, may steal, kill, commit adultery, or eat on the Day of Atonement. As for the positive commandments, women are obligated to observe only those for which there is no set time, such as returning lost items to their owners. Any positive commandment for which there is a set time does not obligate women, such as praying three times daily.[10]

Although these are the rules, exceptions abound, especially in holiday-related commandments. Reciting the kiddush to welcome the Sabbath and the havdalah to usher it out, attending a Seder on Passover, lighting Chanukah candles, and hearing the Book of Esther read on Purim are all positive time-bound commandments that do obligate women.[11] Other exceptions include study, an active nontime-bound commandment from which women are exempted,[12] and the priestly code of purity, a set of negative commandments that do not obligate women.[13]

The Talmud itself questions the validity of these rules, given the large number of exceptions. It concludes that just because a rule exists, one may not infer that it is universally applicable.[14] The rule is more like an observation based on a large number of cases rather than a prescription for all possible contingencies.

The reason for the exemption of women from certain commandments is not recorded in the Talmud, probably because it was so obvious. Role differentiation in Talmudic society was determined by sex, and therefore if a woman who was occupied with child rearing and caring for her husband and home was obligated to fulfill all the commandments, she would find that religious and familial obligations made conflicting demands on her time. For instance, if both she and her husband were supposed to appear three times daily in the synagogue, their family would be neglected at those times. Since ideal observance of Jewish practices presupposed a smoothly functioning family unit, and since it was a woman's job to keep the home functioning smoothly, the rabbis exempted her from the time-bound positive commandments, those most likely to create conflict.

A slightly different interpretation is hinted at in the Tosefta, the companion volume to the Mishnah, in the phrase "because her husband has authority over her."[15] Since a woman looked to her husband for support and protection, and was under his care, she was not obligated by positive time-bound commandments, because they would make too many inroads into her time and much of her behavior independent of her husband's approval or consent.

What, then, is the reason for the numerous exceptions to the rule, especially in connection with the holidays? If a woman were exempted from attending a Seder, the central ritual of Passover, which retells the story of the Exodus and of God's timely intervention in history, and were her Passover observances limited to eating matzo, her religious experience, on holidays in particular, would be reduced to form without content. The fact that the rabbis obligated a woman to participate in the more meaningful holiday rituals reveals their concern for her total Jewish experience.

There are two further significant developments that affect women's participation in ritual life. According to the Jewish tradition, in order to foster more cohesive bonds among the members of a family or larger social grouping, one member of the group may be empowered by the others to perform a ritual on their behalf, provided that that member is himself obligated to perform the ritual act. For instance, on Friday nights the head of the household, with the permission of the other members of the family, may recite the blessing over wine for them all. They need only respond "amen" at the end of the blessing in order to fulfill their individual obligations. One could think that a woman, too, could recite this blessing for the family. However, no woman does so. The Talmud says, cursed be the man who lets his wife recite the blessing for him Friday night.[16]

Another privilege denied women was being called up to read a portion from the Torah, a regular part of the prayer service. Although no legal argument prevents a woman from being called to read from the Torah, it was not customary to call her up because of the "dignity of the congregation."[17] What this means, apparently, is that it did not seem appropriate for a woman to display her knowledge and ability in front of the male members of the congregation.

Balancing this loss of opportunity is a parallel trend in the opposite direction. Certain commandments in the course of time became labeled "women's commandments," because it was the women who became responsible for fulfilling them. Men left home observance of the dietary laws to their wives. Later rabbis, when questioned on the details of these laws, would consult the women. This phenomenon is already observable in the Talmud in the discussion on whether flour may be sifted a second time on a holiday. To prove that it may, the Talmud cites Rav Joseph's and Rav Ashi's wives, both of whom did so. Rav Ashi relies on the correctness of his wife's practices, claiming that had she not seen it done in the home of her father, a famous rabbi, she would not have done so herself.[18]

Another commandment in this category is the lighting of candles Friday night, a symbol of the festivity and the holiness of the Sabbath. These candles may be lit by any member of the household, but it naturally evolved that the woman, caretaker of the home, assumed exclusive responsibility for the carrying out of this ritual.

The cumulative effect of these exemptions and shifts of responsibility was to exclude a woman from performing publicly, in the synagogue, or even in front of the members of her own family. Her presence certainly was welcome at services, and was necessary at most family celebrations, but her religious role was glorified and her involvement was greatest in the seclusion of her own home and kitchen. Furthermore, the general effect of releasing women from certain commandments, in particular from the obligations to pray and study, has been to turn the synagogues and the academies over to the men. Prayer, an ongoing quest for an I-Thou confrontation with God, and study, the intellectual encounter with God's revealed word, require much time, effort, and skill. Women, because their role in life does not permit them to make the effort or acquire the skills, do not pray with regularity, nor do they delve into the study of the Jewish tradition. These two essentially spiritual experiences of Judaism are, therefore, most regrettably, not part of a woman's religious experiences.

CIVIL AND CRIMINAL LAW

The one area in which no essential distinction is made between men and women is in matters of civil and criminal law. If a woman commits a crime, she is judged in the same way that a man is; if a crime is committed against a woman, she has access to the same avenues of legal retribution as a man.[19]

A few exceptions to this equal treatment can be found, but they concern details. For instance, if two groups of litigants come to court simultaneously, the case in which one of the litigants is a woman is to be heard first.[20] If a man is sentenced to stoning, he is stoned bare, whereas a woman is stoned clothed.[21]

The only significant differentiation pertains to privilege, not personal rights. A woman was excluded from giving testimony in most cases and from serving as a judge.[22] Since women were not trained in Jewish law, it was inconceivable that they should be able to sit in judgment. Why a woman could not give testimony is more difficult to ascertain. However, if it is true that in those days women were more marginal members of society, then it would not seem valid to accept in court their representation of reality.

Some apologists explain this exclusion in terms of women being too emotional, and therefore unable to testify with objectivity.[23] According to this line of reasoning, a woman could not serve as a judge because anyone whose word was not accepted as testimony was consequently not capable of judging, of weighing the testimony of one against another.

LAWS OF INHERITANCE

According to the Bible, a man may bequeath his property only to his sons. We read in Numbers 27 that when Zelophehad died leaving only five daughters and no sons, the women petitioned Moses to grant them their father's share of land in Israel so that his name would not be "lost to his clan." Moses granted their request after first consulting with God. But aside from families with no sons, women did not inherit.

In the time of the Mishnah, some change had come about in these laws, reflecting an initial stage of social redress.

> In the case of one who dies and leaves sons and daughters; if the estate is large, the sons inherit and the daughters are maintained from it. If the estate is small, the daughters are maintained from

it and the sons shall go begging on the doorsteps. Admon exclaimed: "Am I to lose out because I am a male?" Rabban Gamliel said: "Admon's view has my approval."[24]

In this law of the Mishnah we find evidence of a struggle against the injustice done to women by excluding them from the inheritance laws. Although the daughters do not inherit property, they do inherit a certain amount of money to cover their expenses until they mature or marry. Also, depending on the size of the estate, the daughters can inherit amounts greater than the sons. Thus in a few cases women are favored over men, as made clear by Admon, above.

What seems to underlie this concept of maintaining daughters, however, is not so much an effort to equalize women's rights as a protective attitude toward them, making it unnecessary for them to resort to begging. For that reason, in the instance of a small inheritance the daughters took all, and the sons had to go begging. But in the disposition of large estates women still did not get their fair share.

Parallel to this Mishnaic development was another one, also aimed at securing some share for the daughter in the father's property. The rabbis determined that the minimum dowry a father could give his daughter upon marriage was fifty zuzim.[25] If he were rich, he had to give her more, according to his means. Should the father die before his daughter married, the court would determine the amount he would have given her and expropriate it from the estate before it was divided up among the heirs. In such a case she was to receive no less than one-tenth of her father's assets.[26]

The rabbis in later generations defined a way for a father to effect a large property transfer to a daughter after his death, thus circumventing her inability to inherit. If a man who is fatally ill makes a gift of property to a daughter and does not couch the gift in inheritance terminology, after his death she has the right to take possession of her "gift," or in other words, her inheritance.[27] Depending on her father's instructions, in such a case she could be treated equally with her brothers, or in some instances she might even be favored.

These inheritance laws, in addition to the divorce laws, illustrate how rabbinic legislation responded to changing values in society and in turn were in the forefront of effecting desired social changes. The thrust of these laws was to narrow the gaps between women's rights and men's, and to obliterate them completely in this area in the course of time.

"THAT THOU DIDST NOT MAKE ME A WOMAN"

It would be impossible to ignore in this discussion one of the blessings that an adult male Jew recites every morning, not because the prayer is so significant but because it, more than any other passage, has generated so much anger and scorn. The blessing reads: "Blessed be God, King of the universe, for not making me a woman." Women in general, and the women's liberation movement in particular, are incensed by these words, because they seem to imply that women are inferior, and that discrimination against them is in order.

The earliest written record of this blessing dates back to the second century. In the Tosefta, Rabbi Judah comments that this blessing expresses a man's gratitude for being created male, and therefore for having more opportunities to fulfill divine commandments than do women, who are exempted from a good many.[28] Given this interpretation, the words lose most of their sting. They merely reiterate the social facts of life, namely, that a woman's primary concern was with husband and children, and that she was instructed to give familial obligations priority over religious ones.

Another interpretation of this blessing is that it is simply expressing the joy any man feels at being exactly who he is. Similarly, the ancient Greek used to express his thanks for being born a man and not an animal, male and not female, a Hellene and not a barbarian. It is possible that either the Greek formulation influenced the Jewish, or else that they developed independently, since such feelings are natural to all human beings.[29] This understanding of the blessing, too, is not inflammatory, because nothing negative is being said about women, only something positive about men.

Only when this blessing is removed from its context in the prayerbook and divested of its historical background does it assume the pernicious content that is currently read into it.

AGGADAH

Parallel in importance to the legal sources of the Talmud are the Aggadic ones: the portions that record rabbis' opinions on a variety of subjects, legends about biblical characters, and stories about contemporary rabbis and their families, some with legendary elements and others wholly believable. All of these Aggadic materials are included in the Talmud because they are morally charged, because they reflect the editors' attempt to educate the body of readers via a story with whose characters they could identify. The general adulation of many of the saintly rabbinical figures introduced into some of these stories an exaggerated representation of the facts, but at the core of every one is a kernel of truth.

One of the biggest pitfalls of trying to extrapolate a general view of the Talmud on any particular subject is the error of projecting the view of an individual rabbi onto the body of rabbis at large. On any given subject, views can be found that range from one end of the continuum to the other, and no view can be called normative unless it is the basis of some piece of legislation adopted by majority vote, or unless it can be verified by a number of anecdotes about real occurrences.

On the basis of the behavior, characteristics, and treatment of women by others in Talmudic stories, we will try to synthesize an image of a typical woman, or of typical feminine characteristics and reactions in Talmudic times. Any trait that occurs quite frequently will be taken as a trait common to many women and not just to the particular women cited.

A woman's prime function in life is to concern herself with man's welfare and to provide for his physical comfort. A statement reported in the name of Elijah the prophet, and therefore most authoritative, explains how a woman serves as man's helpmeet: she converts grain into food and flax into clothing, thereby bringing light to his eyes and standing him on his feet.[30] Or put succinctly by Rabbi Yossi: "I have never called my wife 'my wife,' only 'my home.'"[31]

Supporting these contentions, the Talmud cites many references to woman's solicitous care of man. Rabbi Eleazar's wife

cooked him sixty different kinds of food to help him regain his
health, and still she was reluctant to let him return to the academy
for fear that the rabbis might torment him.[32] When Mar Ukba and
his wife sought a hiding place and found it in a hot oven, he burned
his legs on the embers, and she suggested that he rest his feet on
hers to alleviate his suffering.[33] This devoted care is also seen in the
ways that rabbis' wives devised to serve their husbands food and
pour them wine during the wives' menstrual periods, when contact
between husband and wife was forbidden.[34]

A second function of a wife is to satisfy her husband's sexual
needs. Such satisfaction will not only cause him pleasure but will
also greatly diminish his inclination to commit sexually immoral
acts. The Talmud assumes that were a man not married, he would
not be able to resist temptation, and that even after marriage he is
continuously waging a battle against his inclination to extramarital
sexual sin. It relates, for instance, that Satan appeared to Rabbi
Akiba, and again to Rabbi Meir, in the form of a beautiful woman
atop a date tree. Both began climbing, but halfway up, their lust
abated, because God had warned Satan to desist in deference to
the rabbis' great Torah knowledge.[35]

An ideal wife, in addition to satisfying her husband's sexual
needs, actively tries to remove temptation from him. Rava's wife
found out that Huma, the widow of a prominent rabbi, had perhaps inadvertently enticed her husband, whereupon she chased
Huma out of town, exclaiming that she would not let Huma kill
another man.[36]

A third highly applauded duty of the wife is to enable her
husband to study Torah. Rabina claims that parallel to a man's
obligation to study is the dual obligation of the wife: first, to
encourage her husband to leave her to go away, even to another
town, to study for long periods of time; and second, to begin the
education of her young sons at home.[37] She, however, is not obligated to study.

The woman in Talmudic literature who fulfilled the first part
of this obligation in a most exemplary fashion was Rachel, the wife
of Rabbi Akiba. It was she who first discerned Akiba's intellectual
ability while he was only a shepherd employed by her wealthy
father, who proposed marriage to Akiba on the condition that he
would leave her to study, who forfeited her inheritance when she

married Akiba against her father's will, and who, once they were married, lived alone and in poverty for twelve years while Akiba studied with the great rabbis. Her reward was that when Akiba returned home, accompanied by thousands of his own students, he told them that all the knowledge that he and they had acquired in reality belonged to her.[38] She was also blessed with a daughter who made the same sacrifice for her husband, Ben Azzai, that Rachel had made for Akiba.[39]

Further evidence of this function of women is found in the story that Rabbi Dosa ben Harkinas' mother used to bring his crib to the academy so that even as a very young child he would grow accustomed to the sounds of Torah,[40] and in the incident in which Rabbi Ahadboi forgot all his Talmud because he acted disrespectfully to his teacher, Rav Sheshet, until his mother beseeched him to forgive her son.[41]

The Talmud chastises men who exploit their wives' sacrifices on their own behalf. A rabbi left his young wife to go away and study for twelve years, and by the time he returned she had become barren. Only after her father, Rabbi Judah the Prince, prayed for her did she become fertile again.[42] Hanania ben Hachinai returned home unannounced after twelve years of study and so surprised his wife that she died of shock. He prayed to God saying, "The poor woman, is this to be her reward?," and she was revived.[43]

The most poignant story of all, containing the sharpest criticism of a husband, is about Rav Rehumai, who used to return home from the academy each year on the eve of the Day of Atonement. One year he did not come home on time because he had become engrossed in his studies. His wife grew anxious and began to cry. At that moment, while he was sitting on a balcony studying, the balcony collapsed; he fell and was killed.[44]

These anecdotes point out that man's academic success depends not on himself alone but on his wife too, because she maintains the home in his absence and anxiously awaits his return. If he abuses her or denies the value of her efforts on his behalf, he is severely punished: either his wife becomes barren, or she dies, or he dies because he mistreated her. In each of the two cases in which the wife was afflicted in order to punish the husband the affliction was only temporary. In the third story the husband bore his own punishment, and no reprieve was granted.

Another one of the demands made upon a wife is to be fiercely loyal to her husband and not to tolerate any assaults on his dignity. When Rabbi Eleazar ben Arach moved to another town, his students did not follow him there. He was willing to move back to where his students were, but his wife would not permit him to do so, because he would be belittling himself in their eyes. Eventually they did come to him, but by then he had forgotten his Torah, an indication that he should not have followed his wife's advice.[45] Although it was her duty to offer it, it was not necessary for him to heed her warning. In another instance, Yalta, the wife of Rav Nahman, advised him abruptly to dismiss his guest, a prominent rabbi, because the guest was mercilessly embarrassing her husband.[46]

Women, of course, raised the children. In Rabban Gamliel's blessing to his daughter upon her marriage he expressed hope that she would never come home again and would always have something to complain about. What he meant by this odd wish was that she should live happily with her husband and not leave him to return to her father's home, and should give birth to sons and constantly say, "Dear me, my son hasn't eaten, or hasn't drunk, or hasn't gone to the synagogue today."[47]

From these stories we conclude that a woman's role in life is only supportive, that a man whose life is devoted to the worship of God, study, and productive, meaningful work outside the home cannot achieve these goals unless a woman stays at home to care for him and his children. In short, a woman's mind and energies are to be directed to fulfilling a man's needs, so that a man's mind and energies can be directed to fulfilling the broader needs of God and man.

Emerging from the numerous references to women in the Talmud is an image of woman's character, or more exactly, of how men recorded the characteristics of hundreds of different women. Needless to say, some of the displayed characteristics are admirable, while others are base. One recurrent trait is woman's great compassion for the poor. Although a man may give the poor money, he does not come into direct contact with them. A woman senses the immediacy of their needs, and responds in her own way by giving them food to appease their hunger. A consequence of her deeper involvement with real human suffering is that a woman's prayers, in particular her petitions for mercy, are generally more effective than a man's.[48]

Illustrating these ideas, we find the following three incidents. Hillel's wife was about to serve him dinner one day when a poor man appeared who was going to be married but had no money for a wedding feast. She gave him the very meal that she had cooked for her husband, and kept Hillel waiting until she prepared another.[49] The people once came to Abba Hilkia to ask him to pray for rain. He and his wife went upstairs, stood in separate corners of the room, and petitioned God for mercy. The first cloud that appeared came from the direction in which his wife was facing.[50] When Mar Ukba and his wife found themselves in danger of being burned by a hot oven, she told her husband that as a reward for her kind treatment of the poor, no harm would come to them.[51]

A woman's compassion for those in pain also seems to be deeper than a man's. When Rabbi Hanania ben Teradion was burned at the stake, it was his daughter who stood at his side and cried out in grief.[52] When Rabbi Judah the Prince was in great pain and lay dying, the rabbis prayed for him, and were thus able to prolong not only his life but also his suffering. His loyal maidservant, who could no longer bear to see him in such pain, smashed a pitcher to the ground, silencing the rabbis, thereby giving the rabbi's soul a chance to escape.[53]

Despite a woman's sensitivity to suffering by others, she herself seems better able to cope with poverty, pain, and adverse circumstances than a man. Her faith in God is not easily shaken by a tragedy. Rabbi Meir's twin sons died one afternoon. When he saw their dead bodies he cried out in despair, whereas his wife, resigned to the tragedy, reacted in a more self-contained way, exhibiting a noble attitude toward death.[54] Rabbi Hanina ben Dosa's wife had no food in the house to cook for the Sabbath; nevertheless she lit a fire on the hearth to fool the neighbors, save face, and avoid charity. When God rewarded her, she chose to postpone the good life until the world-to-come.[55]

"Women are light-headed"[56] is a statement frequently quoted by the rabbis. Many stories describing the actions and sayings of women disprove this statement. A woman's cleverness is revealed in a broad range of circumstances. It is evidenced in a retort made by a rabbi's widow to the rabbis who were in the process of determining the size of her weekly allowance from her late husband's estate. She persuaded them to include an allotment for expensive garments of silk by arguing that they would be embarrassed for her were she forced to curtail her style of dress after her husband's death.[57] A woman in captivity in a brothel succeeded in discouraging men from approaching her by shrewdly directing their attention to other women more beautiful than herself.[58] The mother of Antoninus, later the Roman emperor, temporarily exchanged babies with Rebbe's mother so that the Jewish child, circumcised despite the Roman decree against this, would be saved.[59] A childless couple was once about to separate, and the husband instructed his wife to return to her father's home, taking with her any object of value that she desired. When he fell asleep she transported him, her most highly prized possession, to her father's home.[60] These examples, in addition to many others, disprove the contention that women were considered inferior in intellectual ability. Actually, the "light-headedness" of women usually referred in context to the theoretical ease with which they could be seduced.

On occasion a woman's mind is portrayed as even sharper than a man's. Rabbi Meir used to pray that all sinners would perish from the face of the earth. His wife chided him, pointing out that the verse at the end of Psalms 104 meant that all sin should disappear, not all sinners.[61] A young girl once scolded Rabbi Joshua for taking a short cut across a field. He replied self-righteously that he was only following the path, but she retorted that it was trespassers like him who had beaten out the path.[62]

Several times a woman outsmarts a heretic whose tactic it was to ridicule Jewish beliefs by questioning particular verses of the Bible. An outstanding anecdote in this category relates how Rabban Gamliel's daughter handled the heretic who accused God of being a thief, a claim based on the verse in Genesis that says that when Adam was asleep, God took, or stole, a rib from him. After hearing this accusation, Rabban Gamliel's daughter cried out in distress in order to summon a guard. When asked by the heretic why she was so upset, she answered that thieves had come upon her the night before, had taken her silver pitcher, and had left a gold one in its place. The heretic laughed, commenting that he would be delighted if only such "thieves" were to attack him, leaving him richer than before. She then explained her parable by saying that

Adam was similarly delighted when God removed a rib from him only to replace it with a woman to serve him.[63] In this incident a woman with a keen mind succeeds in refuting the heretic, demonstrating her own ability, and making a laudatory statement about women in general.

Summing up, we find that in all of the stories in which women outsmarted men, the men were deserving of such humiliation. Rabbi Meir had displayed intolerance for people with low resistance to sin, Rabbi Joshua had been insensitive to the property rights of others, and the heretic was guilty of denying God. It was therefore most appropriate that the arrogant behavior of all three men was quashed by a woman.

Another group of stories displays a woman's intimate knowledge of Bible and Talmud. It is difficult to determine what kind of education women received in those days, because educating his daughters was not one of the father's responsibilities. He did teach them Bible, and in some cases, Greek.[64] Rabbi Eliezer, dissenting from popular opinion, declared it preferable to burn the words of the Torah than to give them to women.[65] Despite this view, we find women who knowledgeably quoted Jewish traditions.

One woman is singled out in the Talmud for her scholarship. It is reported that Bruria, the wife of Rabbi Meir, learned three hundred new laws every day and that legal decisions were reached that accepted her opinion over the opinion of a rabbi.[66] In several incidents her knowledge of the Bible appears to have been superior to that of her husband and his students. One day she found a young man studying silently, not making the customary sounds, whereupon she kicked him as a reprimand for not paying attention to the verse in the Bible that says that the only way to retain knowledge is to involve every part of the body in study.[67]

Other women knew the Bible too. A woman once came to Rabbi Eliezer to ask why three punishments, differing in gravity, were meted out to those who worshiped the golden calf, even though all three groups of people had apparently committed the same sin. Consistent with his opinion stated above, he refused to answer, telling her that a woman should apply her wisdom to the distaff side exclusively.[68] But the Talmud does record an answer to her question, indicating that it was certainly a legitimate one.

Women display knowledge of Talmudic traditions also. Bruria

quoted a favorite saying of the rabbis, that a man should not indulge in excessive conversation with a woman, in order to mock Rabbi Yossi, who spent too many words asking her for travel directions to the city of Lod.[69] A woman innkeeper, who asked Rabbi Joshua why he did not eat the food she had set before him, quotes to him what seems to be a rather obscure law, that one does not leave a portion for the poor on the plate but rather in the pot.[70] Rabban Gamliel's sister, Ima Shalom, quoted traditions that she had heard from their grandfather.[71] Samuel's daughters not only quoted Jewish law but actually utilized it in a shrewd way in order to obtain permission to marry a cohen after having been returned from captivity.[72]

Women even participated in courtroom discussion. Rav Hisda was determining whether the precious stone a man had presented his wife for betrothal was worth the prescribed minimum amount. As he was computing its current value, his mother volunteered her opinion that it would be more accurate to determine its value at the time of betrothal.[73] Even though Rav Hisda did not take his mother's statement into consideration for good reasons, of which she was not aware, it is significant that his mother was present at legal proceedings, was able to speak her mind freely, and that her opinion was recorded in the Talmud.

What is rather disconcerting is the fate of some of these learned women. Bruria, it seems, was seduced by one of her husband's students.[74] Samuel's daughters married but died untimely deaths.[75] Perhaps these unhappy consequences are to be taken as a warning to fathers who want to educate their daughters, or to women who want to educate themselves, that they had better abandon their plans for self-improvement.

Another quality widely held as characteristic of women is saintliness. The rabbis comment that the Jews were released from slavery in Egypt thanks to the saintly women of that generation;[76] that when jewelry was collected to melt down into the golden calf, the women refused to contribute their trinkets for idolatry;[77] that when ten of the spies sent to scout the land of Israel returned with discouraging reports, the women refused to lose faith, and were therefore spared the punishment of dying in the desert.[78] Women brought sacrifices to the Temple which they were not obligated to bring.[79] The Talmud quotes a list of restrictions that women accepted for themselves over and above what was necessary, such as extending the period of abstaining from work through Saturday night instead of ending it at sundown, or not working on the new-moon holidays.[80] Some rabbis felt that women fulfilled the ritual observances with greater alacrity and enthusiasm than did men.[81] The Talmud is also full of stories about individual saintly women. It relates how one widow purposely attended a synagogue at a distance from her home so that she would be credited by God with the effort she made in getting there, and how a young girl fervently prayed that no man would unwittingly be led astray by her and thus lose his place in Paradise.[82]

Along with all these positive qualities, the Talmudic stories run the entire gamut of negative evaluations. One of the best known criticisms is summed up in the following saying: Ten measures of talk were assigned to earth; nine were appropriated by women, and the remaining one had to be shared by the rest of the world.[83] Supporting this comment are stories that show women to be excessively talkative, sharp-tongued, arrogant, and outspoken. For instance, when Rabbi Shimon bar Yohai would find his mother chattering on Saturday, he would say to her: "Mother, don't you know that today is the Sabbath?"[84] A certain woman's case was decided by Rabbi Judah. Annoyed at his adverse decision, which obligated her to pay damages, she told him that she doubted whether his teacher, Samuel, would have judged her in the same way. When asked if she knew Samuel, she replied that he was a short, potbellied, and large-toothed rabbi, a description that so incensed Rabbi Judah that he excommunicated her.[85]

Among women's other ugly traits are cruelty, jealousy, vengefulness, and their mean treatment of one another, symptomatic perhaps of their need constantly to compete with one another for men's affections. One woman drove another out of town,[86] the neighbor of a starving woman came over to see what she was cooking for the sole purpose of embarrassing her,[87] and two women bickered with such animosity that they began to curse each other.[88] Women also appear to be superstitious, suspected of being witches, desirous of luxury, and quick to anger.

In this survey of women's characteristics portrayed in the Talmud we have tried to disprove some of the popular ideas of prejudice against women and to show through the recurrence of admirable traits, in stories of one woman after another, that they, too, are part of the composite picture of the Jewish woman of those days. We have concentrated least on the negative qualities, because these are the ones more frequently bandied about, whether in jest or seriously.

We have seen that despite statements to the contrary, women are shown to have minds, use them, sometimes outsmart men, and even educate themselves in Jewish law, long considered to be an exclusively male domain. We find also that women seem to be singled out for their greater involvement with the poor, with the resultant greater efficacy of their prayer in comparison to men's, astonishing in light of later developments in Judaism which released women from the obligation to pray three times daily. The last positive characteristic mentioned, women's saintliness, is perhaps least surprising, because it is still considered an attribute of much of womankind today.

A third area of discussion is the rabbi's attitude to their wives and to the marital relationship. We will investigate whether marriage was a significant enough part of their lives to make them concerned about a harmonious marital relationship and whether a wife was an important enough person to be able to wield any influence on her husband's emotional and social well-being.

To begin with, we will note the very special treatment accorded brides. The two famous schools of rabbis, the Houses of Hillel and Shammai, discussed in detail how to entertain a bride at her wedding. Later rabbis are reported to have danced before her, one did a juggling act for her amusement, and another raised her on his shoulders. Some rabbis felt that it was not proper for a rabbi to compromise his dignity in public in such a fashion, but they were overruled.[89]

This effort to please the bride, even at the expense of personal dignity, reveals the great value the rabbis attached to marriage. Only in marriage, they felt, could a husband and wife fulfill their greatest potential as human beings. The rabbis hoped that the joyous celebration of a couple's wedding would inform the reality of their married life, and that its pleasant memory would help maintain a harmonious relationship.

A man who did not marry merited the strongest criticism of the rabbis because he would not be living what they considered to be a normal life with a wife and children, one that was most conducive to serving God's and man's needs. According to Rabbi Eliezer, a man who does not marry is not a man (Yevamot 63a),[90] and in Rabbi Tanhum's view, a man who lives without a wife lives without happiness, without blessing, and without goodness. Others added, without Torah and without peace (62b).

An ideal marriage in the eyes of the rabbis is one in which a man loves his wife as much as himself, and respects her even more than himself (62b). This attitude toward wives was so important that the rabbis incorporated it into the formula of the marriage document. A man promises that in addition to his legal responsibilities to take care of his wife, he will "worship, esteem, and treat her kindly, as is the custom of Jewish husbands."

That the rabbis considered a poor marital relationship to be a source of great displeasure can be concluded from their numerous statements about unhappy marriages, the cause of which was usually the wife. Rav used to reiterate the declaration in Ecclesiastes (7:26), "and I find woman more bitter than death" (63a). Abaye defines a bad wife as one who serves good food and good curses. Rava defined her as a woman who serves good food but turns her back on her husband (63b). According to the commentators, this phrase means that either she refuses him the pleasure of her company and thereby torments him, or else, euphemistically, she refuses to share his bed (63b, Rashi *ad locum*).

Some of the very same rabbis who lamented the evils of womankind were those who had less than ideal relationships with their own wives. The Talmud records the following information in conjunction with Rav's negative assessment of womankind. Whenever Rav asked his wife to make him lentil soup she made him pea soup, and whenever he asked for pea soup he got lentil (63a). It is not surprising that personal frustration led to general calumny, but one cannot consider Rav an objective, detached critic of womankind whose statements reflect general attitudes.

It is clear from this preoccupation with unhappy marriages that men, although they legally could dismiss a woman on the basis of any pretext, did not do so. Instead, they endured the unpleasantness of poor marital relationships, and contented themselves with making bitter statements about their wives' ability to make them miserable.

It also follows that woman's status in those days was not one of total subordination to her husband. As seen above, the Talmud abounds in complaints about women. This information that wives did defy their husbands provides strong evidence that wives felt themselves on a relatively equal footing with them.

That husbands did not divorce their wives even when they had good reason to do so, and that wives felt confident enough of themselves to seek their own pleasure at the expense of their husbands, could not have been predicted from the legal sources alone. What was legally permitted—what was morally correct—and what was actually practiced could vary greatly. Through evaluation of case histories the extent of these differences can be estimated.

CONCLUSIONS

Emerging from this survey of legal and Aggadic sources is the image of a woman whose role in life was well defined along traditional sociological lines as caring for husband, children, and home, and who was always dependent upon a man, be it her father, husband, or son, for satisfaction of her needs.

Given this framework, the rabbis endeavored to evolve specific ethical guidelines for the treatment of women. Careful not to erode man's dominant position, they attempted to secure the greatest possible good for women. Their most intense concern was for the least fortunate women, the orphan, the divorcée, the widow, and the "anchored" woman. Married women, too, merited fair and sensitive treatment as a result of rabbinic insights into their social, emotional, and sexual needs.

The reasons that the rabbis chose to maintain the status quo—that of a woman's confining herself to her home and not seeking fulfillment elsewhere—were both positive and negative. In order to preserve high standards of sexual morality they had to limit severely the social contact between men and women. With these same goals in mind, they also set down strict regulations for a woman's modesty in dress and behavior.

Second, and even more important, the rabbis guided themselves by their ultimate goals. Since they defined Jewish commitment in terms of activism, an ongoing concern for the welfare of the community, and a quest for a dialogue with God, they had to regulate family life in a way that would lead to optimum achievement of these goals. Before they could engage a man's help for his fellowman, or his devotion to God, it was necessary to provide for his family. The easiest and most obvious way of doing so was to keep the woman where she had always been, at home, because her efficient efforts there would free her husband to fulfill his religious and ethical duties outside the home.

Women's characteristics, as they emerge from these Talmudic anecdotes, also reflect social conditioning. It is undoubtedly true that a woman was taught to accept a supportive role in life, was inspired by Rachel-type stories to make sacrifices for her husband (or rather for his study of Torah), was trained to be soft and feminine, to relieve suffering and ease poverty, and to be content with and make the most of life's circumstances.

Most encouraging are the numerous anecdotes in which women buck the tradition, in which they assert themselves and speak their own minds. Women did not suppress their ability to think and arrive at more logical conclusions than men's in life's situations and in legislative problems. Wives, whether they were justified or not, often defied their husbands, perhaps in a subconscious effort to assert their independence. That Bruria, in many ways the antithesis of Rachel, is recorded in the Talmud, even at the risk of her potentially subversive influence, is most indicative of the fact that womankind was not monolithic in those days, and that men did not force women into being docile, insipid, and shallow helpmeets.

Another observation of this survey concerns the dynamic nature of the rabbinic legislation. Guided by the eternal ethical principles of the Torah, such as the pursuit of social justice, the rabbis found it necessary to alter details of existing legal institutions in order to adjust them to refined social values and the changing perception of man. This trend is true of rabbinic legislation in general, and of their treatment of women in particular. They initiated, for instance, ways for a woman to terminate a marriage. The techniques for legal change based on social considerations which were developed in the rabbinic era were used from that time on to confront similar kinds of problems.

Not all areas affecting women were discussed in this chapter.

The issues of abortion and birth control first became vital problems in the later Talmudic period, and therefore the main body of literature dealing with them is found in post-Talmudic responsa.

Other topics, such as the ability of women to make and keep vows, the rights of a minor sold by her father as a maidservant, the separation of husband and wife during the wife's menstrual period, levirate marriage and a women's release from its bonds, were not discussed because they abound in technical terms and complex issues. However, the purpose of this chapter is not so much to be comprehensive as to probe the relationship between men and women in the Talmudic period by investigation of selected issues.

The implication for contemporary life of the conclusions reached here is that, as a result of the great changes in the technological age and woman's increasing sense of her own value and her potential contribution to society at large, a re-examination of the legal institutions and social structures dictated by rabbinic literature is urgently needed. All traces of legal and social discrimination against women—which usually reflect an outdated social structure—should be discarded. Ways must be found to involve women more in the religious life of the community. Women should be encouraged to develop their individuality in the same way as men. To paraphrase Kant's definition of the equality of all human beings, women should no longer be used as the means with which men achieve their ends.[91]

NOTES

1. All parenthetical references in the text in the section "Betrothal" are to Kiddushin.
2. All parenthetical references in the text in the sections "The Marriage Document" and "The Marriage Ceremony" are to Ketubot.
3. Kiddushin 41a.
4. Ketubot 63b.
5. Ibid., 61b, 70a–77b.
6. Yevamot 113b; Gittin 19a.
7. Gittin 26a.
8. Yevamot 122a, 121b.
9. Ibid., 122b.
10. Ketubot 29a.

11. Berakhot 20b, Pesahim 108a, Shabbat 23a, Megillah 4a.
12. Kiddushin 29b.
13. Ibid., 29a.
14. Ibid., 34a.
15. Tosefta Kiddushin 1:11.
16. Berakhot 20b.
17. Megillah 23a.
18. Bezah 29b.
19. Kiddushin 35a.
20. Yevamot 100a.
21. Sanhedrin 44b.
22. Yerushalmi Sanhedrin 3:9.
23. Katriel, Fishel Tchorsh, *Keter Efraim* (Tel Aviv: Moreshet Publications, 1967), p. 194.
24. Baba Batra 139b.
25. Ketubot 67a.
26. Ketubot 68a.
27. Baba Batra 131b.
28. Tosefta Brahot 7:18.
29. Saul Lieberman, *Tosefta Kifshuta*, I, 120.
30. Yevamot 63a.
31. Shabbat 118b.
32. Baba Mezia 84b.
33. Ketubot 67b.
34. Ibid., 61a.
35. Kiddushin 81a.
36. Ketubot 65a.
37. Sotah 21a.
38. Ketubot 62b–63a.
39. Ibid., 63a.
40. Yerushalmi Yevamot 1:6.
41. Baba Batra 9b.
42. Ketubot 62b.
43. Ibid.
44. Ibid.
45. Kohelet Rabbah 7.
46. Kiddushin 70.
47. Bereshit Rabbah 26.
48. Ta'anit 23b.
49. Derekh Eretz 6.
50. Ta'anit 23a, b.
51. Ketubot 67b.
52. Abodah Zarah 18a.
53. Ketubot 104a.
54. Midrash Mishlei 31.
55. Ta'anit 24b–25a.

56. Kiddushin 80b.
57. Ketubot 65a.
58. Abodah Zarah 18b.
59. Ibid., 10b, Tosafot amar lei.
60. Shir Hashirim Rabbah 1.
61. Brahot 10a.
62. Eruvin 53b.
63. Sanhedrin 39a.
64. Yerushalmi Shabbat 6:1.
65. Yerushalmi Sotah 3:4.
66. Pesahim 62b; Tosefta Kelim Baba Mezia 1:6.
67. Eruvin 53b–54a.
68. Yoma 66b.
69. Eruvin 53b.
70. Ibid., Ibid.
71. Baba Mezia 59b.
72. Ketubot 23a. The only men who are not permitted to live with their wives after the wives' return from captivity are the "cohanim," descendants of Aaron the High Priest.
73. Kiddushin 12a.
74. Abodah Zarah 18b, Rashi *ad locum*.
75. Yerushalmi Ketubot 2:6.
76. Sotah 11b.
77. Bamidbar Rabbah 21.
78. Ibid.
79. Hagiga 16b.
80. Yerushalmi Ta'anit 1:6.
81. Shmot Rabbah 28.
82. Sotah 22a.
83. Kiddushin 49b.
84. Yerushalmi Shabbat 15:3.
85. Nedarim 50b.
86. Ketubot 65a.
87. Ta'anit 24b–25a.
88. Baba Mezia 84b.
89. Ketubot 17a.
90. All following Talmudic references are to Yevamot.
91. Erich Fromm, *The Art of Loving* (New York: Harper & Row, 1956), p. 12.

Equality of Souls,
Inequality of Sexes:
Woman in Medieval Theology

ELEANOR COMMO MCLAUGHLIN

Medievalists today are often sensitive to the issue of the "relevance" of their chosen field of study. When the topic is the theological definition of the female sex, there is apparently even more question as to the timeliness of the medieval perspective, for surely the years between the decline of antiquity and the Renaissance seem to have been a Dark Age for the woman. Because I suspect that this is a widely held view even among readers with some professional interest in the history of theology, I begin this paper with a note on the importance of the medieval period for the history of the woman. Little has been written on the problem of the woman in medieval theology in comparison with other eras of Church history.[1] The New Testament and patristic ages and the sixteenth century have attracted far more attention. Even the spate of interest arising out of the late nineteenth- and early twentieth-century feminist movement produced primarily the "great women in history" type of literature. Those few books on women and the Church that include a chapter on the Middle Ages paint an undifferentiated and quite unanalytical picture of medieval misogyny.

213

There is thus a need for the most basic historical investigation in this area, which is only just now getting under way.[2]

The student of the woman in the Christian tradition needs to look to the medieval centuries to discover what transformations occur in the biblical and patristic traditions during the period that saw the emergence of Western Christian civilization. The classical, antique Christian and Germanic components of that civilization merged and reformed each other into a new spiritual, intellectual, and sociopolitical reality that in many respects created the limits and possibilities of our own twentieth-century world. It is, therefore, a medieval reinterpretation of the antique and Christian heritage that we have inherited, especially at the unconscious and symbolic level. The medieval world was a self-consciously Christian society that produced not only a high theology but also a rich and variegated popular piety of which we have ample record in sermon, saint's life, and Mary legend, song, and drama. Here is the level at which theology touched the lives of the ordinary priest, monk, or nun, layman or laywoman. This paper will at times move from high theology to this second level of discourse, for popular belief, unarticulated assumption, and prejudices, however mysteriously passed on over the generations, are possibly a more persistent portion of the medieval inheritance today than the logical and carefully qualified statements of Thomas Aquinas. As a historian and a reasonably "conscious" woman, I have been continually amazed at the extent to which these attitudes toward the female regarding her sexuality, her roles, and her personality characteristics, reflected in medieval popular piety and theology, remain with us today. By "us" I do not mean solely those who stand closer to a continuity with the medieval Christian tradition—Roman Catholics, Eastern Orthodox or Anglicans—but I refer also to our secularized society, which in its assumptions about the woman and all her works has deep and unconscious roots in medieval culture. True liberation from the androcentrism and misogyny of those assumptions can come only when that past is made explicit and clear in its implications. I trust the accuracy of this statement will emerge from the material itself without any particular effort on my part to draw the parallels and relationships between these medieval assumptions and our modern notions of the female polarity.

A millennium of human history, despite certain continuities

and common themes, is too vast and variegated for summary treatment. The life of Christian perfection open to an eighth-century Anglo-Saxon abbess, and the attitudes toward the female religious displayed by the mendicant orders of the thirteenth century differ greatly in accord with a changed religious as well as social environment. In what follows I will therefore avoid wide-ranging generalization and deal rather with several topics or problems in the theology of the woman during the period 300–1300 A.D. The paper will fall into four sections: first, a summary theoretical statement, based primarily on Thomas Aquinas' *Summa Theologica*, of the theological presuppositions about the female human being. In this section some allusion will be made to the extent of Thomas' revision of the Augustinian monastic tradition, a revision in certain areas revolutionary, but ultimately loyal to the Augustinian patterns. The second and third sections will deal with the two institutions that on both theoretical and concrete levels embraced the actual life possibilities for women—marriage and the religious life with its idealization of virginity. These two life states will be explored at both the levels of formal theology and, to a lesser extent, institutional practice. A final section will refer to the popular misogynist tradition as an illustration of the ways in which the theological world view reinforced social and psychological presuppositions. In each of these areas I have only touched the surface, for the basic research on these questions is yet to be done. However, the outlines of the theological construct and its reflection in popular piety are here evident. The medieval Church's view of *femina*, in all its ambivalence, ambiguity, and even sometimes perversion, must become part of our consciousness if we are to overcome and build creatively on the past.

I

A representative theological framework for our study is appropriately drawn from the work of the Dominican Doctor of the Church Thomas Aquinas, not because he dominated the thirteenth-century theological scene (which he did not) but rather because of his mediation between the patristic and predominantly Augustinian inheritance, which had shaped theological speculation through the twelfth century, and the new naturalistic world view of Aristotelian metaphysics and natural science that became known to scholars in his lifetime. From the perspective of the problem of the female creation, Thomas' enthusiastic adaptation of the naturalism and empiricism of Aristotelian Greek philosophy afforded the possibility of an amelioration of the patristic tradition's dualism and spiritualism with its explicit androcentrism. On the other hand, Aristotle brought to Thomas a complete biology, as well as an androcentric anthropology, which gave a "scientific" basis to the antifemale tradition inherited from the Fathers. The excitement of reading Thomas on women, sex, and marriage is found in the unraveling of the Aristotelian and Augustinian threads woven together into a new whole that is at once more androcentric and less misogynist than the patristic inheritance. This contrast is symbolized by a reference to the personal lives of our two authorities—Thomas, an oblate at five, and Augustine, a young man of passion, father of an illegitimate son; Thomas thus wholly ignorant of women, but at the same time neither frightened nor apparently preoccupied with his own sexuality or the female who by definition threatened to arouse it. I leave further comments on such a comparison to the psychohistorian.

Thomas' discussion of the creation of the human being, focusing, as did the Fathers, on the Genesis 2 account, does depart from Augustine's in a way that has important implications for the nature of the female human being. In accord with Aristotelian hylomorphism, man (homo) is a composite of body and soul, in contrast to the platonized patristic anthropology that defined the human being as a soul imprisoned in the materiality of the flesh.[3] This more integrated view of the relation of body and soul made possible for Thomas an escape from the patristic dualism that identified vir, the male, with spirit, and the female polarity with the earthward drag of the body. Thomas not only defines the human being (homo) as an integrity of body and soul, he gives a positive valuation to the body. The body has an excellence with respect to its end as long as it serves that end.[4] This view might have helped overcome the patristic pessimism about sex and the body, a pessimism that always fed a fear and denigration of women. However, Thomas followed Aristotle and his patristic authorities in their intellectualist definition of man, homo, so that the body-denying dualism and its associated androcentrism were reinvigorated. He did this by determining that the end for man, the final fulfillment of the human being, life with God, is achieved by the operation of the rational soul.[5] Ultimately, therefore, the body is again left out.

Furthermore, in his discussion of the bisexual creation of mankind, male and female, Thomas follows Aristotle in his view that the male is ordered to the more noble activity, intellectual knowledge, whereas the female, although possessing a rational soul, was created solely with respect to her sexuality, her body, as an aid in reproduction for the preservation of the species.[6] Thomas also follows Aristotelian biology in his assertion that the girl child represents a defective human being, the result of an accident to the male sperm, which was thought to contain the complete human being *in potentia* and to reproduce by nature the likeness of its origin, that is, another male.[7] This finality of the female as a mere instrumentality, an aid to reproduction, is the only explanation Thomas can offer for the existence of a "second sex," since for any other activity—work or play—man would have been better served by a male helpmate. Thomas asks reasonably why human beings were not created in pairs like the other animals, answering with the litany of female subordination familiar from our patristic sources: that it is appropriate to the dignity of the first man to be the principle of the totality of the species, as God is principle of the totality of the universe; that the monogamous marriage might be better preserved, for man will love the woman all the more if he knows her to have been made from his flesh; also, as man in society is the head of the family, "in which each has his or her particular duty," it is fitting that the woman be formed out of him.[8] Finally, as the Church takes her origin from Christ, so sacramentally it is proper that woman be formed of man. Her creation from his side rather than his head is a reminder that she is not to be despised.[9] The subordination and inferiority of Eve—and therefore of all womankind—to the male are thus established before the Fall in the order of God's original creation: first, by reason of the primacy of Adam's creation, who was not only first in time and the founder of the human race but also the material source of the first woman; and second, by reason of finality, for Adam displays the peculiar end and essence of human nature, intellectual activity, whereas Eve's finality is purely auxiliary and summed up in her bodily, generative function.

Despite this natural prelapsarian subordination, the male and female do share an essential equivalence in that God created the human race to know and love Him, and both sexes are thus marked by the *imago dei* (the image of God) and the possession of a rational soul.[10] As soon as this is said one must quickly add that Thomas follows Augustine in the view that the male possesses the image of God in a way different from and superior to the image found in the woman, using the analogy of the differences in degree between superior and inferior angels.[11] Ultimately this difference resides in the fact that the rational faculties appear more strongly in the male than in the female, a proposition that Thomas supports with the Aristotelian notion that the inferior quality and finality of the female body inevitably works a deleterious effect on woman's soul.[12] Her sexuality, which is identified with her essence as a woman, involves a weaker and more imperfect body, which in turn affects the intelligence upon which moral discernment is based.[13] The inequality between male and female relates thus to the moral as well as physical and intellectual realms, and it seems to be the woman's body that is the ultimate source of her inferiority and subordination to the male. In addition, even that which is peculiarly the woman's, the generative function, is inferior to the male equivalent, for the man is the active and fecund force, the woman but a passive and receptive instrument. On every level she is subordinate and auxiliary. It is significant that nowhere does Thomas discuss in an extended and complete fashion the inferior and subordinate nature of the female, simply because he assumes this state of affairs and therefore makes little effort to prove what all perceive as given.

The role of the prototypical woman Eve in the Fall of man worsens this natural subordination into the punishment of male domination. Yet a careful examination of Eve's role in the Fall deprives her even of the dignity of clear responsibility for her own situation. The essential sin of the first parents, pride, the desire to be like God, is the same for both, but the motivation was different, and the course of events assigns differing responsibility. Eve, rather than Adam, was approached by the serpent, for she was recognized as more credulous, easier to seduce and, as his mate, more capable of seducing the male.[14] Eve's inferior reasoning ability accounts for her actual belief that she could equal God, whereas Adam never really believed the serpent's promise, but acceded to the temptation out of hope that he might attain the knowledge of good and evil, and out of love for and solidarity with his spouse.[15] Adam's loyalty to Eve diminishes the gravity of his sin; his superior intellectual powers, however, make him more responsible for his act than Eve. Furthermore, in Adam the species of the human race fell, for Thomas feels that if Eve had fallen to the snake's temptation and Adam had resisted, there would have been no expulsion from Paradise.[16] Eve's role was instrumental but not decisive. On the other hand, Thomas argues that Eve's pride was more serious, her sin more grave, for she actually believed the snake, and she sinned against her neighbor as well as God in occasioning Adam's fall.[17] It would seem that Eve's sin was more grave than that of Adam, but somehow less effectual. From our perspective, she is denied even the "dignity" of being successful and independent in evil.

The punishment for the Fall which relates to human bisexuality differs according to the proper function of each sex. The male of the species, who in the original creation was responsible as the head of the family for its material support, must now procure bread by the sweat of his brow. The woman, whose punishment Thomas considered the more grave, suffered an aggravation of her natural state of subordination.[18] After the Fall she became subject to male domination, under which she must obey her husband even against her own will. Also, her peculiar function as aid in generation becomes a painful burden, with the introduction of the fatigue of pregnancy and the pain of childbearing. Even the woman who by reason of sterility avoids that pain is punished by the opprobrium brought on the female who does not fulfill her natural purpose.[19]

Only within the order of salvation, that which defines the end of mankind, the beatific vision and life with God, does one meet with an area of equivalence between male and female grounded in the fact that both sexes are created in the image of God and both by nature desire to know their final cause, God. But the Fall of man requires that this end can be achieved only through the incarnation and redemption of mankind in Christ, and an essentially androcentric Christology fundamentally weakens the theoretical equivalence of the order of salvation. The maleness of the first human being, Adam, is underlined by the maleness of the Second Adam and Redeemer. Thomas deals explicitly with the question, Why did Jesus Christ take on human flesh in the male form, why did he not appear as the sexless Logos? The answer affirms at once the goodness of God's creation, which was in sexual form; sex belonging to human perfection, Christ must assume also that sexuality. But it was specifically a male sexuality, because the masculine sex is more nearly perfect and strong, and because the roles of the Redeemer, as doctor, pastor, and defender, are incompatible with the subordinate status of the woman.[20] Intimately connected with the maleness of Christ is the exclusion of the woman from the work of applying the grace of Christ's action to sinful mankind, the sacramental and teaching function of the priesthood. The priest acts as instrument of Christ's work, an extension of the humanity of Christ, whose duties are incompatible with the subordination peculiar to the female sex. It should be noted here that while Thomas, in his discussion of women and Holy Orders, does make this Christological argument, a large proportion of the rationale focuses not on female disabilities with respect to the divine nature of Christ but rather on biological and sociological grounds for a male priesthood. I will give some attention below to these arguments, which reflect the patriarchal character of medieval feudal and familial structures and Aristotelian biology and are not, therefore, properly speaking, theological.

In Thomas' discussion of the redemptive role of Mary he partly balances this otherwise wholly male Christology. Mary "began" the work of salvation as Eve "began" the work of perdition. That the female sex might not be excluded from this saving work, Christ took his flesh from his mother, but the nature and role of Mary still remains necessarily secondary and derivative. She owes all that she is to the Son.[21]

The true equivalence of the sexes, grounded in the creation of both male and female in the image of God, is given substance only in the resurrected state. There the hierarchical relationships of the order of creation, which correspond to the imperfections of corporeality, are overcome in a resurrected human being, who, though sexed, functions only in a truly human and beatific fashion, that is, with a spiritual/intellectual enjoyment and love of God. Thomas denies the view, held by some authorities, that all resurrected persons will be male. He insisted that equal perfection is granted to males and females in Paradise—a less androcentric position than that of Augustine, who envisaged a paradisical equality of asexual souls.[22] However, the type of activity ascribed to the resurrected state by Thomas is that which on earth is peculiarly male—intellection. The animal operations of sexuality required on earth to preserve the species will be of no use in Paradise, where the individual rather than the species is the focus of attention. Hierarchy remains a characteristic of Paradise, but it will be a hierarchy of spiritual merit rather than one determined by sex.[23] In Paradise there will be neither the pangs of childbirth nor wet dreams nor sweat—a promise that reflects the paradisical freedom from concupiscence with its accompaniment of the pain of childbearing and the involuntary, irrational movement of the male member.[24] Thus the logical equivalence on a religious level of the male and female equally endowed with a rational soul in the image of God is finally and unambiguously fulfilled in the Resurrection. It is, however, an equivalence without active sexuality, in which both male and female function equally as angels rather than as men and women, but an equivalence in which the woman loses that which has defined her very being, the ability to bear children.

As Børresen has so well demonstrated, for Thomas there is in every aspect of the woman's life a tension and often a confusing ambiguity between the subordination of the order of creation and the equivalence of the order of salvation, a tension that can be overcome only when the woman is able to renounce or escape that which has been considered essential to her femaleness, her reproductive function. Unsatisfactory to a post-Freudian world as this spiritualized anthropology may be, it must be pointed out that the paradisical male also was "freed" from his sexuality. For a more nearly complete appreciation of this tension between equivalence and subordination in the relationship between the sexes we need to turn from Paradise to the two earthly institutions that were the arena of confrontation between these theories and the social realities—marriage and the monastic life. We look at marriage and the virginal life—in truth, the only roles officially open to women—as a means of illustrating the Church's attempt to do justice to the equivalence while assuming and reinforcing the subordination.

II

Marriage always gave the Christian Church great difficulty insofar as it empirically involved physical sex. Despite Thomas' Aristotelian naturalism, the married state never quite escaped the Pauline/patristic brush of dualist pessimism, for coitus was associated with concupiscence and irrationality—a disorder from both Greek and Christian viewpoints. Thus Thomas felt it necessary to insist that marriage was not a result of the Fall, but existed as an institution at creation for the purpose of fecundity the multiplication of souls to know and love God.[25] However, he agreed with Augustine that prelapsarian sexuality was rational, without passion, the man implanting his semen as the farmer sows his seed. But within this hypothetical prelapsarian marriage the female was still subordinate to the male, her end auxiliary, procreation. Only the extent and harshness of her submission was less; and as noted, the absence of lust in the procreative act was balanced by an absence of pain in childbirth. Significantly, Thomas follows Augustine in speculating that this paradisical copulation would occur without destroying the woman's hymen: her virginity would remain undisturbed. In this Thomas follows the patristic view that defloration is a corruption of the female body.[26]

It must first be noted that in this fallen world marriage was the least acceptable of the three states of life open to the woman, the first being the virginal religious life, the second continent widowhood, the third "if you must" marriage.[27] After the Fall, marriage became a remedy for the sin of lust, in addition to being the natural institution for the procreation and education of children to love and honor God. By the thirteenth century the sacramental character of marriage was gaining in importance, symbolizing the indissolubility of the bond between Christ and His Church, and conveying grace to the married couple for the fulfillment of the "goods" of marriage. We turn now to the place of the woman in Christian marriage in the context of these three "goods": procreation, remedy for sin, sacrament.

It must be remembered that the woman, defined with reference to her ultimate reason for being as an aid in reproduction, is more essentially involved in marriage than is the male. Her position in the marriage relationship is, however, subordinate and auxiliary from a number of different perspectives.

First, biologically, the woman assumes a passive and auxiliary role in conformity with the inferiority of her body. Thomas grounds this view in Aristotelian physiology, in which the active principle of procreation is carried wholly by the male sperm containing the human embryo *in potentia*, which needs only the mother's "inner space" for growth and nourishment.[28] The sex act performed with the intention to prohibit conception is sinful, not because the woman violates her potentiality as mother but because the teleology of the male sperm is violated.[29] The marriage act also has a fundamentally different and unequal effect on the male and female bodies, for in defloration the woman loses her virginity, and thereby loses irretrievably her bodily integrity. She is never again whole She is as if castrated, despite the integrity of her sexual function, and, for example, is unable to enter certain rigorist religious orders.[30] The biological consequences of marriage—the loss of virginity, the getting and bearing of children—are for the woman, in the medieval perspective, not simply natural processes but poignant and painful symbols of her status as the daughter of Eve and of the inferior nature of her body.

One might expect to find in the second aspect of the procreative end of marriage that these children must not only be produced but must be educated in the fear and love of God, a more honorable and primary role for the woman. But here, too, Thomas emphasizes that the responsibility for the education of children lies with the father, who alone possesses the force and authority deemed necessary for instruction.[31] One of the penitential *summae*, a guidebook for confessors, indicates that in the case of a separation the children should be sent to the father from the age of three years—that is, shortly after weaning—for their nurture as godly Christians, unless there is a weighty reason for leaving them with the mother.[32] Of course, the facts of medieval life deviated from this, for, especially in the later Middle Ages, didactic handbooks addressed to young women and wives witness to the educational role of the mother, especially in religious instruction. Indeed, there is good evidence that in the later Middle Ages among the laity, female literacy (in the vernacular) was far more frequent than literacy in the husbands, especially among the noble classes.[33] However, the theological perspective tended to limit the woman to the purely physical procreation and nurture of the children. The principal end of marriage, according to Thomas, was fecundity, the procreation and education of children, a task in which the man functioned as head of the family community biologically and morally. The physical, intellectual, and moral weakness of the woman required male dominance for her own spiritual and moral direction as well as that of the children.[34] There was occasional mention of the necessity for cooperation between the marriage partners, but this in no way mitigated the hierarchical relationship between the man and his wife. Although Thomas admitted also the greater importance of the mother in the life of the children, he did not see this priority as in any way modifying the subordinate position of the woman.[35] The mystique of motherhood does not seem to have attached to the life of the ordinary woman, but rather to have functioned at the supernatural level: our Mother Mary, Mother Church. In the piety of the mystics one reads of Christ our Mother. An important question is here raised. What impact, if any, did this cultic "motherhood" have upon the life or consciousness of ordinary Christians, male and female?

The second end of marriage, according to Thomas, was that of remedy for sin, *remedium peccati*, a means of taming the fires of lust. (As a method of dealing with lust, marriage was considered morally inferior to continence, the preferred response to concupiscence.)[36] The burning of sexual desire was a part of the punishment for the Fall. According to Thomas, it reflected the loss of original justice, and was a result of the habit of disordered appetites common to all human beings after the Fall. Thus, although Thomas modified the widely held Augustinian view that sexual lust was the cause of the transmission of original sin, still the tone of theological and religious thinking on the subject of the sex desire was heavily marked by the extreme dualism of the patristic view.[37] Sex, even married sex, was in some sense evil, and the sexual drive insatiable and well-nigh irresistible. Hence, throughout our period, in discussions of marriage as remedy for sin, there is great emphasis on the ever-present threat of adultery, as if each partner were driven by endless sexual appetites, which, if not satisfied and tamed within marriage, would inevitably lead to adulterous orgies.

Interesting with respect to our topic is the assumption that the sex drive was stronger in the female, as her whole being was identified with the reproductive function. Accordingly, it was held that the female was the morally weaker sex and more frequently adulterous than the male. "For in women the humors are more abundant, wherefore they are more inclined to be led by their concupiscences." Emil Brunner, writing a Christian anthropology in 1937, also opined that the woman is more sexual than the man.[38] The medieval theological view, framed in accordance with accepted medical opinion, is reflected in sermon exempla and popular tales in which the male authors feature the adulterous wife far more frequently than a guilty husband. Of adultery more will be said below, but first we must look to the means by which marriage dealt with lust.

Central to the concept of Christian marriage as remedy for sin is the notion of the marriage debt, the right that each partner has to the body of the other. This mutual right reflects the element of equivalence that Christian theology, based upon Paul (I Cor. 7:4), introduced into marriage, a truly revolutionary concept that decreed a genuine reciprocity in the sexual relationship.[39] Medieval medical theory assumed that the sexual needs of the woman were as great as if not greater than those of the man. This reciprocity in the responsibility to respond to the needs of one's partner was however defined with reference to the goods of marriage, the procreation of children or the prevention of sin. Thus the general rule established that the partner could never refuse the sexual petition of the other partner, lest such a refusal force the petitioner into adultery.

When we look at the exceptions to this general rule which Thomas and the canonists work out, we find that a pervasive androcentrism undermines this theoretical equivalence and reciprocity. For example, although a woman may not seek sexual relations during menstruation, lest the child then conceived be malformed, a wife may not refuse her mate during her menses, for she would thus expose her husband to the danger of sin, and the remedy for sin takes precedence over the good of the child.[40] A woman must also accede to demands of a leprous husband, though the children are threatened with leprosy; but lest her own health be endangered, she need not live under the same roof with her husband. Thomas assumed greater danger of infection from cohabitation than from intercourse.[41] There is rarely reference to these difficult cases initiated by the wife's petition, for Thomas assumes that the natural shyness of the woman is such that the male must usually initiate the sexual act;[42] this despite the belief that a higher level of concupiscence is to be found in the female. There was another element of medical and folk belief that undermined sexual equivalence—the widely held notion that a male was physically harmed by "bottling up" his semen. Thus the woman in some sense existed to relieve the man, and prostitution could be acceptable as a necessary evil, since male nature requires such a safety valve. The attitude of a society toward prostitution can be a barometer of the degree to which the woman is reduced to mere instrumentality.

The ambiguity of this theoretical mutuality in the sexual relationship is especially well represented in Thomas' discussion of the problem of vows of continence, which are by definition a greater good than the marriage vow. There seems to be an absolute rule that neither partner may, after marriage, take a vow of continence without the consent of the other.[43] As a man has absolute control over his body—a right that a woman does not have—he may take Holy Orders, but he may not exercise his priestly duties unless his wife consents to mutual vows of chastity.[44] On the other hand, some authorities hold that a husband may go on a Crusade (which involves a temporary vow of chastity) without the wife's consent, whereas she has no such right to take the crusader's vow without his permission.

> It is sufficiently probable that the wife ought to be willing to remain continent for a time, in order to succor the need of the universal Church. Hence in favor of the business for which the cross is given to him, it is laid down that the husband may take the cross without his wife's consent, even as he might go fighting without the consent of his landlord whose land he has leased. And yet the wife is not entirely deprived of her right, since she can follow him. Nor is there a parallel between wife and husband: because, since the husband has to rule the wife and not vice versa, the wife is bound to follow her husband rather than the husband the wife. Moreover there would be more danger to the wife's chastity as a result of wandering from country to country,

than to the husband's and less profit to the Church. Wherefore the wife cannot take this vow without her husband's consent.[45]

There is clearly a conflict between the Christian view of sexual reciprocity and medieval society's deeply held belief that a man belongs to himself and a woman belongs to a man. Thus Thomas admits that since a man may dispose of his own person as he wishes, he may send himself into serfdom without his wife's consent, but his new master must allow this wife to claim her conjugal rights. The wife, however, has no right to sell herself.[46] The subordination of the woman, who belongs to the man (although, Thomas insists, less completely than a slave or a child), breaks through even into the one area of equivalence, the sexual relationship. But it is characteristic of medieval society that the tension between the Christian imperative and the pressures of a patriarchal society never disappeared. The capitulation was not complete.

If we turn to the sins of adultery and fornication, which marriage is intended to prevent, we find again this same ambiguity; a revolutionary equivalence and mutuality in theory is frequently undercut by a pervasive androcentrism found on examination of cases. In Roman and Germanic law, only the woman was bound by the law against adultery, for a man became an adulterer only if he lay with a married woman. The Christian teaching on marriage, however ineffectual in practice, did signify a major advance toward a true mutuality between the sexes in its insistence on monogamy for the husband as well as the wife.[47] However, in Thomas, adultery is evil not so much as an offense against the mutual bond of loyalty and affection, but rather because it is harmful to the principal end of marriage, the children, who require a stable and monogamous household if they are to be properly educated to love and honor God. This primacy of the children rather than any community between man and wife accounts for Thomas' view that, in fact, adultery in the wife is more serious than in the husband, for, as she has greater responsibility for the children, her sin touches the whole family. This view is balanced, if you will, by Thomas' reminder that since the man is the morally stronger partner by nature, the sin itself, adultery, is more grave in the male. However, when it came to motives for separation, in actual legal practice it was easier to repudiate an adulterous wife, for despite his insistence on parity, even Thomas held that "in comparison with the good of the offspring, there is more reason for divorce in an adulterous wife than in an adulterous husband."[48]

When we move from high theology to the more popular didactic literature, the "double standard" that we find implicitly in Thomas is represented in all its vigor, as for example in the tract that sets forth the duty of the widow to raise and educate the bastards of her husband's infidelities after his death.[49] We are not surprised to discover these androcentric attitudes toward infidelity in the strongly patriarchal medieval society; what is significant is the fact that despite a theoretical and revolutionary insistence on the reciprocity of fidelity by the medieval Church, the androcentric tendencies of the social milieu permitted, even at the theological level, the introduction of a double standard with respect to adultery.

From a modern perspective, one might look for the beginnings of a sense of mutuality in the context of the third good of marriage, marriage as *sacramentum*. It is important to see that the recognition of the sacramental character of marriage represented an evolution away from the more negative patristic viewpoint in which the evil of sexuality was barely balanced by the goods of children and remedy for sin. In Thomas, the sacrament confers what it symbolizes; thus the sacrament of marriage, symbolizing the union of Christ and his Church, confers grace, which neutralizes and legitimizes conjugal sexuality.[50] The sacramental character of marriage also cements that indissolubility distinguishing a Christian union from the marriage of unbelievers, an indissolubility that was a Christian innovation of great importance for the protection of the woman. However, the indissolubility of the sacramental bond was grounded in the necessity of permanency for the children, and secondarily the moral well-being of the partners (protection from lust).[51] The indissoluble bond was present if mutual consent established a common life together in which children could be reared; sexual consummation was not essential in the view of many authorities.[52] By implication the sacramental character of marriage could raise the sex act from the level of mere animality to a focus of religious and personal meaning. Yet one searches in vain in Thomas for a development out of the sacramentality of marriage of a concept of sexual union as an outward sign, a sacrament, of marital love, fidelity, community. Thomas is undoubtedly the wrong place to look for such a new direction; Dante might prove more fruitful.

This absence of a notion of marriage as a physical relationship that could express or nurture a spiritual partnership for mutual growth and love is striking to the modern mind and requires some comment, for there is an important link between this pessimistic view of sexuality in marriage and the pervasive antifemale bias of of the medieval Church. What is absent here, from our perspective, is the conception of a truly mutual I-Thou relationship within marriage, although this is not surprising in a society in which marriages were arranged with a view to economic or political realities, a society in which the ideal life of love was that lived by the monk. Thomas, following Aristotle, speaks of a "friendship" between husband and wife, but it must be that of inferior to a superior, a hierarchical love comparable to the love of the soul for God.[53] It was a received opinion that a woman was incapable of true friendship, for she lacked the stability and the requisite moral and intellectual capacity.[54] Ziegler suggests that the medieval ethic was wholly focused on *religio*, the vertical bond between the soul and God, and therefore had difficulty evolving a doctrine of loving reciprocity on the horizontal plane.[55] A second and certainly a vital factor is the spiritualized dualist anthropology that Thomas, with all his Aristotelianism, never overcame. Thus physical sex was always suspect and could never be the vehicle of love, which was defined in wholly spiritual terms. The medieval theologian, as well as the poet, made a clear distinction between the satisfaction of carnal desire, concupiscence, and the love that exists between friends or between the soul and God. This theological pessimism about sexual love—and by extension about the female, who was perceived as the principal arouser of concupiscence or lust—was deepened by popular attitudes far older in origin and darker in hue, a demonizing of sex and especially of female sexuality. I refer, for example, to the common beliefs that no Christian should receive the eucharist the morning after he or she had sexual relations, or that a menstruating woman should not receive communion, or even enter a church.[56] Menstrual blood was thought to be attractive to devils and unclean spirits, and a menstruating woman would by her presence sour milk and kill the grass she walked upon, according to popular belief. Similar views on the uncleanness and spiritual danger of the natural sexual functions of the female are implied in the service of the "Churching of Women" that followed childbirth.

This unbridgeable gap between a materialized sexuality and the life of the spirit made very difficult or impossible a development of a view of marriage as a mutually supportive relationship, a school of charity, different from but parallel to the monastic school of love. Furthermore, marriage was always regarded as an instrumentality, excused only by fecundity and its function as remedy for lust. What mutuality the Church affirmed was justified in terms of the needs of the children, not the needs of the partners, except in the negative sense of avoidance of sin. Finally, the mutuality symbolized by the sacramental character of Christian marriage was never seen to move beyond the marriage bed, for in every other aspect the woman's subordination was affirmed, with biblical, biological, and social buttressing. Yet at the same time the role of mother and nurturer of children was by no means accorded the honor given it in the post-Reformation world. Here again Aristotelian biology assured a passive, auxiliary, and subordinate status, so that the mother in Thomas reminds one of the Nestorian Mary, a tube through which the male semen passes to emerge, if nothing untoward happens, a man child, educated and trained by his father after a brief period at his mother's breast.[57] The ambivalence of the Church toward the institution of marriage corresponds with and reinforces the morally and spiritually suspect nature of the female. Both marriage and women are necessary for the preservation of the species, but no positive spiritual values other than biological necessity seem to be found in either.

A sense of the concrete meaning of Christian marriage for the woman in our period can be conveyed by looking briefly at some examples of popular didactic literature addressed to wives and young girls. These can be roughly divided according to two sorts of authorship: those written by clerics or pious laymen (occasionally a pious laywoman), and those written by laymen in the context of a courtly love ethic. There are some very interesting differences between these two genres which will be noted below.

All of these works reflect the fact that, according to the accepted views, two life styles were available for the woman, either that of the obedient wife and fruitful mother or that of the religious; for both the young unmarried girl and the widows of whatever age were supposed to live like nuns even in their own homes.[58] Augustine's view long remained normative, at least among churchmen: that the fecundity of a married woman was not comparable in value to the fecundity of the virgin, who produced souls for Christ.[59]

Instructions addressed to the wife typically emphasize that the domain of the woman is the house. She should not wish to go out too often or ask about her husband's business, says one tract addressed to the good wife which Hentsch suggests may have been written by a woman.[60] Another recurrent theme is the necessity of obedience and honor to the husband, for "God has commanded that the woman be always in submission; as a young girl, she obeys her parents and masters, later her husband, or if she becomes a religious, the rule and her superior."[61]

Books written for girls in the context of courtly love are characterized by an emphasis on adapting behavior so as always to please the men, with great attention to appearance. The girl must be clean, bathe often, use perfume so that her lover believes her body full of flowers.[62] The treatis *La Cour d'amour* reminds the girl that she should speak only rarely and never at meals, and that she needs little intelligence; Philippe de Novaire would not have her learn to read lest she be exposed to evil.[63] Both the clerical and courtly literatures rail against the presumed female characteristic of endless and meaningless chatter. The courtly literature insists that a girl's sole aim in life is to prepare herself to marry. An Italian nobleman describes the two duties of a married woman: to be faithful to her husband, even if he is unfaithful, and to want to have children. The education of those children is rarely mentioned; in this Italian tract it is included among the widow's duties, for as long as the father is alive, he remains responsible for the children's schooling.[64] The Chevalier de la Tour Landry, a late fourteenth-century English gentleman, in a well-known instruction for his three daughters, also refers to the necessity of avoiding jealousy and giving the husband complete liberty. Obedience must be implicit, especially in public, and the husband must be supported even if evil, "for God has given him to you—and besides, the more evil a husband, the more important is a good wife."[65] Here we see the emergence of the more familiar double standard, the identification of the wife with virtue and piety.

Our observation of the relatively unimportant role of the psychological in contrast to the physical aspects of motherhood in the theological picture of the woman and marriage during the early and high Middle Ages is borne out by this popular literature, which gives almost no attention to child rearing in the instructions to the wife; the stress is wholly on the importance of her fecundity. In general, the emphasis in the popular courtly literature is placed on learning the modes of external behavior that will please a husband. However, there is discernible an important difference in tone between the more religious tracts and those written within a courtly context. Despite the brief compass of my sample, I find it possible to see in those instructions written in a religious vein a far greater respect for the woman as a person with a mind. Saint Louis, Louis IX of France, in an admonition to his daughter Isabelle insisted that she learn to read and be able to discuss religious subjects with serious persons.[66] The manuals for women written by courtiers give more attention to the smell and appearance of the lady, explicitly de-emphasize her mind, worry about her constancy, and in general discuss the female as an object of pleasure whose first duty is to please men and whose indispensable quality is beauty. If morality is dwelt upon, it is that which touches the male ego, honesty and constancy.[67] Any idealization of the woman is chastened by social realities. One thirteenth-century courtier observes that the value and fame of a woman depend on the standing and fame of her lover; therefore choose well, advises the gentleman.[68] In contemporary language, the secular texts treat the woman as a sex object, whereas those written in the context of piety reflect, if ever so dimly, that twofold nature of Christian marriage of which the theologians spoke—an area of equivalence remains alongside the natural subordination. There is no question but that the evolution during the twelfth and thirteenth centuries of the Church's insistence on *consent* as the prerequisite of Christian marriage marked a significant advance for women over the earlier Germanic view of marriage as a purely financial contract often involving abduction or unilateral repudiation. Furthermore, within the religious context the woman had a choice: she could elect virginity and the religious life as an alternative to marriage.

The root of this freedom is, of course, the theological fact that the woman, possessing an immortal soul, can be called to follow God rather than an earthly father, husband, or lover.[69] There is thus a limitation, at least in theory, to the totality of the bondage. And there is also an alternative.

III

We turn now to that better life through which the woman can in theory escape the natural subordination and inferiority to which she is ordained by her sex. That option is the virginal life, to which both males and females may be called by God for the pursuit of religious perfection while on earth. The monastic life, which is the highest institutional expression of the call to virginity, is also the single institutional reflection of the religious equivalence of the sexes. Yet here, too, as in marriage, we find that a deep-seated androcentrism, reflecting on ambivalent theology and a patriarchal society, permeated even those areas theoretically committed to equivalence.

First we look to the theoretical basis, the call to virginity, as the prerequisite of religious perfection. While under the old law the command "be fruitful and multiply" was a precept, it was assumed that after the Incarnation the world population had reached an adequate level and the task before the Christian peoples was the conversion of existing souls. The call to fecundity abrogated, the more perfect life was that of sexual abstinence. There were two fundamental reasons for this view: first, all human action, thought, and love should be directed toward God, but sexual activity and attachments distract from that proper end for man; second, sexual activity involves a loss of consciousness and rational control, thus enfeebling intellectual activity. Continence stimulates that which is properly human, the power of reason, and promotes the recovery of the state of human nature before the Fall. Virginity involves the human being in spiritual rather than corporeal goods. It promotes the proper finality of the individual—life with God; whereas marriage promotes only the good of the species—procreation. Thomas, citing Augustine, expressed these values in a baldly androcentric fashion: "I consider that nothing so casts down the manly mind from its heights as the fondling of women, and those bodily contacts which belong to the married state."[70]

We have already indicated the revolutionary character of Christianity in its insistence on the equivalence of the sexes with respect to sexual fidelity in marriage. That equivalence is spelled out with insistence in the patristic era with respect to the call to virginity and religious perfection. Ultimately the Fathers of the early Christian centuries agreed that both sexes are created with a rational soul in the image of God, and accordingly, that both are called to the same end, life with God. Despite subordination on the level of creation, the order of salvation offers equality between the sexes. This was a new ideal in the late Hellenistic world, in which religion and philosophy often limited the heights of spiritual perfection to males. The startlingly prominent public role taken by women in the New Testament Church is probably reflective of the impact of this revolutionary Christian attitude in the first century of the Church's life. However, it is important to see how that theoretical equivalence between the sexes on the religious level was from the first undercut by fundamentally androcentric conceptions. In the patristic world the very idealization of virginity, which made it possible for a woman to pursue a religious life equal to that of the male, free of male domination, contained within itself the heavy burden of fear of the female as the ever-present threat to continence that underlies much of patristic misogyny.[71] The association of the mind/flesh dualism with the male/female bipolarity, of which Rosemary Ruether speaks in Chapter 5 of this book, lays the groundwork for a different and unequal definition of virginity as it is applied to the female. Thus only the female, whose whole existence and finality are bound up in her auxiliary procreative function, must deny what the society defined as her nature in order to follow the religious life. This suggestion is illustrated in the patristic adaptation of the classical ideal of the *virago*,[72] the female military hero who achieves equivalence, or indeed eminence, in the world by becoming not a great woman but, as it were, a man (*vir*).[73] For the female, virginity is not an affirmation of her being as a woman but an assumption of the nature of the male, which is identified with the truly human: rationality, strength, courage, steadfastness, loyalty. Early medieval saints' lives display this ideal quite as openly as did the more misogynist Fathers; Ratherius of

Verona writes of the manly Christian woman who forgets her natural weakness and through God's grace wins great battles against evil.[74] But even the masculinized female saint never wholly escapes her female dependence and weakness, for in the idealized portrait she is often the bride of Christ, her weakness by nature overcome by the strength of Christ.[75] One might object that the ideal of virginity demanded of both men and women a denial of their sexuality, of fatherhood as well as motherhood. That is of course correct, but what I am saying is that the male, already defined in terms of a superior rationality, with its possibility of self-transcendence, was upon entering the religious life, in contrast to the woman, denying something quite literally external to his being. There is need to examine the medieval literature of instruction and admonition for male and female religious to explore these suggestions further.

In another aspect of the theoretical realm the religious equivalence of male and female is fundamentally undermined by the Church's development of a rationale for the denial to the woman of Holy Orders. Here the maleness of God and the Incarnation provide the foundations for this aspect of female insufficiency, for as Christ's humanity was of necessity male, the instrument of his grace, the priest, corresponding to the instrumentality of His flesh, must also be male. Furthermore, ordination confers a superiority of rank that cannot be received by one who is by the order of creation in a state of subjection. Thus the woman, like the slave, may not validly receive Holy Orders.[76] As the Church lives in the world, it properly follows the laws of society with respect to the subordinate status of the female. These arguments reflect the fundamentally sociological character of much of Thomas' discussion of the prohibition of women in Holy Orders. They presuppose the patriarchal and hierarchical structures of a premodern society. Thomas never explicitly forbids the priesthood to women, nor does he say directly, as Bonaventura did, that because Christ was male, so also his priests must be men.[77] Indeed, in Thomas' discussion of baptism, in an emergency he allows a laywoman as well as a layman to baptize validly as Christ's minister, citing Galatians 3 that in Christ there is neither male nor female. However, a woman performs this office instrumentally, by virtue of Christ's power, not by virtue of her spiritual equivalence to a layman, and her subordinate status is symbolized by the fact that she can baptize without incurring sin only privately and in the absence of an available male.[78] Without doubt for many reasons, having perhaps most of all to do with ancient and subconscious cultic taboos, Thomas would have abhorred the idea of female priests, but given the overwhelmingly androcentric character of thirteenth-century society and theology, he was less insistent on the theological necessity of a male priesthood than he might have been.

The equivalence of the female soul to that of the male here on earth is acknowledged only in the admission of the possibility of a woman receiving gifts of the Holy Spirit, gifts of prophecy. But even these outpourings of the Spirit of God may not be exercised publicly, for (1) the woman stands under the punishment of domination and may not exercise authority, (2) her public activity could endanger men by arousing lust, and (3) her lack of wisdom limits her to the private sphere.[79] The inadmissability of a female priesthood is an excellent example of the Church's ambivalence toward its own insistence on the spiritual equivalence of the sexes.

We turn for further examples of this ambivalence between spiritual equality and androcentrism to the historical development of the monastic life, in which the call to religious perfection was institutionalized. Again no claim is made here to completeness; we cannot survey the history of the role of women in the monastic tradition, for such a history is yet to be written. Rather, we look at selected examples from monastic history which illustrate the ambivalence, ambiguity, and conflict between subordination and equivalence, hoping to raise questions and problems in the history of monasticism which can be a useful focus for further study.

As already indicated, there was, in contrast to Jewish practice, an astonishing level of female participation in early Christian religious life. Even after the suppression of the orders of deaconesses and widows, partially in response to the Gnostic threat and its female eccentrics, numbers of the Fathers of the first five centuries accepted individual women as their spiritual friends, as equals, even mentors in the spiritual life.[80] Women also shared in the early history of monasticism. Female hermits, anchorites, and cenobites were widespread in East and West. Especially interesting is the early medieval institution of the double monastery, which probably had its origins in the practical needs of the female conventuals, who required agricultural help in the fields and priests to celebrate mass, hear confessions, and provide pastoral guidance.[81] What is interesting with respect to later developments is the authority and jurisdiction given to the abbess in some of these early double foundations, especially in Anglo-Saxon England, where the double monasteries were prevalent in the seventh and eighth centuries and were frequently led by women. Furthermore, this female leadership was not perceived as unusual by witnesses such as Bede. In addition to their administrative and teaching functions, a number of these women actually became missionaries, requested by Boniface to help him in the conversion of Germany. Othlon records six men and six women who left England to aid Boniface, the women founding monasteries, as did the men—Chunitrud in Bavaria, Tecla in Kitzingen, Leoba at Bischofsheim, Walpurgis succeeding her brother as abbess of Heidenheim. Leoba was Boniface's special companion whom he requested to have buried beside him after their death. These women were learned in scripture; they taught; they administered great religious houses; they missionized alongside the men, and without any hint in the sources that these public roles were improper for women.[82] Their life was active; not, as in the case with the later type of medieval female religious, wholly cloistered and contemplative. One irresistibly asks for an explanation for this unusual equivalence, an explanation for the existence of female saints and abbesses so indistinguishable in action from their male counterparts. Some suggest that the predominance of royal blood among these eminent Anglo-Saxon women provides an answer, for queens and noblewomen were always less tainted by Eve's disabilities in medieval society than their more humble sisters. Perhaps even more fruitful is the sociological approach, involving a close analysis of pre-Norman English society with respect to the relationship between its still relatively simple structures and the functional roles assigned to males and females in various status groups.[83] Whatever the answer, there seems to be found in Anglo-Saxon monasticism an effective equality between the sexes which belies the closeness of those centuries to the deeply misogynist patristic tradition.

What a different and infinitely more complex situation is to be found when we move into the high Middle Ages, the era of the first great revival and revolution in monastic piety, the idealization of the *vita apostolica,* a life of poverty and preaching, with its new rigorism and new forms of monastic organization. The students of this "religious movement," beginning with the fundamental work of Herbert Grundmann, have all remarked on the broadly based and numerically important response of women to these new modes in the pursuit of religious perfection.[84] Indeed, Grundmann suggests, without really pursuing the idea, that the flood of women to the hermitages, to the wandering preachers, and to the newly rigorist and observantist monastic foundations may well have powerfully shaped the content of the rich ideal of the *vita apostolica* rather than simply representing a female response to ideals originated and articulated by the men alone.[85] This possibility needs to be explored, just as the role of women in the formulation of thirteenth- and fourteenth-century mystical piety requires further examination. However, the aspect of this outburst of female enthusiasm for the new forms of piety to which we turn here is more institutional in focus. Specifically I wish to point out the host of unsolved questions surrounding the ambivalent response of the male religious orders to these women and their spiritual aspirations.

Initially the explosion of female piety following the Gregorian reform was greeted with open enthusiasm both by those men who called for a more rigorous observance of Benedictine monasticism and by those wandering preachers of the *vita apostolica* who advocated a new ideal of poverty and mission to the world in imitation of the life of Christ and his apostles. Prominent examples of this male acceptance of female religious equality, the right to be a religious of the new and more perfect variety, are seen in Dominic's initial foundation, the female monastery Notre Dame de Prouille, by which he hoped to attract young women to the Catholic faith away from the austerities of the heretical Cathari, who had until then found favor among the most seriously spiritual women of Provence.[86] Women flocked to Dominic's call, and before his death he oversaw three female convents, not realizing that this was but a trickle compared to the numbers who would seek the status of Dominican nun in the years to follow. We will turn in a moment to the negative reaction that this flood of female converts brought forth.

Robert of Arbrissel illustrates even more the initially favorable but ambivalent response of male religious reformers to the desire of women to share this new spirituality. He was an early twelfth-century hermit and wandering preacher whose call to penitence was especially addressed to women, the outcasts and the fallen. In his ideal of the *vita apostolica* he saw Jesus surrounded by both men and women as a model for his own preaching and mission. Complaints brought by his bishop of the inappropriateness of encouraging such groups of undisciplined, wandering female followers led Robert to found a convent for them, in itself a concession to the view that women should not be out in the world, but rather should be gathered protectively behind cloistered walls.[87] However, Robert's foundation was again unique in its ostensible dedication to true religious equivalence between the sexes, insofar as the double monastery that he established at Fontevrault was to be led by the women, under the spiritual as well as economic jurisdiction of the abbess. This was a radical innovation, at least on the theoretical level, for never before had there been an explicit acceptance of a woman's preeminent spiritual authority, as for example, in the abbess' possession of the right of punishment over the monks.[88] The basis for Robert's arrangements lay in a peculiar combination of New Testament exegesis and long-accepted attitudes toward sex roles. He referred to Christ's commandment to the apostle John to care for his mother as the basis for the relationship of the male and female religious at Fontevrault, the men serving and caring for the women. In addition, the more general insight of the *vita apostolica*, that those who follow Christ are called to serve, seems to have played some part in his thinking.[89] In any case, he speaks of the women as the weaker and more delicate sex, for whom the life of contemplation and psalmody is appropriate. The men, stronger, fitted for the active life, are called by their patron, the Beloved Apostle, to a life of service and obedience. Thus the women's cloister dedicated to the Virgin Mary and the monk's cloister to John the Evangelist represent these reciprocal roles, in which the male is servant and subordinate to the nuns, who rule. Contemporary scholars tend to look upon Fontevrault as an extraordinary exception to the rule of female subordination within monastic institutional history. Recently Ernst Werner, from a Marxist viewpoint, has considered Robert of Arbrissel's devotion to the spiritual life of women an important "step towards *Humanitas* in the history of female emancipation."[90]

Robert's originality, especially on the theoretical level, may not be disputed, but I would like to suggest that Robert's foundation at Fontevrault is an excellent symbol of the deep-seated ambivalence toward women of the medieval Church, even in its most adventurous spirits. This point can be made without adding to the information available to us. In the first place, there is Robert's assumption of female weakness, which did not permit a woman to follow a religious ideal that involved contact with or a mission to the outside world. Instead of using this female characteristic as a justification for the male headship of the monastery, as does Peter Abelard in his discussion of the rationale of the double monastery,[91] Robert chooses to give the direction of his monastery to an abbess, an unusual decision for his time. Because the sources, later lives of Robert, tend to attribute to him motives acceptable to the writers, it is very difficult to discover actually what spiritual ideal he intended to set forth in his monastery. There is evidence that the monks were to function as servants and providers for the women. The apostolic ideal of service and solicitude, exemplified by the care of their patron John the Evangelist for the widow Mary, requires a ruling abbess to whom the men must submit themselves for service to the weaker sex. Werner points out the parallels between this arrangement and the later secular ethic of courtly love, in which the knight is spiritually and morally purified by his service and submission to the pure and tender lady.[92] Yet Werner does not see that this relationship could reflect the same androcentrism that permeated the thought and institutions of medieval society. Is not the abbess, despite her canonically revolutionary authority, in some sense instrumental to the fulfillment of the monk's spiritual calling; the nuns instrumental to the achievement of the apostolic ideal of humble service? A clearer instance in which the nun is unconsciously used as a means to a religious ideal, which in its fullness was limited to the monk, is seen in the chronicler's report of Robert's habit of sleeping among the women he had converted from a life of sin.[93] This practice Robert called a *martyrium*, by which he did penance for the sins of his youth. It was historically a form of asceticism which had roots in the primitive Church and endured into the early Middle Ages as a means of practicing an unusual degree of control over the temptations of the flesh. Here again the woman functions in a most traditional fashion as temptress, embodying the lusts of the flesh, as an auxiliary in the monk's pursuit of virtue through resistance to her presence. As seen from a critical perspective, Robert of Arbrissel's mission to women, his foundation of a female order involving a double monastery headed by an abbess can be interpreted as still reflective of the subordinate and auxiliary role of the woman rather than as an expression of a true equivalence between male and female in the pursuit of religious perfection. In any case, it should not uncritically be reckoned as a "step towards *Humanitas* in the history of female emancipation." The positive in Robert's work emerges when we compare his serious concern for the spiritual welfare of women with some of the developments of the later twelfth and thirteenth centuries in monastic history.

If we turn from this specific exemplar of the new piety of the eleventh and twelfth centuries to the more general problem of the growing numbers of women who sought entrance to the new and reformed orders, we find once more evidence of this same ambivalence with respect to female religious equality. The initial welcome to female converts given by some of the reformers—the Premonstratensians, Cistercians, Dominicans and Franciscans—was very quickly abandoned in the face of the overwhelming numbers of women who flocked to the proponents of a new and more rigorous spirituality. This negative reaction was universal.

The Premonstratensians never actually permitted their female houses to function in accord with their founder's ideals, for the women were strictly cloistered, limited to menial work, narrowly dependent on male leadership. The female followers of Norbert of Xanten were closer to being lay sisters than true religious, and in 1137 the general chapter of the order forbade the foundation of any further women's houses.[94] The Cistercians also by 1134 formally declared that they would not welcome any more female communities in their order; in the first place, women had often been provided for only because they were the abandoned womenfolk of Cistercian monks. The female convents frequently were not even officially recognized as Cistercian houses, although some few following the Cistercian Rule were tolerated. Jacques de Vitry gives one of the very few direct explanations of the opposition of the Cistercians to female conversions: "It was not thought desirable that the female sex submit itself to such rules of austerity and approach such summits of perfection."[95]

Both the Franciscans and the Dominicans, after the initial interest of their founders in the spiritual development of women, forbade their female branches the status of true membership in their respective orders. Both struggled throughout the thirteenth century to shut off the stream of conversions and disallow the creation of more female houses. The rejection is explicit: the women, both Dominican and Franciscan, wanted and struggled for union with the Friars, the privilege of following the rules adhered to by the Friars, especially with respect to strict poverty. Both also wanted their pastoral care to be carried out by the Friars rather than by local secular clergy. The papacy during the thirteenth century quite consistently supported the women, wishing to attach the *cura* of female religious to the new orders rather than permit the women to organize their own religious communities, a solution that, as one might expect, seems not to have occurred to these women.

It is significant that very little explanation of the reasons for the reaction is given; the honesty of De Vitry's passage is rare. Often we read that, as the women were cloistered, the half-dozen or so Friars who would have to serve each convent would thus be prohibited from following out the evangelical essence of their rule, to preach and teach to the world as their master Jesus had done.[96] The economic argument is often heard: the support of unproductive nuns was resented by the male religious. There is also the implication that any association with women is simply too dangerous for the health of the soul. In each case the spiritual well-being of the male religious is used as the justification for the refusal to permit women to aspire to the religious life. A Premonstratensian chapter statute of the late thirteenth century presents the most direct and misogynist justification for the resistance to the cure of female religious.

. . . that the iniquity of women surpasses all iniquities which are in the world, and that there is no wrath greater than the wrath of a woman, that the poisons of vipers and dragons are healthier and less harmful for men than familiarity with women

. . . wanting to provide our descendants with things necessary for the well-being of their souls as well as their bodies, we shall receive under no condition any more sisters for the increase of our perdition, but rather we shall avoid accepting them as if poisonous beasts.[97]

The results of this conflict between the fact of large numbers of women aspiring to religious perfection and the disinclination of the new, reformed orders to take responsibility for the direction and pastoral care of these women was usually a compromise, a limited number of women following a rule quite different from that of the Founder, under the explicit domination of the abbots.[98] And, of course, the overflow, the large numbers of pious women who were refused by the orders or who remained loyal to the new religious ideal of an apostolic life in this world, made up the crowds of Beguines, the semireligious laywomen who pursued a life of charity and prayer in free communities barely recognized by the Church, always on the borderline between heresy and reform. For the student of the role of women in the medieval Church, however, it is not the aristocratic Benedictines but the Beguinal movement, with its close ties to many forms of late medieval piety, that may be the most fruitful area of research.[99]

Southern summarizes the situation for women in the monastic life of the high middle ages succinctly: "In the great period of monastic foundation from the early tenth to the early twelfth century the position of women in the monastic life suffered a sharp decline."[100] The male monastic world failed ultimately to meet the demand of large numbers of women for the religious life. In theory the pursuit of spiritual perfection was an area of equality between the sexes. In fact it was not. Not only were considerable numbers of women kept out, but those who did become religious followed rules that in important ways differed from male monastic rules; and these differences reflected the subordinate, inferior, and auxiliary character rather than the equivalence of the female human being. A few of these differences will serve to illustrate this point. First, there is the universal tendency to submit women to an ever more strict *clausura*, or total separation, from the world and especially from males, even those who of necessity administered to them the sacraments. The movement toward a total separation from the world was confirmed in 1293 by Boniface VIII's bull *Periculoso*, which forbade to a nun any movement outside the convent without permission of the bishop. This development, in fact as well as theory, limited the female religious to one form of the religious life, albeit one generally considered the most perfect, the contemplative, just at a time in Christian history that saw the creative proliferation of new ways to know, love, and follow God. These new ways, the preaching and teaching, a direct imitation of the life of Christ and his apostles in the humility of poverty, were thus, with few exceptions (notably the Third Orders and Beguines), closed to women by the fact of their sex. The female religious, even though she had denied her sensuality and sex in embracing the virginal life, never escaped the male assumption that she was a danger, a source of contamination, and that, in addition, her sex made her incapable of resisting the temptations of any contact with the male or the world. For example, elaborate curtains were erected lest a dying nun see the priest who administered last rites, and we read that in double monasteries the sisters were not allowed to sing the offices lest their song, like that of the Sirens, arouse male passion. While the *clausura* was more or less characteristic of all religious, male and female, the universality of its application to women was symptomatic of the inability of the medieval Church to deal with the woman at the level of spiritual equivalence.

On a more practical level, the duties assigned to women in the double monasteries remind us of the strength of the typology of the female role. The nuns were always in charge of the housekeeping, kitchen, cellar, the economy of the two houses, although monks performed these duties when there were no women about to do them. The description of the prerogatives of the Cistercian abbess reflected the maternal and affectionate correction she was to exercise, for her powers had no force of juridical authority.[101] Even in rules written solely for women, as the *Ancren Riwle*, there is the same stereotype of the female that we find in frankly misogynist literature. For example, the nun was to speak as little as possible, for if Eve had not spoken, she would have not fallen. Even the sins mentioned seem peculiarly trifling and "female": for example, the nun must be careful not to laugh, or break a dish, or soil her habit. The nun must be especially careful to guard her eyes, and no man may look at her eyes without express permission.[102] The female religious is not here dealt with on the level of religious equivalence, a soul who has, by free will and grace, put away the life of the senses, but rather she is still regarded as a sexual animal, a peril to herself, and especially to men. Literature that set forth the ideal of the nun often enumerated the weaknesses of the woman rather than focusing on the spiritual problems of the religious. Once again the woman, even the woman who had denied her essential womanhood, was identified not as a rational being bearing the *imago dei*, sharing in the life of grace a foretaste of the equivalence gained fully only in Paradise, but rather she was reduced to *femina*, the daughter of Eve. The nunnery was "a place where mature women who were tired of matrimonial licence might purge their past errors and be worthy of attaining the embraces of Christ."[103] Research needs to be done at the very fundamental level of comparison of rules, rule commentaries, and didactic literature for male and female religious to test further this suggestion that different and unequal levels of perfection were expected of the two sexes.

The equivalence of male and female in the order of salvation theoretically breaks through into the created order within the institutions of marriage and the religious life, but, as we have seen, that theoretical equivalence is sharply undercut by the dominant androcentric assumptions of the medieval world view and patriarchal society. Repeatedly in the literature the darkness of the picture for women is admitted, but authors brighten when they refer to that development in medieval theology and piety which, they aver, more than balanced the scale—the growing interest in the cult of the Blessed Virgin.[104] I enter upon this subject, the implications of the Mary cult for the theological understanding of the woman, with some trepidation, for it is a topic of immense scope which, to my knowledge, has yet to be studied in depth. Here I can only offer some questions and suggestions for further exploration. However, these suggestions may be surprising, for although preliminary, they are quite contrary to the standard interpretations of the relevance of the cult of the Virgin to the history of womankind.

The prominent role of Christ's mother in theological speculation and popular piety has a long history that extends into the first centuries of the Christian Church. The cult of the Virgin was prominent most especially among Greek-speaking Christians in the patristic era, and was a focus of lively theological speculation in the Carolingian age.[105] Therefore, when one speaks of the "rise" of the cult of the Virgin in the twelfth century, this is a relative statement that, to have any meaning, must be placed in the context of an ancient and important tradition of Mariology. This intensification of interest in Mary in the Western Church, along with the evolution of the ethic and literature of courtly love, have been cited, usually without much in the way of evidence, as a force on the intellectual and emotional level for a more positive evaluation of the woman. It is true that Mary was, at least externally, female, and she provided a "feminizing" element in an otherwise wholly masculine religion. Yet I suggest, in contrast to this accepted view, that the medieval cult of the Virgin at every level, theological and popular, displayed an androcentric bias that, rather than deepening an appreciation of the bipolarity of God's creation or female equivalence, underlined the weakness, inferiority, and subordination of real females. The reasons for this suggestion are in essence two. The first is Mary's theological isolation from human femaleness, which, by implication, degrades the real woman and which often prevented Mary from functioning psychologically as a model for female personhood even in the medieval context. The second lies in the roles given to Mary in the divine plan by theologians and popular myth: her actions, reactions, her personality, all of which can be seen to reflect the theologically supported popular misogynism of the medieval period.

From the very beginning the tendency, especially among the Byzantine Fathers, was to divinize Mary; Mary Queen of Heaven, Mary *Theotokos*, without whom no man is saved.[106] These themes from the East entered into the Western theological tradition especially during the Carolingian era, and we find, for example, intense discussions between Ratramnus and Radbertus in the ninth century on the question of Mary's freedom from original sin, focusing on the problem of the "closed uterus." Ratramnus opposed those who held the common view that a woman's uterus is unclean, indecent, and that therefore Christ could not have emerged from Mary's womb in a natural fashion. Ratramnus insisted that Christ was born normally and that Mary, like any other mother, underwent the rite of purification after his birth. Radbertus supported the opposing position, which by the thirteenth century was commonly accepted, that Mary's womb remained closed, for she was never "infected" with original sin (through coitus), and that therefore Jesus was born in a supernatural fashion, free of sin.[107] This insistence on Mary's freedom from sin—original as well as actual sin—was a source of continual debate (both Bernard and Thomas rejected the doctrine of the Immaculate Conception, although it was a widely held popular belief), but the tendency, well established in Eastern theology, was to insist that Mary's purity was unlike that of other ordinary women, which involved temptation and struggle.[108] Mary, ever virgin, of the *uterus clausus*, was in some sense a model for the nun, but in fact she never experienced the conflicts between flesh and spirit of the earthbound virgin. In the history of piety one hears much of the *imitatio Christi*; was there also in female popular piety an *imitatio Mariae?*

The emphasis in popular devotion, and ultimately in high theology, upon Mary's unique sinlessness was matched in its implications by the speculation regarding her death and the nature of her body. By the eleventh century some were asserting that Mary's body was like that of Christ—that is, not subject to corruption. These tendencies to remove Mary from the human sphere were opposed by certain theologians, in particular Saint Bernard, whose Christ-centered mysticism involved a much more human Mother Mary. But even though one must recognize the larger scope to sensuality and human feeling in the twelfth-century accounts of the Virgin, there is still a great distance between Mary's motherhood and that of the ordinary woman. Some held that the birth of Jesus in the absence of original sin was without pain, as in Paradise. The marriage of Mary and Joseph, idealized as the model Christian marriage, was, of course, grounded in consent, and never involved the union of two bodies. This chaste marriage could not function as an achievable standard for the majority of couples, who were incapable of such heroic discipline.[109]

A different, more human, more sensual Mary does begin to appear by the twelfth century. Some monastic authors give evidence of a frankly erotic conception of the Virgin, frequently using the sensuous imagery of the Song of Songs. For example, Rupert of Deutz writes of Mary:

Your Creator has become your spouse; he has loved your beauty
. . . He has coveted your loveliness and desires to be united to
you . . . Hurry to meet him, that you may be kissed with the
kiss of the mouth of God and be drawn into His most blessed
embraces . . .[110]

Rupert writes of a human Mary who contrasts sharply with the
Byzantine Queen of Heaven. She suffers the pains of childbirth,
and when her son hangs on the cross, she openly agonizes and
laments as any mother would. The more erotic conception of Mary
is reinforced by and probably reinforces the secular cult of courtly
love, and one can read in the Cistercian Aelred of Rievaulx that
men must honor Mary as their mother and serve her as the true
knight serves his mistress.[111]

What do these contradictory elements mean for women: Mary
the impassible Queen of Heaven, Mary the Bride, the Mother of
God, the Mother of all faithful Christians? Far more research into
popular piety is necessary before this question can be answered,
but the indications are that this almost divine woman was at once
removed and unrelated to the reality of earthly femaleness. She
was also perceived as a fulfillment of the sexual fantasies of the
celibate men who wrote about her. Indeed, it is possible to discern
in this cultic and psychological function a feminizing balance in
medieval Christianity that was lost to the Protestant traditions
after the Reformation, which not only removed Mary from popular
religion but also stressed Old Testament patriarchy in a way foreign to medieval Christianity.

Was there a Mary for women in the Middle Ages? There is
evidence that by the end of our period a more human vision of
Mary had evolved, a figure who could relate to the life of the
married as well as the celibate woman.[112] A fruitful area of study
in which to examine these questions would be the writings of the
great female mystics of the later Middle Ages who evolved a
Christian piety written by and for women, and second, the popular
Mary legends, tales and sermon *exempla*, which could give us some
insight into the beliefs and feelings of the common folk.

Let us turn from Mary's being to her work for mankind as a
means of exploring her character and personality in her roles as
refuge of the sinner and mother of mercies. As Christ was the

second Adam, so Mary was the new Eve, beginning the work of redemption, as Eve began the work of sin. Thomas tells us that Mary was necessary in the work of redemption to ensure universality, for Christ represented the masculine sex in general, Mary the female sex in general.[113] Her role in human salvation, however, is appropriate to her sex—secondary, passive, auxiliary—in comparison with that of Christ the Redeemer. The development of the notion of Mary as coredemptrix during the Middle Ages is a problem for Roman Catholic Mariology, for it can move without much difficulty into an unacceptable Quadrinity.[114] But in the context of our interest, it provides another example of the proposition that no matter how high Mary was exalted, her peculiarly female nature as auxiliary was never lost.[115] Bernardino of Siena sees her as adding the dimension of corporeality to God's creation, again in accord with the material nature of the female.[116] Bernardino's rhetoric in his discussion of Mary's relationship to God is a magnificent example of the duality of the cult of Mary in our period, exalting the Mother of God above all mothers and yet assuming a character, a personality, that reflected the male picture of the female. Bernardino wrote:

> . . . one Hebrew woman invaded the house of the eternal King. One girl, I do not know by what caresses, pledges or violence, seduced, deceived, and if I may say so, wounded and enraptured the divine heart and ensnared the Wisdom of God . . .[117]

When we turn to more popular literature, the Mary legends and sermon *exempla*, we find in Mary's activities as font of mercy and refuge of sinners other character traits that, like that of the seductive female depicted above, correspond to the androcentric and often misogynist *Weibsbild* of the medieval world. A rhymed *vita* of the twelfth century depicts Mary in a Martha-like role, as temple virgin, polishing the ornaments. When this author describes Mary beneath the cross, she is completely hysterical and out of control, again a perhaps less than admirable female model. So frequently we find Mary functioning either as the impassible Queen of Heaven, or at the opposite pole, as an irrational female.[118] The thirteenth-century Mariale, until recently attributed to Albertus Magnus, finds Mary full of every grace a creature can share, perfect in knowledge of created as well as uncreated things, but she could not receive the grace of Holy Orders, for the disability of the female can never be surmounted even by the virtues and graces of the Mother of God.[119]

Most revealing of Mary's personality are the Mary legends which depict her as the merciful refuge of the sinner. We see Christ, the distant Judge, rationally deliberating over the just punishment of a notorious sinner. Mary the merciful comes to the sinner's rescue, not necessarily because he repents, but for his loyalty to her, expressed perhaps in a daily salutation.[120] A favorite story tells of the abbess, away from her convent for two years with her lover, yet she always prayed to Mary, who therefore took her place and concealed the sin until the day she forgot the prayer.[121] This exemplifies a recurring theme of Mary's emotional and perhaps irrational mercy, contrasted to the rational and deliberate justice of Christ. Is not Mary here the "typical female," softhearted, illogical, even vengeful? Mary the nourisher, the mother, frequently saves lives by offering the sick or the starving her breast,[122] an example of how the sexuality of the human Mary, where that arises, is seen from a male point of view. The popular literature, in depicting Mary as a mediator between the punishing God and the sinner needful of mercy, gives to her a necessary and a praiseworthy role in the divine economy, but still it is a woman's role: auxiliary, subordinate, marked by emotionalism, irrationality, sensuality, and ultimately a lack of dignity. Now, it is very possible that what we have here is a medieval expression of a divine complementarity in which the warm, emotional, the giving, even quixotic, finds its place alongside the more deliberate and impersonal rationality of God the Son. The Middle Ages were not an age of reason, and my perceptions of Mary's "lack of dignity" may be an anachronistic imposition of rationalist values upon the medieval past. Nevertheless there was, so to speak, a division of labor, hierarchically ordered, between Mary and her son. Even their complementarity reflected to some degree the role and characterological super- and subordination of men and women on earth.

I do not see in the growing interest in the Virgin as object of theology and popular devotion from the eleventh and twelfth centuries an unambiguous sign of a heightened appreciation of the female or a movement in the realm of ideas toward female dignity.

The cult of the Virgin, complemented by the ethic of courtly love, fashioned the female element according to male perceptions and needs. As an embodiment of the ideal of virginity, Mary did function as a symbol of female equivalence in the order of salvation, a model for the nun and the chaste wife. But that equivalence was, in heaven as in this world, always qualified by the subordinate, auxiliary, and ultimately inferior character of female personhood relative to the masculine norm.

IV

The Virgin Mary in so many ways represents the ambivalence of the medieval Church in its relations with the female sex, for in the theology of Mary there is a conscious attempt to undo the evil attributed to Eve and to glorify the feminine principle. Yet I have suggested that in its very act of venerating Mary the medieval world could not escape fundamental androcentric and even misogynist assumptions. It is appropriate to conclude this investigation of the woman in medieval theology with some reference to the frankly misogynist tradition, which, in fact, was a literary genre of some importance, having its roots in classical antiquity, and extending in one form or another into the present age.[123] We look at this misogynist literature, some of it clerical and didactic, some more popular in origin and audience, as a means of exploring the impact of high theology on the popular mind. Just as the Mary legends reflect unconscious expectations of female behavior, so the misogynist portrait of female faults reflects, at least in part, the theological expectations of the age. One must stress that qualifier "in part," for in addition to strong classical and patristic traditions of misogyny well known to our medieval writers, there was the impact of strongly patriarchal social structures. Also, one must beware of forging too strongly direct links between theological speculation and male attacks on unfaithful mistresses or cuckolding wives. Still, it shall be apparent, the theological tradition played an important role in the popular negative perception of women.

The sermon literature has yet to be explored with this topic in mind, but Bennett notes that in the Dominican sermons women are scarcely mentioned except in connection with the sin of luxury or superstition, sins associated with the woman's sensuality and lack of intellectual development.[124] The typical thirteenth-century preacher harped on the danger of women, stringing out his biblical exemplars—Eve, Jezebel, Delilah, Bathsheba, Salomi.[125] A most fruitful source of explicit works or chapters on the evil and danger-ous character of women is in monastic literature, mainly didactic works for the instruction of novices in the religious life. Hildebert of Tours (1057–1133) writes of the three dangers to the monk: "Hurtful to holy men are women, avarice, ambition" (and note that the woman comes before avarice and ambition).[126] Bernard of Morlaix, a twelfth-century Cluniac, writes of the insatiable sensu-ality of women, even nuns, and declares there to be no good women on earth—all delight in misdeed and hanker after the destruction of men.[127] Alexander Neckam, again in the context of instructions for the monastic life, writes a long section in the *De vita mona-chorum* on the female sex. He touched on a theme well known from classical antiquity, the use of "cosmetics" to disguise the ugliness of their bodies, the telltale signs of sin. All that is natural they attempt to change by artificial means, and the purpose of all this artifice is to snare the unwary man. According to Alexander, even the married man is plagued by his woman, for if she is ugly, she depresses him; if beautiful, she invites adultery. Alexander's discussion reminds us that these monastic tracts on women are not merely didactic works railing against evil women but are warnings against the dangers of the female sex as such. For although he admits that not all women are as he describes, he quickly adds that hardly a virtuous woman can be found, and that even in the cloister a man is not safe.[128] The continual theme of this monastic literature is the woman as danger, as source of discord, as continual threat to peace and quiet and the contemplative life (all women talk too much), and above all as persons whose *values* are perverse. Repeatedly we hear that women do not keep faith, they are fair-weather friends, they seek only gold and treasure, and as soon as a man comes on bad times they will desert him.[129]

It has been suggested to me that a thorough exploration of the monastic literature might reveal that it was human sexuality itself, not primarily the woman, that was feared by the monk. Homo-sexuality was more of a daily threat to the chastity of the monk than seduction at the hands of a beautiful woman. Could the frequent outcries against the dangerous female be a projection of that fear of the implications of friendship among the brothers? Here again is a problem that requires investigation and that at present eludes a simple answer.[130]

Even marriage, despite its sacramental character, comes under direct attack in a genre of didactic literature reflecting the Gregorian reformers' efforts to enforce clerical celibacy. Here we see the insatiable woman, sexually boundless in her appetites, ever after greater riches, subject to violent rages and irrational inconsistency, careless of all law or social order, of loyalty and steadfastness, the destroyer of men, rich and powerful as well as the poor.[131] Deceit and indirection are the woman's weapons, for she lacks the force to proceed otherwise. In short, the wife brings more cares than pleasures, and marriage, ruined apparently by the female partner, is to be avoided. Repeatedly in these attacks on women, the image of Eve, mother of sin, seducer, betrayer of Adam, is presented as the ultimate *ratio* for this fear and mistrust of the female sex. It would seem that the ascetic tradition requires this devaluation of the female, perceived to embody all that is inimical to the celibate religious life.

One of the most emotionally striking examples of medieval misogynism, which visually reflects the theological roots of this fear, is the figure *Frau Welt*, which appears in the portal sculpture of numerous German churches in the thirteenth and fourteenth centuries. Stammler traces the evolution of this powerful symbol as it moves from literature to sculpture, where the Prince of this World, *Mundus* (John 12:32 and 14:30), appears in a portal of the Strasbourg cathedral, luring the foolish maidens to their perdition, while Christ and the wise maidens appear on the opposite side. *Mundus* is an attractive, enticing figure from the front, but if one moves around to his back, one sees that the clothes are ripped away to reveal an ugly body eaten through by worms and frogs and snakes—a revelation of the moral reality of the pleasures of the world and the flesh.[132] By the thirteenth century this traditionally male figure, the Prince of this World, in both literary and sculptured form, is found transformed into a woman, *Frau Welt*, with the same courtly aristocratic beckoning smile and hand seen from the front, and a behind eaten through by the creatures of hell and the grave. She is often accompanied by the iconographical symbol of fleshly lust, the goat, and sometimes appears as a fanciful creature, half human, half animal, the demonic devil's wife, who, just like the beauteous courtly lady, leads men to their destruction through preying on the lusts of the flesh. How does one account for the transformation of *Mundus*, the Prince of this World, with its scriptural basis, into *Frau Welt*, the woman, as the embodiment of the seductive and damning blandishments of the world? Stammler amazingly gives us primarily a linguistic explanation, suggesting that with the emergence of an important vernacular literature, the Latin concept *mundus*, male in gender, was translated in the literature into German, whence the feminine *Frau Welt*.[133] He makes brief reference to the strength of the patristic and medieval misogynist tradition, but does no more than allude in a paragraph to that possible source for the shift in sex of this personification of evil, a shift that occurs just at the moment when the developing cult of the Virgin and the love ethic of the Goliards were supposed to have injected some positive notes into the medieval picture of the female sex. Surely the problem is far more complicated than the change in gender from Latin to German. Stammler points to instances in France of *Frau Welt* in church portal sculpture. But rather than grapple with the inconsistency of the masculine French noun, *le monde*, he takes the appearance of *Frau Welt* as evidence of the German origin of the convention.[134] Whatever further research concludes with respect to this interesting problem, *Frau Welt* remains a public symbol of the high medieval Christian association of the feminine with the evils of sensuality and self-indulgence, for in *Frau Welt* the woman personifies worldly evil, that "materiality" and "fleshiness" which the theological tradition has identified with womankind.

As a final example of the popular theological misogynist tradition, one must allude to the phenomenon of witchcraft, which grew in importance during the late medieval centuries, to blossom into its full power and terror in the sixteenth and seventeenth centuries. Those accused of witchcraft were overwhelmingly of the female sex, although the accusers tended to be randomly divided between the sexes. Although very few contemporary students of witchcraft have dealt satisfactorily with this obvious question, why so many witches and so few warlocks, our medieval commentators raised and answered the query in familiar terms.[135] Women are by nature lacking in intellect. They are weaker, more easily misled by the devil, more superstitious, endowed with greater sensitivity to the supernatural than men, and women have a natural tendency toward the sins of the flesh to which witches are especially given. These were the principal reasons offered when medieval authors asked, as they often did, why so many practitioners of the black arts were women. Women, we are told, were finally attracted to witchcraft because, lacking real power and authority themselves, they sought revenge through supernatural means.[136] (This perception of the importance of powerlessness in female behavior is an observation by our medieval authorities that is possibly still valid.) The role of the woman in witchcraft is an important topic that needs to be thoroughly explored, especially from the vantage point of modern sociology and anthropology.

V

The devilish figure of the witch side by side with the seductive, sensual *Frau Welt* and the shrewish, yapping, unfaithful wife gave pictorial power to the misogynist tradition transmitted by the medieval world for embellishment and some modification to the age of Renaissance and Reformation. What is the role of the theological tradition in this unhappy trinity of female vice? Can one lay it all at the feet of the Fathers' selective use of the biblical tradition, and their medieval interpreters? Obviously the question cannot be answered in so simplistic a fashion. Medieval misogyny had many sources: for example the antifemale rationalist bias of classical antiquity, the strongly patriarchal traditions of a Germanic warrior society, sexual and cultic taboos common to many civilizations, and the sexual projections Freud has taught us to recognize. The deeply androcentric and misogynist character of the medieval concept of the woman cannot be wholly accounted for by reference to the realm of theological ideas, for society, psychology, and experience also played their roles. Comparative studies of medieval and other premodern societies reveal, despite important differences in religious ideology, extensive similarities in attitudes toward women, sex-role differentiation, and sexuality in general. Yet the evidence is overwhelming that the medieval Christian theological tradition and the symbols that it generated, many of which are still with us, did provide important stimuli and a convenient ideology for the dehumanization of the female sex. Despite the truly revolutionary implications of the biblical admonition, "There is neither male nor female, for ye are all one in Christ Jesus" (an equivalence graphically illustrated by the single initiation rite, baptism, alike for men and women), at every level, theological, legal, institutional, popular piety, that paradisical equivalence of souls was undermined by a deeply felt androcentrism and misogyny.

The misogynist elements of the medieval Christian tradition had their theological basis in the dualist and spiritualist anthropology inherited from New Testament and patristic sources, reinforcing the patriarchal character of the religion of the Old Testament. This dualism between flesh and spirit, body and intellect, was clearly androcentric in its identification of the male with the element of spirit or mind, the female with flesh and sexuality. Although the medieval centuries saw some amelioration of the patristic sexual pessimism in admitting a more positive view of Christian marriage, ultimately our medieval commentators deepened the androcentric and antifemale character of the tradition under the influence of a strongly patriarchal Germanic society and with the scientific support of the wholly androcentric Aristotelian biology. Aristotle's intellectualist definition of human nature combined with the inherited ascetic tradition to further strengthen the limitation of the female human being to the auxiliary and instrumental role of sexual procreation, defining the woman as a misbegotten and wholly subordinate creature, hedged about with fear and loathing as an embodiment of the sensuality that threatens the purity of male mind and spirit. By giving a "scientific" basis to the earlier patristic attitudes, the Middle Ages guaranteed the survival of this antifemale anthropology long after rigorist ascetic attitudes had ceased to dominate Western society.

In addition, the Middle Ages, in its philosophical presuppositions as well as its theology, assumed a hierarchical cosmos in which difference in being and function implied difference in dignity and order. Thus in medieval society inequality was rationalized and perhaps even softened by a strong sense of mutual responsibility: God for the soul, lord for the serf, man for woman. The standards of post-eighteenth-century individualism and egalitarianism should not be applied to the medieval world. Women were subordinate in this hierarchy, as were also serfs, but we are not yet wholly sure how either group perceived its "place" in that *ordo*. We are certain that the rationale of hierarchy, superordination and subordination, no longer is convincing, at least for those on the bottom. Yet hierarchical modes of thinking still dominate in our feelings, if not in our thinking, about relationships between the sexes.

What is to be done? The first task is to make explicit the assumptions received from this tradition about male/female difference and hierarchy, and to expose with the help of historical understanding the now patently invalid intellectual foundations of these typologies. For example, have not the insights of the social sciences already called into question the implicitly rationalist definition of human nature by which the feeling and responding side of our being is denigrated and perceived as specifically feminine? The twentieth-century person may well believe himself to be free of Adam and Eve mythologies and the monastic imperative to virginity, yet still think and feel in terms of an identification of the mind/body dualism with the male/female bipolarity which supports our stereotypes of the passive, emotional, and seductive woman and the rational, idealistic, and active male. Behind the recently popular discussion of male and female complementarity lies some very traditional symbolism and feelings about the "eternal feminine" which need to be brought into the open.[137] The woman and the man must be demythologized.

More difficult, and ultimately more important, will be the constructive work, the evolution of a new Christian anthropology that first takes seriously the biblical affirmation of the goodness of creation and affirms the positive role of human sexuality as a vehicle of human love and true mutuality. This anthropology for human liberation calls for the building of a new model of sex identity which permits individual personality to flourish without the constraints of sex stereotypes or hierarchical power relationships.

For this reconstruction it will be necessary to affirm the fundamental moral equivalence of the sexes, not simply within the sexual relationship, as did the medieval church, but also in the world beyond the family, in which world, with fewer children and longer life spans, modern men and women are destined to spend more than half of their lives. This means that a new anthropology will be grounded in a recognition of the role of work in human self-fulfillment and the right, therefore, of women as well as men to meaningful work. In the medieval tradition work was a punishment for the Fall, assigned particularly to the sons of Adam; in Protestant capitalist societies work has become an alienating exploitive mode for dominating nature, both human and inanimate. The women's movement could well encourage the basic reconstitution of both economic structures and attitudes toward work, which would make possible a new balance between familial nurturing and socially productive work in the lives of women and men who share these roles and are not limited by their sex to a life of the hearth or the hunt.

A third aspect of a new anthropology will reside in the recognition that the categories underlying the theologians' or the psychologists' accounts of sex difference and role can be as time-bound as the dogmas of Aristotelian biology. A Christian view of the nature of woman and man needs to be dynamic and prophetic, not antiscientific, but also not taken in by the faith systems of the Freudians or their successors.

The medieval theological tradition does have, as we have seen, a positive core that can contribute to a new anthropology for free people, female and male. The medieval Church insisted in theory on a true mutuality and moral equivalence between the sexes in the area of sexual fidelity within marriage. In this regard the Church opposed the then newly emergent ethic of courtly love and condemned the romantic view of a sexual relationship based on "feelings" rather than on mutual commitment and self-giving. Some careful thought will reveal that the idea of the woman as sex object—idealized, even unattainable, but existing ultimately for the gratification of the male sense of well-being—has important origins in the medieval courtly love tradition.[138] That tradition was condemned by the Church out of the conviction that mutual fidelity, reflecting the ultimate value of each partner as a child of God, is the only basis for the relationship between man and woman in marriage. In some sense, a woman never belonged wholly to her husband, was never completely defined in terms of her sexuality, for there was always the prior bond of the soul to God, in the context of which all other commitments were judged, the practice of medieval canonists notwithstanding. This medieval condemnation of the romantic ethic is a strong instance within the tradition of the rejection of the concept of woman as a purely sexual being. Insofar as the "new morality" sanctions the abandonment of a relationship when it ceases to please, or feel good, the medieval tradition opposes that reduction of the human being to a sensual instrumentality with an insistence that neither partner, female or male, exists to be used for the gratification of the other.

The eschatalogical dimension of the medieval theology of the sexes could also be of interest to those who seek to formulate a new anthropology. In the simplest of terms Thomas tells us that in Paradise all the inequalities and subordination of the order of creation shall be overcome. There will still be hierarchy, but it will be an ordering by merit, rather than by sex or status. So much of Christian eschatology has been secularized and brought down to earth. If one must have superiors and subordinates, why not on the basis of merit?

But is this hierarchical universe, with its fixed and ranked functions and orders, a positive basis for a new anthropology? Is it not rather of our inheritances from the past the most pervasive and difficult to bring into line with the needs of twentieth-century persons in their individuality and society? It is easy to find recent literature within the Christian theological tradition that insists on a nondualist anthropology and on an unambiguous moral equivalence of the sexes, but dwells at the same time upon the differences between women and men that imply not only separate function but also an unambiguous superordination and subordination, grounded paradigmatically in the relationship of God to his creatures. Thus Karl Barth has spoken of man and woman as an A and a B; in respect of order woman is B, ". . . and therefore behind and subordinate to man."[139] The problem here is not a medieval anthropology but a medieval doctrine of creation and sociology, by which a specific order and precedence was assigned by divine fiat to man and woman, which order we are yet bound to maintain. There is indeed implied an inadequate definition of human nature: static, ahistorical, hierarchical, Platonizing in its assumption of ontologically fixed relationships between the sexes. The reader will pardon me if under every bush of "complementarity" I espy this hierarchical cosmos, this Great Chain of Being, in which difference becomes rationalized subordination.

In conclusion, despite this ambiguous legacy, the medieval Christian tradition did not only speak of the woman's spiritual equivalence with her brother. The Church provided an institution, and a calling, the monastic life, which symbolized and often gave concrete opportunity to exercise that spiritual equivalence in which all persons, female and male, are called alike to Christian perfection. Only within those portions of Christendom which after the sixteenth century renounced the dual ethic of monasticism and celibacy was the woman wholly limited in her Christian vocation to the home, to her role as procreator and nurturer. However often the medieval commitment to spiritual equivalence was undermined by androcentric and patriarchal assumptions, the institution of monasticism was for the Christian woman a real and concrete option, a little world occasionally run by and for women. She had an alternative to the authority of father and husband. She had a choice.

NOTES

1. There is a considerable body of journal literature in French and German, but much less in English. See Sr. Emma Therese Healy, *Woman According to St. Bonaventura* (Erie, Pa., 1956) and D. S. Bailey, *The Man-Woman Relation in Christian Thought* (London, 1959).
2. An excellent recent work is Kari Elisabeth Børresen, *Subordination et équivalence, Nature et rôle de la femme d'après Augustin et Thomas d'Aquin* (Paris, 1963)—hereafter cited as "Børresen."
3. Thomas Aquinas, *Summa Theologica*, ed. English Dominican Province, 3 vols. (New York, 1947), I, 76, 1. For the summary of Thomas' views that follows I am indebted to K. E. Børresen, *Subordination et équivalence*.
4. *ST* I, 91, 3; Børresen, p. 126.
5. *ST* I, 92, 1; Børresen, p. 129.
6. Ibid.
7. *ST* I, 92, 1, ad 1; "Woman is said to be a misbegotten male, as being a product outside the purpose of nature considered in the individual case: but not against the purpose of universal nature" (*ST* I, 99, 2, ad 1).
8. *ST* I, 92, 2.

9. *ST* I, 92, 3.
10. Børresen, p. 136.
11. Børresen, p. 137.
12. *ST* II–II, 70, 3, concl.; *ST* II–II, 156, 1, ad 1; Børresen, p. 143.
13. Børresen, p. 143; e.g., the woman, like a child or a fool, may not take a valid judicial oath.
14. *ST* II–II, 165, 2, ad 1.
15. *ST* II–II, 163, 4, concl.
16. *ST* I–II, 81, 5, ad 2; Børresen, p. 174.
17. *ST* II–II, 163, 4, concl.
18. *ST* II–II, 163, 4, concl.
19. *ST* II–II, 164, 2; Børresen, pp. 169–170. This punishment appropriate to each sex is in addition to the general effect of the Fall, the loss of the gift of original justice, which entails mortality and a diminishing of the natural inclination to virtue.
20. Børresen, p. 188.
21. Ibid., p. 180.
22. Ibid., p. 253.
23. *ST* Suppl., 81, 3, ad 1, 2, 3.
24. Josef G. Ziegler, *Die Ehelehre der Pönitentialsummen von 1200–1350* (Regensburg, 1956), p. 181.
25. *ST* I, 98, 1 and 2; Børresen, pp. 150–151.
26. *ST* I, 98, 2, ad 4; Børresen, p. 153.
27. Within the first two states the woman can escape the special penalty laid on the daughters of Eve—direct subordination to a male.
28. Børresen, p. 199.
29. Ibid., p. 221. Thus masturbation in the male has often been felt to be a more serious problem than the same act performed by a woman.
30. See n. 26 above. It would be useful to know to what extent men who were not virgins were equally excluded from religious vocations.
31. Thomas Aquinas, *Summa contra Gentiles*, III, 122.
32. Ziegler, *Die Ehelehre*, p. 133.
33. See H. Grundmann, "Die Frauen und die Literatur im Mittelalter," *Archiv für Kulturgeschichte*, XXVI (1935), 129–161.
34. Børresen, p. 199; Thomas, *Contra Gentiles*, III, 123.
35. *ST* Suppl., 44, 2, ad 1: "Although the father ranks above the mother, the mother has more to do with the offspring than the father has. Or we may say that woman was made chiefly in order to be man's helpmate in relation to the offspring, whereas the man was not made for this purpose. Wherefore the mother has a closer relation to the nature of marriage than the father has."
36. *ST* II–II, 152, 4, concl.
37. *ST* Suppl., 41, 3, ad 3; 49, 4, ad 4; Børresen, p. 220.
38. *ST* Suppl., 62, 4, ad 5; Ziegler, *Die Ehelehre*, p. 118. So many

examples in the casuistic of legal reasons for separation seem to assume a guilty wife. See E. Brunner, *Man in Revolt, A Christian Anthropology* (London, 1939), p. 354.

39. *ST* Suppl., 49, 2, ad 3; Børresen, p. 204.

40. *ST* Suppl., 64, 3, concl.; 64, 4, concl. On popular beliefs about the evils of menstrual blood, see Ziegler, *Die Ehelehre*, pp. 259–274.

41. *ST* Suppl., 64, 1, ad 4; Børresen, p. 222. A woman may refuse to accede to her husband's demands if she is ill so that the carnal act would endanger her health further (see *ST* Suppl., 64, 4, concl.).

42. *ST* Suppl., 64, 2; 64, 5, ad 2; Børresen, p. 222.

43. *ST* Suppl., 64, 6; Børresen, p. 205.

44. *ST* Suppl., 53, 4; Børresen, p. 206.

45. *ST* Suppl., 64, 6, ad 1.

46. *ST* Suppl., 52, 3; Børresen, p. 201.

47. *ST* II–II, 154, 8; Suppl., 62, 4.

48. *ST* Suppl., 62, 4, ad 3 and 4; Børresen, pp. 207–208; see also A. Esmein, *Le mariage en droit canonique* (Paris, 1935), II, 100–108.

    It was apparently most unusual for a man to remain loyal to his wife, as observed the chronicler of Baldwin of Hainaut: "although it is rarely found in any man that he should cleave only to one woman and be content with her alone." See *La Chronique de Gislebert de Mons*, ed. L. Vanderkindere (Brussels, 1904), pp. 191–192, cited in John F. Benten, "Clio and Venus: An Historical View of Medieval Love," *The Meaning of Courtly Love*, ed. F. X. Newman (Albany, N.Y., 1968), p. 24.

49. Francesco da Barberino, *Del Reggimento e costumi di Donna* (ca. 1307–1315) in Alice A. Hentsch, *De la littérature didactique du moyen-age s'adressant spécialement aux femmes* (Halle a.S., 1903) p. 113—hereafter cited as "Hentsch."

50. *ST* Suppl., 42; Børresen, p. 212.

51. *ST* Suppl., 42, 2–3; ". . . since in divine matrimony man receives by Divine institution the faculty to use his wife for the begetting of children" (a.3).

52. *ST* Suppl., 44, 1, concl.; Børresen, pp. 216–217. This decision that *consensus* rather than *copula* was the determinant element in Christian marriage was necessary in order to admit the sacramentality of the marriage of Joseph and Mary, which involved consent but not physical consummation. In this view Thomas followed P. Lombard, who insisted that carnal union was not the essential component of Christian marriage.

53. *ST* II–II, 10, 2, ad 3; Børresen, p. 229. This is a hierarchical relationship based on love, however, not on fear, as between master and servant.

54. Ziegler, *Die Ehelehre*, p. 199.

55. Ibid., p. 223, n. 78.
56. Ibid., pp. 263–264. The sexual parts of a woman's anatomy were known as "turpitudo feminarum" (p. 181).
57. Francesco da Barberino in his instructions to mothers prefers that a woman suckle her own children, but if a nurse must be used, better that her own child should be a boy—presumably the milk is better (Hentsch, p. 116).
58. Ibid., p. 7.
59. Ibid., p. 32.
60. Ibid., p. 161.
61. Philippe de Novaire (d. 1270), *Des quatre tens d'aage d'ome*, in Hentsch, p. 83.
62. *La cour d'amour* (early 13th cent.), in Hentsch, p. 56.
63. Philippe de Novaire, in Hentsch, p. 84.
64. Francesco da Barberino, in Hentsch, pp. 109–113.
65. Chevalier de la Tour Landry, in Hentsch, pp. 131–132.
66. Saint Louis, *Enseignements à sa fille Isabelle*, in Hentsch, p. 81.
67. See *La cour d'amour*, in Hentsch, pp. 56–57.
68. Sordello, *Ensenhamens d'onor*, in Hentsch, p. 67.
69. Saint Louis, *Enseignements*, No. 15. It is necessary to obey one's husband and parents, but against God you must not obey anyone (Hentsch, p. 81).
70. *ST* II–II, 151, 3, ad 2 (Augustine, *Soliloq.*, i, 10); 186, 4, concl.; Suppl., 41, 3, ad 2; I–II, 34, 1, ad 1; II–II, 15, 3; Børresen, p. 231.
71. *Reallexikon für Antike und Christentum* (Stuttgart, 1941 ff.), Lfrg. 58 (1970), "Frau," p. 258. It would be useful to explore comparatively instructions to male and female religious to determine if the female ascetic perceived the opposite sex with the same fear and even horror that is found in ascetic literature addressed to men.
72. Marie-Louise Portmann, *Die Darstellung der Frau in der Geschichtsschreibung des früheren Mittelalters* (Basel, 1958), pp. 19–20.
73. Saint Jerome, *Lettres*, Collection des Universitiés de France, 8 vols. (Paris, 1949–1963), IV, ep. 71 ad Lucinum, 10: ". . . from a spouse, she has become your sister, from a woman, a man, from a subject, an equal . . . under the same yoke she hastens with you towards the kingdom of heaven."
74. Ratherius of Verona held up the ideal of the manly woman, modeled after Judith and the martyrs, "And thus a man in mind, a woman in body . . ." (Portmann, *Die Darstellung der Frau*, p. 22). One must not forget that in a primitive agricultural society, power over crop fertility and domestic skills were necessary for survival. The typical Germanic goddess was a mother goddess, from whom mankind learned the arts of housekeeping and agriculture. These characteristics were "taken over" by many early medieval virgin saints, who were not the less powerful for their

domestic and agricultural prowess. See Lina Eckenstein, *Woman Under Monasticism* (New York, 1963; orig. ed. 1896), pp. 23–27.

75. Fortunatus, *Vita Radegundis*, in Portmann, *Die Darstellung der Frau*, p. 38.

76. *ST* Suppl., 39, 1, concl.; Børresen, pp. 183–184. For a recent discussion of this position, see Joseph A. Wahl, *The Exclusion of Women from Holy Orders*, Studies in Sacred Theology, 2d Ser., No. 110. Catholic University of America (Washington, D.C., 1959).

77. Børresen, p. 188.

78. *ST* III, 67, 4.

79. *ST* II–II, 177, 2, concl.; III, 27, 5, ad 3, on the Virgin Mary, that she did not teach or perform miracles, but did prophesy. See also Børresen, 184–185.

80. See Ernst Wolff, "Das Frauenamt im Amt der Kirche . . ." *Peregrinatio*, II (Munich, 1965), 179–185.

81. See Stephanus Hilpisch, *Die Doppelklöster, Entstehung und Organisation* (Münster, 1928).

82. G. E. Browne, *The Importance of Women in Anglo-Saxon Times* (London, 1910), pp. 32–39.

83. Betty Bandel, "English Chronicler's Attitude Toward Women," *Journal of the History of Ideas*, XVI (1935), 113–118.

84. Herbert Grundmann, *Religiöse Bewegungen im Mittelalter*, 2d rev. ed. (Darmstadt, 1961), esp. chs. 4, 5, and 6.

85. Ibid., pp. 170–203.

86. Micheline de Fontette, *Les religieuses à l'âge classique du droit canon: Recherches sur les structures juridiques des branches féminines des ordres* (Paris, 1967), p. 90.

87. Ernst Werner, "Zur Frauenfrage und zum Frauenkult im Mittelalter: Robert v. Arbrissel und Fontevrault," *Forschungen und Fortschritte*, XXIX (1955), 269.

88. Fontette, *Les religieuses à l'âge classique*, pp. 46–47. Some abbesses did in fact exercise such jurisdiction—receiving professions, confessing, distributing the Sacrament—but this was always perceived as uncanonical and illegal.

89. Werner, "Zum Frauenfrage und zum Frauenkult," p. 270.

90. Ibid., p. 276.

91. Hilpisch, *Die Doppelklöster*, p. 75, epistles to Heloise, II and VIII.

92. Werner, "Zum Frauenfrage und zum Frauenkult," p. 275.

93. Ibid., p. 272.

94. Fontette, *Les religieuses à l'âge classique*, pp. 16–17.

95. Ibid., pp. 29–30.

96. Ibid., p. 116; Grundmann (*Religiöse Bewegungen*, p. 203), refers to a disinclination to take the "trouble and responsibility," but probes no further for explanation.

97. Hilpisch, *Die Doppelklöster*, p. 83.

98. Ibid., pp. 103–151. The rules for female Dominicans and Francis-

can Clares were characterized by strict enclosure and great austerity, with none of the elements of preaching, teaching, and mission that reflected the original ideals of the founders.

99. See Grundmann, *Religiöse Bewegungen*; Ernest W. McDonnell, *The Beguines and Beghards in Medieval Culture* (New Brunswick, N.J., 1934); J. Greven, *Die Anfänge der Beginen* (Münster i.W., 1912).

100. R. W. Southern, *Western Society and the Church in the Middle Ages* (Harmondsworth, Middlesex, England, Penguin Books, 1970), p. 310.

101. Hilpisch, *Die Doppelklöster*, p. 74; Fontette, *Les religieuses à l'âge classique*, p. 37.

102. Hentsch, pp. 58–59.

103. Hildebert, *Vita S. Hugonis*, ii, 11 (*Patrologia Latina*, vol. 159, p. 868), in Southern, *Western Society and the Church*, p. 311.

104. August Wulff, in his study of misogynist literature in the West, sees the cult of the Virgin as the countervailing tradition (*Die Frauenfeindlichen Dichtungen in den Romanischen Literatur des Mittelalters, bis zum Ende des XIII. Jahrhunderts* [Halle, 1914], p. 1.

105. See Leo Scheffczyk, *Das Mariengeheimnis in Frömmigkeit und Lehre der Karolingerzeit* (Leipzig, 1959).

106. Hilda Graef, *Mary, A History of Doctrine and Devotion* (London, 1963), pp. 165–167.

107. Ibid., pp. 176–179.

108. Ibid., p. 183.

109. Hannelore Bühler suggests that Mary stands not as a model for Christian marriage but as an alternative bride (*Die Marienlegenden als Ausdruck mittelalterliches Marienverehrung* [Köln, 1965], p. 113.

110. Graef, *Mary, A History of Doctrine and Devotion*, pp. 215–216. See Bühler (n. 109, above) on the legends surrounding Mary the Bride—of Christ or of her earthly devote (pp. 112–115).

111. Graef, *Mary*, p. 249.

112. In the Vatican grottoes is a fifteenth-century chapel dedicated to *Maria praegnans* to which women came to pray for a safe delivery.

113. ST III, 31, 4, concl.; Børresen, p. 180.

114. Bühler, *Die Marienlegenden*, p. 110.

115. Dionysius the Carthusian, using the traditional Mary/Eve parallel, wrote that as Eve shared in the Fall, so a man redeemed the world, but not without woman as an additional cause (see Graef, *Mary*, p. 320).

116. Graef, *Mary*, pp. 317–318.

117. Ibid., p. 317.

118. Ibid., pp. 259–261.

119. Ibid., p. 272.

120. Bühler, *Die Marienlegenden*, pp. 55 and 60.

121. Ibid., p. 63.
122. Ibid., p. 57.
123. An excellent recent monograph in English on this subject is Katherine M. Rogers, *The Troublesome Helpmate, A History of Misogyny in Literature* (Seattle and London, 1966).
124. R. F. Bennett, *The Early Dominicans* (Cambridge, Mass., 1937), p. 107.
125. A. Lecoy de la Marche, *La chaire française au moyen-age* (Paris, 1886), p. 429. Jacques de Vitry said the first woman had no rest until she drove her husband from Paradise and condemned Christ to suffer on the cross.
126. Wulff, *Die Frauenfeindlichen Dichtungen*, p. 22.
127. Ibid., p. 26.
128. Ibid., pp. 28–30.
129. Jacques de Vitry, *The Exempla*, ed. Thomas F. Crane (London, 1890), CCXLI, 100. Another priest was given his option by the bishop to abandon his concubine or give up his parish. He preferred to quit his parish; but when the woman saw that he had resigned a rich parish and had become poor, she forsook him.
130. I am grateful for this suggestion to Prof. Giles Constable of the Department of History, Harvard University.
131. Wulff, *Die Frauenfeindlichen Dichtungen*, pp. 35–41.
132. Wolfgang Stammler, "Frau Welt, Eine mittelalterliche Allegorie," *Freiburger Universitätsreden*, N.F. 23 (Freiburg i.d.S., 1959), pp. 23–24.
133. Ibid., p. 35.
134. Ibid., p. 76.
135. E. William Monter points to the need for an interdisciplinary study of this problem in "The Historiography of Witchcraft: Progress and Prospects," *Journal of Interdisciplinary History*, II, No. 4 (1972), p. 450.
136. Nikolaus Paulus, *Hexenwahn und Hexenprozess* (Freiburg i.B., 1910), devotes an entire chapter to the medieval sources on this question of the preeminence of women in witchcraft and sorcery (see pp. 195–247).
137. See for example, F. X. Arnold, *Woman and Man, Their Nature and Mission* (Freiburg and London, 1963), p. 50: "The focal point of woman's nature is her heart, her affections and emotions. Man's focal point on the other hand is more in his intelligence."
138. John F. Benton, "Clio and Venus: An Historical View of Medieval Love," *The Meaning of Courtly Love*, ed. F. X. Newman (Albany, N.Y., 1968), p. 35: "Courtesy was created by men for their own satisfaction, and it emphasized a woman's role as an object, sexual or otherwise."
139. Karl Barth, *Church Dogmatics* (Edinburgh, 1961), III, Part 4, p. 171.

Canon Law and the Battle of the Sexes

CLARA MARIA HENNING

A world on the move and an innovative Church council have forced the Catholic Church to look at itself. Sister churches, but more so secular society, are scrutinizing the Church's external appearance and its internal attitudes. Although they themselves have only in the very recent past taken steps to alleviate practices of the most overt type of discrimination against women, other groups are pointing out that the Catholic Church still insists on treating one half of her membership as *auspicia*, people whose descent disqualifies them from communion with God. The *auspicia*, of course, are Catholic women, and their negative treatment is sanctioned by a vast system of law.

"Canon law" elicits an awesome reverence from most of us, even though it has in many quarters fallen into such disrepute that many will scoff at its very existence and negate its usefulness *in toto*. It is so much identified with strictures, prohibitions, and pretentious authority that it has discouraged lay people in general from making a serious study of canonical science. And yet a full understanding of the Catholic Church requires a study of canon law, for it contains literally all thinking relative to the Church—its history and theology, political makeup, and sociology. Women

267

especially should apply themselves here. The law of the Church is used, on the one hand, as an excuse for many ills, and on the other hand, as an excuse not to correct the ills that beset the Church; both rationalizations are especially true in regard to the status of women. If more women were to interest themselves in Church law, if nothing else, a full understanding of it would make them realize that "working and waiting from the inside" may not be the most effective approach to changing women's status in the Church.

The study of canon law is not the healthiest undertaking for women; the dust that has accumulated over several hundred years gets into one's lungs and does, to be sure, very little for peace of mind. But canon law does demonstrate better than perhaps any other discipline the inordinate degree to which Christianity has guided Western civilization in its attitudes toward women, and it is through this study that women would come to realize the immense credibility gap that exists between their aspirations toward full integration and the various organizational definitions that support the status quo. Women would find the study of canon law intellectually stimulating and enriching but at the same time most frustrating. A modern woman could not help but find herself overcome by feelings of indignity and at other times by wild bemusement at the immense naïveté with which the laws affecting her sisters seem to have been written.

Everybody is studying the status of women. Every Christian and non-Christian denomination has a committee under way, and I never fail to marvel at the courageous application and decisiveness that the Canon Law Society of America brings to its own investigation. It was in 1971 that the society first decided to study the status of women in canon law, and absolutely nothing has come of it.

In reality, of course, the subject has been researched quite enough. Some of our best theological minds have applied themselves to the question of women's role in Church life and have concluded that, at least in theology, there is no valid reason for denying women full participation in the active ministry. Once their researches and opinions are given some consideration, it only remains to ask, "So why are women still not given the opportunity and right to study toward the priesthood?" The answers inevitably involve the law of the Church; it simply does not permit it. A most sensible counterreply is, "Then let us change the law," and there are undoubtedly many, many canonists who would gladly go along with that suggestion if it were that easy. However, canonists are by no means legislators, and unlike contemporary secular law, canon law is not changed by lobbyists, courts, or the deliberations of legislators but depends in a curious way on the will of a small group of men, who, by the Church's definition, would have to be moved by the Holy Spirit. These men not only are all past the virile age and were trained in seminaries—literally—to believe that women are quite inferior beings, but they have, moreover, been trained to regard canon law as a somewhat static discipline that reaches far back into the Church's past. They are taught that this past must by all means be respected and continued.

The 2,414 laws of the *Code of Canon Law* of 1917 are not, by any means, the exclusive body of law the canonist works with. Also involved are some thousands of decrees and decretals, thousands of laws promulgated by local Church councils in the past, and dozens of law compilations of many hundreds of years ago. No one has ever counted how many instructions, not to speak of decisions, there are that serve to elucidate and explain the law. All this material is the canon law, at the same time that it explains the more contemporary *Code* of 1917. Every one of these systems of legislation reaches at some point into the life of a woman, either directly or by negative manipulation of her place in the Church politic.

In the following pages we shall have the opportunity to refer to only a very few of these laws and canonical sources. Two of the very early sources we will be using are the *Didascalia Apostolorum* and the *Apostolic Constitutions*. Without engaging in an academic discussion of their true origin, let us just accept that the *Didascalia* is a pseudoapostolic collection that probably was written in the second half of the third century in either Syria or Palestine, and that the *Constitutions* were written in Syria in approximately 380 A.D. (The latter actually comprises a partial adaptation of the *Didascalia*.) A third reference source of canon law was the *Concordia discordantium canonum*, by the great canonist and compiler Gratian, of the twelfth century. This is a massive compilation of Church law before and up to Gratian's time and is regarded not only as a source book but as an authoritative teaching manual. The current *Code of Canon Law* relies heavily on Gratian's work as source material. In any case, together these few sources from the past present us with a convenient cross section of canonical jurisprudence. The first two documents depict the extreme dependence of contemporary law on ancient writings, and Gratian's work builds for us a bridge between the mass of older canon law and our own times.

It is very important to keep in mind that the opinions of the Church Fathers on any subject have always carried the voice of authority and that, in fact, their pronouncements were and still are regarded as laws in their own right.[1] Therefore, we must appreciate that if any law in the *Code* of 1917 requires elucidation, the canonist will research into the past sources, whether they are ancient documents, Church councils, teachings of the Fathers, or compilations of canon law and papal pronouncements, all of which will carry the weight of authority to this very day. This looking backward is in a real sense a constraining influence, but it is also a principle that is written into the *Code*, whose Can. 6, nn. 2, 3, 4, stipulates that other canons must be interpreted in the spirit of the old law.

The law of the Church is designed to elevate one group at the expense of another: women are sacrificed as human beings to elevate priests to the status of sanctified beings. The law was written over the centuries by men for men, and by men who regarded sex (which is still today very hard to come by without women) as quite undesirable. In that men wrote for men, and then celibates for celibates, women were written out of the organization of the Church and out of the sanctuary. As far as the spirit of canon law is concerned, the Church seems to assume that it can do very well without women.

Anyone who has spent a few years among a large group of men must conclude that men have a singularly exclusive feeling about themselves. They like each other. Men find women alien, and this, I believe, is particularly true of celibate men, who, after all, have gone through years of conditioning that agitates against women and is in favor of proposing the priesthood as a pure and superior club. I often felt in canon law school like an intruder in a boys' club tree house: the prevalent spirit was "No girls allowed."

In the following pages we shall discuss some of the canonical rules that affect women in the Church. Perhaps the difficulties involved in changing the organizational Church's attitude toward females will become apparent if we trace, even to an inadequate degree and, to canonists, in a devastatingly simplistic fashion, the origins of some of the more overt laws that discriminate against females.

There are, of course, many rules that are an insult to women in addition to the famous Can. 968 which forbids females the sacred ministry. That prohibition must be viewed in connection with other discriminatory laws and their origins as they developed over two thousand years of antifemale theology and legislation.

Modern Catholic women can marvel at diocesan statutes that required, until almost only yesterday, that a priest make a woman rider sit in the rear of his car, even though—indeed, especially when—the seat next to his was unoccupied. Were the legislators worried that the priest would succumb to the woman's female presence, or did they perhaps fear that the woman would be overpowered by the godly person next to her and start fondling the priest? We may safely exclude the possibility that the legislators had traffic safety in mind. We said that such rules existed until only yesterday because we would like to give certain western, midwestern and southern dioceses the benefit of the doubt. . . . The fact remains that such rules are an insult to both adults involved because they presume an extreme lack of self-restraint on the part of both priest and rider.

The contemporary woman might be equally surprised to learn of statutes in relation to the above that require a person observing a priest riding in a car with a woman next to him to report it to the bishop. Mankind's justified outrage at totalitarian countries that encourage citizens to spy on one another finds no parallel in the law of Christ's Church.

The modern woman must be distressed to realize that canon law (reiterated by many diocesan statutes) requires that only mature women over the age of fifty may serve as housekeepers in parish houses. It is again insulting to both priests and women, for this rule presumes that all sorts of illicit sexual activities might occur if anyone below the age of menopause vacuums a priest's bedroom and dusts his stereo set. In keeping with changing conditions, the Church should be concerned to update this law, because, as we all know, there are now many snappy seventy-year-old women —and priests.

How could such sexual innuendos possibly have been worked into a body of law? A fully satisfactory answer would require volumes of historical and theological, as well as juridical, analysis. Let us remind ourselves that the Catholic Church is defined on the basis of many sexual allusions that surface into the governing constitution. Think, for example, of the gospel visions of the Church as the bride of Christ (Eph. 5:23 ff.). This seems quite naturally to encourage like descriptions, such as the bishop as bridegroom to his bride the diocese, among others.[2] Such analogies invite visions of honeymoons, blushing young things and ardent lovers, and probably rely heavily on the ancient, erroneous belief that the male alone effects life in the act of copulation: Christ therefore creates life in his Church, the bishop in his diocese, the priest in his congregation, and so on, toward the delegation of women as mere receptacles of men's life-giving forces. It is a philosophical approach to order which over centuries established the ecclesiological concept that the Church must be guided by men only.

It would be very hard to deny that the Church is intimately sexist. Sexist attitudes abound, reflected in laws, for example, that require women to cover their heads in church,[3] discourage women from singing in Church,[4] still prohibit women from approaching the altar during celebration, and do not admit girls or women as Mass servers.[5]

If we accept that one reason for these laws is a misinterpreted view of biological processes that saw the male as the initiator of life, perhaps another is a general fear of women. One reason, however, that must in any case be accepted is men's inordinate fear of and disgust with women's menstrual cycle. The male's peculiar awe and discomfort regarding the female's menstruation is, in fact, very pronounced in the canonical sources. It militated against an acceptance of deaconesses, of whom we will come to speak shortly. Several contemporary authors are convinced that a major factor for the exclusion of women from liturgical roles and organizational law lies in this discomfort. Thus Erling Brodersen writes: "I must

. . . emphasize that the biological fact of menstruation is the main obstacle to women's participation in liturgical functions: one always shied away from it with fear. The demand for cultic cleanliness won out against the deaconess."[6]

As we shall see, even a most liberal role of deaconesses in Antioch was amended to read "if she is not in the way." The fear of menstruation is found in discussions of women in general and deaconesses in particular. Thus Dionysius of Alexandria (died c. 264 A.D.) declared that a menstruating woman may not take communion or go to church,[7] and Theodor Balsamon taught that "the uncleanliness of menstruation banished the deaconess from her role before the holy altar."[8] We might further quote Theodores of Canterbury, who declared that "women may not step into a Church during the period of their menstruation. Neither lay women nor nuns should attempt this."[9]

The above may serve as a context in which to view a few of the general laws that forbade women all liturgical functions. For a woman, her menstrual cycle is only a very minor part of her identity, and at worst an annoyance, whereas from reading men's comments about this biological process, one might be led to believe that woman's destiny is conditioned by a debilitating loss of blood and the need for constant transfusions. In any case, although the above comments are no longer listed as "reasons" for confining women, these ancient rationales continuously lowered woman's place in the Church until we learn of laws affecting our very lives, such as the law that views a woman as the very last possible candidate to perform a baptism.

Canon 742/2 establishes that in baptizing, a priest is preferred to a deacon, a deacon to a subdeacon, a cleric before a layman, and a man before a woman. There is a perverted charm to the innocence with which canon law assigns women the lowest rank in this little hierarchy of values, but it does so on the authority and by extension of a very ancient rule found in the *Apostolic Constitutions* which even in the fourth century declared that baptism by women is "dangerous and godless."[10] Gratian incorporated this ancient principle into his own work seven hundred years later;[11] Pope Urban II (1088–1099) seems to have been one of very few exceptions in conceiving of the idea that women might possibly be harmless ministers of baptism,[12] and the contemporary Can. 742

consequently appears in the twentieth century as a compromise.

Ida Raming, a contemporary German theologian and canonist of truly exceptional ability and commitment to women's rights, cleverly points out that the enlightening element about the prohibition against women as ministers of baptism in the *Constitutions* lies in this document's view of the act of baptizing as a show of rather worldly power. It depicts woman as the body of the man. She was created from man's rib, and was chosen to bear the pain of childbirth; and granted this demeaning position, how could she possibly perform the "governing" act of baptism?[13]

Canon 813, which forbids women to serve at Mass unless there is no man present, and which further requires the woman, if she does serve, not to go near the altar and to give answers only from afar, more readily depicts the seemingly contaminating effect of woman's presence. Precedents of this law comprise, among others, ancient prohibitions against cohabitation of priests and women,[14] and are related to the very interesting Can. 845, which until recently prohibited lay persons from spending communion. Whereas Can. 845 affects all lay persons, its meaning for women lies in the precedent of Can. 2 of the Synod of Reims (c. 624), which first denied women the right to spend communion. Gratian again adopted this synodal law six hundred years later, and Can. 845 appears once more as a compromise between the mores of very old and more "contemporary" times. Still, today it appears pitifully backward when the Congregation of the Sacraments eases the restrictions of Can. 845 by granting the privilege of spending communion to male lay persons or nuns when priests are not available.[15] The sense conveyed by such manipulation of the law is that if they be women, at least let them be undefiled by sex.

It has further become apparent how very much resistance there is against ordinary women in the role of lectors. The Church can and does again rely on the ancient laws. It can once more rely on the *Didascalia* and the *Apostolic Constitutions*, because (on the basis of I Cor. 11:3 and Eph. 5:23, 28) both discourage women from teaching.[16] The *Constitutions* reason that Jesus chose to send only men, not women, and that, after all, the man is the head of his wife, with the conclusion that consequently a woman cannot pretend to be in a teaching position "over a man." Gratian, of course, drew upon these sources to support his own teaching that women should not be heard preaching the word of God,[17] and we find this feeling fresh and forceful in Can. 1342/2.

The above is but a very simplistic exposition of historical canon law, its attitudes, and the influence the past has on our present times. No respectable canonist would dare ignore this past completely.

The exclusion of women from minor liturgical functions and finally the priestly ministry is intimately tied to the entire historical phenomenon of deaconesses. We cannot ignore the historical and legal record pertaining to deaconesses, because this conditions any discussion of women ministers in the Catholic Church. If one looks at the footnotes to Can. 968 (which reserves ordination to baptized males), it is surprising that this very important canon is not supported by at least a score of the literally hundreds of ancient laws that denied to women ordination of any kind.[18] The hundreds of laws that might have been cited in the footnotes involve ancient pronouncements against female Christians in general, but, very important, the many comments against deaconesses.

Several books have been written on deaconesses during the past three years, and there is under way a strong movement to have deaconesses reintroduced into the orders of the Church. The re-establishment of the deaconate for women is seen as a touchstone for female advancement in the Church. But when viewed in relation to our desire for women ministers, it may actually be a "cop-out," and may indeed be a step backward. The legal status of deaconesses in the first few centuries seems to have been that of ordained servants and nothing more. We must be very much on the alert in seeing that this status will not be reintroduced along with the order. The early deaconess was placed under severe restrictions. Indeed, the ancient record indicates that the Church sought from the very beginning to eliminate the order from the life of the Church.

The Greek term *diaconein* suggests a voluntary and personal self-spending in service (in contrast to *doulenein*, which connotes a slavelike submission in service). The concept of *diaconein* was instituted even during apostolic times to describe a recognized office in the early Christian community; indications of it are found in Phil. 1:1, I Tim. 3:8, and II Tim. 4:5, while Acts 6:6 describes the rite of ordination proper to this office for women and men without difference: "They brought them before the apostles, and they, after prayer, laid their hands upon them." We are immediately reminded of Phoebe, whom Paul recommends as "our sister, a deaconess of the church of Cenchreae. Please give her a Christian welcome, and any assistance with her work that she may need. She has herself been of great assistance to many, not excluding myself" (Rom. 16:1–2). A main issue would be whether or not Phoebe's office can be regarded as having had significance as a sacerdotal ministry—equal to that of men—in the Church of Christ, but so very much in our investigations would have to rely on presumptions, and we are forced to turn to the more generous historical record of succeeding centuries.

Saint Ignatius of Antioch, in 117 A.D., was the first to mention a stratification in orders according to bishops, presbyters, and deacons, male and female. The functions of these early deaconesses were clearly roles of service in the sense of the Greek *diaconein*, but it becomes apparent that their main obligations throughout the first centuries involved assisting in the ministering to women. The important *Apostolic Constitutions* in the second half of the fourth century still allude especially to their original teaching function, but describe their role primarily as messengers, keepers of the door at church, and as assistants at baptism.[19] Although such assignments point to women's active participation in the ministry of the Church, it is clear from the record that deaconesses were in no way self-assertive. Perhaps we might term their activities rights rather than obligations, rights that were strictly defined: deaconesses were cautioned not to give quick answers and to answer only as much as necessary when giving instructions; to be cautious in explaining the mysteries of the faith; not to preach in a holy place; further, not to enter into theological disputations; not to serve at the altar; and to refrain from baptizing on their own authority.[20] Male deacons were not given such restrictive guidelines in which to function.

Whatever ministries were initially assigned to women were apparently removed with every succeeding century. If the right to attend to the care of women, minor teaching functions, and other such minor services as lighting lamps (a task traditionally reserved for the mother in Jewish religion) was their ministry, even those limited opportunities for involvement apparently were regarded as a threat. Saint Epiphanius by the middle of the fourth century scolds those who would extend the ministry of the deaconesses to include sacerdotal functions, and warns not to call them "presbyteridas," lest anyone suppose they actually have sacerdotal powers.[21] Perhaps he was relating more to such liberal usages as described in the *Testamentum Domini nostri Jesu Christi*, of the fifth century, which tells us that deaconesses carried the éucharist to women who were ill at home (II, 20); but the opinion of Epiphanius obviously reflected the majority opinion. As we have already mentioned, this privilege was finally denied to deaconesses by the Synod of Reims in about 624 A.D.

Significant for our short evaluation are the titles and status given to the order of deaconesses. For instance, it is complicated to relate the order of deaconess to the order of widow. These titles were often used interchangeably and at times synonymously in the sources to describe women who carried out the same duties. Also, widows and deaconesses are often placed in different hierarchical order. The *Apostolic Constitutions* in the fourth century commands widows to obey deaconesses,[22] while the *Testamentum Domini nostri Jesu Christi*, one century later, places widows above deaconesses.[23] Mary Daly, Mary Lawrence McKenna, and Erling Brodersen, among others, present the history of deaconesses, widows, and virgins as a definitive development that may be very misleading because it conjures up in the mind of the reader a smooth evolution of their offices. In our view, these titles reflect the utter confusion of early churchmen as they were trying to come to terms with the problem of having to deal with women in areas of activities they felt were reserved to males. The confusion of names reflects their confusion of sentiments toward females. We may have a parallel in contemporary solutions to the demands of liberationist groups on companies to promote more women to managerial posts; secretaries are given new, important-sounding titles, such as "vice-president" or "administrative assistant," while they continue to perform the same secretarial chores.

A few more words about the rank accorded deaconesses. Generally they fell below bishops, priests, and deacons, while they outranked exorcists and minor clerics, but significantly the *Apostolic Constitutions* subordinated deaconesses to the extent that deacons

could excommunicate these women![24] Their low position in the
scheme of a hierarchy is further indicated in that deaconesses had
to share one-tenth of the gifts of the faithful at Mass with sub-
deacons, lectors, and singers—that is, not with their "equals," the
deacons.[25]

Therefore, we might propose that if you light lamps, you are
doing one of many boring chores priests do not want to bother
with. We are, of course, concentrating on the many negative aspects of the historical record, hoping that others will present the
bright side. We are trying to depict the dangers involved in blindly
demanding the reintroduction of the order of deaconesses "as it
existed in the young Church," and we are thereby running the danger of complicity in a crime committed over the centuries by
thousands of canonists who have quoted the negative record to rationalize their prohibitions against women's active involvement in
the ministry. This is forcefully impressed upon us by Erling Brodersen, the young Danish theologian of astounding insight and
learning who in 1970 earned a doctorate by presenting a dissertation
whose fury at the past and present treatment of women in the
Church impresses us as nothing less than inspiring. Brodersen cites
the very liberal usage of the Monophysitic Church of Antioch, as
told by Johannes of Tala (c. 538 A.D.), where deaconesses were permitted free access to the sanctuary (if they did not have their
monthly period, N.B.!) and where they functioned as the spenders
of communion.[26] Brodersen comments:

> Those authors with whom we have been dealing, whether on pur-
> pose or not, have either not mentioned this passage or have hidden
> it into a corner of their works. If one can detect it at all under-
> neath the dust, one would in any case need a strong magnifying
> glass. Behind this silence there probably hides a super radical tabu
> attitude which is particularly at home in Roman Catholic circles.
> . . . A mis-formed male ego can not comprehend how such per-
> mission could have been granted.[27]

Central to our present-day understanding of the early deaconess as a predecessor to future women ministers is the question
of whether deaconesses were or were not ordained—and, if the laws
of Church councils are an indication, they most certainly were not.

The *Apostolic Constitutions*, three and a half centuries after Paul, and the Council of Chalcedon, in 451 A.D., give us the ritual of ordination proper to deaconesses, which is the same as depicted in Acts 6:6. The latter describes their ministry as a *leitourgia*.[28] But even before, and certainly later, this important issue became more and more obscured.

The *Apostolic Traditions* of Hippolytus, in the early third century, describes widows as chosen and thereby conveniently neglects to mention a separate act of ordination.[29] The Council of Nicea, in 325 A.D., orders that women who were ordained in the Paulicean sect are to be considered laywomen upon entry into the Catholic Church—which gives rise to the suggestion that the Church did not have an order of ordained women in 325.[30] The Council of Laodicea, of the mid-fourth century, explains, "It is not proper to ordain priestesses or presidents of the assembly,"[31] and the Council of Orleans (535 A.D.) outrightly prohibited the ordination of women, offering us as a reason the fact that women are a weak sex.[32]

The ecclesiastical record in the West in general offers a picture that makes the reader believe that ordained women existed only *par accidens*, that is to say, in spite of prohibitions against the practice, but possibly because of the definite albeit rapidly fading tradition in the East. Without going into a detailed history, let us just say that the record provides a pattern of slow evolution from the deaconate of women as an instituted ministry of individual service to a ministry of service that finds its institutional expression with the rise of religious communities. With the growth of monastic life the phenomenon of charismatic and committed women slowly merges with the phenomenon of convent life.[33] Synods and councils between the fourth and sixth centuries (Nimes in 394, the Council of Orange in 441, Epaeon in 517, and Orleans in 523) repeatedly denounce the deaconate for women as an institution, while they occasionally, though vaguely, acknowledge that such an institution exists "in other places."

Whatever later sources we might find comfort in—such as sources that mention nuns, a queen, or a pope's wife who was given the breviary, maniple, and in certain cases the stole—the fact remains that by the time of Saint Thomas women in general had finally been delegated to a place where they are, as a group, distinguished even from lay people. As far as women are concerned, the Church had impressed its sanctions against them to the extent that one finds after the tenth century very few pronouncements in Church legislation for or against women.

To argue whether ordination during the early six centuries was one of sacramental character that could be revived today seems inconclusive from the start, simply because the sources are so ambiguous. Our clues would have to come from the very first decades rather than centuries, but as R. J. A. van Eyden has already pointed out, such a question has to be a juridic question while the Church was not yet juridic in outlook.[34] The only reliable conclusion we can draw seems to be that the activities of deaconesses were quite distinct from those of presbyters and also deacons, and that the deaconesses were gradually confined in their functions to an ever more limited sphere of activities, until women who wished to serve became walled in by convents. If we therefore wish to reinstitute the deaconate for women, we must be clear in our deliberations whether we really want the order as it was many hundreds of years ago. For one thing, we must as women involve ourselves wholly in any legislation that seeks to design this order for our times. But at a time when some of us are demanding the power to absolve, to celebrate Mass, and to otherwise fully minister to the needs of people, will we be satisfied with the offer of an ordained role that allows us little more than the lighting of lamps? And we must be aware of the possibility that a sophisticated power play may be in the offing if the Church does decide to ordain deaconesses but continues to prohibit women ministers with full sacerdotal powers. Since deaconesses still will not be full ministers, they will support the priesthood by taking over many of the minor chores, and thereby inadvertently conspire in the preservation of an all male and celibate—albeit increasingly shrinking—priesthood, making it thus a more elite group than it is even now.

The history of deaconesses extends one message to Catholic Christian women: *Get thee to a nunnery!* The various sources taken from councils, early documents, and the teachings of Church Fathers (and we have mentioned perhaps one half a percent of the entire record) have over the centuries contributed to a solid juridical foundation on the basis of which at least the ruling body of our Church cannot conceive the integration of females in the active ministry.

There is one area of canon law that is rarely mentioned in connection with the desire for equality between men and women, and this is women's position in relation to the procedural law of marriage cases. There are several rules that are particularly arrogant in this specialized area of law, and the reader may enjoy a short discussion of these. I believe a few points in the procedure are especially indicative of negative attitudes toward women and depict as well a curious relationship between these attitudes and what may be indigenously celibate male fantasies. For the most part our discussion will involve rules involving the physical examination of women. Such examinations are most often called for in non-consummation cases in which the question presents itself whether or not two married partners have engaged in sexual intercourse.

Because consummation is under normal circumstances most easily detected in the woman partner to a marriage, the norms for the physical examination of a person center more often on an examination of her body than that of her husband. Of course, if a woman or a man points to some physical problem associated with the man, or if the wife's physical integrity cannot be established absolutely, the man will be asked to submit to a physical examination.

To explain some of the references to follow, we should mention two documents issued by the Sacred Congregation of the Sacraments in 1923 and 1936. These serve to explain, elucidate, and complement the procedural law concerning marriage cases as laid down in Book IV of the *Code*,[35] and are appropriately enough referred to as 1923 *Instruction* and 1936 *Instruction*.[36] Both documents are quite thorough in reiterating the laws of the *Code* when applicable and are therefore usually referred to without further cross-reference to the *Code*.

The Instruction of 1923, issued specifically for non-consummation cases, specifies that two midwives with proper certificates and experience should be appointed for the physical inspection of the woman. However, the woman to be examined may ask that two physicians instead of midwives undertake the examination. If neither physicians nor midwives are available, two married women (matrons), who are selected by the court, may examine the woman. In the latter case the matrons' reports must be submitted to one or two experts in medicine, so that their conclusions may be checked authoritatively.[37] The 1936 *Instruction* essentially repeats these simple rules.

However, later in 1942 an attempt was made to clarify the above through an instruction from the Holy Office. In this new instruction, male doctors are referred to as "physicians" and female doctors as "women with a doctor's degree," the latter then being lumped together with "women who have at least a legal certificate of fitness for the practice as midwives." The instruction then declares that, "After the inspection has been performed by the women, they shall be orally examined by the Tribunal itself, but always in the presence of a physician who is genuinely learned in these matters and entirely honorable; and the latter may make remarks and put appropriate questions."[38] What the law here establishes is that the opinion of a woman doctor giving testimony before the court must be corroborated by a male colleague. Lest it be said that this is perhaps an individualistic interpretation of the law, the reader is referred to George Evans,[39] and further invited to enroll in the School of Canon Law, where this interpretation is still taught today. I do not know personally of any case where it has been employed, but, then, I know of many instances where some very worthwhile and equitable laws on the books are rarely if ever employed by the courts.

One aspect of the provisions for male and female physicians or midwives which seems particularly out of tune with evolving contemporary attitudes toward both patient and the medical profession is the fact that the law establishes a double standard in the examination of men and women. The rules establish that two male physicians will examine a man in the case of alleged impotence, and that two female physicians, midwives, or matrons will examine a woman. But as we have seen, male physicians are also allowed for the woman "if she consents" or if males are assigned by decree of the court. Since the distinction between male and female doctors and other female examiners is made only in regard to the examination of the woman, the law must be interpreted to exclude the same choice of female doctors from an examination of a male.

The physicians a woman may ask for according to the 1923 *Instruction* are clearly meant to be males, and the question presents itself whether a man may request female doctors or midwives or matrons for his examination. The law is in any case still operative and has only recently met with some thought from the Canon Law Society of America and the Canadian Canon Law Society; both propose a simple reformulation to the effect that "an expert shall be designated."[40]

The procedural norms further prescribe how physicians or other competent persons should proceed in their examination. When an ecclesiastical judge orders the examination of a woman, he must also instruct the woman to be examined to take a bath for one half hour unless the examiner advises him that this would be harmful or useless.[41] A man to be examined is not likewise instructed to take a bath. Perhaps someone is missing her big chance by not making a canonical investigation of the historical law on this point and selling it to the feminine-hygiene-deodorant people.

Only the most innocent among us will fail to grasp exactly the evidence on which an expert will base his diagnosis regarding the fact of consummation. It is clear that the examiner will investigate whether or not the woman's hymen is broken;[42] and there are ample provisions for how this determination should be made. The examiner is thus told to provide in his or her report detailed information about the woman's hymen, such as its form and type, and the size as well as position of the orificium. Of great importance is a determination as to the degree of elasticity, and thus penetrability, observed in the hymen.[43] The rules further provide that the above examination should be "visual, digital, and instrumental."[44]

Canon lawyers are usually trained to regard testimony of an intimate and sexual nature with clinical professionalism, but unfortunately many, many priests who work in tribunals and consequently send women to these examinations and then evaluate the results are not canonists. Most tribunal officials are not only not canonists but also are quite young and hence often do not have the experience to realize what effects their questions about the intimacies of a marriage can have on a distressed woman who seeks a divorce from a man with whom she cannot have relations. It is of course altogether amazing that the laity is expected to subject itself to a system that allows itself outrageous violations of privacy of the most intimate kind. It is even more amazing that the laity still subjects itself to such procedure.

Church law as it pertains to marriage in general and ecclesiastical trial law as it applies to marriage cases seem unduly voyeuristic. I cannot imagine that any group of women, over no matter how many centuries and under no matter what primitive conditions and times, would compose laws that make detailed inquiries into the thickness of a woman's hymen. Nor can I believe that women would devise laws that inquire into the length of a man's foreskin—speaking of which, we should in all fairness mention that the length of a man's penis under special circumstances also enters the picture. Of course, we could further examine enough volumes that discuss the length of a woman's vagina to fill a small but respectable library, whereas the length of a man's penis has over the years been treated in but a few articles of minor length. However, all this might involve us in further discussions about artificial vaginas, missing uteri, and the fascinating topic of how peasant folk in olden times would fake "unimpaired" hymens. But we will leave these topics to the dustbin of canonical history.

A writer at the turn of the last century made the observation that "the woman of today [1896] who realizes that the home circle as at present constituted affords insufficient scope for her energies, had a precursor in the nun who sought a field of activity in the convent."[45] Women in medieval times realized that Church work was not open to them except within the religious life, and convents as instituted *diaconein* were still the only means of serving the Church open to women who felt themselves called until—it seems incredible—only a very few years ago. Today Catholic Christian women no longer accept this form as the only possibility. They are holding onto the tail end of the forces of feminism.

It would not be respectable to close without mentioning the Second Vatican Council. The powerful theme of the common priesthood of all believers (I Peter 2:9–10) has been advanced with new vigor in the document "The Church in the Modern World": "Those who believe in Christ, who are reborn not from the flesh but from water and the Holy Spirit, are finally established as 'a chosen race, a royal priesthood, a holy nation, a purchased people.' "[46] These are not only the echoes of Paul but, from the East, the echoes of Justin Martyr (165 A.D.), who attributed priesthood to Christians as a race,[47] Irenaeus, at the beginning of the third century, who explained that "all just possess the priestly rank,"[48] and Origen (253 A.D.), who taught that "all who have been anointed with the oil of sacred chrism are made priests."[49] It will be remembered, however, that Tertullian, who also held the notion of the common priesthood of all believers, taught simultaneously that "it is not allowed to a woman to speak in church, but neither to preach, nor to baptize, nor to claim a part in any man's duty, much less to share the duty of the priestly office."[50] Also Vatican II speaks of "the royal priesthood" of the laity, of all. The laity—and it does include women—is mentioned in almost every document of the council. The laity's and women's contributions are vital.[51] But where are they welcome? Where is woman's place in the common priesthood? One might assume in the liturgy if we did not know better. We cannot ignore the fact that very ancient misogynistic attitudes still dominate the thinking of churchmen: Only yesterday the German diplomat Elizabeth Mueller was denied diplomatic recognition at the Vatican because "a woman would be upsetting."[52]

It would seem that woman's place still is that assigned her over the centuries in the home, in convents, and more recently perhaps in such worldly occupations as time has shown she can successfully perform—and of the latter there are hardly any left besides the sacred ministry in the Catholic Church. Today more and more writers are pressuring the Catholic hierarchy to grant women full participation in the Church, that is, in the planning of Church affairs as well as in functions that are its essence—the ministry of souls. But in recent months we have noticed a change of emphasis in this pressure. If enlightened men and women asked yesterday why a modern, educated, and charismatically endowed woman should not be able to enter the sacred ministry, we now hear occasionally that women are not asking for a privilege but that they may demand a right. There are today many women and men who would join Brodersen when he declares: "Today, it is not a question of the commandment to love, but solely a matter of legal rights. One has totally neglected to accord the woman a right as such, and it is rather a fact that the woman has been legally suppressed under the pretense of equality."[53]

This writer's position is that concerned Catholics should abandon a position of appeal to the hierarchy for one of assertion. This position demands revolution, and if we want to see radical change in the position of women in the Catholic Church we must remember that at no time in history and nowhere in the world were changes brought about solely by women in mantillas praying demurely before an altar. We find ourselves in the unfruitful and ridiculous position of arguing with churchmen that we are worthy of their recognition, when we should ask ourselves how these men can believe themselves authorized to deny us rights over and beyond Gospel passages that declare the equality of all in the eyes of God.

The operative law of the Church is designed to grant men—specifically priests—the absolute controlling position. Since it is only human to enjoy and defend power, we should not expect a radical change of attitude to come from them. Neither should we expect to find convincing reasons for a change in the historical record of canonical jurisprudence, because the few charitable voices we will hear from the past will drown in the fury of pronouncements against women. We are confronted with a system that will in every likelihood continue to write discriminatory new laws on the basis of the discriminatory old law.

Let us quickly interject that there are of course many ordinary priests and even some churchmen in ruling positions who would not hesitate to grant women their human rights, and those who have spoken out openly should be commended by all women for bridging the vast credibility gap that exists between their training, the law, and their sensitive positions. But how long are we to wait until one of them does anything concrete about women's lowly status? When will the first liberal bishop ordain one of the several women who are presently fully qualified and waiting for the priesthood?

It may be validly said that research into the history whereby women in the Church are not able to exercise their talents and ambitions is a mere academic game. But this research has its value in the same way as have investigations into the reasons for which black-skinned Americans were forced to ride in the back of public buses, even if it serves no other end than to bare the frustrating possibility that there is no other solution but revolution. Again, some among us may indeed get a charge out of knowing the etiology of Can. 742, and the anthropologists and behaviorists among us may analyze the laws' sexual allegories evident in the descriptions of the bishop's relationship of bridegroom to his diocese as male fantasies sublimating male desires for the power to give birth. But the time comes when we must leave such academic indulgences to the forum of universities and Newman Center lectures. How do we get into the sacristies?

It is most difficult to chart a course of action. What means could possibly be devised to force the institutional Church to a showdown? We have tried petitions, have tried to gain interviews with Church leaders, only to be either refused or smiled at. We have studied theology, Church history, religious education, and canon law, but all for nought—unless we use these areas of knowledge aggressively.

The sad fact is that women are organizationally far stronger than they dare realize. This strength lies in a newly awakening intelligentsia of women in homes, universities, and convents, and in the magnificent organizational structures of our religious orders. We seem to be waiting for God to show us through some dramatic sign how to combine these forces, and they would indeed be formidable forces. Who if not nuns and women in general are in charge of millions of young minds? Who if not women support the Church through labor and money? Should we ever make up our minds that we want to influence the course of the Church's future, a unified effort by all women of the Church—involving concrete education programs in high schools and colleges, and economic boycotts—would surely prevail against empty theological excuses, discriminatory laws, and the collectively self-righteous ego trip of the all-male hierarchy.

When I follow moon launchings and say "Godspeed" to Mars and Venus probes, I shudder to think what our Church will be all about in another few hundred years. I envision a future doctoral dissertation in canon law on the problem of whether or not a child born in orbit around Jupiter and baptized in reconditioned water may be considered properly baptized. Complications worthy of at least an additional two volumes would arise if that ceremony was conducted by a cloned person, and to boot, a cloned woman.[54] The Church's ossified thinking and fearfully reactionary attitudes toward women must be done away with in our lifetimes or it cannot survive. The scientific community is allowing us to appreciate that reproductive processes soon need no longer be tied to the act of copulation. Sperms are being frozen in sperm banks, and soon the female uterus will be reproduced with an ideal environmental glass comforter in the laboratory, while our Church will continue to be concerned about consummation and the thickness of a woman's hymen! Fearful threats as well as astonishing new possibilities are being opened up to us through science. But the Church will have less and less to say to this new world unless it can adopt a philosophy that is genuinely equal to the task of speaking about the dignity of humanity—both female and male.

NOTES

1. C. Munier, *Les sources patristiques du droit de l'Église du VIIIe au XIIIe siècle* (Mulhouse, Ger., 1957), p. 167. Canon 1366 of the *Code* prescribes adherence to the principles set by Aquinas.

2. *Pontificale Romanum* (Regensburg, 1888), I, 84.

3. Can. 1262/2; S.C. Conc. 12 Jan. 1930, *Acta Apostolicae Sedis*, 22–26.

4. Can. 1264; S.C. Rit. 18 Dec. 1908.

5. Can. 813.

6. Erling Brodersen, "Der Spender der Kommunion im Altertum und Mittelalter," unpubl. doctoral dissertation, Studies in Sacred Theology, 2d Ser., No. 213 (Washington, D.C.: The Catholic University of America, 1970), p. 98. See also Sr. Albertus Magnus in *National Catholic Reporter*, Jan. 5, 1966, p. 6; Ida Raming, "Zum Ausschluss der Frau vom Amt in der Kirche," unpubl. doctoral dissertation (Muenster in Westfalen: Westfaelische Wilhelms-Universitaet, 1969), *passim*.

7. Dionysius of Alexandria, *Epistolae*, in C. L. Feltoe, ed. *The Letters and Other Remains of Dionysius of Alexandria*, Cambridge Patristic Texts (Cambridge: Cambridge University Press, 1904), pp. 102 ff. See Brodersen, "Der Spender der Kommunion," p. 94.

8. *Florilegium Patristicum*, Bonnae, Theodor Balsamon, *Responsa ad interrogationes* Marci (Interrogatio 35), pp. 42, 64. See Brodersen, "Der Spender der Kommunion," p. 97.

9. In P. W. Finsterwalder, *Die Canones Theodori Cantuariensis und ihre Ueberlieferungsformen* (Weimar: Hermann Boehaus, 1929), D. 41, p. 234. See Brodersen, p. 115.

10. *Apostolic Constitutions*, III, 9, in F. X. Funk, ed. *Didascalia et Constitutiones Apostolorum* (Paderborn, Ger., 1905), pp. 199, 201.

11. C. 4, C. XX, *De cons.*

12. C. 30, C. IV, q. 3.

13. Raming, "Zum Ausschluss der Frau," pp. 22–23.

14. C. 1, X, *De coh. cleric et mulierum*, III, 2. In line with that thinking, Can. 133 of the *Code* makes a point of admonishing clerics to stay away from women of dubious social standing. Regarding women as Mass servers, attempts to ignore this rule were made as early as the mid-sixties; see "Those Girl Servers at Mass," *Homiletic and Pastoral Review*, LXVI (1965–66), 427–428.

15. *Notitiae*, I (1965), 139, nn. 41, 44.

16. *Apostolic Constitutions*, III, 16; *Didascalia*, III, 5, in F. X. Funk, ed. *Didascalia et Constitutiones Apostolorum*.

17. C. 4, C. XX, *De cons.*

18. Raming, "Zum Ausschluss der Frau," p. 9.

19. *Apostolic Constitutions*, III, 16.

20. *Loc. cit.*

21. Epiphanius, *Adversus Haereses*, in J. P. Migne, *Patrologiae Cursus Completus, Series Graeca* (PG) 161 vols. (Paris, 1857–66), LXXIX, 3, 4.

22. *Apostolic Constitutions*, III, 16.

23. *Testamentum Domini nostri Jesu Christi*, in I. E. Rahmani, ed. *Testamentum Domini nostri Jesu Christi* (Moguntiae, 1899).

24. "Diaconus excommunicat subdiaconum, lectorum, cantorem, diaconissam, si absente presbyero res id postulet," *Apostolic Constitutions*, III, 26.

25. *Apostolic Constitutions*, VIII, 31.

26. See text and commentary in Brodersen, p. 89.

27. Ibid., pp. 89–90.

28. *Apostolic Constitutions*, VIII, 19–20; J. Mansi, ed. *Sacrorum conciliorum nova et amplissima collectio*, 53 vols. in 59 vols. (Paris, 1901–27), VII, 363.

29. *La Tradition Apostolique de Saint Hippolyte*, in *Liturgiewissenschaftliche Quellen und Forschungen* (Muenster, 1963), XXXIX, passim.

30. K. J. Hefale, *History of the Christian Councils*, 5 vols. (Edinburgh, 1894–96), I, 431.

31. Can. 11, Mansi, II, 578.

32. Can. 18, Mansi, VIII, 837.

33. See Mary Lawrence McKenna, *Women in the Church* (New York: P. J. Kenedy and Sons, 1967), pp. 11–146.

34. R. J. A. van Eyden, "Die Frau im Kirchenamt; Plaedoyer fuer die Revision einer traditionellen Haltung," *Wort und Wahrheit*, XXII (May 1967), 354.

35. Book IV discusses three essential forms of trial procedure for various marriage cases which we will not deal with separately here. The most basic of these forms is "formal procedure," another involves summary procedure for the adjudication of six particular impediments to marriage, and the third form involves procedure for non-consummation cases.

36. S.C. de Sacramentis, decr. *De processibus in causis dispensationis super matrimonio rato et non consummato*, 7 May 1923, AAS, 389–413; S.C. de Sacramentis, *Instructio servanda a tribunalibus dioecesanis in pertranctandis causis de nullitate matrimoniorum*, 15 Aug. 1936, AAS, 313–361.

37. *1923 Instruction*, n. 89/1.

38. Decree June 12, 1942, AAS, 34–200.

39. George R. Evans, "Ratum et Non-consummatum Procedure: Regulations Concerning Corporal Examination," *The Jurist*, XVI (April 1956), 170–179.

40. "Resolutions of the Canon Law Society of America, September, 1968," Art. 18, *The Jurist*, XXIX (Jan. 1969), 26–27; Canadian Canon Law Society, "Recommendations Submitted to the Canadian Catholic Conference by the Canon Law Society for the Revision of Procedural Law," II, Art. 8, unpubl., Ottawa, June 25, 1969.

41. *1923 Instruction*, n. 92.

42. There are of course several ways by which a hymen can be broken without sexual intercourse (suppositories, horseback riding, dancing, karate lessons). The procedures provide for thorough inquiries into such possible causes.

43. Edward L. Heston, "Some Practical Hints on the Preparation of 'Super Rato' Cases," *The Jurist*, XVIII (July 1957), 279–286, 284; Joseph A. Hickey, "Requirements of the Ratum et Non-consummatum Process," *The Jurist*, V (Jan. 1945), 1–19, 16.

44. See Evans' treatment in "Ratum et Non-consummatum Procedure" (n. 39, above).

45. Lina Eckstein, *Women Under Monasticism: Chapters on Convent Life Between A.D. 500 and A.D. 1500* (Cambridge University Press, 1896), p. 479.

46. Walter M. Abbott, ed. "Dogmatic Constitution on the Church," *The Documents of Vatican II* (New York: The American Press, 1966), p. 25.

47. *Dialogus cum Tryphone*, in PG, VII, 745.

48. *Adversus Haereses*, 4, in PG, VII, 995.

49. *Leviticum Homilium*, 9, in *Die griechischen christlichen Schriftsteller der ersten Jahrhunderte* (Leipzig, 1920), XXIX, 418.

50. *De Virginibus Velandis,* in J. P. Migne, *Patrologiae Crusus Completus, Series Latina,* 221 vols. (Paris, 1844–66), II, 950.
51. See the "Decree on the Apostolate of the Laity," in Abbott, ed. "Dogmatic Constitution on the Church," pp. 487–520.
52. D. Barsotti, "Il fondamento della vocazione al Sacerdozio," *L'Osservatore Romano,* Jan. 24, 1970, p. 1.
53. Brodersen, p. 121.
54. Cloning is a procedure by which organisms (presently confined to certain vegetables) are reproduced by the furthering of a host organism's cells rather than through manipulation of its reproductive systems.

Women and the Continental Reformation[1]

JANE DEMPSEY DOUGLASS

The Reformation brought some fundamental changes in the Church's way of looking at women and marriage which greatly influenced society both in the short- and the long-run perspectives. Roland Bainton has written, "The reform, in my judgment, had greater influence on the family than on the political and economic spheres."[2]

Luther found in his biblical studies much evidence to persuade him that marriage had been seriously depreciated by the Roman Church. Even since the Fall, marriage is intended by God to be the normal—rather the ideal—life for human beings, a life that must not be considered ethically inferior to celibacy, as medieval theology had taught. Women and sex came to be seen as fundamentally good. The ensuing attack on monastic institutions had profound consequences, socially and economically. And the home became the new center of women's religious vocation.

This study will begin by sketching briefly the new theology: the protestant rejection of the distinction between life according to the precepts and life according to the counsels of perfection; the teaching of the sinner's justification in God's eyes by grace through faith in Christ and the active life of service that flows from it; the doctrine of Christian vocation in the world; and the priesthood of all believers. Then it will focus directly on the Reformation view of marriage, women and the home, using materials drawn primarily from Luther of Wittenberg, Bucer of Strasbourg, and Calvin of Geneva.

The second section will deal with a few of the practical consequences of these ideas in the realms of marriage law, education, and Church life. Within the familiar structures of home and Church, presided over by men as they had been before, women nevertheless were seeing their old tasks differently and discovering new roles.

In the third section we will look at the role of women in the Reformation as seen through the eyes of a contemporary nun in Geneva, Sister Jeanne de Jussie, who was writing a journal of the city's troubled years from 1526 to 1535.

A NEW THEOLOGY OF MARRIAGE

Rejection of the "counsels of perfection": Medieval theology had distinguished between Christian life according to the precepts and life according to the counsels of perfection. The first, obedience to the law of God, was binding on all Christians, and the ordinary Christian found it difficult enough to meet this requirement. The second was a higher calling, possible for a few, which demanded virginity—among many other disciplines—and merited greater reward in heaven. Luther, quite early in his reforming career, ruled out this distinction as untenable. There cannot be two classes of Christians among the baptized. All law given by God is binding on all men, Luther thought, including such hard commandments as "Love your enemies" (Matt. 5:44), which had previously been considered among the "counsels of perfection."[3]

Justification by grace through faith: But however binding the law may be on all, it is also impossible for any person, however saintly, to fulfill the law, Luther believed. Without the gift of God's grace, no one wants to obey God's will at all. But even the Christian person, justified in God's eyes on the grounds of Christ's righteousness claimed by faith, remains at the same time a sinner. He is unable to claim any reward from God as though he had earned it, however much "religious" activity he may engage in.[4]

Rather, the Christian person, trusting God's promise to him of eternal life, is freed from all preoccupation with merit and reward. In thanksgiving for Christ's gifts he pours out his love joyfully and freely in service to his fellowmen. As he remembers Christ's becoming a servant and dying for sinners like himself, he thinks, ". . . why shall I not do freely, joyfully, with my whole heart and spontaneously everything which I know will be pleasing and agreeable to Him? I shall give myself therefore as a kind of Christ to my neighbor." And since he is free from the need to be occupied with meritorious religious duties, he resolves to do what is rather necessary, useful, and salutary for his neighbor.[5]

The family as a school of faith: Thus the Christian who can receive only as a gift his faith in Christ and His promise of salvation turns to the world actively in loving service, pouring out the love he has received, doing whatever needs to be done for the meeting of human needs. This is the life of the saint. And the family is the most immediate context for this service. One of the constantly recurring themes in Luther's commentary on Genesis is that

> The legends or stories of the saints which we have in the papacy are not written according to the norm of Holy Scripture. For it is nothing to wear a hood, fast, or undertake other hard works of that sort in comparison with those troubles which family life brings, and the saints [i.e., the patriarchs] bore them and lived in patience.[6]

Moses in describing the life of "the most holy patriarch Abraham" does not create a monastic image with miracles but makes him "a very plebeian man who is occupied with household affairs, for he has a wife and has children." The papists do not understand this sort of sanctity because they do not see his faith.[7] Rebecca is a good example because she was a holy and good mother, flesh and blood, not other than we are, one who suffered and was tempted too.[8] Luther saw marriage as a school of faith where the saints learn to live by faith while struggling with the "worldly" problems of affection and alienation, birth, washing diapers, feeding and educating a family, and death—sometimes of the aged but often of children.[9]

Christian vocation: "Vocation" is no longer reserved for the religious life, that of clergy or monks. Luther believed that just as a secular magistrate by faith can exercise a Christian vocation in the world, so can the housewife.[10] A wife should realize that her many tasks, caring for children and helping or being obedient to her husband, are "golden, noble works."[11] A wife in childbirth should not be encouraged by "foolish" legends of the saints but rather by this: "Think, dear Greta, that you are a wife, and God gives you this work. Take comfort cheerfully in His will." Do your very best to bring forth the child, but if you die, you die in a noble work and obedient to God.[12] Luther clearly contrasts her God-given vocation with "religious" activities.

> If a mother of a family wishes to please and serve God, let her not do what the papists are accustomed to doing: running to churches, fasting, counting prayers, etc. But let her care for the family, let her educate and teach her children, let her do her task in the kitchen . . . if she does these things in faith in the Son of God, and hopes that she pleases God on account of Christ, she is holy and blessed.[13]

Superiority of married life: Luther in his enthusiasm for marriage goes beyond merely affirming it as a good gift of God.[14] "The married state is not only equal to all other states but preeminent over them all, be they Kaiser, princes, bishops . . . For it is not a special, but the commonest, noblest state."[15] He takes Jesus' words, "Have you never read that the Creator made them from the beginning male and female? . . . For this reason a man shall leave his father and mother, and be made one with his wife; and the two shall become one flesh" (Matt. 19:4–5), as a commandment as strong as the ones against killing and adultery. "You should be married, you should have a wife, you should have a husband."[16]

Possibility of voluntary celibacy: Yet at other moments Luther acknowledges that in addition to the physically incapable, there are others who have the gift to live in celibacy and are free to do so— but let them not damn the home![17] He assumes that this gift is a rare one. Calvin, too, grants that God bestows the grace for celibacy

> on certain men, in order to hold them more ready for his work . . . Let no man rashly despise marriage as something unprofitable or superfluous to him; let no man long for celibacy

unless he can live without a wife. Also, let him not provide in this state for the repose and convenience of the flesh, but only that, freed of this marriage bond, he may be more prompt and ready for all the duties of piety. And since this blessing is conferred on many persons only for a time, let every man abstain from marriage only so long as he is fit to observe celibacy. If his power to tame lust fails him, let him recognize that the Lord has now imposed the necessity of marriage upon him.[18]

The possibility of celibacy here is clearly a gift of God, a grace, rather than a state that can be achieved by human discipline; it has a practical function in circumstances in which marriage would hinder a person exercising a particular vocation, rather than any ethical superiority; and it should be practiced with the expectation that its need may be temporary, rather than on the basis of a life-long vow.

Marriage and the clergy: The protestant tradition saw no reason why the clergy should be bound to practice celibacy. In fact, it saw the ancient tradition of clerical marriage in the whole Church and the continuing practice of marriage at least for the lower clergy in the Eastern churches as excellent precedent for married pastors. And it rejected on principle the requirement of a vow of celibacy from anyone.[19] In the early years of the Reformation, in fact, priests felt considerable pressure to marry in order to witness to their new theological view of marriage.[20]

Priesthood of all believers: One reason why the clergy were not expected to live according to a different moral standard than the laity was the new protestant understanding of the Church. By faith in Christ's work and by baptism, Luther understood that for all Christians,

> just as we are co-brothers, co-heirs, and co-kings, so we are also co-priests with Him, daring with trust through the spirit of faith to appear before God and cry "Abba, father," and to pray one for the other, and to do all those things which we see performed and figured by the visible and corporal office of priests.[21]

He even specifically includes the task of teaching each other the things that are of God.[22] Calvin, too, taught that "every member of the church is charged with the responsibility of public edification according to the measure of his grace, provided he perform it decently and in order."[23]

Note that the priesthood of all believers was not seen primarily in terms of a Christian's intercession on his own behalf before God, but rather in the context of community, the intercession of one for another, the announcing of the Word to one another. But this doctrine did not preclude in the mainstream of the Reformation the necessity for ordained ministers. For the sake of order, educated men were selected to serve on behalf of the community in the public functions of the conduct of worship, the sacraments, and preaching. Yet a theological basis for equality of responsibility between the clergy and the laity—including laywomen—had been established.

Against the despisers of women: Since the state of marriage was now viewed as the noblest way of life for clergy and laity alike, it is not surprising that Luther was eager to refute the "papists . . . and all who despise the female sex. And at the same time they produce examples of fathers and saints who were married. By them is adorned the marriage which the whole world depreciates and disparages, just as can be seen in the poets Juvenal and Martial."[24] Luther acknowledges the sins often recounted of historical women, particularly of Eve, but feels they should be remembered "without insult of the sex," for vice is common to both men and women.[25] Though there is no scorn in his observation, he thinks that the female sex is "weaker, carrying about in mind and body several vices. But that one good, however, covers and conceals all of them: the womb and birth."[26]

For Luther, Eve's name reveals her glory—the mother of all men. "God placed his creation of all men in woman, and the use of creation, that is, to conceive, give birth, nurse, educate children, serve the husband and administer the home. Thus among the worst vices and evils this unspeakable good shines forth."[27] Even after the Fall her punishment, the bearing of children in pain, should be rightly seen as a "cheerful and joyful punishment." Eve was not abandoned by God. "She saw that she retained her own sex and was a woman. She saw that she was not separated from Adam to live alone and isolated from a man. She saw that the glory of motherhood was left to her," and was doubtless much encouraged,

Luther thinks.[28] Though Luther sees a woman's role closely tied to her capacity to bear children, this is for him a happy and fortunate destiny rather than the curse it so often seemed for writers of earlier centuries. In his thought it is barrenness that is cursed.[29] He has been deeply influenced by the Old Testament texts upon which he commented so often.

Sexual union in itself is good: Luther believed that all of the shame associated with sexual intercourse is the result of sin. There was no shame in Paradise, since God established and blessed sexual union. Adam and Eve then had an "honorable pleasure" in sex such as they had in food and drink. But today, because of the Fall of Adam and Eve, man cannot know woman without a "dreadful madness of lust." The work of conception is linked with "such a shameful and dreadful pleasure that it is compared by the doctors with epilepsy."[30]

The contrast between purity of sex as practiced in Paradise and the shame associated with it because of sin can of course be found in various forms in the whole previous Christian tradition. For Christianity generally opposed dualistic positions that made the body inherently evil. But in the context of Reformation thought, the emphasis fell on the positive acceptance and use of creation, damaged as it is by sin. For it can still be seen as good through the eyes of faith.

If a man burns at the sight of a girl, Luther explains, the sin is not of the eyes but of an impure heart, for eyes, feet, hands are gifts of God.[31] The proper remedy for sexual desire is not to hide as a monk in a monastery to avoid the sight of women but to learn how to use the gifts of God; for vice is not cured by abstaining from things given by God but by proper use and governance of them.[32] When a man is himself without vices, "he uses things piously and in a holy manner and faithfully. May you do the same also, whether in marriage or the magistracy . . . and you will use things well: wife . . . things which are good in themselves."[33]

If the modern reader is offended by Luther's including a wife among "things" to be "used," it can be pointed out that elsewhere Luther carefully distinguishes a wife from the household possessions that are subject to a husband's disposition. For only God alone, through the Word and the Gospel, can rule the human soul.[34]

Calvin, too, is eager to repudiate what he considers a deprecia-
tion of marriage by the Roman doctrine. He finds it absurd that
Roman theologians should on the one hand call marriage a sacrament and on the other hand call it "uncleanness and pollution and
carnal filth," from which priests must be barred, even denying that
the Holy Spirit is ever present in copulation.[35] He shares generally
Luther's conviction about the goodness of marriage. Yet in commenting on the seventh commandment, he can warn married couples not to pollute their marriage with "uncontrolled and dissolute
lust. For even if the honorableness of matrimony covers the base-
ness of incontinence, it ought not for that reason to be a provoca-
tion thereto."[36]

Wives subject to their husbands: All the reformers presume in
biblical fashion that the husband is the head of the household, and
that the wife should be obedient to him.[37] Bucer, following the
imagery of Ephesians 5:23–24, indicates that the husband should
teach his wife in order that she may have all sanctity and piety of
life, should call her away from sin, feed her, cherish her like his own
flesh. The wife in turn should offer her body and aid wherever possible for the worship of God and for all other things useful in this
life.[38]

Calvin in commenting on Ephesians 5:22–33 clearly does not
mitigate the requirement for wives to subject themselves humbly to
their husbands. Yet he emphasizes here as elsewhere[39] that Christians are to be subject one to another, men as well as women. The
husband's authority is "more that of a society than of a kingdom."
He is not to oppress his wife.[40]

Evidence of the seriousness with which the wife's duty of obedience is taken can be found in the *Register* of the Company of
Pastors of Geneva. In 1552 an unsigned letter was received from a
noble lady who had become persuaded of the evangelical faith since
her marriage to a militantly Catholic husband. She explains the
unpleasantness with which she is treated because of her faith, the
pressure exerted on her to conform to Catholic practices, the way
in which she is spied upon and confined, assaulted in spirit and
body, unable to confess her faith openly, sing the psalms in French,
or possess books about Jesus Christ. Then she inquires whether the
law of marriage requires her to remain with her husband, or whether
she would be free in the Gospel to go to a place where she could

worship God in liberty, and whether Geneva would give her up to
her husband if she were to flee to Geneva and be pursued by him
there.[41] A Christian husband will love, not despise, his wife and
cherish her companionship and aid. The reply, probably written by
Calvin, expresses pity and compassion for her anguish and perplex-
ity. But it makes clear that scripture does not permit believers to
leave an unbelieving partner voluntarily merely because of hostility
or suffering. Rather, Christian wives are to strive to fulfill their
duties to their husbands in such a way as to win them to the faith.
Flight, if a way is provided, is justifiable only in persecution where
extreme danger exists. And since the wife is presently complying
with her husband's demands of "idolatry" in silence, she is far from
such extreme danger. She must pray for courage and constancy to
resist demands that would be sin against God and to show her
faith with sweetness and humility. If her husband then persecutes
her almost to the point of death, she is permitted to escape. And
the gentleman carrying the letter will reply further orally concerning her personal security.[42] One fundamental point made here, of
course, is that marriage with an "unbeliever" is nonetheless valid;
and this point would be applicable equally to the case of a man
married to an unbelieving wife. But the husband's legal right to
rule over the wife seems to be accepted even to the point of physical abuse, with two exceptions: the wife may escape if she is in
danger of death, and she should refuse to obey commands causing
her to sin against God.

A briefer reply by Calvin to another unidentified woman suffering similarly dates from 1559, and essentially the same advice is
given. But he is more explicit about abuse:

> We have a special sympathy for poor women who are evilly
> and roughly treated by their husbands, because of the roughness
> and cruelty of the tyranny and captivity which is their lot. We do
> not find ourselves permitted by the Word of God, however, to
> advise a woman to leave her husband, except by force of necessity;
> and we do not understand this force to be operative when a hus-
> band behaves roughly and uses threats to his wife, nor even
> when he beats her, but when there is imminent peril to her life,
> whether from persecution by the husband or by his conspiring
> with the enemies of the truth, or from some other source . . .

we exhort her . . . to bear with patience the cross which God
has seen fit to place upon her; and meanwhile not to deviate from
the duty which she has before God to please her husband, but
to be faithful whatever happens.[43]

Submission applied to politics: At least one of the Reformers,
the Scot John Knox, who worked for a time in Geneva, could see
nothing but evil in the fact that women, contrary to nature and
Scripture, as he believed, were usurping men's authority in his day
by ruling nations.[44] Though God has occasionally raised up remarkable women to commanding positions, women by nature are "weake,
fraile, impacient, feble, and foolishe; and experience hath declared
them to be unconstant, variable, cruell, and lacking the spirit of
counsel and regiment."[45] Even without the help of scripture, Aristotle rightly understood that even a man too much dominated by
his wife is a poor ruler.[46] Eve's malediction after the Fall to be subject to her husband's will (Gen. 3:16) and the New Testament injunctions to silence in the congregation (I Tim. 2:9–15 and I Cor.
14:34–35), together with the Fathers' writings in the same tone,
gave Knox confidence that Mary, "Jesabel of England," would soon
be put down from her tyranny by God.[47] And in fact she died a few
months later.

Mutual love of the spouses: In protestant thought about marriage one can discern a gradual shift away from the older emphasis
on procreation as justification for sexual intercourse, and even away
from an emphasis on marriage as the remedy of incontinence.[48]
Luther himself had defined marriage as a "divine and legitimate
union of a husband and wife in the hope of offspring, or at least for
the sake of avoiding fornication and sin for the glory of God."[49]
But he can also say, "What is more desirable . . . than a happy
and tranquil marriage, where there is mutual love and the most de-
lightful union of souls?"[50]

It is true that the Augsburg Confession of Lutheranism, 1530,
focuses on marriage as commanded by God to avoid fornication.[51]
The Second Helvetic Confession, however, of the Reformed tradition, in 1566, in the section on marriage mentions the remedy of
incontinence only parenthetically. God wishes man and woman to
cleave inseparably to each other and to live in one highest love and

concord. No mention is made of procreation, here.[52] The Westminster Confession of Faith, 1647, also Reformed, declares that "Marriage was ordained for the mutual help of husband and wife; for the increase of mankind with a legitimate issue, and of the Church with a holy seed; and for preventing of uncleanness."[53] The order in which the three traditional purposes appear seems significant. In general, without losing sight of the traditional discussions of the role of marriage to remedy incontinence and provide offspring, protestant thought tended to increase the importance of the mutual cherishing of husband and wife, which had earlier been subservient to the purpose of procreation.

This emphasis can be seen particularly in Bucer in the early years of the Reformation. For him, "The true and entire purpose of marriage is that the spouses serve one another in all love and fidelity, that the woman be the aid and the flesh of the man and the man the head and saviour of the woman."[54] In his later definition of marriage, in *On the Kingdom of Christ*, he retains the same elements: the fellowship and union of a man and woman for the mutual participation in the whole of life with the greatest benevolence and love, after the imagery of Ephesians 5:23–24. He adds explicit reference to the duty to exhibit the communication of divine and human law and to offer the use of the body for sexual intercourse if required. But he makes no mention here of procreation.[55]

The priority of the spouses' mutual love seems also to be present in the treatise of the Spanish humanist Juan Luis Vives, *The Education of the Christian Woman*, dedicated to England's Queen Catherine of Aragon. But the context in which it appears seems to give it a very different function. Vives advises a wife that "the union was not instituted for progeny, but for the communion of life and indissoluble fellowship."[56] But in another context it seems that his point of view is more monastic than protestant. In discussing the possibility that no children are born to a marriage, he reminds the woman of the perils of pregnancy and birth which should hardly be desired. The ancient curse of barrenness is past; today virginity is better than marriage. A woman can choose children to adopt and love as her own. She should receive as a gift of God that she does not bear children or lose them.[57]

VISIBLE CHANGES IN THE STATUS OF WOMEN

It is difficult to find evidence that any conscious effort was made by the Reformation to change the social status of women. Yet the new theology did contribute to greater freedom and equality for women, though certainly not immediately.[58] In marriage law, in education, and in Church life changes were made that immediately benefited men and women alike but provided motivation for more sweeping changes in women's role in later centuries.

Marriage law: The Reformers in general no longer saw marriage as a sacrament.[59] They urged that laws concerning marriage should be revised, often by the secular authorities,[60] to reform many abuses. One example would be the elaborate system of prohibited relationships, including "spiritual relationships," which limited a person's choice of marriage partners.[61]

Among the actual changes brought about was the increased effort to make all marriages publicly recognized. The banns were conscientiously published, the marital status of strangers desiring to marry investigated, and in Geneva provision was made for marriages to be celebrated in the framework of the normal public-worship services. Considerably more emphasis than in the past was placed on parental consent to marriage.[62]

But the most striking change was the permission given, however seldom, for divorce and remarriage of the injured party. Until the Reformation, separation of bed and board had in some cases been possible, but the marriage bond remained and prevented remarriage so long as both spouses lived. The Reformation as a whole continued to be extremely reluctant to grant divorce.[63] Luther is well known to have declared that he preferred bigamy to divorce, but he is talking of grave pastoral problems, and his statement seems to convey more his horror of divorce than his approval of bigamy.[64] Bucer is the exception to this rule. He tried, though unsuccessfully, to persuade Strasbourg and then England to permit divorce and remarriage whenever the fundamental conditions for marriage, according to his definition, including love, were lacking.[65]

In some cases an effort was made in the legislation to treat

women equally with men; in other cases clear discrepancies exist.
For example, the point is made in the Geneva Marriage Ordinances
adopted in 1561 that, "Although in ancient times the right of the
wife was not equal with that of the husband where divorce was
concerned . . . If a man is convicted of adultery and his wife demands to be separated from him this shall be granted to her also,
provided it proves impossible by good counsel to reconcile them to
each other."[66] Yet in the case where one of an engaged couple dis-
appears before the marriage and the other wishes to be released
from the promise, it appears that under certain circumstances a
a girl would be required to wait a year for her freedom, whereas a
man would not.[67]

Public education: Reformation teaching of the "priesthood of
all believers" made it very important that all Christians should be
capable of reading the Bible and other religious literature. Some
public education had existed prior to the Reformation, as early as
1428 for boys—but not girls—in Geneva,[68] part of a general improvement in education of the laity in the later Middle Ages. But
the Reformation provided the impetus to expand and develop these
small beginnings.

Luther as early as 1524 called on the civil authorities to establish schools to educate the children.[69] After 1536, the official beginning of the Reformation in Geneva, all Genevese children were
required to attend school. Those families that could pay for tuition
were expected to do so, but the schoolmaster was to be paid by the
city so that he could feed and teach the poor children without
fees.[70] Girls and boys learned reading, arithmetic, catechism, and
writing. After 1541, girls seem to have had their own school for
primary instruction, but there were complaints for many years
that no public secondary school for girls existed in the city.[71]

Another impetus to the development of women's education
must certainly have been the contemporary example of learned
noblewomen of the Renaissance who patronized the arts and letters and sheltered religious refugees, as Renée of Ferrara did for
Calvin.[72] When one adds to the educated noblewomen of the Renaissance the list of those who actually ruled in the sixteenth century, such as Elizabeth of England and Marguerite of Austria, it is
easy to understand why a Renaissance enthusiast can call it the
"century of illustrious women."[73]

A number of humanists of the late fifteenth and early sixteenth centuries urged that women, too, should be taught the classics and share more fully the intellectual life of the day: Lionardo
Bruni was followed by Agrippa's *De nobilitate et praecellentia
feminei sexus* of 1529, Domenichi's *Nobilita della Donna* of 1544,
Thomas Elyot's *The Defense of Good Women* of 1534, Bercher's
Nobylytye of Wymen of 1552, Juan Vives' *De institutione femi-
nae christianae* of 1523, and even Erasmus.[74] Some, like Vives, propose a very modest program of education thoroughly oriented toward protection of women's chastity and humility.[75] But in Bercher's *Nobylytye of Wymen*, around 1552, appears a statement of
the equality of women's gifts with men's. "I have noted in some
[women] learning, in some temperance, in some liberality . . . and
I have compared them with men that have been endowed with like
gifts and I have found them equal or superior."

> The bringing up and training of women's life is so strait and
> kept as in a prison, that all good inclination which they have of
> nature is utterly quenched. We see that by practice men of small
> hope come to good proficiency so that I may affirm the cause of
> women's weakness in handling of matters to proceed of the
> custom that men hath appointed in the manner of their life, for
> if they have any weak spirit, if they have any mutability or any
> such thing, it cometh of the diverse unkindnesses that they find
> of men.[76]

This interest in improving the education of women flourished
in humanist circles, always restricted, where women's social equality with men came to be accepted. A new education was needed to
prepare women for new roles. But even at a time when such social
equality existed in the governing classes of Florence or Ferrara, for
example, it did not exist in the lower or even the middle classes of
those cities, and it was seldom to be found in northern Europe. In
German, French, and English society down to the Reformation, if
women received any education at all, it was geared to the domestic
duties that were considered theirs by nature: reading, writing, calcu-
lation, elementary nature study (as preparation for nursing the
sick), needlework, spinning, music, astrology, religion.[77]

It may well be true that humanism took the lead in transforming the image of women's place in society in the fifteenth and six-

teenth centuries. But it must not be forgotten that this was a period of enormous social and economic change, which produced greater social mobility in the lower classes of society as well. The general improvement of educational standards among the laity in this period would work to the advantage of women to some degree. And, on the other hand, one can hardly forget the Renaissance delight in criticizing and satirizing women's foibles.[78]

Church life: With the disappearance of the nuns in protestantism, women lost one visible, official role in the Church that was not immediately replaced, even by the revival of the deaconesses later in the century. Women were not ordained to the ministry in mainstream Continental protestantism for centuries, nor were they permitted to be elected as laymen to the official boards that governed the churches.

Yet the protestant encouragement of a married clergy gave rise to the new role of the pastor's wife, who has been called the "pilot model of the new woman" created by Reformation influence.[79] Luther's former nun Katherine von Bora has acquired a familiar place in histories of the Reformation for her firm though simple faith, her eagerness to help Luther experience the goodness of marriage of which he had been writing, and her valiant skill in managing the enormous household domiciled in the old monastery: the Luther family with their children, theological students, visiting relatives and distinguished theologians, religious refugees—all with a painfully limited budget.[80] No one can read Luther at any length without being deeply impressed by the influence of his experience of marriage on his pastoral theology. The story of Calvin's search for a properly virtuous wife and his marriage to Idelette de Bure is far less generally known, partly because Calvin is far less free than Luther with personal references in his writing. But evidence of his warm affection for his wife can be gleaned particularly from his correspondence.[81]

But genuinely heroic is the story of Wibrandis Rosenblatt. Already widow of the humanist Ludwig Keller, with a child, she was married to the reformer Oecolampadius and bore three children before his death. In the same month the reformer Capito's wife died, and several months later Wibrandis was married to Capito, bearing five more children before the plague took Capito and three children. Bucer's wife perished in the same outbreak of the plague, but on her deathbed urged her husband to marry their friend Wibrandis and be father to her children. Of Bucer's thirteen children only one still survived at the time of his marriage to Wibrandis, but two more children were born and a niece adopted. Like Katie Luther, Wibrandis, in addition to the burdensome tasks of managing a large household, with a husband deeply immersed in his work, shared the anxieties of the early years when the Reformation had not yet been established officially and when persecution, exile, and death for the new faith were close at hand. In fact she shared Bucer's exile in England, and was left to care for the family after his death (Bainton, *Women of the Reformation*, pp. 79–95).[82]

Not all of the new breed of pastors' wives limited their activities to the household. Katherine Zell, wife of the Strasbourg reformer, began her more public career immediately after her marriage when the bishop excommunicated her husband for marrying and scurrilous tales of his morals were circulating. She published her denial of the tales and a strong defense of clerical marriage, adding:

> You remind me that the Apostle Paul told women to be silent in church. I would remind you of the word of this same apostle that in Christ there is no longer male nor female and of the prophecy of Joel: "I will pour forth my spirit upon all flesh and your sons and your *daughters* will prophesy." I do not pretend to be John the Baptist rebuking the Pharisees. I do not claim to be Nathan upbraiding David. I aspire only to be Balaam's ass, castigating his master (p. 55).

There soon followed her letter of protest to the bishop, and a published tract about which the bishop protested to the council (p. 57). She also published a small treatise of consolation for a magistrate of the city suffering from leprosy (abridged in Bainton, pp. 69–71), and four pamphlets of hymns written by others, to which she added a preface (p. 72). Katherine made a public address at her husband's death, arousing criticism for her action. She replied, "I am not usurping the office of preacher or apostle. I am like the dear Mary Magdalene, who with no thought of being an apostle, came to tell the disciples that she had encountered the risen Lord" (pp. 66–67). Freed of much domestic responsibility by the death of her only two infants, she cared for the floods of refugees and did extensive visiting of the sick and prisoners; after living for a time in the hospital for syphilitics with a sick nephew, she complained to the town council about conditions and saw her recommendations largely adopted (pp. 59, 61, 63, 65, 71). Just before her death she conducted an interment service quietly at 6 A.M. for a dead Schwenckfeldian woman—and was duly criticized by the town council. The woman's husband had requested a pastor to conduct the funeral, but the pastor had insisted on announcing her apostasy from the true faith, a condition that the husband refused to accept. Katherine's outspokenness caused her to be called a "disturber of the peace of the Church" by one pastor whose sermon she criticized, and Bucer called her "a trifle imperious" (pp. 73, 72, 63).

Other protestant women, too, entered into the controversies of the day. Argula von Grumbach, a Bavarian noblewoman of the house of Hohenstaufen, in 1523 wrote a bold letter to the faculty of the University of Ingolstadt protesting their requiring a recantation of Lutheran theology from a young teacher. Concerning her role in the affair, she says,

> I am not unacquainted with the word of Paul that women should be silent in church (I Tim. 1:2) but, when no man will or can speak, I am driven by the word of the Lord when he said, "He who confesses me on earth, him will I confess and he who denies me, him will I deny" (Matt. 10, Luke 9), and I take comfort in the words of the prophet Isaiah (3:12, *but not exact*), "I will send you children to be your princes and women to be your rulers." (pp. 97–98; cf. p. 104)

She sent the duke of the region a copy of her protest, but she also wrote to him and the magistrates in general a broader tract against the conduct of the clergy, reminding them of their responsibility not to encroach on God's authority. The authorities left her to her husband's discipline, and he maltreated her in his anger at losing his position. She consulted with nobles in hopes of persuading them to the Reformation, visited Luther, and was twice imprisoned for her subversive activities: circulating non-Catholic books, conducting private services in her home, and conducting funerals at

cemeteries without authorization (pp. 97–108). Elisabeth of Braun-
schweig, for five years ruler of her land, was deeply influential in
the politics of the Reformation and wrote a tract on government
for her son, one on marriage for her daughter as well as one on
consolation for widows (pp. 125–144).

Despite their lack of public office in the Church, these—and
many other—spirited and courageous women did have theological
justification for their involvement in the protestant doctrine of the
priesthood of all believers. This understanding of the nature of the
Christian community gave a powerful impetus to the teaching of
the laity so that they could carry out their responsibilities. Not only
did laymen need to learn to read the Bible, but parents were expected to teach the faith to their children and servants. Catechisms
were prepared for teaching the basic elements of theology to all the
laity; and in most of the Reformed cities there were regular lectures on the Bible which laymen as well as pastors frequented.

This new way of understanding the Church also required revision of the liturgy so that the laity could become full and active
participants—singing, confessing the faith, praying, and hearing the
Word in their own language.[83] Laywomen as well as laymen found
a new understanding of their ministry in the Church, both in public worship and in their Christian service to the world through their
secular vocations.

THE IMAGE OF WOMEN IN
SISTER JEANNE DE JUSSIE

Having now seen something of the image of women through protestant eyes of the period, we can check our impressions against
those of a nun of the Order of St. Claire, Jeanne de Jussie, who was
living in a convent in Geneva during the years just before the Reformation, when protestant adherents were increasing. A young nun
who had learned to write in a Geneva school before entering the
convent,[84] she chronicles the events of the years 1526 to 1535 in
her volume *The Leaven of Calvinism, Or the Beginning of the
Heresy of Geneva.* It is a spirited account, if not a very elegant one
in style, with far more references to women than one is accustomed
to find in sixteenth-century documents! Sister Jeanne ends her

work with the sisters filing out of the city of Geneva, which they now found so hostile to their vocation, and re-establishing themselves at Annecy in France, where she eventually became the abbess.[85]

Sister Jeanne has the strong conviction that the women were more loyal to the Catholic faith than the men.*[86] Though many monks and priests disgracefully married, she reports, only one of all the sisters of St. Claire was perverted, and she had not come with good intentions. The others were all strongly persuaded of the heresy of the new faith.[87] There were often torn loyalties in divided families, but Sister Jeanne tells enthusiastically of the firmness in faith of many "good Catholic women" whose husbands were heretics. There was the woman who suddenly died of sadness when her husband had the new baby baptized by the protestant pastor, Farel.[88] Many others were "more than martyrs," beaten and tormented for their unwillingness to desert the true faith. Three, locked in a room because they would not attend the protestant Easter communion, escaped by a window to attend Mass.[89] Two "notable bourgeois Catholic women" came, in 1535, at some risk to the convent to console the sisters when protestant men were ransacking it, destroying pieces of art, and trying to persuade the nuns to give up their vocation (Jussie, Le Levain du Calvinisme, pp. 146–150).[90]

On Good Friday of 1533 the population of the city was lining up in two armed camps. The Catholics were eager to root out the "infection" that was troubling the city (pp. 54 ff.).

The wives of the Christians assembled, saying, that if it happens that our husbands fight against those infidels, let us also make war and kill their heretic wives, so that the race may be exterminated. In this assembly of women there were a good seven hundred children of twelve to fifteen years, firmly decided to do a good deed with their mothers: the women carried stones in their

---

* The same point is made in the chronicle of a contemporary Protestant minister, Anthoine Fromment: Les Actes et Gestes merveilleux de la Cité de Geneve, Nouvellement convertie a l'Evangile faictz du temps de leur Reformation et comment ils l'ont reçue redigez par escript en fourme de Chroniques Annales ou Hystoyres commençant l'an MDXXXII, ed. G. Revilliod, Geneva, 1854, pp. 4–5, 11, 17, 45–6.

laps, and most of the children carried little rapiers . . . others
stones in their breast, hat and bonnet. (pp. 54–55; cf. pp. 70–72)

The same day, after a Catholic man had been fatally wounded by
a blow on the head, the "Christian women" let out a great cry and
turned on the wife of a Lutheran shouting, "As the beginning of
our war, let's throw this bitch in the Rhone!" She escaped into a
house, but the women in their anger threw everything in the shop
on the ground. Meanwhile the nuns of St. Claire in tears and great
devotion prayed for the victory of the Christians and the return of
the erring to the path of salvation. Some "good Christian women"
came to warn the sisters that if the heretics won, they planned
to force all the sisters, young and old, to marry. But the day
passed without bloodshed (pp. 56–57), and a truce was eventually
arranged.

The protestant women are never portrayed as violent. Nonetheless by 1534 two sorts of aggravation are attributed to them:
they ostentatiously work on feast days, and they try to persuade the
nuns to leave the convent.

While the Catholics were in festival procession in the streets,
the Lutheran women sat in their windows for everyone to see them
spinning and doing needlework. There were reprisals. After some of
them did laundry on the day after Easter and Pentecost, their
clothing was thrown in the Rhone. A big Lutheran woman was hit
in the head with the distaff someone had snatched from her, then
she was trampled in the mud (pp. 89–90).*

As early as 1534 a Lutheran woman, a relative of one of the
nuns, came to visit the convent and used the opportunity to pour
out her "venom" on the "poor nuns." She claimed that the world
had been in error and idolatry till now, that the commandments of
God had not been truly taught, that their predecessors had lived
wrongly, and finally added "detestable words" on the Sacrament.
When the nuns did not succeed in quieting her by their objections,
they finally barred the door in her face while she continued to talk
(pp. 86–88).

Twice when city officials came with protestants to ascertain

---

* Fromment tells of a protestant woman who took up the sword enthusiastically to defend her family in a battle outside the city (p. 195).

whether the nuns were being constrained in any way to remain in the convent against their will, they brought protestant women with them. One, Marie d'Entière, of Picardy, had been an abbess, but now was married and "meddled with preaching, and perverting people of devotion." In spite of the nuns' scorn for her defection, she persevered in her attempt to persuade them to her new view. Sister Jeanne reports that she said,

> O poor creatures! If only you knew that it is good to be with a handsome husband, and how agreeable it is to God. I lived for a long time in that darkness and hypocrisy where you are, but God alone made me understand the abuse of my pitiful life, and I came to the true light of truth. (p. 164)

Regretting her life in "mental corruption and idleness," she took five hundred ducats from the abbey treasury and left that "unhappiness." "Thanks to God alone, I already have five handsome children, and I live salutarily" (p. 165). The sisters replied by spitting on her in detestation.

Another time Lady Claude, wife of Levet, an apothecary, was brought to the sisters, for she also "meddled in preaching." When the protestants asked "that diabolical tongue" to "do her duty," she began to preach, disparaging the Virgin Mary, the saints, and the state of virginity, praising marriage, and claiming that all the apostles had been married, quoting Paul's approval of being two in one flesh, and "perverting Holy Scripture." When the nuns vigorously protested and asked her to be taken away, they were told by the protestant men that she was a holy creature, illuminated by God, who had won many souls to the truth by her holy preaching and divine teaching (pp. 176–177).*

It is interesting that Lutheranism for Sister Jeanne is primarily identified with contempt for the Sacrament, iconoclasm, and this new lauding of marriage. A new form of marriage service is reported in 1534 as performed by Farel, consisting in no solemnity or devotion but "only their commandment to join together and multiply the world," and "some dissolute words that I do not write at

---

* Fromment's chronicle adds many details about her conversion and preaching (pp. 15–21), and confirms Sister Jeanne's story of the Catholic mob's destruction of her husband's apothecary shop (p. 44).

all, for it is shameful to a chaste heart to think them" (p. 86; cf. p. 110).

Apart from the "false" sister who became protestant and married, publicly maligning the sisters' way of life, they believed, only one nun emerges from the journal as a personality. That is the Mother Vicar, who first assists the frail and elderly abbess in dealing with the protestants and city officials who come to disturb their way of life and then is asked by the nuns to take charge of them (pp. 118–156). When ordered to attend a public disputation on religion, she and the abbess decline respectfully on the grounds that they have vowed to live the cloistered life. Furthermore, "it is not the task of women to dispute, it is not ordained for women . . . since it is forbidden to uneducated people to meddle in interpreting Holy Scripture, and a woman has never been called to dispute or witness" (p. 118). But she proves to be a very aggressive and vocal advocate of her own way of life, brashly telling off the protestant men with as much irreverence as they show her. When she was asked why the nuns wear such garments, she replied that they like them, then in turn asked the questioner why he was dressed so pompously (p. 163). When Farel and Viret came to preach to the nuns, she put up such a racket of protest that she was removed from the room. But she continued to beat on the wall and cry warnings to the sisters not to listen, telling the preacher he was wasting his effort, till Farel forgot what he was talking about (pp. 131–132). After this experience he decided not to return to preach there again (p. 134).

Our glance at the Reformation as seen by Sister Jeanne gives evidence that protestant teaching in praise of marriage seemed to unsympathetic contemporaries to be of considerable importance in the new faith and a radical departure from the tradition. Furthermore, her journal helps to confirm our impression that women played a more active role in bringing about the Reformation—and opposing it—than has usually been assumed. However colored by her limited experiences and personal preferences the journal may be, it is nonetheless a useful and fascinating complement to other sorts of sources for the period.

The only "women's liberation" of interest to the sixteenth-century Reformation was the elimination of the monastic view of women, sex, and marriage which had flourished both in the monastery and among the laymen. Protestants wanted to give monks and nuns as well as laymen the freedom to take up their Christian vocation *in the world* by providing a new theological understanding of life as well as an opportunity to leave the convent. But we see in Sister Jeanne's account that though the protestants talked of "freedom," to the nuns they seemed to bring a new sort of constraint, a constraint to marry and be subject to husbands. For to protestantism the patriarchal structures of society of the day were biblically sanctioned and needed only to be humanized by Christian love.

Yet the protestant doctrines of Christian vocation and the priesthood of all believers, along with a new view of marriage, did in fact tend to change the image and role of women in the direction of greater personal freedom and responsibility, both immediately and over the centuries.

NOTES

Biblical quotations are from the New English Bible (Oxford and Cambridge, 1970); quotations from John Calvin, *Institutes of the Christian Religion*, are from the edition of The Library of Christian Classics, Vols. XX, XXI, ed. John McNeill, trans. Ford L. Battles (Philadelphia, 1960); unidentified translations of other works are those of the author.

WA (Weimar Ausgabe) refers to *Kritische Gesamtausgabe der Werke D. Martin Luthers* (Weimar, 1883 ff.). References are to volume, page, and line; dates of first publication are in parentheses.

CO (Calvini Opera) refers to the Corpus reformatorum edition of Calvin's works, *Johannis Calvini Opera quae supersunt omnia* (Brunswick, 1863–1900). References are to volume and column.

1. This paper is in fact limited to three centers of that part of the Reformation often known as the Magisterial Reformation, excluding regretfully the Radical Reformation and the Catholic Reformation for lack of space.
2. Roland Bainton, *Women of the Reformation in Germany and Italy* (Minneapolis, 1971), p. 9.
3. E.g., see Luther, *Von weltlicher Oberkeit, wie weit man ihr Gehorsam schuldig sei* (*On Secular Authority, To What Extent It Should Be Obeyed*) (1523), WA 11, 249, 9–23; see also Calvin, *Institutes*, II, viii, 56–57, and IV, xiii, 11–13.

4. Luther, *Tractatus de libertate christiana* (*Treatise on Christian Liberty*) (1520), WA 7, 52, 25 to 53, 14; WA 7, 53, 24–33; WA 7, 54, 31 to 55, 36. See also *In epistolam S. Pauli ad Galatas commentarius* (*Commentary on Paul's Letter to the Galatians*) (1535), WA 40-I and 40-II.

5. Luther, *Tractatus de libertate christiana*, WA 7, 66, 1–8.

6. *Enarrationes in 1 librum Mose* (*Commentary on Genesis*) (1535–45), WA 42, 585, 11–14.

7. *Enarrationes in 1 Mose*, WA 43, 101, 7–12; see also 42, 432–433.

8. Ibid., WA 42, 390, 7.

9. See, e.g., *Von ehelichen Leben* (*On Married Life*) (1522), WA 10-II, 275–304.

10. *Von weltlicher Oberkeit*, WA 11, 257, 16 to 258, 11. See Gustaf Wingren, *Luther on Vocation*. (Philadelphia, 1957), *passim*.

11. *Von ehelichen Leben*, WA 10-II, 296, 13. See also Calvin, CO 53, 225–229.

12. Ibid., WA 10-II, 296, 14–24. For other examples of evangelical works on marriage, see W. Kawerau, *Die Reformation und die Ehe* (Halle, 1892), pp. 64–86.

13. *Enarrationes in 1 Mose*, WA 43, 20, 31–36.

14. E.g., *Von ehelichen Leben*, WA 10-II, 294, 27–33.

15. *Deudsch Catechismus* (*German Large Catechism*) (1529), WA 30-I, 162, 6–11.

16. *Vorrede zu Justus Menius' Oeconomia christiana* (1529), WA 30-II, 61, 4–7.

17. *Enarrationes in 1 Mose*, WA 43, 21, 1–3.

18. *Institutes* II, viii, 43. See also Martin Bucer, *De regno christi* (*On the Kingdom of Christ*), ed. F. Wendel (Paris, 1955) (Martini Buceri Opera Latina, XV), II, ch. xlv, pp. 226–231; "The Second Helvetic Confession" (1566), ch. xxix, 1, ed. P. Schaff, *The Creeds of Christendom, With a History and Critical Notes* (New York, 1877), III, 304.

19. Luther, *De captivitate babylonica ecclesiae praeludium* (1520), WA 6, 541–542; WA 6, 557, 11–23; *De votis monasticis* (*On Monastic Vows*) (1521), WA 8, 573–669; Calvin, *Institutes*, IV, xii, 22–28, and IV, xiii, 17–19.

20. See Bainton, *Women of the Reformation*, pp. 56, 81, 159, 162.

21. *De libertate christiana*, WA 7, 57, 28–33; see also pp. 56, 35 to 58, 3; *De captivitate babylonica*, WA 6, 564, 6 ff.; *An den Christlichen Adel deutscher Nation* (1520), WA 6, 407.

22. *De libertate christiana*, WA 7, 57, 26.

23. *Institutes*, IV, i, 12. Calvin does not spell out this doctrine as systematically as Luther, but the elements of it are present.

24. *Enarrationes in 1 Mose*, WA 43, 344, 25–29.

25. Ibid., WA 42, 282, 34, 39–40.

26. Ibid., WA 43, 344, 4–6.
27. Ibid., WA 43, 344, 15–20.
28. Ibid., WA 42, 148, 23–31.
29. Ibid., WA 42, 642–644.
30. Ibid., WA 42, 89, 37 to 90, 2; see also WA 42, 177, 1–7.
31. Ibid., WA 42, 497, 1–2.
32. Ibid., WA 42, 496, 25–30.
33. Ibid., WA 42, 497, 22–26.
34. *Predigten über das 1. Buch Mose* (1527), WA 24, 421, 9–19.
35. *Institutes,* IV, xix, 36.
36. Ibid., II, viii, 44.
37. For Luther, see F. Wendel, *Le Mariage à Strasbourg à l'Époque de la Réforme, 1520–1692* (Strasbourg, 1928), p. 41.
38. *De regno christi,* II, ch. xxxix, ed. Wendel, p. 209.
39. *Institutes,* III, vii, 5; CO 49, 737–763; esp. CO 53, 207–222.
40. CO 51, 735–746, esp. 740. A strong statement of men's role as channels of grace for women can be found in CO 49, 730.
41. CO 14, 337 ff.; trans. by P. E. Hughes, ed., *The Register of the Company of Pastors of Geneva in the Time of Calvin* (Grand Rapids, 1966), pp. 193–6.
42. CO 10, 239 ff.; trans. by Hughes, ed. *The Register . . . ,* pp. 196–198.
43. CO 17, 539; trans. by Hughes ed. *The Register . . . ,* pp. 344–345.
44. *The First Blast of the Trumpet Against the Monstrous Regiment of Women* (1558), in *The Works of John Knox,* ed. David Laing (Edinburgh, 1885), IV, 366–373.
45. Ibid., p. 374.
46. Ibid., p. 375.
47. Ibid., pp. 377–400, 420.
48. See, e.g., Thomas Aquinas, *Summa Theologica* III, q. 29, art. 2c.
49. *Enarrationes in 1 Mose,* WA 43, 310, 24–26.
50. Ibid., WA 43, 313, 4–6.
51. Art. VI, ed. Schaff, *Creeds of Christendom,* III, 52.
52. Ch. xxix, ed. Schaff, *Creeds of Christendom,* III, 304. There is, however, another section of Ch. xxix dealing with parents' duties.
53. Ch. xxiv, ed. Schaff, *Creeds of Christendom,* III, 655.
54. *Von der Ehe,* p. 12a, quoted and discussed by Wendel, *Le Mariage à Strasbourg,* p. 46.
55. *De regno christi,* II, ch. xxxix, 209.
56. Loys Vives, *L'Institution de la femme chrestienne,* trans. Pierre de Changy Efevier (Lyon, 1543), p. 125.
57. Ibid., pp. 203–204.
58. Here we can agree with Maurice Bardèche, *Histoire des femmes* (1968), II, 144–145 and 155, in his conclusion, but for totally different reasons. One must look beyond the changed ideals for

family life to which he refers. In fact the "Luther text" that he quotes at length, without giving its source, is almost entirely a quotation from Prov. 31:10–28.

59. Luther, De captivitate babylonica, WA 6, 550–553; Calvin, Institutes, IV, xix, 35; H. Thielicke, Ethik der Geschlechtlichkeit (Tübingen, 1966), pp. 108–136.
60. See esp. Bucer, De regno christi, II, cap. xv, ed. Wendel, pp. 152–153.
61. See Luther, De captivitate babylonica, WA 6, 553–560; Calvin, Institutes, IV, xix, 37.
62. See Wendel, Le Mariage à Strasbourg, pp. 101 ff.; Pierre Bels, Le Mariage des protestants français jusqu'en 1685 (Paris, 1968); "Marriage Ordinances of Geneva," in Hughes, ed. The Register . . . , pp. 72–81.
63. Wendel, Le Mariage à Strasbourg, pp. 146–149.
64. De captivitate babylonica, WA 6, 559, 20–21; see also pp. 558–559. There was, however, the notorious case of the bigamy of Philip of Hesse, a Lutheran noble.
65. See Wendel, Le Mariage à Strasbourg, p. 48; also his introduction to Bucer, De regno christi, pp. xlix–l; Bucer, De regno christi, II, caps. xxii–xliiii, ed. Wendel, pp. 165–226.
66. Hughes, ed., The Register, pp. 77–78.
67. Ibid., p. 80.
68. Jules Le Coultre, Maturin Cordier et les origines de la pédagogie protestante dans les pays de langue française (1530–64) (Neuchâtel, 1926), p. 117; Henri Naef, Les Origines de la Réforme à Genève (Geneva, 1968), I, 297.
69. An die Ratherren aller Städte deutsches Lands dass sie christliche Schulen aufrichten und halten sollen, WA 15, 27–53; see also Eine Predigt, dass man Kinder zur Schule halten solle (1530), WA 30 II, 517–588; for Bucer, see De regno christi, II, ch. xlviii, ed. Wendel, pp. 238–240.
70. Le Coultre, Maturin Cordier et les origines de la pédagogie protestante, p. 117.
71. Thérèse Pittard, Femmes de Genève aux jours d'autrefois (Geneva, n.d.), pp. 148–149, 151–152.
72. Bainton, Women of the Reformation, pp. 239–250; for other examples see pp. 171–268.
73. A. Chagny and F. Girard, Une princesse de la Renaissance: Marguerite d'Autriche-Bourgogne, Fondatrice de l'Église de Brou (1480–1530) (Chambéry, 1929), p. 5.
74. William H. Woodward, Studies in Education During the Age of the Renaissance (1400–1600) (New York, 1965), pp. 124, 204, 205, 207–209, 264, 270.
75. Vives, L'Institution de la femme chrestienne, pp. 30–32, 37, 83, 107.

76. Quoted in Woodward, *Studies in Education During the Age of the Renaissance*, p. 265.
77. Ibid., pp. 205–206.
78. See Katherine Rogers, *The Troublesome Helpmate* (Seattle, 1956); Kawerau, *Die Reformation und die Ehe*, pp. 41–63.
79. Bardèche, *Histoire des femmes*, II, 145.
80. See Bainton, *Women of the Reformation*, pp. 23–43.
81. Richard Stauffer, *L'Humanité de Calvin*, Cahiers théologiques 51 (Neuchâtel, 1964), pp. 19–29.
82. All parenthetical page references in the text will be to Bainton until the next footnote.
83. Translations of many of the Reformation liturgies can be found in B. Thompson, *Liturgies of the Western Church* (Cleveland, 1961).
84. Jeanne de Jussie, *Le Levain du Calvinisme, ou Commencement de l'hérésie de Genève* (Chambéry, 1661; repr. Geneva, 1853), pp. 164, 167.
85. Naef, *Les Origines de la Réforme à Genève*, I, 297–9.
86. Jussie, *Le Levain du Calvinisme*, p. 106.
87. Ibid., pp. 33–35.
88. Ibid., pp. 88–89. Undoubtedly the reference is to William Farel, although Sister Jeanne consistently calls him "Faret."
89. Ibid., pp. 106–109. See also Pittard, pp. 134–135, for women disciplined in the 1540s for not attending sermons or learning French prayers.
90. All parenthetical page references in text hereafter will be to Jussie.

The Protestant Principle:
A Woman's-Eye View
of Barth and Tillich

JOAN ARNOLD ROMERO

In much the same way as blacks have experienced the white Jesus in a white church preaching an alienating message, a number of women, too, are becoming conscious of the alienation from a masculine God, a masculine Church, and a masculine theology. For women the situation has in many ways been worse, for they form the bulk of the population of the Church, while in the structures of authority as represented both theologically and institutionally, it is men who have had the role of representing God to the people.

> But this hierarchy of authority [stemming from God] is compounded by *His*. As a symbol of God *His* maleness profoundly affects both our theological thinking and ecclesiastical practice; and thus our general social attitudes. In theological thinking the unconscious "syllogism" appears to run:
> God is male
> God has the right to dictate and to demand (bully) obedience
> Males share this right with God.[1]

319

There are strong signs that traditional modes of theology and institution are breaking down today. The Jesus movement and Pentecostalism represent a search for a more authentic relationship to God, while the movements of secular theology, theology of hope and theology of liberation, at the other end of the spectrum, seek to come to grips with the fact of an advanced industrial society whose oppressive aspects are being felt more and more, not only by blacks and by members of the Third World but also by many women (as well as men) in their everyday lives.

Thus women today (at least some of them), like other groups of people who have experienced oppression or suppression by a dominant group, discover themselves as protesters. This protest is sometimes open, but often silent, as women are becoming increasingly unhappy with the Church and social structures that do not allow them effective room to be themselves and to speak for themselves. In a sense they might be called the new "Protestants," who speak prophetically against alienating structures. To use Tillich's term, the "Protestant principle" is a protest against the identification of the ultimate concern with any particular creation of the Church, including its theology. In effect, protest works to relativize both theology and ecclesiastical institutions that have become demonic insofar as they have become absolutized and oppressive.[2]

This chapter is an attempt to come to grips with two important Protestant thinkers of this century, Karl Barth and Paul Tillich. Obviously, other figures might have been chosen. The aim of the chapter is to discover within the very different structures of their thought elements that falsify the experience and aspirations of women, as well as those elements that can prove useful to women in naming their own reality. As the story of human existence began with Adam's naming of his world, and continued with man's description of God's action in narrative form (as in the Old and New Testaments), or in conceptual form as in most of the Christian theological tradition, the time has come for women to describe their own reality and perhaps even to develop new forms to speak about it.

Rereading Barth and Tillich in this light, I was very much struck by the differences: where Barth's theology is characterized by structures of domination that entail authoritarianism both in the Church and in social relations, Tillich's theology appears to be not

only nonauthoritarian but a real attempt to integrate male and
female polarities in Church and in culture. Where Barth continu
ally stresses that the male-female relationship is the model of relations for society, Tillich hardly touches that relationship, and only
indirectly in the *Systematic Theology*.

The approach of the paper will be twofold: first, to lay out
the structure of each man's theology as it relates to questions of
domination, and second, to show how Barth *explicitly* relates these
themes to women, while Tillich speaks rather in terms of polarities
in general, and refers them only indirectly to women. Finally, we
may perhaps discover some clues that emerge from the study of
these men in order to indicate some new theological directions.

KARL BARTH AND THE DIVINE LORDSHIP

In the sense of crisis after the First World War, Barth sought for
resources from the Christian tradition to revitalize the Church.
The time itself revealed to him very clearly the failure of the tradition of Christian liberalism, and like the early Protestant reformers,
he looked for new life in a return to the resources of the Word of
God as witnessed to in the scriptures. During the Hitler regime his
theological stance provided both truth and power for resistance to
the encroachments of the Nazi power on the Church. The great
NO for which Barth is famous served the churches well as a way of
saying NO to the regime in a new, prophetic style.

Barth takes as his starting point the primacy of the divine revelation of God, where God reveals himself in his Word. This revelation takes place first and foremost in the person of Jesus Christ, to
whom the biblical writings bear witness. The Scripture is the
Word of God for us, and it is through the proclamation of this
Word in preaching that we come to knowledge of God. This knowledge cannot be known antecedently from man in any way, but is
known insofar as God makes himself known to us, miraculously.[3]
Thus our human experience is of no account in coming to know
God. One cannot question experience or speak the language of the
philosophers or any secular language and so come to find God. Not
only is the hearing of the Word a miracle but God himself must
take care of our understanding of it.[4]

In the Word as Revelation, God's act of speaking is seen to be indistinguishable from the divine I that confronts man as Thou. This Word is directly identical with God in God, and only indirectly identified with God's speech in man, that is, in scripture, and even more remotely with theology, for the human is never a determining factor of the way the infinite exists in itself. Rather, we must always read off our doctrine from the original datum of revelation, the Word that the scriptures reveal, and not from any knowledge we may have about it. In this encounter the Word appears less as means of communion than as an "other," not to be identified with man. But "the boulder of a Thou which does not become an I, but is here cast on our path," is seen as an encounter that can never be "dissolved in fellowship" (Church Dogmatics, I/1, 159–160).[5] This Word appears in humanity, veiled and yet made visible to us. The infinite boundary that exists between God and us is bridged by God himself in a bodily way, so that the Word of God is Christ himself. If the Scripture may also be identified as the Word of God, it is primarily because it witnesses to Christ, who is the Word *par excellence*. Scripture itself always remains a relative word, a word related to Christ, from whom it derives its meaning and its communicability. That is the only sense in which it is relative, it would seem.

It is only in the Holy Spirit that revelation can be known as such, and the Spirit is defined variously as God's freedom to present to the creature his presence from within, or as the ground of man's possibility of personally participating in revelation (I/1, 516). The YES of God is the act of the Holy Spirit, who always remains other than man, in such a way that man who "is as it were called in question within his own house [to be] present at God's revelation as a servant is present at his master's action," can say Yes to God in obedience (I/1, 535). Man does not yet appear as partner of God, though later in the Church Dogmatics Barth does seem to make room for such a role. Yet the Holy Spirit does establish communion of man and God within revelation. Only there does God seek us "as those who can let themselves be found . . . as a Person with persons" (I/1, 466).

On man's side, the presence of the Spirit means the subjective possibility of faith. which, in spite of the idea of communion that Barth has, does not allow for reciprocity, but only for the "act of renouncing reciprocity, the act of acknowledging the one Mediator beside whom there is no other" (I/2, 146). Only God is Subject; in relation to God the human person is never subject of action, but rather always subject to the divine action. Mary as true hearer of the Word is the model for mankind. Her virginity (which leads Barth into an interesting discussion of the worth and validity of signs as themselves participating in the reality to which they point) is a sign of faith, "the denial, not of man in the presence of God, but of any power, attribute or capacity in him for God." As woman, she is precisely non-everything—"non-willing, non-achieving, non-creative, non-sovereign," as opposed to willing, achieving, disobedient man (I/2, 188). This view of the woman's role as the prototype of humanity in relation to God is, of course, firmly grounded in the theological tradition, but perhaps it has not often been stated in such absolute terms.

If God speaks to man in revelation, man enters into relationship with God by hearing the Word, a hearing understood as obedience in faith. The mind is subjected in the process not of seeking the truth but of hearing the Word and surrendering to it. Theology finds its place as the attempt to understand the Word of God, which is Christ, while preaching is the speaking of the Word in human words within the Church.

Knowledge of God is, then, a privileged knowledge that operates in a sphere over and above merely human knowledge. Ministry is primarily the preaching of the Gospel, and the preacher, for all that he must remember that the word he speaks has power only by the power of God, is nonetheless the privileged place where the Word of God is spoken. Though God may speak independently of the actual words of the preacher, he actually speaks only through the preaching. Thus the relation of God to man as Master and Lord finds an echo in the relation of the preacher to the congregation, at least in the act of preaching. And in as male-dominated an institution as the Church, God speaks with a masculine voice. Women are the listeners, and the congregation takes on a kind of feminine role, passive and dependent.

While the theme of the Word of God is a prevailing theme for Barth, it is by no means the only theme. In later volumes of the *Church Dogmatics* Barth takes up the notion of man as image of God, and particularly as image of Christ as the man for his fellowmen. In the third volume he comes back to the discussion of person, which he sees to be essentially constituted by the relation for others, both in terms of the Trinitarian relation and on the model of Jesus Christ as the Man for others. Where he had defined the person earlier in terms of God as "an I existing in and for itself with a thought and will proper to it" (I/1, 354), he now defines the person as "I am in encounter," a being fulfilled in his relations with others (III/2, 243).

The problem arises in the way that man images the Trinity. We are told that man was created in the basic form of the duality of man/woman as image of the God who is not solitary. But whereas in man the I and the Thou are two different individuals, in God the I and the Thou are the same individual (III/1, 196). Man/woman as image is not an image of the Trinity *per se*, but rather "the correspondence of the unlike" (III/1, 196). What Barth is driving at, I think, is the unity of the I-Thou relationship in man and woman together, a relationship taken as paradigmatic for man's relation to his fellowman. Where the relation is one of equality and oneness in being in the Trinity, in man the relation is one of duality and inequality. God did not create man alone, Barth tells us, "but the unequal duality for man and woman in the basic form of duality" (III/1, 288).

Barth rejects any view that would make men and women equal, because the sexual differentiation itself is the sign of limitation proper to the creature. Where in the Trinity there is distinction without inequality or separation—perfect union with one will and freedom—on the human level, union is achieved by the superordination/subordination relation. Recognition of sexual differentiation is recognition of weakness and limitation. To attempt to overcome that differentiation is described as a kind of *hubris*, or pride, because, in fact, one is attempting to overcome the separated condition that is human existence. Such an attempt could only be a form of *gnosis*, a false spirituality (III/4, 157).

It is interesting that in this discussion it is woman who represents the creature, as in Barth's understanding of the Virgin Mary. She is subordinate and unequal, who must understand and keep her place. It apparently does not occur to him that perhaps male domination is in reality a usurpation of the role of God, that man in that relation is attempting to escape the subjection that belongs to creaturely status, according to his own theology.

In partial recognition of that point, Barth admits that man and woman transcend their sexuality at one point, but at one point only, in their relation to God. In other words, on earth the polarity is total, and the attempts to overcome it only show "the undeniable power of the temptation to seek to evade one's sex as the form of an aspiration to neutral humanity (III/4, 157). To be faithful in the hearing of the Word, the "requirement of faithfulness to sex [i.e., the sexual differentiation] is made at every point by both men and women" (III/4, 155).

Thus he rejects the falsification of the image of Christ by the addition of female elements. Christian art has wrongly given Christ "that well known and frightful mixture of masculine and feminine traits . . . instead of honourably at least in the form of a man" (III/4, 161). One might question at this point, as Tillich does, whether this feminization of Christ is not in fact an attempt to humanize Christ, a response to the rejection of the feminine elements of the tradition.

For Barth the qualitative difference between God and man has been extended to man and woman. The relation of lordship is constitutive in Christ, so that generic man's salvation is in faith in Christ and in his lordship. This is paralleled on the human level, for woman, in her relationship to the (specific) man who is her lord, and to whom she is bound in obedient love, always, as he adds, without prejudice to her dignity (whatever that may mean). The prevailing model is the hierarchical model of master to servant, or occasionally, of father to child, from God to man, from Christ to man, from man to woman. The form of communion is obedience, because of the fundamental inequalities. Only in the Trinity can communion mean something else.

The third heme of importance is Barth's understanding of freedom. In many ways his theology expresses a fear of human freedom, understandable enough in the context of the breakdown of culture and law of the two world wars. God alone as Subject is fully free for himself. Man participates in divine freedom insofar as he is "free for Him, who as the Creator, willed and always does will to be free for his creature" (III/1, 195). Elsewhere true freedom is described, not as freedom of choice, which Barth rejects, but as freedom for God; that is, freedom to obey him (III/4, 13).

Divine freedom is initiative, choice, lordship, inspiration, while human freedom consists in following that initiative to act on the divine choice/command, to accept the divine lordship. Woman in turn stands in the same relation to man—"properly speaking, the business of woman, her task and function, is to actualize the fellowship in which man can only precede her, stimulating, leading, inspiring" (III/4,171). Insofar as woman is understood to be subject to man, without detriment to her dignity of course, she is already free, because in obeying her husband she obeys God. On the other hand, Barth does recognize that women have often been actually oppressed. To be truly liberated, that is, free by Barth's definition, she should not protest, because, in fact, her rebellion may be an indication of the same contempt for divine order as man's oppression of her is. Her response in faith is to keep her proper place, to follow man's initiative, and in that way to bring him to repentance. By that analogy, Jews should go quietly and with dignity to the gas chambers; blacks should "keep their place" and convert whites from their sin. The only trouble is that this advice has always benefited those who hold power in an oppressive structure. To accept this advice may encourage arrogance in the superordinate (superior) class. In addition, there is little evidence that this moral superiority of the dominated has ever had much power to convert the powerful of this world.

Part of Barth's problem is his mode of reading revelation. Insofar as the Bible—Old or New Testaments—is taken as complete expression of the Word of God, theologians cannot adequately take account of the present aspirations of women. An increasing number of women reject the patriarchal view of society that characterizes the biblical world, a view that Barth has, in fact, absolutized. Women find few enough images of themselves in that world with which they can connect. By contrast, theologians of black power and of the Third World liberation movements are able to find some models in the Exodus story. While there are indeed models of active and creative women, particularly in the Old Testament, they are clearly exceptional. In any case, Barth does not refer to them. Even the Galatians passage (3:28) "In Christ there is neither Jew nor Gentile, slave nor free, male nor female" he understands in the weakest sense. Woman is truly woman with man, as (and the comparison is apt in Barth's system!) the free man is only free with the slave.[6] Woman remains in the position of subordination, and all Barth's insistence on her proper dignity has a hollow ring.

The fundamental problem, as I see it, in the Barthian understanding of theology is its acceptance of the master-servant relationship as normative; God speaks and men obey, a structure which becomes the model for relations of domination both within the Church and within society. It would seem that if one rejects this norm in order to seek alternatives in Church, politics, family or natural environment, one must also question the mode of relation to God.

In *The Humanity of God*, written in 1956, Barth recognizes the need to correct some of his earlier positions, not, however, in order to deny those positions, since he still thinks it was necessary to speak that way at that time. Here he understands man as called to be the covenant partner of God, though he still underscores the absolute nature of the difference between God and man. He even comes to evaluate culture more positively than in his earlier work, as "the attempt of man to be man, and thus to hold the good gift of his humanity in honor and to put it to work."[7] In creative human activity God is able to produce parables of his own goodwill.

Theology, too, insofar as it is a form of culture and of human effort, may be dialogue with God. As dialogue the relationship includes the human partner in his (her?) full reality as one who must in some sense participate in the Word in order to understand and communicate it.

It is clear that Barth sees the change in his thought to be the result of a deeper understanding of the role of Christ in the world of men. Once Christ has appeared, the world *is* different. The original concept of the Word, interpreted as absolute initiative of God (which, of course, it remains)—but apart from and to the detriment almost of man, to whom it was spoken—has now given way to an understanding of the graciousness of God present in our midst in Christ Jesus. The word that then appeared to be a word spoken to man, who received it from above by a kind of miracle, is now a Word that really enters incarnationally into the conditions of human life. Barth can even go so far as to say that once Christ has appeared, "What is *Christian* is surely but fundamentally identical with what is *universally human*."[8] But he still means that we do not understand what is Christian from our experience of the human. Rather, from Christ we understand what "universally human" means.

With the understanding of Christ as real communication of God to man for communion, Barth emphasizes more than he had in his earlier writing God's presence to man in love. Yet his discussion of the dimension of love in the speaking of the Word leaves one curiously cold. It is clear from what he says of prayer as the atmosphere of theology that he himself understands that one cannot know God apart from love, but somehow it is not a warm human love.

Barth, I think, does not mean to devalue women. He really sees their life of submission as being truer to what it means to be before God than the masculine ideal, at the same time that he thinks that men cannot and must not imitate women in their ideal life. In one sense he agrees with Schleiermacher, whom he quotes almost with approval:

> Women are more fortunate than we in that their business affairs take up only a part of their thoughts while the longing of the heart, the beautiful inward life of imagination, always dominates the greater part. . . . Wherever I look, it always seems to me that the nature of women is nobler and their life happier, and if ever I toy with an impossible wish, it is to be a woman.[9]

Barth is even willing to concede that

> There have always been far too many male or masculine theologians. And in Schleiermacher for all our reservations, we can learn so much with regard to the understanding of women and the whole question of sex-relationship that we gladly accept the possibility that . . . the phenomenon had in his case a positive significance. . . . But it is to be noted that not all similar phenomena in men of the same tendencies, not all feminine thought, feeling and conduct on the part of men, has this positive significance.[10]

What he means is that it was a nice idea, but rather sentimental, and we can agree. Nevertheless one wonders what difference his appreciation of "feminine thought" actually made. Male thinking is, after all, complete in itself.

TILLICH AND THE POWER OF BEING

Tillich, like Barth, was concerned with the breakdown of Western culture experienced after the crisis of the First World War. But where Barth saw the crisis negatively, and sought to overcome it in the assurance that comes from the reassertion of the Divine Sovereignty through the return to the Word in the scriptures, Tillich felt the time contained not only chaos but also *kairos*, a time pregnant with the future. Tillich was unhappy about Barth's solution, and saw it as an attempt on the part of the theologian to escape his own finitude, and thus as an expression of a very real arrogance. More than Barth, he understood the impact of historical awareness and the need to take the demands of the present seriously. For Tillich history itself contains revelatory moments, and his concern was to discover not only power from the tradition but also power in the present for a new future.

The basic theme of Tillich's theology is the notion of God as Being, something that was more than a concept for him, as we shall see. This was the basis for a nonhierarchical view of reality. In coming to grips with historical existence and culture he attempted to overcome the many dualities that he found. It is interesting that these dualities are not described directly as male/female, though some of them do relate to male/female stereotypes. At only one point, in the discussion of the Trinity, does he deal directly with the polarity of male/female. Out of the attempt to deal with these polarities, a triadic structure emerges, not only the Trinitarian doctrine of God but also a triadic structure of man and history. Perhaps more important than the triadic structure *per se* is the sense of a new age beyond the divisions.

The themes that are significant for our study may be described briefly as follows. The theme of Being as creative Ground from which man has his being, and in which he participates; revelatory experience that overcomes the polarities of subject and object, or reason and emotion; Tillich's view of the person as centered self related to others in community; and his understanding of history as openness to the future.

Tillich calls his method one of correlation. Human existence in its quest for salvation from the negativities of existence and for fulfillment seeks answers to such questions as: What is the meaning of life? Is an unambiguous life possible? How can we find the courage to be in the midst of anxiety? The questions he sees are those raised by philosophers, poets, painters—that is, from culture. While men can raise the questions, they cannot give answers. The answers are to be found in the Christian tradition, though not in any simple way. It is the work of the theologian to take the questions seriously, and to show the ways in which the Christian insight can provide the answers, a task that needs to be done anew in each generation. Thus theology implies a continuing reinterpretation of the myths and symbols of the tradition, and even a critique, in order that the answers may appear in the present with full clarity. Where Barth rejected culture as in any sense revelatory, Tillich takes up the question of revelation in history and in culture, not only in the attempt to make the Christian answer relevant but even to understand it better. In some sense revelation itself may be relative to the questions that are asked in a particular historical period.

This view implies two things. First, it implies a recognition and a coming to grips with the fact of historical relativity, in that past expressions of faith have attempted to answer the questions of their own times in the philosophical framework of those times. Second, it implies that the work of reinterpretation is not only a theological task but is itself in some sense revelatory, as any other aspect of culture, in the creation of a new symbol or myth. The new myth will have meaning insofar as it expresses the depth of Being, insofar as it "speaks" to modern man; and this is something that cannot be programmed. Rather, says Tillich, "a new myth is the expression of the reuniting power of a new revelation, not a product of formalized reason."[11]

Central to Tillich's project is the examination of the nature of reason. He rejects the quest for scientific knowledge as the only form or the norm for reason, and insists that the classical concept of reason was much fuller and richer. Ontological reason is reason in relation to Being, to the whole of reality. Subjective reason, the human mind, is attuned to the *Logos* structure of being, in which it participates. Reason in this sense has to do with human meanings and ends, while technical scientific reason has to do with means.[12] As he pursues the analysis he exposes other polarities in the structure of reason: the subject-object dichotomy, detachment and participation in the exercise of reason, static and dynamic elements, formal and emotional elements in reason. Insofar as reason is characterized by one side of the polarity, it is inadequate. Tillich's concern, then, is to discover the unity and the wholeness of reason by overcoming these crippling dichotomies, which he understands to be the result of the cultural development of the West, and perhaps also, in part, symbolic of the human situation of estrangement.

To take one example, reason unites both formal and emotional elements. In Western culture, detached knowledge for the purpose of control is accepted as the proper form of reason, while emotion is understood to be irrational. The consequent suppression of emotion is a distortion, as is detached reason when it is made a way of life. Furthermore, the suppression frequently leads to emotional reactions, and even overreactions, which appear irrational and are certainly destructive. The formal and emotional elements together form perfect knowledge, which is a form of union in which the split between subject and object is overcome. The biblical sense of *gnosis* is precisely this kind of knowledge, Tillich points out, and it includes sexual union as well as mystical knowledge. It is knowledge as communion. Intrinsic to knowledge, then, is eros, not in the narrowly sexual sense, but as drive toward union with being and fulfillment. Knowledge goes beyond the intellect, and it may well be, as depth psychology has shown, both healing and transforming.[13] Tillich does not make the point, but it is clear enough that the dichotomy of formal reason and emotion relates to the stereotypes of masculine and feminine thinking. Masculine thinking is not the only form of thought, we might say, extrapolating from Tillich; full understanding comes from the integration of the polarity.[14]

Reason, for Tillich, is neither opposed to nor denied by revelation. It is reason in the integrated sense that receives revelation, through the experience of being grasped by the ultimate concern, which may be an ecstatic or mystical experience. It may also arrive through the experience of anxiety, the shock of possible nonbeing

(*Systematic Theology*, I, 163).[15] But while there may be many revelatory experiences, the revelation of Jesus as the Christ is the supreme revelation, the definitive revelation; but the biblical witness is not the last word. Christianity itself is in history, and is not final itself, though it witnesses to the final revelation (I, 134).

What does Tillich mean by Being? He certainly does not mean the concept of being derived from the grammatical use of the verb "to be" as a copula. It is rather the wholeness of reality, grasped in a unifying experience, an experience of being at home in the world, fleeting though that sense may be in the estrangement of existence. He describes Being as creative Ground, a notion that reflects the mothering and nurturing aspect of reality, reminiscent of the New Testament expression of the God "in whom we live and move and have our being" (Acts 17:28). In the context of existential anxiety, where nonbeing is an active threat, Being is experienced as victorious power, the power to give and sustain life, and the power finally to overcome nonbeing.

The full Christian answer to this sense of anxiety and estrangement from being, from one's own true self and from others, is to be found in Christ as the New Being. But in order to understand Christ as New Being, one must understand the full implications of the estrangement implied in actual existence. The notion of estrangement is related to the Marxist notion of alienation, as well as to existentialist analyses of existence. Tillich accepts the existentialist understanding of *ex-sistere*—"to stand out or away from"—and applies this to man's relation to Being. Thus the Christian symbol of the Fall is interpreted to make sense out of this alienation or estrangement from the Ground of Being.

The Fall is for Tillich an example of historicized myth, a symbolic expression of a state of things told in story form. It does not relate to the first couple only—at least that gets Eve off the hook! It is the story of each individual in the passage from essence (where one is united to the Ground of Being) to existence. The state "before the Fall" is one of potentiality, of "dreaming innocence," and the Fall itself is the drive toward actualization, the passage from dreaming innocence to knowledge. He gives two examples suggested by the Genesis story itself. The first is the sexual awakening of the adolescent, the discovery of sexual feelings and the consequent sense of guilt. The dilemma in which the adolescent finds himself is that if he actualizes himself sexually, he becomes guilty, but if he fails to realize his sexual power actually, he loses himself altogether (II, 36). The second experience is the desire for forbidden knowledge; to gain knowledge is to gain control, but with the gain comes a sense of guilt (cf. III, 73).

Tillich seems to be ambivalent about the Fall, the process through which man becomes estranged. On the one hand, it is a necessary stage of actualization, but on the other, it is sin and estrangement. It is the reverse side of creation, of God's othering himself in creating finite beings separated from himself. While the Fall has always been a problem for theologians and others to understand, Tillich admits that it is the one irrational element of theology (II, 30, and III, 284).

It is interesting that he does not refer to the male/female question in the discussion of estrangement. Likewise, his description of Jesus as the Christ—the One who brings the new state of things and who conquers the situation—understands Him from the point of view of His personhood, not His maleness (cf. II, 120). He comments on the feminization of images of Jesus, as already mentioned, as a reaction to an overly masculinized form of religion.

The only place where Tillich speaks directly to the question of male and female is in his discussion of the Trinity, the triadic structure of Being as creative power, saving love and ecstatic transformation. He is sensitive to the fact that orthodox Protestantism in eliminating the Virgin Mary has also succeeded in eliminating feminine elements in God. He is concerned both to be faithful to Protestant symbolism in its genuine elements, but also to overcome the one-sided male symbolism that has so often appeared in Protestant forms. Thus he suggests that the Ground of Being points to the mother qualities of giving birth, carrying, and embracing, as well as to the father qualities of calling back, of resisting independence of the created, and (curiously) of swallowing it (III, 294). With respect to Jesus as the Christ, the element of self-sacrifice (so often in fact felt to be characteristic of women) is in fact proper to neither male nor female as such, but is the negation of one or other in exclusion. With respect to the Spirit, he points out that the feminine element of the Spirit brooding over the earth was lost very early in Jewish symbolism, but the ecstatic mystical character of the Spirit transcends the male/female dichotomy—a character that Protestants have generally mistrusted, he points out.

More than Barth, Tillich understands the human person as centered self, having his/her own dignity as a responsible subject and creator of culture. Within the self, however, there is a polarity between individualization, the search for self-identity, and participation, being with others, living and acting in a world. When self-identity is overemphasized, the individual is lonely and cut off from his world; when participation is overemphasized, the person is cut off from his/her own selfhood. Participation in being, in the group and in culture, means that Tillich cannot talk about the individual apart from culture and history.

Yet there are certain elements that Tillich understands to be beyond history. The fundamental questions that men ask are basically the same: the question of being, the question of meaning and purpose, the question of the good and of fulfillment. Art, too, does not progress in any historical sense. When individual freedom is decisive, in the individual free act *per se*, the moral act, there is no progress; there is progress only with respect to ethical content and educational level. Progress takes place in the cultural element within the moral act, but not in the moral act itself (III, 333). Similarly, in the history of thought, there is progress and development in the content of the answer, but not necessarily in the question or in the initial insight.

In culture the depth of Being continually manifests itself in the course of history, under different forms and symbols. The content of the symbols is always to be understood historically, though that to which they point is absolute. Any symbol that is absolutized, even religious symbols (perhaps especially religious symbols), become demonic and idolatrous.

Man is essentially a historical being, someone who is free insofar as he sets and pursues purposes and transcends the given situation in a kind of breakthrough toward the future (III, 303). He is free insofar as he has a vision of the Kingdom and can create worlds other than the given world. Thus, for Tillich, there is a real sense that the Kingdom of God as symbol finds partial realization as a future to be striven for, but never adequately achieved. In some sense, human freedom is part of the struggle—the content of the partial realization is not set ahead of time, though its full realization is possible only in the *eschaton*, beyond time. At the end of time all the partial realizations of being will be taken up into Being itself, and all the ambiguities of existence will be overcome. This is the return movement to unity and fulfillment, which Tillich describes as the return to essentialization (III, 400).

History contains both surprise and novelty. In the realm of Spirit, the active divine presence in history, there is always room for the inbreaking of the qualitatively new. At key moments of history, possibilities for transformation emerge, which will in turn create a new tradition. These moments are *kairoi*, times filled with the promise of the future and expectation of new revelatory experience. At this juncture man can respond either by seeking to hold onto the past, out of anxiety about the new and untried future, or he can take the risk of the new.

In what ways might we as women respond to Tillich's thought? First, it is clear that Tillich when he says "man" means either the individual person or the human race. He means to speak about the human situation, the situation of men and women in the world. The human spirit is estranged spirit, and this is the universal situation. Tillich's analysis is theoretical at this point, precisely because he does not differentiate between different forms of estrangement, and thus is not very helpful to women. It is too general.

Tillich's theology of Being as creative Ground avoids the whole problem that we found so intimidating in Barth's theology —the basic authoritarianism that related man to God as slave to master, or as child to a Father who retained the characteristics of the master. Tillich's understanding of God is nonauthoritarian, and he is able to allow the human person real power by participation in the power of Being. In some sense, human beings act along with and under the Spirit in history. In that sense the democratic insight that all persons have their own dignity and have the destiny of participating as creators of culture is not alien to Tillich, though some of us have found it lacking in Barth's theology.

Tillich is more a theologian of culture than of politics. In his sense, theology of culture includes a theological analysis of all cultural expressions, the discernment of the ultimate concern in philosophy, political systems, artistic styles, or ethical/social principles (I, 39). He is looking at culture reflectively as object of man's creation, and as it contains elements and symbols of the divine Spirit. Politics, however, is a more difficult matter to approach for an idealist, and Tillich concludes that in the last analysis it is the individual rather than the group that is related to the transcendent. Similarly, alienation is not experienced by the political group, by which he means the state, but only by individuals within the group. He is very conscious of the oppressive use of power, which he sees to be demonic. If there are ambiguities throughout the whole of existence, they appear to him to be most obvious in the political realm. In his discussion of history, little importance is given to smaller groups within the State, because he normally identifies the State as the history-bearing group (III, 309).

It is no accident, surely, that women theologians have found Tillich a more sympathetic figure than Barth. The structure of his theology is nonauthoritarian and allows for genuine human dignity and freedom for both men and women. His attempts to revalue and integrate those aspects of thought devalued by the masculinized culture of the West are significant. His view of history, with its possibility of genuine newness, allows a new vision of the future to emerge, a vision that is not dominated by either social or theological structures of the past, though it is able to draw on the resources of the tradition. The theological work is also understood as something more than a reinterpretation of the past, it is understood as openness "for new experiences which might even pass beyond the confines of Christian experience"—this, he says, is "now the proper attitude of the theologian" (I, 45).

If we must fault Tillich, it is for his overemphasis on the universal, his inattention to the functions of differentiation in human life. Though he claims to speak of the human person as a whole in the universal experience, one has the feeling that his description is the universalization of the inner life of the European middle-class male, a particular feeling made universal. His idealization of the person as spirit expressing itself in culture tends to sell the body short, as well as politics. While his emphasis on the importance of eros as cohesive force in the body politic is important, perhaps a theological analysis needs to be made of the acceptance of institutional violence in our culture—violence to persons and groups through inequality, poverty, institutionalization of the unfit, and other hidden means. Recognition that the characteristics of our own culture and its history are not identical with "original sin" or "the Fall" may open up freedom to study other cultures and to discover ways of living together constructively rather than destructively

CONCLUSION

For both Barth and Tillich the subject/object scheme is crucial.[16] For Barth, to be subject is necessarily to control and to dominate; this is why God alone can be subject with regard to man. Tillich, however, attempted to go beyond the split of subject/object, so that the Ground of Being was seen as primal ground, out of which subject/object came, and where, in the experience of union, the split was overcome. By specifically setting up the possibility of an other form of knowledge beyond scientific knowledge, where the dichotomy (and domination) of the object reigns supreme, Tillich points the way toward another form of knowledge and of being together in community, a mode of participation and concern. Yet on the specifically political level he was not able to go beyond the present definition of politics as manipulation of power to a politics of participation, though there are real clues in his thought.

Other Christian themes related to structures of domination in Church and theology have been the teachings on suffering and sin, which are not unrelated to the man/woman theme, as we saw in Barth. The teaching on sin has frequently had the effect in the Church of reinforcing the status quo through fear of the repressive aspects of utopia and the fear of utopia as *hubris*. Likewise, Jesus' teaching on poverty of spirit and submission to the Father's will has reinforced oppressive regimes that have demanded obedience because they have seen themselves as part of the divine will. What was meant to be preached to the rich and powerful, and thus to be a potent force for change, when preached to the poor becomes a continuation of the suffering of the poor and the oppressed. By such preaching the hunger and thirst for justice has been castrated by becoming an impotent longing for the hereafter. Willy-nilly, theology is linked with politics, and we had better discover and make explicit what the connections are.

Once theology becomes self-critical, aware of the fact that it does not speak of a disembodied eternal truth but of the truth understood as social reality, then theology is free to become critical of the present, prophetic in its vision of the future, and active in its working toward that future.

First, theology must become critical to demythologize the forms of domination canonized in our theology as much as in our ecclesiology and our politics. Liberation theologians in Latin America have been working in various ways on the theologico-political analysis of the sources of power in their own society, the links between oppressive government and Church, and the ways in which people are excluded from participation in power. These theologians are no longer concerned with sin in general but with the concrete oppression that is revealed in day-to-day existence. Beyond this, they look for ways of overcoming the sense of defeat of the poor, who are getting poorer every day, who have internalized the oppression in their own sense of fatalism and despair.

Second, in times of the breakdown of culture, such as our own, the theological task is less the consolidation of the tradition by looking back than the building of a new vision. The prophetic work in our time may replace the systematic work in importance for some time to come. Prophecy is understood in this sense of pointing toward the future, discovering sources of hope and uncovering new alternatives. Today the structure of competition, as well as other forms of domination, is being questioned in our society by old as well as young. We are beginning to understand the destructiveness of the competitive order, and an increasing number of people want out—not always openly, however. It would be interesting to know just how many people "have lost faith" in the electoral process and democratic government in this country. That loss of faith may be quite a subversive act.

The third task of theology is the practical work in politics, understood in the sense of action by communities for the realization of value. A theology for the liberation of women, in particular, must address itself to the question of the liberation in *praxis* of people from old forms of domination and of destruction. Such a theology is not and cannot be developed in the abstract, but will grow out of actual involvement in the work of liberation, out of new forms of life in community, new life styles in which people experience what it means to become free of oppression and repression in their day-to-day lives. Through the struggles of these communities, struggles that are both personal and political, will come new forms of life and celebration, and a form of theological reflection that can drive the quest for the future ahead.

In some not altogether frivolous sense God needs to be liberated from our theology. Theology is not a tabernacle to contain the One who is Ahead, but it is a sign on the way, and thus is provisional. Thus the theologian is not only protester and prophet, if she is lucky, but also pilgrim.

NOTES

1. "Towards a Theology of Sexual Politics," an anonymous article from South Africa, quoted in Letty Russell, "Human Liberation in a Feminine Perspective," unpublished ms.
2. Paul Tillich, *Systematic Theology*, 3 vols. (Chicago: University of Chicago Press, 1951–63), I (1957), 227.
3. Karl Barth, *Church Dogmatics*, trans. G. T. Thomson *et al.*, 4 vols. (Edinburgh: T. & T. Clark, 1936–62), I/1, 282.
4. Karl Barth, *The Humanity of God* (Richmond, Va.: John Knox Press, 1960), pp. 58–59.
5. All parenthetical references in text until n. 6 will be to Barth, *Church Dogmatics*.
6. Barbara Hall, in an unpublished paper, makes the case that Paul is here really speaking of the new age, when the distinction between Jew and Gentile, man and woman, slave and free has ceased to be decisive in the Church.
7. Tillich, *Systematic Theology*, I, 4.
8. Karl Barth, *Christ and Adam: Man and Humanity in Romans 5* (New York: Harper & Bros., 1957), p. 111. Emphasis is Barth's.
9. *Schleiermachers Leben*, I, 412, quoted in Barth, *Church Dogmatics*, III/4, 155. I wonder how many women would identify with that description of them today!
10. Ibid., III/4, 155.
11. Tillich, *Systematic Theology*, I, 92.
12. Ibid., I, 72–73.
13. Ibid., I, 89–97.
14. At this point one can probably not say with any assurance that certain polarities are biologically based on sex-linked differences. It may be that biological determination influences women to value affection, and men to value achievement. Or it may be that women have not been fully socialized into the dominant male system of competitive achievement, and that mothering and

nurture require other values. What is at stake here (and I think Tillich is quite right) is that the kind of knowledge that we value in our society is a distorted knowledge. Its results have been at best ambiguous, and at worst destructive.

15. All parenthetical references in text until the final footnote will be to Tillich, *Systematic Theology.*

16. "The subject/object relation defines subjectivity as a function of domination, the domination of objects and the reduction of other subjects to objects. Western selfhood, certainly in its male forms, is a selfhood of appropriation and manipulation in its very self-definition and definition of relationships . . . domination permeates almost universally the prevailing mode of experiencing reality" (Murray Bookchin, "On Spontaneity and Organization," *Liberation* [March 1972], p 13)

Epilogue: The Coming of Lilith

JUDITH PLASKOW GOLDENBERG[*]

In the beginning the Lord God formed Adam and Lilith from the dust of the ground and breathed into their nostrils the breath of life. Created from the same source, both having been formed from the ground, they were equal in all ways. Adam, man that he was, didn't like this situation, and he looked for ways to change it. He said, "I'll have my figs now, Lilith," ordering her to wait on him, and he tried to leave to her the daily tasks of life in the garden. But Lilith wasn't one to take any nonsense; she picked herself up, uttered God's holy name, and flew away. "Well, now, Lord," complained Adam, "that uppity woman you sent me has gone and deserted me." The Lord, inclined to be sympathetic, sent his messengers after Lilith, telling her to shape up and return to Adam or face dire punishment. She, however, preferring anything to living with Adam, decided to stay right where she was. And so God, after more careful consideration this time, caused a deep sleep to fall upon Adam, and out of one of his ribs created for him a second companion, Eve.

For a time Eve and Adam had quite a good thing going. Adam was happy now, and Eve, though she occasionally sensed capacities

* With Karen Bloomquist, Margaret Early, and Elizabeth Farians.

within herself that remained undeveloped, was basically satisfied with the role of Adam's wife and helper. The only thing that really disturbed her was the excluding closeness of the relationship between Adam and God. Adam and God just seemed to have more in common, being both men, and Adam came to identify with God more and more. After a while that made God a bit uncomfortable too, and he started going over in his mind whether he might not have made a mistake in letting Adam talk him into banishing Lilith and creating Eve, in light of the power that had given Adam.

Meanwhile Lilith, all alone, attempted from time to time to rejoin the human community in the garden. After her first fruitless attempt to breach its walls, Adam worked hard to build them stronger, even getting Eve to help him. He told her fearsome stories of the demon Lilith who threatens women in childbirth and steals children from their cradles in the middle of the night. The second time Lilith came she stormed the garden's main gate, and a great battle between her and Adam ensued, in which she was finally defeated. This time, however, before Lilith got away, Eve got a glimpse of her and saw she was a woman like herself.

After this encounter, seeds of curiosity and doubt began to grow in Eve's mind. Was Lilith indeed just another woman? Adam had said she was a demon. Another woman! The very idea attracted Eve. She had never seen another creature like herself before. And how beautiful and strong Lilith had looked! How bravely she had fought! Slowly, slowly, Eve began to think about the limits of her own life within the garden.

One day, after many months of strange and disturbing thoughts, Eve, wandering around the edge of the garden, noticed a young apple tree she and Adam had planted, and saw that one of its branches stretched over the garden wall. Spontaneously she tried to climb it, and struggling to the top, swung herself over the wall.

She had not wandered long on the other side before she met the one she had come to find, for Lilith was waiting. At first sight of her, Eve remembered the tales of Adam and was frightened, but Lilith understood and greeted her kindly. "Who are you?" they asked each other, "What is your story?" And they sat and spoke together, of the past and then of the future. They talked not once, but many times, and for many hours. They taught each other many things, and told each other stories, and laughed together, and cried, over and over, till the bond of sisterhood grew between them.

Meanwhile, back in the garden, Adam was puzzled by Eve's comings and goings, and disturbed by what he sensed to be her new attitude toward him. He talked to God about it, and God, having his own problems with Adam and a somewhat broader perspective, was able to help him out a little—but he, too, was confused. Something had failed to go according to plan. As in the days of Abraham, he needed counsel from his children. "I am who I am," thought God, "but I must become who I will become."

And God and Adam were expectant and afraid the day Eve and Lilith returned to the garden, bursting with possibilities, ready to rebuild it together.

Suggested Further Readings

Baer, Richard, *Philo's Use of the Categories of Male and Female.* Brill, 1972.

Bailey, D. S., *The Man–Woman Relation in Christian Thought.* Longmans, 1959.

Bainton, Roland, *Women in the Reformation in Germany and Italy.* Augsburg, 1971.

Beauvoir, Simone de, *The Second Sex.* Bantam, 1953.

Culver, Elsie, *Women in the World of Religion.* Doubleday, 1967.

Daly, Mary, *Beyond God the Father.* Beacon Press, 1973.

———, *The Church and the Second Sex.* Harper & Row, 1968.

Hayes, H. A., *The Dangerous Sex: The Myth of Feminine Evil.* Pocket Books, 1972.

James, E. O., *The Cult of the Mother God-dess.* Praeger, 1959.

———, *The Worship of the Sky God: Semitic and Indo-European Religion.* Athlone Press, 1963.

Miegge, Giovanni, *The Virgin Mary.* Westminster, 1955.

O'Faolain, Julia, and Martines, Lauro, *Not in God's Image: Women in History from the Greeks to the Victorians.* Torch (Harper & Row), 1973.

Patai, Raphael, *The Hebrew Goddess.* Ktav, 1968.

Phipps, William, *Was Jesus Married? The Distortion of Sexuality in the Christian Tradition.* Harper & Row, 1970.

Reik, Theodor, *The Creation of Woman.* McGraw, 1960.

Rogers, Katherine, *The Troublesome Helpmeet: A History of Misogyny in Literature.* Univ. of Washington Press, 1966.

Roszak, Betty and Theodore, *Masculine–Feminine: Readings in Sexual Mythology and the Liberation of Women.* Harper & Row, 1969.

Slater, Philip, *The Glory of Hera: Greek Mythology and the Family.* Beacon Press, 1968.

Stendahl, Krister, *The Bible and the Role of Women.* Fortress, 1966.

Van Buren, Nancy, *The Subversion of Women.* Westminster, 1973

Index

ABOUT THE EDITOR

ROSEMARY RADFORD RUETHER is the author of, among other works, *The Church Against Itself* and *The Radical Kingdom*, and has contributed to many journals and anthologies of religious and scholarly thought. She is a member of the editorial board of the *Journal of Religious Thought* and is a contributing editor to *Christianity and Crisis* and the *Ecumenist*.

Dr. Ruether holds a Ph.D. in Classics and Patristics from the Claremont Graduate School. She served as Assistant Professor of Historical Theology at Howard University's School of Religion from 1967 to 1972 and has been Visiting Lecturer in Roman Catholic Theological Studies and a member of the Faculty of Divinity at the Harvard Divinity School. During the 1973–74 academic year Dr. Ruether is teaching at Yale Divinity School and the Howard School of Religion.